The City & Guilds textbook

Food and Beverage Service

FOR THE LEVEL 2 TECHNICAL CERTIFICATE

John Cousins and Suzanne Weekes

DYNAMIC LEARNING

HODDER EDUCATION
AN HACHETTE UK COMPANY

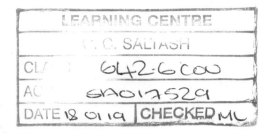
Although every effort has been made to ensure that website addresses are correct at time of going to press, Hodder Education cannot be held responsible for the content of any website mentioned in this book. It is sometimes possible to find a relocated web page by typing in the address of the home page for a website in the URL window of your browser.

Hachette UK's policy is to use papers that are natural, renewable and recyclable products and made from wood grown in sustainable forests. The logging and manufacturing processes are expected to conform to the environmental regulations of the country of origin.

Orders: please contact Bookpoint Ltd, 130 Park Drive, Milton Park, Abingdon, Oxon OX14 4SE.

Telephone: (44) 01235 827720. Fax: (44) 01235 400454. Email education@bookpoint.co.uk

Lines are open from 9 a.m. to 5 p.m., Monday to Saturday, with a 24-hour message answering service.

You can also order through our website: www.hoddereducation.co.uk

ISBN: 978 1 5104 3621 3

First published in 2018 by
Hodder Education
An Hachette UK Company
Carmelite House
50 Victoria Embankment
London EC4Y 0DZ

www.hoddereducation.co.uk

Impression number   10 9 8 7 6 5 4 3 2 1

Year   2022 2021 2020 2019 2018

Cover photo © zhekos – stock.adobe.com

City & Guilds and the City & Guilds logo are trade marks of The City and Guilds of London Institute. City & Guilds Logo © City & Guilds 2018

Typeset in India

Printed in Slovenia

MIX
Paper from
responsible sources
FSC™ C104740

Contents

Qualification map to the Technical Certificate in Food and Beverage Service Level 2

Unit	Learning outcome	Topics	Page
201 Introduction to the hospitality industry	1 Understand the scale and diversity of the hospitality industry	1.1 Sectors of the industry	2
		1.2 Economic importance of the industry	13
	2 Understand career development within food and beverage service	2.1 Departments and job roles	16
		2.2 Methods of career development	20
		2.3 Job applications and interview preparation	25
	3 Understand employability skills required for the hospitality industry	3.1 Work ethics	28
		3.2 Managing online presence	30
	4 Understand the impact of the food service industry on the environment	4.1 Impact of the food service industry on the environment	32
		4.2 Responsible sourcing of food	34
202 Principles of customer service	1 Understand customer service	1.1 Characteristics and benefits of customer service	38
		1.2 Types of customers	40
		1.3 Customers with specific needs	41
		1.4 Consequences of poor customer service	48
		1.5 Legislation for customer service	49
	2 Understand customer service delivery	2.1 Team working	61
		2.2 Meeting and exceeding customer expectations	64
		2.3 Measuring effective customer service	72
		2.4 Impact of customer service on the business	75
203 Safe working practices for food and beverage services	1 Understand personal responsibilities and actions for compliance with health and safety and food hygiene legislation	1.1 Health and safety responsibilities	77
		1.2 Food safety responsibilities	87
		1.3 Maintaining a safe working environment	92
	2 Understand food safety hazards, their key features and how these are controlled	2.1 Food safety hazards and key sources of contamination	99
		2.2 Characteristics of pathogenic bacterial growth	102
		2.3 Reducing the risk from food safety hazards	104
	3 Understand how to maintain a safe and secure service area	3.1 Maintaining a safe working environment	112
		3.2 Maintaining a secure working environment	113
		3.3 Consequences of non-compliance with legislation	115
204 Menu knowledge	1 Understand menu styles and service methods	1.1 Different menu styles	118
		1.2 Food service methods	120
		1.3 Impact of menu styles	121
		1.4 Business impact of menu styles	122
	2 Understand menu product knowledge	2.1 Menu terminology	127
		2.2 Preparation and cooking methods	138
		2.3 Service equipment	139

Introduction

The aim of the book

Food and Beverage Service for the Level 2 Technical Certificate is the essential guide for those studying and/or working in food and beverage service.

The book has been specifically designed to support the City and Guilds Level 2 Technical Certificate in Food and Beverage Service. The book will also be valuable to support the broader-based study requirements of a range of other qualifications and in-company training programmes.

Requirements for professionalism in food and beverage service

Food and beverage service is the essential link between the menu, beverages, services and the customers.

The demand for food and beverages away from the home is increasing and, with a broader range of people eating out, customer needs are changing. Food and restaurant styles are also continuing to diversify to meet the challenges of the demands being made by increasingly knowledgeable and value-conscious customers.

Good food and beverage service in any sector is achieved where customers' needs are met and where management consistently reinforce and support service staff in the maintenance of clearly identified technical standards and service goals.

Although there is less emphasis on sophisticated service techniques in some sectors, there is now a far greater emphasis throughout the industry on the need for professional food and beverage service personnel who have:

- sound product knowledge
- well-developed interpersonal skills
- technical competence
- the ability to work as part of a team.

People working in food and beverage service are the main point of contact between the customers and the establishment. It is an important role in a noble profession, with increasing national and international status. Skills and knowledge, and therefore careers, are transferable between establishments, sectors and throughout the world.

John Cousins and Suzanne Weekes, June 2018

Acknowledgements

The preparation of this book has drawn upon a variety of experience and literature. The authors would like to express their sincere thanks to all the organisations and individuals who gave assistance and support in the preparation of this text. In particular we wish to thank:

Academy of Food and Wine Service, UK; Burgess Furniture Ltd, London; City and Guilds of London Institute; Croners Catering, Croners Publications; Anne Dubberley and Julie Bromfield, Petals of Piccadilly, Birmingham; Dunk Ink; Andrew Durkan, author and consultant, formally of Ealing College, London; Elia International Ltd, Middlesex; Euroservice UK, Welford, Northants; Foodservice Consultants Society International, UK; David Foskett, emeritus professor of Hospitality Studies, Chair of the International Hospitality Council and an education and training consultant in Europe and Asia; the Hilton Hotel, Ealing Common, London; IFS Publications; The International Coffee Organisation; International Standards Organisation; Le Columbier Restaurant, London; Louvet Turner Coombe Marketing; Meiko UK Ltd; National Checking Company UK; PalmTEQ Limited UK; The Restaurant Association of Great Britain; Royal Academy of Culinary Arts, UK; Louise Smith, Flowers by Louise, Birmingham; Snap-Drape Europe Limited; Steelite International; The Tea Council; Uniwell Systems (UK) Ltd; Williams Refrigeration, UK.

Picture credits

Fig.1.1 © Tomas Marek/123RF; Fig.1.2 © Imagestate Media (John Foxx)/London V3037; Fig.1.3 © stocker1970/Shutterstock.com; Fig.1.4 © Lance Bellers/Shutterstock.com; Fig.1.5 © Kzenon/Shutterstock.com; Fig.1.6 © Ministr-84/Shutterstock.com; p.11 © Jean Vaillancourt/123RF; Fig.1.8 © Mangostar/123RF; Fig.1.9 © Andrew Ward/Life File/Photodisc/Getty Images/European Landmarks & Travel 22; Fig.1.10 © Yevgen Belich/Shutterstock.com; Fig.1.11 © Monkey Business/Shutterstock.com; Fig.1.12 © Sorbis/Shutterstock.com; Fig.1.14 © Sergey Bogomyako/stock.adobe.com; Fig.1.15 © JackF/stock.adobe.com; Fig.1.20 © Patryssia – Fotolia; Fig.2.1 © bartsadowski/stock.adobe.com; Fig.2.2 © Ria Osborne/Hodder Education; Fig.2.3 © Sascha Burkard – Fotolia; Fig.2.5 © pololia/stock.adobe.com; Fig.2.6 © trancedrumer/stock.adobe.com; Fig.2.7 © Andrew Callaghan/Hodder Education; Fig.2.9 © Ria Osborne/Hodder Education; Fig.3.5 © olgapavlova/stock.adobe.com; Fig.3.7 © xy/stock.adobe.com; Fig.3.8 © Fotolia; Fig.3.15 courtesy of Russums; Fig.3.16 © khwaneigq/stock.adobe.com; Fig.4.2 a © Vegetarian Society, b © Fairtrade International; Fig.4.3 © Andrew Callaghan/Hodder Education; Fig.4.4 © fazeful/stock.adobe.com; Fig.4.5 © Catherine/stock.adobe.com; Figs 4.6 and 4.7 © Andrew Callaghan/Hodder Education; Fig.4.8 © The Ritz Hotel (London) Ltd; Fig.4.9 © Andrew Callaghan/Hodder Education; Fig.4.10 © dream79/stock.adobe.com; Figs 4.11–4.15 © Andrew Callaghan/Hodder Education; Fig.4.16 © Carl Drury/Hodder Education; Fig.4.17 © Steelite International Ltd; Fig.4.18 © Ria Osborne/Hodder Education; Figs 4.20–4.22 © Euroservice Trolley Manufacturer – www.euroservice-uk.com; Fig.4.25 © Carl Drury/Hodder Education; Fig.5.1 © Ria Osborne/Hodder Education; Fig.5.3 © Carl Drury/Hodder Education; Fig.5.4 © Andrew Callaghan/Hodder Education; Figs 5.5–5.7 © Carl Drury/Hodder Education; Figs 5.8 and 5.9 © Andrew Callaghan/Hodder Education; Fig.5.10 © Carl Drury/Hodder Education; Fig.5.11 image courtesy of National Checking Co; Fig.5.13 © Malcolm Park editorial/Alamy Stock Photo; Fig.5.15 © Carl Drury/Hodder Education; Figs 5.16–5.28 © Ria Osborne/Hodder Education; Fig.5.29 © Carl Drury/Hodder Education; Figs 5.30–5.32 © Andrew Callaghan/Hodder Education; Figs 5.33–5.35 © Carl Drury/Hodder Education; Figs 5.35–5.38 © Ria Osborne/Hodder Education; Fig.5.40 © Ria Osborne/Hodder Education; Fig.5.41 © Euroservice Trolley Manufacturer – www.euroservice-uk.com; Figs 5.42 and 5.43 © Ria Osborne/Hodder Education; Figs 5.44 and 5.45 © Carl Drury/Hodder Education; Fig.5.46 courtesy of the Langham Hotel, London; Fig.5.47 © Andrew Callaghan/Hodder Education; Fig.6.8 © arinahabich/stock.adobe.com; Figs 6.9 and 6.11 © Ria Osborne/Hodder Education; Figs 6.12–6.14 © Carl Drury/Hodder Education; Figs 6.15 and 6.16 © Ria Osborne/Hodder Education; Fig.6.17 mataka_wariatka/Getty Images/iStockphoto/Thinkstock; Figs 6.18 and 6.19 © Andrew Callaghan/Hodder Education; Fig.6.20 images courtesy of Elia®; Fig.6.21 © Konstantin Kulikov/stock.adobe.com; Fig.6.22 © Carl Drury/Hodder Education; Figs 6.23, 6.24, 6.26 and 6.27 © Ria Osborne/Hodder Education; Fig.6.29 © Carl Drury/Hodder Education; Fig.6.30 © Ria Osborne/Hodder Education; Fig.6.32 © Euroservice Trolley Manufacturer – www.euroservice-uk.com; Figs 6.33, 7.1 and 7.4 © Ria Osborne/Hodder Education.

Structure of the book

The content of the book has been created to support the requirements of the City and Guilds 6103–20 Technical Certificate for Food and Beverage Service. The book begins by exploring the hospitality industry and then covers the principles of customer service, safe working practices, menu knowledge and service, beverage knowledge and service, and finance for food and beverage businesses.

- The learning outcomes covered by each chapter are identified at the beginning of each chapter to help you check what you should learn.
- The topics covered are also identified at the beginning of each chapter, so you can identify what is required under each of the learning outcomes.
- Definitions of important key terms are given throughout the book.
- To help with learning, some test your learning questions are given at the end of each chapter.

The content of the book reflects current practice within the industry. However, it is not intended to be a prescriptive book. The actual operation of the service will always be affected by the style and business needs of the individual operation.

Throughout the book we have referred to job titles and job categories such as manager, waiter, supervisor, bartender, server and catering assistant. In all cases these terms, in line with general trends within the industry, refer to both male and female personnel.

HOW TO USE THIS BOOK

The information in the book can be found in three ways:

1 Using the qualification map at the front of the book (page iii).
2 Using the learning outcomes identified at the beginning of each chapter.
3 Using the index at the back of the book (page 336).

The **qualification map** follows the requirements of the City and Guilds Technical Certificate in Food and Beverage Service (6103–20).

The **learning outcomes** covered by each chapter are identified at the beginning of each chapter, together with the list of topics being covered and page numbers for these.

The index is at the back of the book and provides an alphabetical list of key words from the text, together with their page numbers.

INTRODUCTION TO THE HOSPITALITY INDUSTRY

INTRODUCTION

The purpose of this chapter is to help you develop an understanding of the hospitality industry, the way in which food and beverage service links to the overall industry, and the skills and information you require to seek employment within the industry. This is a knowledge-based unit that will provide you with a broad understanding of the industry prior to commencing the technical food and beverage units.

This chapter will help you to:
- identify the types of sectors and establishments that offer food and beverage careers
- know why the hospitality industry is important to the economy
- identify what job opportunities are available in the hospitality industry
- develop the skills you need to find employment in the hospitality industry
- know how food is produced, including the ethical and sustainability issues involved.

1 THE SCALE AND DIVERSITY OF THE HOSPITALITY INDUSTRY

The word '**hospitality**' encompasses all aspects of the hotel and **catering** (or food service) industry. It is a relatively modern word, meaning the friendly and generous treatment of guests and strangers. The word 'catering' refers to offering facilities to people, especially the provision of food and beverages. The more internationally understood term '**food service**' (which can also be written as 'foodservice') means the same as catering in the UK, and is becoming used more often.

KEY TERMS

Hospitality – the friendly and generous treatment of guests and strangers.

Catering – offering facilities to people, especially the provision of food and beverages.

Food service – a more internationally understood term for catering.

▲ **Figure 1.1** Golf courses usually have bars, serve food and offer a range of other hospitality services

KEY TERMS

Hospitality industry – any business that provides for its customers any combination of the three core services: food, drink and accommodation.

Commercial sector – provision of food and beverages as the primary business of the operation.

Service sector (cost provision) – food and beverage operations that provide a service to other businesses where hospitality is not the primary business.

1.1 SECTORS OF THE INDUSTRY

The **hospitality industry** consists of all those businesses that provide any combination of the three core services: food, drink and accommodation. While there is a clear overlap with tourism, there are a number of sectors within the hospitality industry that are sometimes regarded as separate from tourism; for example, industrial catering and those aspects of hospitality that attract only the local community.

Some sectors are considered **commercial** (for profit) while others are classed as **service** (or cost provision). A general summary of the different sectors is shown in Table 1.1, although the contracting out of catering (see page 4) and other services has blurred the division between commercial and service establishments.

▼ **Table 1.1** Summary of sectors in the hospitality industry

Commercial sector	Service sector
Profit orientated (public or private ownership)	Cost provision
Food service as main or secondary activity	
Hotels	Schools
Restaurants	Hospitals
Pubs and wine bars	Halls of residence
Nightclubs	Prisons
Membership clubs	Factories and other workplaces
Event catering	Travel and transport services
Holiday parks	HM Armed Forces
Leisure attractions	
Cruise liners	

Commercial sector

Hotels and other tourist accommodation

Hotels provide accommodation including private bedrooms. Many also offer services such as restaurants, bars and room service.

The level of service offered by a hotel will depend on what type of hotel it is and how many stars it has. Hotels are rated from 5-star (indicating a luxury hotel) to 1-star (indicating more basic accommodation).

The hotel sector is mainly independently owned and hotels come in all shapes, sizes and locations. More than three-quarters of hotels have fewer than 20 rooms and are often family-run. There are many international hotel chains, such as Hilton, Radisson, Mandarin Oriental and Intercontinental, in the 5-star hotel market. There are also budget hotels, guesthouses and bed and breakfast accommodation.

To attract a wide a range of guests, many hotels now offer a variety of services, such as office and IT facilities (for example, internet access and quiet areas to work in), gym and sports facilities, swimming pool, spa, therapy treatments, hair and beauty treatments, and so on.

The hotel sector is divided into distinct categories with their own characteristics:

▲ **Figure 1.2** The Savoy in London is an example of a luxury hotel

- **Business hotels** are geared to the corporate traveller and the emphasis therefore tends to be on functionality. These hotels will usually have a dedicated business centre, up-to-date communications technology in the bedrooms and ample conference and meeting facilities. Business hotels are more likely to be chain-operated, often with a strong brand element.
- **Town houses** are notable for their individuality, intimacy and emphasis on service. These hotels are usually small and, as the name suggests, located in converted town houses with a domestic feel that is emphasised by their decor.
- **Budget hotels** (for example, Travelodge, Premier Inn) are aimed at business people and tourists who need somewhere inexpensive to stay overnight. The rooms are reasonably priced and have tea- and coffee-making facilities. No other food or drink is included in the price. The accommodation is often co-located with a food operation such as Little Chef. They tend to be built near motorways, railway stations and airports. Budget hotels do not employ many members of staff and there is often only provision for a small restaurant area to cater for a simple breakfast. They are usually located close to shops, cafés, restaurants or pubs (which are often run by the same company as the hotel).
- **Country house hotels** are mostly located in attractive old buildings, such as stately homes or manor houses, usually in rural areas or popular tourist areas. They often have a reputation for good food and wine and offer a high standard of service. Country house hotels may also offer the additional services mentioned above.
- **Guesthouses and bed and breakfasts** are small, privately owned businesses. The owners usually live on the premises and let bedrooms to paying guests, many of whom are regular customers. Some guesthouses offer lunch and an evening meal as well as breakfast.
- **Farms** – the rural tourism industry is important in the UK. Farmers understand this and have formed a national organisation called the Farm Holiday Bureau. The farms in the organisation usually offer bed and breakfast and holiday cottages. Most members of the organisation have invested money to improve their bedrooms to meet the standards required by the National Tourist Board. The accommodation is usually on or near a working farm.

▲ **Figure 1.3** Country house hotels are usually located in attractive buildings

▲ **Figure 1.4** Youth hostels provide budget accommodation

● **Youth hostels** – the Youth Hostels Association runs hostels in various locations in the UK. These establishments cater for single people, families and groups travelling on a limited budget. They mainly provide dormitory accommodation, but some also have private rooms. In some locations, they offer a number of sports and leisure facilities. Basic, wholesome meals are provided at a low cost in some hostels and they all have a kitchen that can be used by visitors to store and prepare their own food.

Consortia

Consortia is the plural of consortium. A **consortium** is a group of independent hotels that make an agreement to buy products and services together. For example, they might all pay a specialist company to do their marketing (advertising and so on). This might mean, for example, that the members of the consortium can then use international reservation systems and compete against the larger hotel chains.

Food and beverage provision

The provision of food and beverage services varies greatly between establishments.

● Upmarket hotels are likely to provide a full range of services, usually with at least one *à la carte* restaurant, 24-hour room service and a well-stocked bar.
● Town house properties generally provide little or no food.
● Budget hotels are characterised by the presence of a family restaurant. This is often a stand-alone, branded outlet that also draws custom from the surrounding area.

Some hotels have speciality restaurants. A high profile or celebrity chef may run a restaurant, for example Alyn Williams at The Westbury Hotel or Alan Ducasse at The Dorchester, or it may specialise in steaks, sushi or seafood.

Many hotels have re-examined the place of food and beverage in their operations. While many town houses open with no restaurant at all, other hotels believe that food and beverage provision is an essential guest service. This has led them to consider alternative methods of running a restaurant, such as **contracting** out to a third party or introducing a **franchise** operation.

The contracting out of food and beverage services to third parties will continue to be a major trend in the hotel catering sector. **Outsourcing** is not always a straightforward option, however. To attract walk-in dining customers, ideally a hotel needs to be located where there is easy access to the restaurant and the location of the hotel itself (such as a city centre) needs to fit with the type of customers being targeted – that is, the product must be attractive to passing trade. Despite these constraints, the number of outsourced restaurants is expected to increase considerably.

With increased consumer interest in food and eating out, hotels are more focused on developing attractive food and beverage facilities in-house. The success of in-house catering depends on the willingness of hotels to deliver a product that is attractive to the outside market, to maintain this product and evolve it, according to changing consumer tastes and trends.

KEY TERMS

Consortium – a group of independent hotels that make an agreement to buy products and services together.

Franchise – an agreement where a person or group of people pay a fee and some set-up costs to use an established name or well-known brand.

Contracting/outsourcing – obtaining services from an outside supplier.

Restaurants

The restaurant sector has become the largest in the UK hospitality industry, making up approximately 40 per cent of the commercial hospitality market. Small establishments employing fewer than ten staff make up the majority of the industry, but it also includes exclusive restaurants and fine dining establishments, as well as a wide variety of mainstream restaurants, fast-food outlets, coffee shops and cafés. The south-east of England has the highest concentration of catering and hospitality outlets.

Many restaurants specialise in regional or national food styles, such as Asian and Oriental, Mexican and Caribbean, as well as a wide range of European-style restaurants. New restaurants and cooking styles gain popularity all the time (according to fashion and the introduction of new or different ingredients).

▲ **Figure 1.5** Restaurants often specialise in regional or national food styles

Chain restaurants

Many popular restaurants and coffee shops, as well as shops with restaurants/coffee shops, appear on the British high street up and down the UK and are known as chain organisations. Some of these chains have more than one outlet in a city and others have outlets abroad too. They often serve morning coffee, teas and lunches and may be arranged in the style of snack bars or cafeterias. Chain restaurants are well known and they advertise widely.

Fast food and takeaways

Many customers prefer the option of popular foods at a reasonable price, with little or no waiting time. Fast food establishments offer a limited menu that can be consumed on the premises or taken away. Menu items are quick to cook and have often been partly or fully prepared beforehand, often at a central production point.

Takeaways include Kentucky Fried Chicken (KFC), Chinese food, pizza, and fish and chips. Some cafés and restaurants also offer takeaway services. Fast food operations include MacDonalds and Burger King.

Some fast food operations include drive-thrus, where customers stay in their vehicles and drive up to a microphone where they place their order. As their car moves forward in a queue, their order is prepared and is ready for them to pick up at a service window.

Delivery is available for a range of products such as burgers, Chinese food, curry and pizza using services such as Deliveroo.

Delicatessens and salad bars: these offer a selection of salads and sandwich fillings to go in a variety of bread and rolls at a 'made-to-order' sandwich counter. The choice of breads might include panini, focaccia, pitta, baguette and tortilla wraps. Fresh salads, homemade soups and chilled foods can be sold, as well as a hot 'dish of the day' and baked jacket potatoes with a variety of fillings. With such a variety on offer, these establishments can stay busy throughout the day.

▲ **Figure 1.6** Fast food is often available as a takeaway

▲ **Figure 1.7** Many pubs now offer food

Pubs

There are tens of thousands of licensed public houses (pubs) in the UK and almost all offer some type of food. Pub food is ideal for many people as it is usually quite simple, inexpensive and quickly served in a comfortable atmosphere. In recent times, many pubs have reviewed their menu as part of the total pub experience in order to stay in business. For example, by adding a separate restaurant area, offering a wider selection of bar snacks and putting on live entertainment.

Nowadays, there is a huge variety of food available in pubs, from those that serve ham and cheese rolls to those that have exclusive *à la carte* restaurants.

Nightclubs and casinos

Most nightclubs and casinos are open to the public rather than to members only. As well as selling drinks to their customers, many now also provide food services, such as restaurants.

Membership clubs

Private clubs are usually run by managers who are appointed by club members. People pay to become members of private clubs. Most members will expect good food and drink and informal service, particularly in the fashionable areas of London.

Event catering

There are many specialist companies that provide event management services. In addition, a hospitality operation, such as a hotel, may have a separate event planning department. Event managers plan and organise weddings, parties, dinners, business meetings and conferences. The event management company is responsible for hiring a venue, organising staff, food and drink, music, entertainment and any other requests the client may have.

Corporate hospitality

Corporate hospitality is hospitality provided by a business, usually for its clients or potential clients. The purpose of corporate hospitality is to build business relationships and to raise awareness of the company. Corporate entertaining is also used to thank or reward loyal customers.

Outside (or outdoor) catering

When events are held at venues where there is no on-site kitchen or catering facility available, or where the level of catering required is more than the venue caterers can manage, a catering company may be invited to take over the management of the event. This type of catering is known as 'outside catering' – a business providing services in a location that is not its own. Examples of such functions include:

- a garden party
- agricultural and horticultural shows

- the opening of a new building
- banquets
- parties in private houses
- military pageants and tattoos
- sporting fixtures, such as horse racing, motor racing, football and rugby.

There is a lot of variety in outside catering work, but standards are very high and people employed in this area need to be adaptable and creative. Sometimes specialist equipment will be required (especially for outdoor jobs) and employees need to be flexible as the work often involves a lot of travel, remote locations and outdoor venues.

Holiday parks

Holiday parks (sometimes referred to as holiday centres or holiday complexes) provide leisure and hospitality facilities all on one site and cater for families, single people and groups. Many holiday centres have invested large amounts of money to improve the quality of the holiday experience. Center Parcs, for example, offers sub-tropical pools, indoor sports facilities and other leisure activities in case the weather is bad.

Holiday centres include a range of different restaurants and food courts, bars and coffee shops. They operate all year round.

Leisure

The leisure sector covers a variety of establishments, including cinemas, theatres and sporting events, all of which are likely to offer some form of catering service.

Theme parks

Theme parks are extremely popular venues for a family day out or even a full holiday. Larger theme parks include several different eating options, ranging from fast food to fine dining. Some include branded restaurants such as McDonald's and Burger King.

Theme parks are also used for corporate hospitality and conferences. Many have conference and banqueting suites for this purpose, while larger theme parks may even have their own hotel.

Health clubs and spas

Health clubs and spas are often luxury establishments or hotels that offer their clients a variety of health and beauty treatments. These establishments may provide healthy food restaurants and relaxation therapies. Health clubs provide sports activities to give people an opportunity to improve their fitness, health and general wellbeing.

Museums

Most museums will have at least one café or restaurant catering for visitors. Some run events such as lunchtime lectures, family events and children's discovery days where food is provided as part of the event.

▲ **Figure 1.8** Health clubs and spas offer healthy food

Museums are also used as venues for private events and banqueting during the hours they are closed to the general public. Sometimes outside caterers are employed for the occasion, but many museums have their own catering team to provide a wide range of food.

Historic buildings and visitor attractions

Numerous historic buildings and places of interest have food outlets such as cafés and restaurants. Many in the UK specialise in light lunches and afternoon teas for the general public. Some are also used as venues for large private or corporate events.

Places such as Hampton Court, the Eden Project and Poole Pottery are all categorised as visitor attractions, and will usually have refreshment outlets serving a variety of food and drinks. Some, like Kew Gardens, also stage large theatrical events and concerts in the summer months.

▲ **Figure 1.9** Attractions such as Hampton Court Palace have food outlets

Retail

Many retail operations offer catering services alongside the retail operation. This can range from vending machines and takeaway services, through to a full-service restaurant. Some retail operations include branches of well-known coffee chains or other popular catering restaurant brands. Independent food and beverage operations are located within shopping centres and retail parks.

Cruise liners

Cruise ships or liners are floating luxury hotels. The food provision on a large cruise liner is of a similar standard to the food provided in a 5-star hotel and is usually high quality, banquet-style cuisine. Many shipping companies are known for the excellence of their cuisine.

▲ **Figure 1.10** Modern cruise liners offer a choice of dining rooms and a range of cuisines

Dining is one of the most important selling points for cruise liners. People who take cruises want to dine well, but cooking dinner for 800 people per sitting and giving people what they want takes skill and good management.

Many modern cruise liners are giant ships that have a number of separate dining rooms. Passengers are free to eat in the dining room of their choice, more or less whenever they want.

As well as luxury liners, catering at sea includes smaller cargo ships, ferries or passenger ships, and giant cargo tankers. The food provision for crew and passengers will vary from good restaurants and cafeterias to more industrial-style catering on tankers. On all types of vessel, extra precautions have to be taken in the kitchen during rough weather.

Service sector

Public sector organisations that need catering services include schools, hospitals and halls of residence.

While the aim of catering in hotels, restaurants and other areas of the leisure and travel industry (known as the **private sector**) is to make a profit, the aim of public sector catering is to keep costs down by working efficiently. Organisations are often working within the constraints of a given budget, known as the **cost provision**. Often companies will compete to win a contract to provide the catering for these organisations.

The contract food service sector consists of companies that provide catering services to other organisations – and is a sector that has grown in recent years. Contract food service management provides food for a wide variety of people, including those working in business and industry, schools, colleges and universities, private and public healthcare establishments, public and local authorities and other non-profit-making outlets such as the armed forces, police and ambulance services. Examples of contract companies include Sodexho, Compass Group, Aramark and Baxter Storey.

The contract food service sector also includes commercial areas, such as corporate hospitality events and the executive dining rooms of many corporations, as well as special events, sporting fixtures and places of entertainment and outlets such as leisure centres, galleries, museums, department stores and DIY stores, supermarket restaurants and cafés, airports and railway stations. Some contractors provide other support services such as housekeeping and maintenance, reception, security, laundry, bars and retail shops.

Many public-sector catering **tenders** are won by contract caterers (contract food service providers) which introduce new ideas and more commercialism (promoting business for profit) into the **public sector**. Because much of the public sector is now operated by profit-making contractors, it is sometimes referred to as the secondary service sector.

The type of menu in the public sector may be different from that in the private sector because the food offered must be suitable for the end consumers.

KEY TERMS

Private sector – businesses such as hotels, restaurants and travel companies that aim to make a profit.

Cost provision – this is an agreed amount of money (the budget) that an organisation must work within.

Tender – when companies compete to win a contract they make a written offer to supply goods and carry out work for a fixed price.

Public sector – organisations such as schools and hospitals that provide a service to the general public. Sometimes referred to as the secondary service sector.

For example, school children, hospital patients and soldiers have particular nutritional needs (they may need more energy from their food or more of particular vitamins and minerals), so the menu must meet their needs. Menus may also reflect the need to keep costs down.

Schools

School meals play an important part in the lives of many children, often providing them with their only hot meal of the day.

Local education authorities (LEAs) are responsible for ensuring that the minimum nutritional standards for school lunches are met.

Schools must provide a paid-for meal where parents request one, except where children are under five years old and only go to school part-time. This does not affect the LEA's or the school's duty to provide a free meal to those children who qualify for one.

In 2006, the Government announced new standards for school food, covering all food sold or served in schools (including breakfast, lunch and after-school meals) as well as tuck shops, vending machines, mid-morning snacks at break time and anything sold or served at after-school clubs.

▲ **Figure 1.11** School meals play an important role in providing nutritious food for many children

Hospitals

Hospital caterers need to provide well-cooked, nutritious and appetising meals for hospital patients, and must maintain strict hygiene standards. High standards of food in hospitals can contribute to the recovery of patients.

The scale of catering services in the NHS is enormous. Over 300 million meals are served each year in approximately 1200 hospitals. NHS Trusts must ensure that they get the best value for money within their catering budget.

As well as providing nutritious meals for patients in hospital (many of whom need special diets), provision must also be made for outpatients (people who come into hospital for treatment and leave again the same day) as well as visitors and staff. This service may be provided by the hospital catering team, but is sometimes allocated to commercial food outlets, or a combination of both.

Halls of residence

Universities and colleges offer halls of residence for students. The food and beverages provided have to satisfy all the residents' nutritional needs, as the people eating these meals may have no other food provision.

Prisons

Catering in prisons may be carried out by contract caterers or by the Prison Service itself. The kitchens are also used to train inmates in catering and food service skills so they may gain a recognised qualification to help them to find work when they are released.

In addition to catering facilities for the inmates, there are also separate staff catering facilities for all the personnel who work in a prison, such as administrative staff and prison officers.

Factories and other places of work

Many industries have realised that satisfied employees work more efficiently and produce better work, so have spent a great deal of money on providing first class kitchens and dining rooms. In some cases, companies will subsidise (pay a proportion of) the cost of the meals so that employees can buy food at a price lower than it costs to produce.

In some cases a 24-hour, seven-days-a-week service is necessary, but usually the hours are shorter than in other areas of the hospitality industry. Food and drink is provided for all employees, often in high quality restaurants and dining rooms. The catering departments in these organisations are keen to retain and develop their staff, so there is good potential for training and career development in this sector.

Staff dining rooms and restaurants in industrial and business settings, such as factories, offices and retail operations, provide employment for many catering workers outside traditional hotel and restaurant catering. Working conditions in these settings are often very good. Apart from the main task of providing meals, these facilities may also include retail shops, franchise outlets and vending machines. They will also provide catering for meetings, special functions and conferences.

Travel and transport services

In addition to providing food and beverage operations at ports, airport terminals and railway stations, there is considerable provision for people on the move.

Airline services

Air travel continues to increase in popularity and therefore so do the opportunities and need for food services catering to the airline industry. Food provision varies greatly between different airports and airlines.

Airports offer a range of hospitality services catering for millions of people every year. They operate 24 hours a day, 365 days a year. Services include a wide variety of shops, along with bars, themed restaurants, speciality restaurants, coffee bars and food courts.

In-flight catering is a specialist service provided by companies located at or near airports in the UK and around the world. The meals provided vary from snacks and basic meals to luxury meals for first class passengers. Menus are put together carefully to ensure the ingredients can safely be chilled and then reheated on board the aircraft.

The price of some airline tickets includes a meal served at the passenger's seat. Budget airlines usually have an 'at-seat' trolley service from which passengers can buy snacks and drinks.

▲ **Figure 1.12** In-flight catering can vary from snacks and basic meals to luxury meals for first class passengers

Rail services

Snacks can be bought in the buffet car on some trains, and train operators may also offer a trolley service so that passengers can buy snacks from their seat. Main meals may be served in a restaurant car and at-seat trolley services are provided in first class.

Ferries

There are several ferry ports in the UK, making crossings to Ireland and mainland Europe. As well as passengers and their cars, many ferries also carry freight lorries. As well as competing against each other, ferry companies are also competing against airlines and, in the case of English Channel crossings, Eurostar and Eurotunnel.

In order to win customers, ferry companies have invested in their passenger services, with most offering several shops, bars, cafés and lounges on board. Some also have restaurant and leisure facilities, fast food restaurants and branded food outlets.

HM Forces

Catering in the armed forces includes providing meals for staff in barracks, in the field and on ships. It is a specialised industry, especially when forces are in the field, and it has its own well-established cookery training programmes. However, like every other part of the public sector, the armed forces need to keep costs down and increase efficiency, so they also have competitive tendering for their catering services. The Ministry of Defence contracts food service providers to cater for many of its service operations. See page 9 on for an explanation of the contract food service sector.

1.2 ECONOMIC IMPORTANCE OF THE INDUSTRY

Gross Domestic Product (GDP)

GDP is an indication of the state of the economy in one number. It is a measure of the total value of goods produced and services provided in a country during a specified period of time.

- If the GDP is up on the previous three months, the economy is growing.
- If the GDP is lower, the economy is contracting.

The hospitality industry makes a substantial contribution to the UK economy. The gross value added (GVA) is the contribution of an individual industry to UK GDP. For the hospitality industry, this is:

- the value of the industry's output minus the cost of purchased inputs in the production process.

From 2008 to 2017 the GVA of the hospitality industry grew faster than that of any other industry. The growth in employment and in GVA has been ahead of those rates for the economy as a whole. The direct contribution of the hospitality industry to the UK economy was estimated to be £73 billion in 2016.

Taxation

In the UK, **taxation** involves payments to a minimum of three different levels of government:

1. the central government (Her Majesty's Revenue and Customs)
2. devolved governments (such as the Scottish and Welsh parliaments)
3. local government.

Central government revenues come primarily from income tax, National Insurance contributions, Value Added Tax (VAT), corporation tax and fuel duty.

Local government revenues come primarily from grants from central government funds, business rates in England and Wales, Council Tax and from sources such as parking fees and charges.

The hospitality industry makes a significant contribution to the UK economy through payment of taxes at all of these levels.

Value Added Tax (VAT)

VAT is a tax on the final consumption of certain goods and services in the home market, but is collected at every stage of production and distribution. Most business-related goods and services will therefore be subject to VAT.

There are several UK VAT rates, the standard rate being 20 per cent. Companies must register for VAT if the value of their taxable supplies in a 12-month period is greater than the current VAT registration annual threshold of £85,000 (from 1 April 2017).

All VAT-registered businesses must submit their VAT returns online, and settle any outstanding tax liabilities electronically.

KEY TERMS

Gross Domestic Product (GDP) – a measure of the value of goods and services in a country during a period of time.

Taxation – compulsory payments collected by central, devolved and local government which contribute to the state's revenue.

Value Added Tax (VAT) – a tax on the final consumption of goods and services.

Restaurants must charge VAT on everything eaten and drunk on their premises or in communal areas designated for their customers to use (for example, shared tables in a shopping centre or airport food court). Restaurants must also charge VAT on hot takeaways and home deliveries.

Pay as You Earn (PAYE)

PAYE is the scheme operated by Her Majesty's Revenue and Customs (HMRC) to take income tax from employees as they earn it. This system also includes the collection of National Insurance (NI) contributions.

- For employers, all payroll data must be submitted to HMRC in 'real time', rather than simply at the end of each tax year.
- People running their own business as a 'sole trader' are self-employed and not affected by PAYE. Their tax is calculated based on their tax return.

Corporation tax

A public limited company is an organisation that can sell its shares to the public. It has to pay tax on income or profits, which is known as corporation tax. Payment of **corporation tax** itself is due nine months and one day after the company's 'normal due date' – usually the last day of the annual accounting period. The current corporation tax rate is 20 per cent.

Support services

There are a range of organisations that contribute to the hospitality industry. These are often termed 'support services' and include:

- food and beverage suppliers
- laundry and cleaning services
- insurance services
- travel and transport.

The success of the hospitality industry has a direct impact on the business success of these organisations.

Different types of employment

The hospitality industry accounts for 3.2 million jobs, making it the fourth biggest employment sector in the UK. Generally, the type of employment is determined by how many hours you work, but that may not always be the case.

Part-time contracts

A **part-time employee** works fewer contracted hours than a **full-time employee**. However, they generally also hold permanent positions and their contract contains many of the same details as their full-time counterparts. The number of hours a part-time employee is scheduled to work per week should be clearly visible within their contract, but they may have the option to work overtime, if and when desired.

KEY TERMS

Pay As You Earn (PAYE) – the scheme operated by HMRC to take tax from employees as they earn.

Corporation tax – a tax on business profits.

Part-time employee – regular employment of usually less than 35 hours per week.

Full-time employee – employment of usually 35 or more hours per week.

Benefits of part-time employment include:

- a more flexible schedule
- allowing individuals to fit their work around other commitments
- the opportunity for people to try out new roles without having to give up vast amounts of their time.

Full-time contracts

The most common type of employment contract is full-time. These contracts are generally offered for permanent positions, and usually set out the employee's salary or hourly wage. Other details included within a full-time contract are holiday entitlements, pension benefits, parental leave allowances, and details on Statutory Sick Pay (SSP).

There is no set minimum number of hours that you must work on a full-time contract. However, most employers recognise full-time work as 35+ hours per week.

Seasonal work

Some hospitality establishments may be busier at certain times of the year. For example, hotels in holiday resorts may only be open in summer months and closed in the winter, or may require more staff in busier periods, and therefore they will offer **seasonal work** on fixed-term or temporary contracts.

Fixed-term, temporary contracts are offered when a contract is not expected to become permanent. Usually they will have some form of end-date included; however, these may be subject to change. As such, temporary workers may have their contracts extended in line with demand and availability. Despite their short-term status, temporary workers are entitled to the same rights as any other member of staff. Benefits of temporary contracts include increased flexibility, the ability to manage work around study or other interests and building experience within a specific sector.

Casual work/zero-hour contracts

Also known as **casual work** contracts, zero-hour contracts specify that an employee works only when required by their employer. The employer is under no obligation to provide a set number of hours to work and the employee does not have to accept any work that is offered to them.

Zero-hour workers are, however, entitled to the same annual leave as permanent workers, and their employer must pay them at least the National Minimum Wage. Individuals on a zero-hour contract may also seek employment elsewhere. In fact, their contract would not be valid if it prevented them from looking for, or accepting, work from another employer.

Indirect employment

There are a range of jobs in support services (see page 14) which contribute **indirect employment** to the hospitality industry. The types of employment available in these sectors are generally the same as those for the hospitality industry.

KEY TERMS

Seasonal work – fixed-term contract for employment during business periods such as summer months or the Christmas period.

Casual work – not employed on a regular basis.

Indirect employment – employment in support services.

2 CAREER DEVELOPMENT WITHIN FOOD AND BEVERAGE SERVICE

2.1 DEPARTMENTS AND JOB ROLES

Departmental hierarchies

Hospitality organisations need a structure for their staff in order for the business to run efficiently and effectively. Departments of hospitality organisations include:

- restaurant
- bar
- reception
- room service
- lounge service
- conferences and banqueting.

Different members of staff have different jobs and roles to perform as part of the team so that the business is successful. In smaller organisations, some employees become multi-skilled so that they can carry out a variety of duties. Managers may have to take on a supervisory role at certain times.

Types of job roles

A hospitality team will consist of operational staff, supervisory staff, management staff and, in large organisations, senior management.

Operational staff

Operational staff are usually practical, front-line, hands-on staff and include waiters and bar staff as well as chefs, reception staff and accommodation staff.

Supervisory staff

Supervisors oversee the work of the operational staff. In some establishments, the supervisors will be the managers for some of the operational staff.

Management staff

Managers are responsible for making sure the operation runs smoothly and within budget. They are accountable to the owners to make sure that the products and services on offer are what the customer expects and wants, and to provide value for money. They may also be responsible for future planning of the business.

Managers are required to make sure that all the health and safety policies are in place and that health and safety legislation is followed. In smaller establishments, they may also act as the human resources manager.

A hotel will normally have a manager, an assistant manager(s), an accommodation manager, a restaurant manager and a reception manager. Within each section of the hotel there could be a manager with departmental responsibilities – a head chef is a manager, for example.

KEY TERMS

Operational staff – practical, front-line hands-on staff in the hospitality industry.

Supervisors – oversee the work of the operational staff.

Managers – responsible for finances and making sure the operation runs smoothly. They may also be responsible for future planning.

The restaurant manager or supervisor has overall responsibility for the organisation and administration of specific food and beverage service areas. These may include the lounges, room service (in hotels), restaurants and possibly some of the private function suites. The restaurant manager sets the standards for service and is responsible for any staff training that may be required, either on or off the job. They may make out duty rotas, holiday lists and hours on and off duty and contribute to operational duties (depending on the size of the establishment) so that all the service areas run efficiently and smoothly.

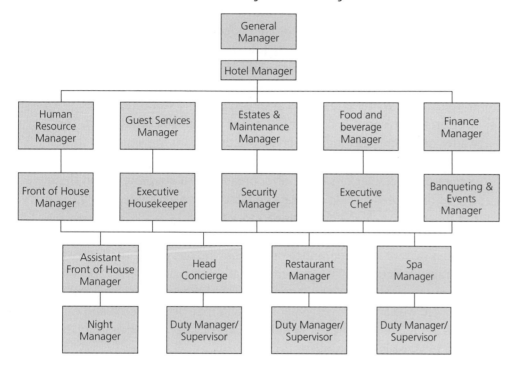

▲ **Figure 1.13** Staffing structure of a 4-star spa hotel

Figure 1.13 shows a typical organisation chart for a hotel and identifies various food and beverage job roles. Food and beverage operations outside hotels often have a similar type of organisation, although different terminology may be used for the various job roles depending on the type of establishment.

Some of the most common job roles in food and beverage service are described below. In smaller operations, some of these job roles may be combined.

Waiter/station waiter/runner

There are a number of waiter roles in a restaurant. These include:

- **Head waiter/maître d'hôtel/supervisor/senior captain.** The **head waiter** has overall responsibility for the staff team and is responsible for ensuring that all the pre-preparation duties necessary for service are efficiently carried out. The head waiter will aid the reception head waiter during service and may take some orders if the station waiter is busy. The head waiter also helps to compile duty rotas and holiday lists and may relieve the restaurant manager or reception head waiter on their days off.

KEY TERM

Head waiter – has overall responsibility for the staff team in the restaurant.

17

- **Station head waiter/section supervisor/service captain.** For large establishments, the restaurant area is broken down into sections. The station head waiter has overall responsibility for a team of staff serving several stations within a section of the restaurant area. A group of tables (which may range from four to eight in number) within a section of the restaurant area is called a station. The station head waiter will also assist in taking food and beverage orders and with the service if required.
- **Station waiter/chef de rang/captain.** The chef de rang or **station waiter** provides service to one group of tables (a station) within the restaurant area. He or she will take food and beverage orders and carry out service at the table with the help of the demi-chef de rang.
- **Assistant station waiter/demi-chef de rang/assistant captain.** The assistant station waiter or demi-chef de rang is the person next in seniority to the station waiter and assists as directed by the station waiter.
- **Waiter/server/commis de rang/assistant waiter/bus boy/runner.** The waiter or commis de rang acts on instructions from the assistant station waiter (chef de rang). They mainly fetch and carry and may do some of the service of vegetables or sauces, offer bread rolls, place plates upon the table and so on, as well as help to clear the table after each course. They will carry out much of the cleaning and preparatory tasks.
- **Trainee commis/debarrasseur/apprentice waiter.** The trainee commis or debarrasseur is an apprentice or learner who has joined the food and beverage service staff. The trainee will carry out many of the tasks during the pre-preparation periods. During service, this person will keep the sideboard well stocked with equipment and may help to fetch and carry items as required for the bar or kitchen. As they develop their skills they will begin to assist in table service.

Cashier

The **cashier** is responsible for billing and taking payments or making ledger account entries for a food and beverage operation. This may include:

- making up bills from food and drink checks
- charging customers for their selection of items on a tray (for example, in a cafeteria).

Barista

The word *barista* is of Italian origin. A **barista** is a bartender who typically works behind a counter, serving both hot and cold beverages as well as alcoholic beverages.

Sommelier/wine waiter

The **sommelier** is responsible for serving alcoholic and non-alcoholic bar drinks during the service of meals. The sommelier must also be a good sales person.

This employee should have a thorough knowledge of:

- all drink to be served
- the best wines and drinks to go with certain foods
- the liquor licensing laws in respect of the particular establishment and area.

▲ **Figure 1.14** A barista at work

KEY TERMS

Station waiter – provides service to a group of tables called a station.

Runner – does some of the service, clears tables and does much of the cleaning and preparatory work.

Cashier – responsible for billing and taking payments.

Barista – a bartender who makes hot and cold drinks and alcoholic beverages.

Sommelier/wine waiter – serves alcoholic and non-alcoholic drinks during the service of meals.

Bar person/mixologist

This role may also be known as a **bartender**. The staff working within bar areas must be responsible and competent in preparing and serving a variety of wine, drinks and cocktails. They should have a thorough knowledge of all alcoholic and non-alcoholic drinks offered by the establishment, the ingredients necessary for making cocktails and understand the requirements of the liquor licensing laws to ensure legal compliance.

Mixology is the art of making mixed drinks, and a mixologist is an employee who mixes and serves alcoholic beverages at a bar. The name is often used for people who specialise in creating new mixed drinks. It can also refer to a person who makes cocktails or is simply a bartender.

Host/greeter

The host or **greeter** acts as receptionist for restaurant operations. Their responsibilities include:

- taking reservations and looking after the booking system
- replying to correspondence
- creating the bookings list for the day
- greeting customers at the restaurant and hanging up their coats
- escorting them to the bar or to their table.

Porters

Porters are the most valuable people in any operation. They help with general cleaning duties and assist in moving equipment and stock.

Staffing requirements

Staffing requirements vary for a number of reasons. Table 1.2 shows the types of food and beverage staff that might be found in different types of food-service operation.

▼ **Table 1.2** Examples of staffing requirements for different types of food-service operation

Medium class hotel	Cafeteria
Hotel manager	Catering manager
Assistant manager	Supervisor
Head waiter	Assistant supervisor
Waiter	Counter service hand
Wine waiter	Clearer
Cashier	Cashier
Popular price restaurant	**Industrial food service/welfare catering**
Restaurant manager/supervisor	Catering manager
Waiting staff	Assistant catering manager
Dispense bar assistant	Supervisor
	Assistant supervisor
	Waiter
	Steward/butler
	Counter service staff
	Clearer
	Cashier

KEY TERMS

Bartender/bar person – staff working in bar areas serving wine, drinks and cocktails.

Host/greeter – receptionist who is responsible for greeting customers when they arrive.

Porter – helps with cleaning duties and moving equipment and stock.

2.2 METHODS OF CAREER DEVELOPMENT

Evaluation of personal skills

Whatever your job role, it is useful to evaluate and check your progress from time to time. Feedback from your peers and managers or a mentor is a useful way of evaluating your performance. Creating a personal development plan provides a way to check your progress, refer back to your targets and think about the outcome.

There are three key stages for monitoring performance in order to check whether targets are being met. These are as follows.

1 Create a **personal development plan**.
2 Identify and evaluate **targets** and then take corrective action when necessary.
3 Keep a **record of performance outcomes** (these must be measurable in order to know whether they have been achieved).

Gathering information to improve your workplace skills is useful – once you have achieved a successful outcome, you can use that information to inform and help others.

KEY TERM

Personal development plan – a plan designed to monitor and measure an employee's performance.

Personal development plan

A personal development plan will help you to:

- identify targets and timescales to improve your skills and knowledge
- advance your career for personal and professional success
- evaluate the performance feedback you receive from your mentor, manager or tutor
- improve your future performance.

An example of an action plan for personal development is shown in Table 1.3.

▼ **Table 1.3** Action plan for personal development

Target	Steps to take in milestones	Indicators of successful completion	Start date	Target completion date	Done
1 Taking beverages orders to establishment standards	a Complete on the job training	Sign off and feedback from supervisor	Start October	End October	To be signed by supervisor
	b				
	c				
2	a				
	b				
	c				

The next step is to identify which skills you need to develop further.

Knowledge advancement and training needs

Table 1.4 shows a personal **target** chart that can be used to identify a skill to be developed or knowledge to be gained, along with any training needs. The chart asks you to explain why the skill is important, to describe how you will achieve it and to provide evidence that it has been achieved successfully.

KEY TERM

Target – an outcome for an employee to work towards as part of their development.

▼ **Table 1.4** Personal target chart

	Target 1	Target 2	Target 3
What is the target?	Wine service to establishment standards		
Importance of the skill and knowledge and why you need it	Essential to be able to fully contribute to wine service		
How you will achieve the skill and knowledge and what training, support and guidance you will need	On job training and experience Attend wine course		
Evidence that you have achieved your aim	Feedback from supervisor		

Skills development

Table 1.5 shows a skills development progress chart that enables a person to assess the skills they currently possess, identify skills they would like to develop and then rank them in order of priority. There are two sorts of skills:

1 **Hard skills** are the physical technical skills required.
2 **Soft skills** are the social skills required to enable successful interaction with colleagues and customers.

▼ **Table 1.5** Skills development progress chart

Knowledge, skills, qualities and experience	Already experienced	Want to know more	Want to develop further	Order of importance
Preparation skills				
Bar skills				
Wine skills				
Service skills				
Order-taking skills				
Billing skills				
Time management				
Identifying barriers to personal success				
Being able to reflect positively				
Knowing what kind of career you want				
Preparing a job application				

Knowledge, skills, qualities and experience	Already experienced	Want to know more	Want to develop further	Order of importance
Writing a job application covering letter				
Writing an attractive CV				
Understanding what is required to be successful				
Teambuilding skills				
Developing professional relationships				
Being assertive				
Dealing with difficult people				
Developing confidence				
Dealing with basic problem-solving				
Being self-motivated				
Evaluating personal competitiveness				
Understanding effective interview techniques				
Preparing for an interview				
Developing personal records				
Recording evidence				

Communication

Listening

Listening is an important part of effective communication. Learn to listen carefully and to understand facial expressions, gestures and body language. Good listeners:

- avoid distractions
- concentrate on what is being said
- think about what is being said
- show interest in the person speaking and do not look bored
- maintain eye contact with the person talking and acknowledge what is being said
- ask sensible questions if necessary
- summarise what has been said in their own words to check they understand what they have been told.

It is important to be an active listener. Show the person you are listening to that you are interested in what they are saying by maintaining eye contact and responding to what they say. Listen before you form your own opinion.

▲ **Figure 1.15** Active listening

Body language

Communication can also be non-verbal, in other words unspoken. It is important to understand other people's body language. Body language refers to:

- posture
- how close a person stands to another person
- facial expressions
- hand movements and gestures
- eye contact.

Speaking

In order to communicate effectively:

- Speak clearly and slowly.
- Remember that not speaking the same language can cause difficulties.
- Avoid using too much unfamiliar terminology and jargon.
- Speak clearly and slowly to those who have a hearing impairment, as they may be able to lip read.
- When writing letters or emails – always read through your message to check for spelling mistakes (use a spelling and grammar check).

Team working

Staff must be able to work as part of a team, both within and between departments. The people in a team depend on each other to be successful and, as a member of the food and beverage department, you will need to be able to work as part of a team.

Aspiration versus limitations

It is great to have aspirations – things that you want to achieve. However, you may be unable to achieve everything you want to for any one of a variety of reasons:

- There is more to learn than expected.
- Some skills take a long time to perfect.
- Your current workplace may offer you the opportunity to learn only basic skills and so this may slow down progress.
- Opportunities for promotion are not always available.

However, having aspirations beyond the current requirement of the job is essential to maintain future career development.

Trial shifts/work experience

You may be offered a trial period of work to see how you get on. These are for set periods and give you and your potential employer the opportunity to make decisions about your potential career development and to see whether or not a particular job is right for you.

Work experience positions are common and available on application for those studying for a qualification in the industry. Work experience in food and beverage services can also be offered to school students.

Part-time employment

The benefits of part-time employment for career development include:

- a more flexible schedule, allowing individuals to fit their work around other commitments
- the opportunity for people to try out new roles without having to give up vast amounts of time.

Apprenticeships

Different to studying at college and university, **apprenticeships** are a way to learn skills within a workplace setting while also getting a qualification. An apprenticeship can be:

- through a day-release course at college, or
- completely work-based, where an assessor monitors the apprentice's learning and development.

KEY TERMS

Work experience or **trial shifts** – being in a workplace for a set period to see how you get on.

Apprenticeship – gaining a qualification while in employment.

Apprenticeships are available at different levels, with the higher apprenticeships being equivalent to a degree.

Information on the various routes to employment and qualifications can be found on the Hospitality Guild website at:

www.hospitalityguild.co.uk/A-Career-in-Hospitality

2.3 JOB APPLICATIONS AND INTERVIEW PREPARATION

When applying for a job you will often be required to complete an application form or send in your **curriculum vitae (CV)**. A covering letter is often required. If the first stage of your application is successful, you will be asked to attend an interview.

Structure of a CV

Your CV lists your educational qualifications and work history, your interests and any other activities in which you participate. Employers will usually want to know where you have demonstrated certain skills, how you have dealt with certain situations in the workplace and whether you carry out any voluntary work.

A CV should follow the following structure:

- personal details
- personal statement
- education
- employment details
- skills
- referees.

When preparing a CV, you should bear in mind the following:

- Make sure your CV is up to date and includes details of all your experience, jobs, dates of employment, names of employers and any professional awards you have won (relevant to the employment you are seeking).
- Always check spelling, layout and punctuation.
- Your personal statement is a short paragraph about yourself that describes your career to date and your personal qualities and skills:
  - Briefly explain what inspires you and how you use existing skills.
  - Specify what your long-term goals are, as well as your immediate goals and targets.
  - Identify how you broaden your outlook, list your skills and emphasise your ability to deal with a range of different people, personalities and cultural diversity.
- Your referees are people who have already agreed are prepared to provide a reference confirming your qualifications and/or work experience. It is acceptable to state that references can be provided on request.

KEY TERM

Curriculum vitae (CV) – lists your contact details, educational qualifications and work history and other details; used when applying for a job to demonstrate your skills to potential employers.

25

Curriculum vitae

Name

Current position:
Home address:
Telephone:
Home email:
Date of birth:

General career overview:

[*Include bullet point list of key features and achievements of career, including key experience and skills*]

- X years' industry experience in food and beverage operations, including X years at craft and supervisory level.
- Experienced in [*give details*].
- Proven record of achievement recognised through promotion and career advancement.
- Hard working and a good team member.
- Commitment to continuing professional development through undertaking various in-company training programmes [*give details*].

Professional experience:

- Dates [*write as month and year in full and include job title and name of place, name of specific place and indication of level of operation, e.g. 5**]
- Reporting to [*give details*].
- Give some descriptive information, such as services provided, for how many people and how many staff responsible for. [*For example, á la carte and table d'hôte all-day dining for up to 000 people, function catering for up to 000 people, with a staffing of 000 people.*]
- List key responsibilities.
- List other job features and unique experience.

[*Then repeat this format for all employment going back in time. Write in the third person as it is easier to write in that format and much easier for other people to read.*]

Professional activities:

- [*Bullet point list of any professional memberships and any contributions to industry activities.*]

Competitions and awards:
Education, training and qualifications:
Hobbies and interests:
Nationality: [*Include visa status if appropriate.*]

▲ **Figure 1.16** An example of a CV

Format of a covering letter

A **covering letter** will usually accompany a CV. The covering letter:

- introduces you to the company
- explains why you are suitable for the job on offer and the skills and qualities you can bring to it
- gives you an opportunity to say how you would be able to contribute to the establishment and the organisation as a whole.

The format of a covering letter includes:

- personal address
- employer's address
- date

KEY TERM

Covering letter – accompanies a CV and explains why you are suitable for the job on offer.

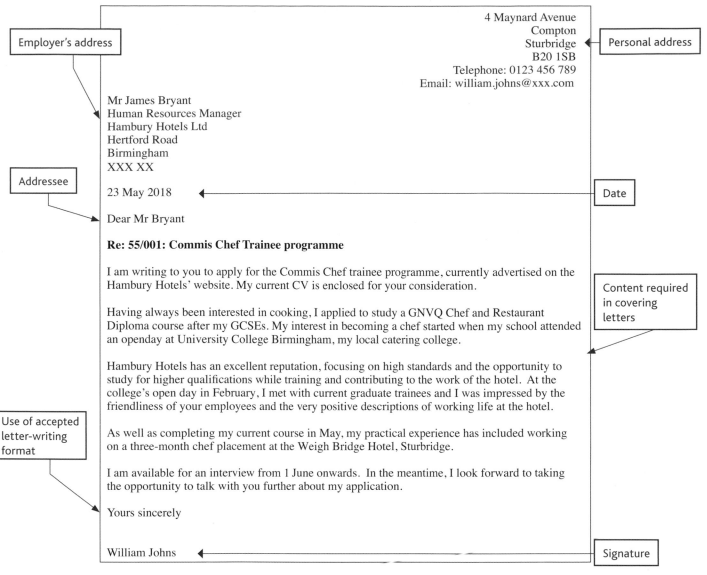

Employer's address

Personal address

4 Maynard Avenue
Compton
Sturbridge
B20 1SB
Telephone: 0123 456 789
Email: william.johns@xxx.com

Mr James Bryant
Human Resources Manager
Hambury Hotels Ltd
Hertford Road
Birmingham
XXX XX

Addressee

23 May 2018

Date

Dear Mr Bryant

Re: 55/001: Commis Chef Trainee programme

I am writing to you to apply for the Commis Chef trainee programme, currently advertised on the Hambury Hotels' website. My current CV is enclosed for your consideration.

Having always been interested in cooking, I applied to study a GNVQ Chef and Restaurant Diploma course after my GCSEs. My interest in becoming a chef started when my school attended an openday at University College Birmingham, my local catering college.

Content required in covering letters

Hambury Hotels has an excellent reputation, focusing on high standards and the opportunity to study for higher qualifications while training and contributing to the work of the hotel. At the college's open day in February, I met with current graduate trainees and I was impressed by the friendliness of your employees and the very positive descriptions of working life at the hotel.

As well as completing my current course in May, my practical experience has included working on a three-month chef placement at the Weigh Bridge Hotel, Sturbridge.

Use of accepted letter-writing format

I am available for an interview from 1 June onwards. In the meantime, I look forward to taking the opportunity to talk with you further about my application.

Yours sincerely

William Johns

Signature

▲ **Figure 1.17** A sample covering letter

- addressee – the person you are writing to
- content (see Figure 1.17)
- the use of accepted letter-writing format (see Figure 1.17)
- your signature.

Interview preparation

First impressions are important. Always make sure you prepare thoroughly as this will help to ensure that you are in control during the interview. Try to remember the following points:

- Research the job you are applying for; make sure that you have read the job description thoroughly. Use this as an opportunity to identify things that you need to ask questions about at the interview.

- Find out about the company by researching how it appears in the news. Look for company performance information and mentions on social media.
- Prepare the answers to possible questions and make a list of questions to ask the employer.
- Remember when answering questions:
  - Use the correct vocabulary when answering questions, and make sure that you can demonstrate good communication skills.
  - Think about the questions before you answer them, and do not waffle!
  - Be clear and concise in your answers.
  - If you do not understand a question, ask the interviewer to repeat it.
- Consider how you are going to introduce yourself at the start of the interview.
- Make sure you are well groomed, smart and look professional. Take account of the type of operation you are applying to work in. More formal operations would expect future employees to wear formal business attire. More casual operations might expect more casual clothing.
- Before the interview, plan your journey and work out the travelling time – allow yourself plenty of time to get there so you do not feel rushed. If possible, visit the premises before the day of the interview. This will help you to calculate journey times and to feel more at home in the premises during the interview.
- Always ensure you have eaten before an interview.

Other interview tips:

- Practise an interview with a friend or colleague beforehand – this is known as role play.
- Show that you understand the importance of time management to the interviewer.
- During the interview, maintain eye contact with the interviewer and smile occasionally. Be confident and polite.

3 EMPLOYABILITY SKILLS REQUIRED FOR THE HOSPITALITY INDUSTRY

3.1 WORK ETHICS

Food and beverage service is the essential link between the customers and the menu on offer in an establishment. The server is the main point of contact between the customers and the establishment, and therefore plays an important role. The skills and knowledge of food and beverage service are also transferable between establishments, sectors and throughout the world.

KEY TERM

Work ethic – positive attitude and competence in contributing to the success of the business.

To be successful in food and beverage service members of staff should have the following attributes:

- sound product knowledge
- well-developed interpersonal skills
- a range of technical skills
- an ability to work as part of a team.

Attitude

Staff conduct should be impeccable at all times, especially in front of customers. The rules and regulations of an establishment must be followed, and respect shown to all senior members of staff. See Unit 205, page 159 for tips on presenting a good attitude at work.

Timekeeping

Punctuality is all-important. Staff who are continually late on duty show a lack of interest in their work, and a lack of respect for both management and customers.

Appearance

Staff should appear professional and hygienic. Their appearance and the first impressions they create reflect the hygiene standards of the establishment and the quality of service.

All staff should be aware of the factors listed in Unit 205 on page 158 regarding hygiene, uniform presentation and personal grooming, and be responsible for ensuring that these are practised in the workplace.

Respecting diversity

Staff must be open-minded and non-judgemental towards customer differences. This helps to demonstrate respect for cultural traditions and diversity in society, including race, colour, creed, ethnic origin, nationality, age, gender, religion or belief, and sexual orientation.

Staff also need to be aware of customers who may have additional needs. Be prepared to deal with people with sight, hearing, mobility and communication difficulties. Also, be prepared and able to deal with children.

Reliability

Success in food and beverage operations is dependent on teamwork. Staff must be able to work as part of a team, both within and between departments. The people in a team depend on each other to be successful and, as a member of the food and beverage department, you will need to contribute to the work of the team by being dependable. Arrive on time, ensure all tasks are completed fully, and ensure a high level of communication is maintained with other members of the team.

Honesty

Trust and respect in staff, customer and management relationships lead to an atmosphere at work that encourages efficiency and a good team spirit.

Resilience

Working in food and beverage service is a demanding job. Staff need to be able to meet the physical demands of the job while maintaining a positive attitude to their work and maintaining a good relationship with colleagues, other departments and customers.

Compliance with the terms and conditions of employment

The obligations and loyalty of staff are first to the establishment in which they are employed and its management. Staff must meet the requirement of the terms and conditions of employment, which are detailed in the employment contract. In addition, there are a range of legal requirements to be observed including, for example, health and safety and licensing. Failure to do so can result in poor performance and possibly dismissal.

3.2 MANAGING ONLINE PRESENCE

Many food and beverage operations use websites as a common way to communicate the product to a wide audience. The organisation's website is one of the first stops for customers when deciding on a product. The website can also provide a platform to:

- receive reservations directly through built-in online booking systems
- provide virtual menus
- stay in contact with customers through blogs and comments.

Third-party booking sites (restaurant marketing portals) provide the opportunity to source bookings and to promote and monitor customer experiences. For example:

www.opentable.com

Beside websites, other online media includes Facebook, Twitter, YouTube, industry blogs and individual blogs. The use of **social media** is increasingly popular, and can offer commercial and personal benefits:

- Commercial benefits – an organisation can promote its products and services.
- Personal benefits – opportunities for professional networking by, for example, setting up a profile on LinkedIn.

Personal integrity

You should always read the terms and conditions of the social media provider. There will be rules about acceptable content both in the text of posts and for images, and various other activities. You must comply with these.

KEY TERM

Social media – internet-based platforms for communication, such as Facebook, Twitter and YouTube.

It needs to be clear if you are posting in a business or personal context.

- Businesses using media are promoting the products and services.
- Individuals using social media are giving information about themselves.

The boundaries between personal and professional use can easily be blurred.

One of the benefits of using social media is the ability to share experiences and opinions, as well as to engage in debate. However, you also need to protect your personal integrity. You should always think about how your current or any future employer's reputation might be affected by any comments you make (or have made), and about the impact your comments might have on your personal reputation.

You should also be aware that information you share with contacts or friends online, or information posted about you by contacts or friends, may be accessible to a much wider audience than you intended. This could be especially important when applying for a job and when in employment. It is now common for employers to check social media of their current employees and as part of the employment selection process.

Use of appropriate language

Operators need to ensure that their websites are easy to use, intuitive, presentable, communicative, current, and an honest reflection of what is offered. Individuals using personal social media also need to follow the same principles.

Content should always be reviewed before posting. This is to avoid posting any content that is, for example, misspelt, incorrect, emotional, misrepresentative or libellous. Content should also be reviewed regularly.

Present and protect a positive business image

When posting anything online you need to think about the legacy of content:

- Once content is posted, it will be seen immediately.
- It is also permanent. Even if it is later deleted it could still be seen through having been repeated or re-posted on other sites.
- There are also malicious pranksters (trolls) who enjoy creating problems for other people who post information online.

To help to present a positive and consistent external image, and also to prevent unauthorised posts or responses by staff, organisations usually have a Social Media Policy. The Social Media Policy will set out the ways in which members of staff in the organisation can engage with social media.

There will also be set procedures to follow when responding to posts. An example of this type of response procedure is shown in Figure 1.18.

Figure 1.18 shows a simple example of a range of similar, and often more complex, response procedures, which are used by many organisations. It is also good advice for individuals.

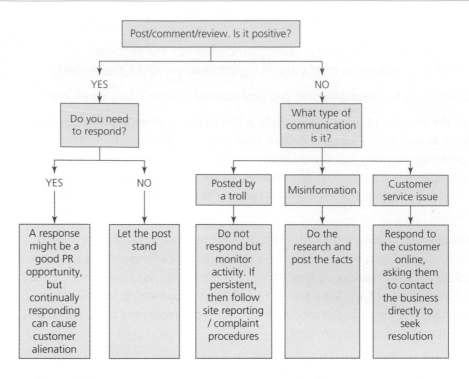

▲ **Figure 1.18** Example of a social media response protocol

Source: Adapted from an illustration from Cousins *et al.* (2016) *Food and Beverage Management*, 4th edition, Goodfellow Publishers

For more information on online security and safe practices see www.getsafeonline.org

4 THE IMPACT OF THE FOOD SERVICE INDUSTRY ON THE ENVIRONMENT

4.1 IMPACT OF THE FOOD SERVICE INDUSTRY ON THE ENVIRONMENT

KEY TERM

Corporate social responsibility (CSR) – business objectives which aim to make an organisation work in more ethical ways.

The hospitality industry is a substantial user of resources. Many organisations have **corporate social responsibility (CSR)** objectives which stress their ethical business aspects.

These can include objectives related to:

- sustainable and responsible sourcing
- fairtrade
- energy saving
- sustainability of the business, and
- concern over pollution and other environmental concerns.

For many organisations, a code of business and social ethics is seen as good for business. Increasingly, businesses will seek only to trade with other businesses that have clear social responsibility policies.

Most businesses now recognise the need for robust CSR strategies. For example, Starbucks is well known for its CSR strategies, which cover each element of its business from sourcing fairtrade coffee through to environmental and community work.

Transport

For the hospitality industry, the impact on transport includes:

- deliveries to the premises
- the need for specialised delivery systems, such as a refrigerated van
- travel distances for food and beverages – often referred to as 'food miles'
- removal of waste from premises
- staff travel costs
- how customers travel to and from the premises.

Reducing the need for transport, especially in reducing food miles, has become a priority for the food service industry. There is greater emphasis on local sourcing and utilising more efficient methods of transport generally.

Energy

The hospitality industry is a huge energy consumer. Lighting, space heating and cooling, and water heating can be a large expense, so controlling energy costs is essential for profitability. Saving energy is also good for the environment: reducing energy production results in less carbon dioxide being emitted into the atmosphere. Energy savings can also help in the operation's sustainability promotion, which is becoming increasingly important to customers.

Steps to reduce energy can include:

- ensuring equipment is turned off when not required
- reducing the amount of energy used during slower times
- using energy-efficient equipment.

Recycling

Businesses in the hospitality industry can recycle significant quantities of materials.

Recycling waste can:

- lower waste-management costs, especially if the business often disposes of heavy materials such as glass
- save space and reduce clutter
- improve the business's environmental credentials
- reduce the business's impact on the environment.

What can you recycle?

Materials that you can recycle include:

- glass bottles and jars
- cardboard
- plastic bottles

KEY TERM

Recycling – reprocessing materials so that they can be reused.

- food and drink cans
- printer cartridges
- electrical items.

Using a recycling waste contractor

Factors to be taken into account when using a waste contractor are:

- what materials are to be recycled
- transport of waste to the facility or collection by the waste contractor
- storage of waste and how often it is to be removed from premises.

Waste

There are a number of benefits from recycling business waste. It will also contribute to saving energy: producing some recycled products (e.g. aluminium) uses far less energy than making it straight from raw materials. However, recycling also uses energy, so the priority should be to reduce waste.

Less disposal to landfill also means less overall harm to the environment.

How to reduce waste

All food service businesses should have an environmental policy. This helps to reinforce the responsibility of the team to be aware that from arriving at the beginning of their shift to leaving the workplace, their actions will have a direct impact on the environment, and on the social responsibility and profit of the organisation.

Ways to reduce waste:

- Have clear allocated responsibilities for controlling waste.
- Monitor the volume and type of waste and measure the costs.
- Recycle everything that can be recycled.

Any sustainability programme should also be aimed at encouraging reduction, reuse and recycling. This is sometimes known as R³, and is depicted in Figure 1.19.

4.2 RESPONSIBLE SOURCING OF FOOD

Food production methods

Food and beverage operations are increasing their knowledge of how food and beverages are produced so that they can ensure more responsible purchasing. This includes purchasing more organic products and taking account of animal welfare and food assurance initiatives.

Use of organic produce

Organic meat and dairy products come from animals that are raised on organic farms. The animals are allowed to roam freely and are given no antibiotics or growth hormones. Organic crops are produced without using artificial fertilisers, pesticides or herbicides.

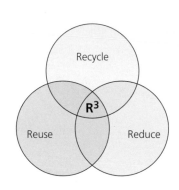

▲ **Figure 1.19** R³: Reduce, Reuse, Recycle

Source: Developed from CESA (2009)

Animal welfare initiatives and food assurance initiatives

Certified foods such as Red Tractor and RSPCA Assured (formerly Freedom Foods) guarantee food safety and higher standards of environmental performance and animal welfare. See Table 1.6 for more sources of information on food production.

▼ **Table 1.6** Sources of information on food production

Organisation	Website
Cert ID – organisation providing food safety certification	**www.cert-id.eu**
Department for Environment, Food and Rural Affairs – Government department dealing with food matters	**www.defra.gov.uk**
Ethical Consumer – magazine providing guidance on how ethical companies and goods are	**www.ethicalconsumer.org**
Fair Trade Foundation – global movement aiming to get a better deal for farmers in developing nations	**www.fairtrade.org.uk**
Food Standards Agency	**www.food.gov.uk**
Red Tractor – food standards scheme which checks that food is responsibly produced	**www.redtractor.org.uk**
RSPCA Assured – ethical food labelling which aims to ensure all farm animals have a good life	**www.rspcaassured.org.uk**
Slow Food Organisation – global organisation promoting the pleasure of eating and biodiversity	**www.slowfood.org.uk**
Soil Association – charity that certifies much of the UK's organic food and campaigns on issues such as pesticides and GM food	**www.soilassociation.org**
Vegetarian Society – organisation supporting those who wish to maintain a vegetarian lifestyle	**www.vegsoc.org**

Provenance of food and beverages

Today, customers are far more interested in where and how food is grown, raised or reared, processed and transported. This can be important in certain cultural contexts (see Unit 202, page 46 for customer dietary requirements) and also includes whether the customer is accepting of practices such as Genetically Modified (GM) foods or irradiated foods.

Product sourcing

More emphasis is also being placed on purchasing so that it is local, sustainable and uses reputable suppliers.

Local

For food service businesses, the benefits of local purchasing can include:

- increased marketing opportunities through making a feature of using locally sourced food and beverage items
- promotions related to local seasons and food and beverage specialities

- improved menu planning, as suppliers can give information in advance on what they are able to provide
- more reliable products and service, with greater flexibility to respond to customer needs.

Sustainable

Sustainability has three aspects:

1 Ensuring the food producers will be able to continue in business through being fair in purchasing practices.
2 Reducing food packaging and food waste.
3 Reducing the effects that food production and food transportation have on the environment generally.

Using reputable suppliers

It is a legal requirement for food service operations to take reasonable precautions and do all that is needed to protect customers. It is important to use reputable suppliers that can be trusted to supply and handle food safely, as well as delivering on time. The UK Food Standards Agency identifies questions that should be addressed before selecting suppliers. These are:

- Is the supplier registered with the local authority?
- Does the supplier store, transport and pack its goods in a hygienic way?
- Does the supplier provide allergen information?
- Does the supplier/contractor supply fully referenced invoices/receipts?
- Does it have any certification or quality assurance?
- How quickly does it respond to your concerns?
- Ask other businesses for trusted recommendations.

Source: Food Standards Agency

Ethical sourcing

Customers have become increasingly aware of **ethical issues** involved in trade relationships. Both fairtrade and direct trade represent efforts to create the best and fairest trade relationships possible.

Fairtrade is about achieving better prices, decent working conditions and a fair deal for farmers and workers in developing countries. The Fairtrade organisation sets social, economic and environmental standards for both companies and the farmers. These standards are assessed independently and a Fairtrade Mark is then allowed to be put on the products.

Direct trade is where an operation trades directly with individual producers. The buyer and producer work together for their mutual long-term benefit.

Seasonality of fresh food products

There is a greater trend towards using more **seasonally sourced** fresh food and beverage items. Buying food which is in season means the quality, taste, freshness and nutritional value are all at their peak, and supplies are more plentiful and cheaper.

▲ **Figure 1.20** Sustainability: separating food waste

KEY TERMS

Ethical issues – purchasing products from sustainable, local and reputable suppliers.

Seasonally sourced fresh food products – food that is purchased during season when it is naturally ready to be picked.

Test your learning

Having worked through Unit 201, see how you can approach the following activities.

1 Name **three** sectors of the hospitality industry that would fall into the commercial or profit orientated sector.

2 Name **three** sectors of the hospitality industry that would fall into the service or cost provision sector.

3 As well as accommodation, food and beverages, hotels now offer an increasing range of services/facilities. Name **three** of these services/facilities.

4 Name **three** ways the hospitality industry contributes to the economy of the United Kingdom.

5 Identify **three** types of employment.

6 State **three** departments of a food service operation.

7 Identify **six** job roles in food and beverage service.

8 What are **three** essential pieces of information that need to go on a CV?

9 If you have produced a CV, give **one** reason for providing a covering letter.

10 If you have been unsuccessful at a job interview, state **one** way you could still learn from the experience.

11 Identify **one** person who you could go to for help in developing a personal development plan.

12 Give **one** reason why is it important to present a good professional personal appearance.

13 List **two** personal attributes that would be helpful when dealing with customers.

14 State **one** reason why it is important to work well as part of a team in the hospitality industry.

15 Give **one** reason why it is important to protect your personal integrity when using social media.

PRINCIPLES OF CUSTOMER SERVICE

INTRODUCTION

The purpose of this chapter is to help you acquire the professional behaviours that have most impact on the way the customer sees you and your organisation.

This chapter will help you to:

- identify your customers
- know your responsibilities in relation to providing customer service
- know how your actions impact on the business and other people
- know what you can do to exceed customer expectations.

1 CUSTOMER SERVICE

1.1 CHARACTERISTICS AND BENEFITS OF CUSTOMER SERVICE

All establishments should aim to offer the highest standards of professional customer service at all times. This should be appropriate to the type and style of the establishment.

The characteristics of excellent customer service in food service operations are:

1 **Provide a professional service**: the level of individual personal attention given to customers. Always:
   - be polite, friendly and well-mannered
   - show respect for the customer
   - listen actively (and do not use jargon when you reply to a customer's question)

- use different methods of communication to meet the needs of customers – for example, those with language difficulties or mobility issues, the elderly or children, cultural differences or people with learning difficulties.
2 **Service consistency**: offer a good standard of service that is consistent every day – and is the same for each and every customer.
3 **Service reliability**: Does the service bring in repeat business?
  Is it exceeding expectations? Are customers made to feel 'at home' in this environment? Are the staff aware of any special features of the service on offer?
4 **Proactively anticipate customer needs and influence change in poor service**: knowing the order of service and observing customer behaviour will enable staff to provide service at the appropriate time. Watch out for trends in consumer demands and stock the product range(s) currently in demand. Being able to meet and exceed customer expectations is vital for excellent customer service.
5 **Aim to achieve 100 per cent customer satisfaction**: set high standards to ensure the customer receives the best experience every time, through thorough training, briefing and service consistency.

▲ **Figure 2.1** A formal restaurant

Benefits of excellent customer service to the organisation and customer

The benefits to the organisation include:

- fewer complaints
- higher levels of customer satisfaction
- increases in repeat business and customer loyalty
- increased sales revenue
- enhanced reputation through word of mouth, reviews, social media
- lower staff turnover.

For the individuals who work in the food and beverages industry, the benefits of providing good customer service include:
- job satisfaction, which leads to increased motivation and pride in the organisation
- job security and training opportunities for advancement
- recognition by management (leading to promotion and bonuses and/or tips).

1.2 TYPES OF CUSTOMERS
Internal customers and their expectations
Other departments/areas of the organisation

- Teamwork – assisting other teams will ensure customers always receive the best service and colleagues are supported when the workload is high.
- Timely/accurate communication – all departments can deliver a high level of service by passing on information quickly to those who need to know.

Accepting diversity

Staff should be aware of, and accepting of, diversity, sexual orientation and cultural differences. This should be taken for granted when serving customers or working alongside colleagues and any other staff member or supplier you may encounter. Be sensitive to the needs and beliefs of others, and always follow your establishment's guidelines on appropriate behaviour.

Behaviour

When dealing with colleagues as customers, staff should still present a professional image and work in a professional manner. Being polite, efficient and knowledgeable should be the standard for all customers, whether internal or external. Staff should be made aware that their behaviour reflects on the business, and that all customers and colleagues deserve to be respected and have the full attention of staff while on duty.

Accurate communication

Passing on information must be done accurately to meet customer and business needs. This will reduce complaints and increase efficiency and profitability. Examples of this might include:

- Reservations informing the Rooms division manager of the room types and tariffs being booked (for example, customers requesting bed and breakfast or room only, any group check-in/check-out times) – from this forecast the Rooms division manager will inform the Food and Beverage manager, who will know when spikes in demand for service are likely and therefore have sufficient staff on duty to cover the demand.
- Writing down customer requirements reduces errors, and repeating back to the customer will ensure the information is correct.
- If orders are written down, staff need to write clearly, in a standardised format. Orders are often taken using an electronic point of sale (EPOS) system (see Unit 205) and care must be taken to make sure information is accurate. Any requests or side comments should be added to the notes section and highlighted before posting to the system.
- An efficient EPOS system will also assist in stocktaking, sales analysis and recording orders. Customer histories can be created to enhance the customer experience for future visits.

External customers and their expectations

External clients can have a range of expectations. These can be split into two categories: business and leisure (see Table 2.1).

▼ **Table 2.1** Customer expectations

Business	Leisure
Speed of service – as time may be limited, service staff should check if the customers are in a hurry.	**Pace of service** – a slower pace of service would usually be expected by leisure customers, but service staff should check if this is the case.
Tact – business customers may be discussing private matters, so any information overheard must be kept confidential.	**Special occasions and celebrations** – weddings, birthdays, anniversaries or awards events come with expectations. These events are often emotional and customers should take away special memories.
Attention to customer needs – service staff should observe and anticipate customer needs without having to interrupt.	**Ambiance** – leisure customers often choose a venue based on an expectation of comfort, service and being cared for. The ambiance should more than a 'home from home', but less formal than for a business customer.
Access to private dining – some customers may prefer a separate area or privacy for their requirements.	
Access to company billing – many business customers will have pre-arranged the bill to be sent to their company. A signature must be obtained to confirm the customer has received the services being billed.	

1.3 CUSTOMERS WITH SPECIFIC NEEDS
Demographics – age, social standing, income

Diverse types of food service operation are designed for the needs people have at a particular time. The customer's demographic will change according to when and where the service is offered. For example:

- A person may be a business customer during the week, but a member of a family at the weekend.
- They may want a quick lunch on one occasion, a snack while travelling on another and a meal with the family on another occasion.
- They may wish to book a special occasion, for example a wedding.
- Younger people may have less disposable income to spend on expensive food and drink in a restaurant and therefore will choose a cheaper option.
- Older people may have a less adventurous palate than younger people.
- Social standing may determine where people go for their leisure and entertainment. This may be a perception of where the individual believes they fit, based on factors such as parentage, education, employment, income and heritage. This however is not definitive and should be used cautiously as a measure of social standing.

Cultural

Staff need to be able to observe and be respectful of cultural differences. To be able to professionally respond to the customer's needs, staff need to know the menu well, including any special offers, and be sensitive to different cultural requirements, such as:

- different preparation methods
- cooking procedures
- the equipment to be used
- dietary requirements
- alcohol content.

Examples of dietary requirements based on religious beliefs are given in Table 2.2.

▼ **Table 2.2** Dietary requirements according to the various faiths

Hindus	Do not eat beef and rarely pork. Some Hindus do not eat any meat, fish or eggs. Diet may include cheese, milk and vegetarian dishes
Jews	Only 'clean' (kosher) animals may be consumed. Jews do not eat pork or pork products, shellfish or animal fats and gelatine from beasts considered to be unclean or not slaughtered according to the prescribed manner. Restrictions are placed on methods of preparation and cookery. The preparation and eating of meat and dairy products at the same meal is not allowed
Muslims	Do not eat meat, offal or animal fat unless it is halal (i.e. lawful, as required under Islamic Dietary Law). Muslims do not consume alcohol, even when used in cooking
Sikhs	Do not eat beef or pork. Some keep to a vegetarian diet. Others may eat fish, mutton, cheese and eggs. Sikhs do not eat halal meat
Rastafarians	Do not eat any processed foods, pork or fish without fins (e.g. eels). Do not consume tea, coffee or alcohol
Roman Catholics	Few restrictions on diet. Usually do not eat meat on Ash Wednesday or Good Friday. Some keep with the past requirement for no meat to be eaten on Fridays; fish and dairy products may be eaten instead

Language

It is important that staff are aware of the words, volume and tone used with customers. Speaking clearly and explaining terms on menus and drinks lists is an important skill to ensure customers have the information that they need. This is especially important if the customer does not understand the language of the menu and beverage lists and is not familiar with technical terms and jargon, such as 'sous vide' or 'VSOP'. Maintaining a polite manner when giving explanations will give a professional impression and keep the customer at ease. For the customer this may be the first time they have heard or read the term, and they deserve to be answered attentively and with respect.

Consider having menus in different languages, and identify members of staff who can speak more than one language.

Different types of customers

See Table 2.3 for ideas on how you might provide the best service for different types of customers.

▼ **Table 2.3** Different types of customers

Type of customer	Description
Groups	Groups would usually be given a set time to eat and a set menu if the numbers are large. Alternatively, a limited menu or buffet-style service would suit large groups. Billing can sometimes cause issues in groups where drinks may not be included, and therefore service staff should be briefed to ensure either a signature to sign to room bills in hotels or payment in a restaurant should be taken
Individual diners	Individual diners may wish to be left alone and this should be respected. However, some customers would be happy to be given the option to share a table with other customers, to strike up conversation and make new acquaintances
Family	When looking after a family dining with young children, the children should receive their food and drinks quickly. The adults can relax once the children have been fed. Items such as colouring books and puzzles can be supplied to keep the children occupied
Business	Business customers may wish to sit at a quiet table and may be limited for time. Service staff should enquire as to their needs and endeavour to conclude the service within the time available. Business customers might be assisted with extras such as a phone or laptop charger, ordering a taxi or local information

Customers with special requirements

Wheelchair users

Customers may have a range of walking difficulties and/or difficulties with stairs. They may use walking sticks, crutches or a wheelchair, or have limitations in manual dexterity. For these customers:

- Offer wheelchair users places at tables where there is adequate space for manoeuvrability, out of the main thoroughfare of customer/staff movement, with easy access to cloakrooms, exits and fire exits.
- Offer a wheelchair user the opportunity to transfer to a restaurant chair.
- Never move a wheelchair without asking the customer first.
- Place crutches/walking sticks in a safe but readily accessible position for the customer.
- Ask customers with manual dexterity difficulties how best they can be helped. Assistance might include, for example, ensuring that all items served or placed on the table are near the customer, offering to fillet/bone fish and meat items and to cut up other food items, and offering alternative cutlery.

Sight/hearing-impaired customers

Communication issues may arise when, for example, customers are blind or partially sighted, deaf or hard of hearing, are unable to speak or have little understanding of the English language.

For customers with impaired sight:

- Be prepared to accept guide dogs into your premises.
- Describe the route to the table, including stairs, changes in floor surfaces, location of walls and potential hazards/obstructions, such as a pillar.
- Seat customers away from excessive noise, which can be distracting and potentially distressing.
- Offer to read menus or wine and drinks lists.
- Consider having larger-print menus and menus in Braille.
- Be prepared to fillet/bone fish and meat items and to cut up other food items.
- Never overfill cups, glasses or bowls.
- Consider using bowls instead of plates for specific food items, but always ask the customer what they would prefer first.
- Be prepared to provide alternative cutlery.
- Ask if you should describe where the food items are on the plate. Use the clock method to explain the location of food on a plate, for example, 6 o'clock for meat, 10 to 10 for vegetables and 10 past 2 for potatoes, as shown in Figure 2.2.

▲ **Figure 2.2** Standard placement of food items

For customers with impaired hearing:

- Seat customers away from excessive noise, which can be especially uncomfortable for customers wearing hearing aids.
- Speak directly to the customer face to face.
- Speak normally but more distinctly.
- Describe food/drink items in simple, precise and plain language.
- Consider including pictures of the dishes on the menus.
- Listen attentively to what is being said and always read back the food or drink order to the customers to confirm all requests.

For customers who have little understanding of the English language similar actions can be taken. Operations can also consider having menus in different languages and pictures of the dishes. It is also useful to have identified members of staff who have ability in more than one language.

Remember:

- Talk to and treat customers with additional needs as you would any other customer.
- Do not talk to a person's companions as if the person was not there.
- The majority of disabled people are not wheelchair users.
- Do not assume anything; always seek to find out from the customer how best they can be helped.

Elderly customers

Elderly customers may experience many of the issues faced by customers with mobility, sight and hearing issues as outlined above. Service staff should be considerate and patient with elderly customers, anticipating their needs and limitations.

Dealing with children

If children are among the customers arriving in the food service area, take the lead in how to care for them from the parents, guardian or accompanying adults. Where applicable, the following factors should be determined.

- Are high chairs/seat cushions required?
- Restrictions on the service of alcohol to minors. (See Unit 206, Consumption of alcohol by young people, page 280 for more information on the legal restrictions for service to 16- or 17-year-olds.)
- Are children's meal menus required?
- The availability and choice of children's meals (make sure you know what the children's meals consist of) including portion size, for example the number of sausages.
- The portion size required if items are ordered from the standard menu.
- For the safety of both children and others, the staff should be aware of children's whereabouts (keep all routes to the kitchen clear).
- If the children are older, then they should be addressed as either 'Sir' or 'Miss'.
- The cost per head in relation to the portion size.
- Any specific requests or amendments to orders, such as no baked beans.
- The importance of not overfilling cups, bowls or glasses.
- Ensuring that children's plates are warm rather than hot to avoid mishaps.

Customers' requests

Customers often make requests for special items such as a birthday cake, champagne or flowers to be delivered in advance. They may also have a specific table request or a seating plan. These requests need to be carefully recorded and communicated to the appropriate departments to ensure the customer receives what they have requested, when they want it.

Staff should always record these requests in the booking diary/events folder and communicate the request to the relevant departments. This should be checked 24 hours before customers are due to arrive to ensure that the request has been acted upon and will arrive in time for the customer. If the request requires an external provider, then details of the provider should also be recorded and delivery instructions should be provided.

Celebrations

If the customer mentions it is a celebration when the booking is taken, this should be recorded in the diary and staff should enquire if they would like the establishment to arrange anything special (champagne, flowers, chocolates, balloons, a cake, etc.).

Dietary requirements

It is now common for customers to have special dietary requirements. The accurate recording of ingredients to highlight allergens, food intolerances and food provenance for **lifestyle preferences** is essential. Service staff need to be fully briefed and have a good understanding of the implications and consequences of serving a customer with something that could make them seriously ill.

To aid the customer in making the appropriate choice, menu items that are suitable for a **vegetarian** diet can be identified with 'V', while menu items containing nuts can be identified with 'N' next to their description. Nevertheless, it is important that the server can accurately describe the dishes so that the customer can make an appropriate choice. The server should never guess and, if in doubt, should seek further information. Some examples of dietary requirements are given in Table 4.20 in Unit 204, page 150.

Allergies

Food items that are known to cause allergies in some people are called allergens and they include:

- gluten in wheat, rye and barley (known as coeliac)
- peanuts and their derivatives
- sesame seeds and other nuts such as cashew, pecan, brazil and walnuts
- milk, fish, shellfish, eggs and tropical fruits.

For more information on allergens see Table 3.6 in Unit 203, page 99.

Sometimes these foods can cause **anaphylactic shock**, resulting in the lips, tongue or throat swelling dramatically over a very short period of time. The result can be fatal, so prompt medical treatment is needed in such cases.

KEY TERMS

Lifestyle preferences – food and beverage consumption based on ethical sourcing.

Vegetarianism – not eating meat or meat-derived products.

Anaphylactic shock – a very serious allergic reaction for which medical treatment is required.

Food intolerances

A **food intolerance** is difficulty digesting certain foods and having an unpleasant physical reaction to them. Unlike an allergy, it doesn't involve the body's immune system as there is no allergic reaction and it is not life-threatening. However, staff should treat an intolerance in the same way they would an allergy as the effects can be severe to the person ingesting the intolerant food.

Lifestyle preferences

Customers have become increasingly aware of ethical issues such as:

- sustainability
- fairtrade
- the acceptance or otherwise of genetically modified foods or irradiated foods
- the need to reduce food packaging and food waste
- the effect that food production and food transportation have on the environment
- vegetarianism.

For food service businesses, the benefits of seasonal and locally sourced foods can also include:

- high levels of nutritional value and freshness when supplies are more plentiful and cheaper
- improved menu planning, as suppliers can give information in advance on what they are able to provide
- more reliable products and service, with greater flexibility to respond to customer needs
- increased marketing opportunities, making a feature of using locally sourced food and beverage items and special promotions related to local and seasonal specialties
- support for training of staff from local suppliers.

See also Unit 201, 4.2 Responsible sourcing of food.

Vegetarianism may derive from cultural, religious, moral, ethical or physiological considerations. It is therefore important that food descriptions are accurate. The various forms of vegetarianism are summarised in Table 2.4 below.

▼ **Table 2.4** Forms of vegetarianism

Vegetarians: semi	Do not eat red meat, or any meat other than poultry, or any meat. Diet includes fish and may include dairy produce and other animal products
Vegetarians: lacto-ovo	Do not eat meat, fish or poultry but may drink milk, eat milk products and eggs
Vegetarians: lacto	Do not eat meat, fish, poultry or eggs but may drink milk and eat milk products
Vegans	Do not eat any foods of animal origin. Diet mainly consists of vegetables, vegetable oils, cereals, nuts, fruits and seeds
Fruitarians	More restricted form of vegetarianism. Excluded are all foods of animal origin, together with pulses and cereals. Diet may include mainly raw and dried fruit, nuts, honey and olive oil

KEY TERM

Food intolerance – difficulty digesting certain foods and having an unpleasant physical reaction to them.

1.4 IMPACT OF POOR CUSTOMER SERVICE

Poor customer service can quickly be communicated to the world via social-media platforms, information-sharing apps and customer review sites. This can have immediate and possibly negative consequences for a business's reputation and therefore profits.

Impact of poor customer service on the organisation

Increase in number of complaints

When there is an increase in the number of complaints, management need to investigate the root cause of these complaints and identify the issues that are causing them. If this relates to customer service, re-training needs to take place or methods and procedures need to be re-evaluated.

- **Loss of business** – complaints, however small, can lead to a loss of business. Reducing the level of complaints as quickly as possible and turning a negative situation into a positive one should be the aim of all staff. Listening to complaints and offering solutions to the customer promptly and politely will often diffuse the complaint and result in the customer being satisfied and returning in the future.
- **Loss of reputation** – poor complaint resolution will result in customers being dissatisfied and complaining to their friends, colleagues and the wider community. A loss of reputation is difficult to recover from, especially if the complaint is made online in the public domain and on social media.
- **Staff demotivation** – management need to look at the causes of complaints and evaluate what has gone wrong with the service operation. It could be due to:
  - staff being put under pressure (due to shortage of staff)
  - a lack of training
  - insufficient stocks of equipment
  - inferior quality of food
  - slow preparation and service of food and drinks
  - disrepair and poor decor of the premises
  - low wages and/or a lack of benefits.

  The above issues will all need to be addressed to show staff they are valued and thus improve morale.
- **Job losses** – ultimately poor customer service resulting in a high level of complaints, loss of business, reputation and staff demotivation will mean that the organisation must either address the issues to improve and regain the customer's loyalty or make job cuts to save the business. Regular staff training, good working conditions and a high standard of service will keep both customers and staff happy so that the business remains viable.

Process for responding to customer problems and complaints

It is important that steps are in place to ensure that customer complaints are properly and professionally responded to:

- Anticipate potential problems – good preparation can help avoid most complaints and knowing what to do when a situation arises will reduce the severity of the situation.
- Actively listen to the customer(s) and apologise – be genuine and listen carefully, repeat back the key points and make notes if necessary.
- Investigate the complaint – talk to all the relevant people concerning the complaint and establish exactly what happened.
- Take action to solve the problem – propose a reasonable solution to the problem within your remit. If this is not possible then refer (escalate) the problem to the relevant person, such as the Head Waiter.
- Refer (escalate) the problem to the relevant person where required – the chain of referral should be communicated to staff in advance of service, so that they are clear on the process. The customer should also be informed whom the problem is to be referred to, for example the Head Waiter or Restaurant Manager.
- Thank the customer for their comments – always thank them for letting you know there's a problem because their 'feedback' will help the business to improve.
- Record information – noting down the details of the incident will not only help to establish if a pattern of issues exists, but also acts as a record for future reference (should this be necessary).
- Follow up procedures – these are put in place to ensure all staff work within company policy and ensure all complaints are handled in a professional manner.
- Undertake further training if necessary – this will reduce the number of incidents and improve the standard of service offered.

Valid complaints provide important feedback for a food service operation and can be used as valuable learning opportunities.

Responding negatively to any online complaints should never happen. Complaints should be acknowledged and then responded to privately and individually to resolve the situation. Negative comments about the complainant will always result in your business appearing to be arrogant and uncaring, however unjustified you may feel the complaint to be.

1.5 IMPACT OF LEGISLATION FOR CUSTOMER SERVICE

▼ **Table 2.5** An overview of the relevant legislation affecting hospitality businesses

Consumer Rights Act 2015	The right to return faulty goods for refund, replacement or repair, and rights on the purchase of digital content
Health and Safety at Work etc. Act 1974	The responsibility of everyone to ensure that they work in a safe manner, in a safe environment and report any unsafe practice. It also places responsibility on employers to provide a safe working environment and safety clothing (PPE) at all times
Food Safety and Hygiene Regulations 2013	This covers temperatures for storing, cooking and display of foods, keeping food safe from contamination and food handling responsibilities

Pricing Act 1974	This requires that prices be clearly displayed and that the customer cannot be misled by displays or statements in regard to prices charged or interest that may be incurred
General Data Protection Regulation 2018	This legislation seeks to give people more control over how organisations use their data and introduces hefty penalties for organisations that fail to comply with the rules and for those that suffer data breaches. It also ensures data protection law is almost identical across the EU
Licensing Act 2003	This informs and guides all premises in England and Wales which are used for the sale or supply of alcohol, provide regulated entertainment or late night refreshment
Weights and Measures Act 1985	Enforced by Trading Standards Offices within local authorities, this act lists packaging sizes and pricing structures that might be used in specific circumstances, such as measurements in which wine and beer can be sold. See also page 276
Equality Act 2010	Legally protects people from discrimination in the workplace and in wider society

Penalties for non-compliance with legislation can be severe, both for the business and for the management and staff. It is important that all members of staff contribute to ensuring compliance with the legal requirements.

Enforcement bodies include representatives of:

- National Trading Standards
- local councils
- police
- weights and measures officials
- Information Commissioner's Office
- Equality and Human Rights Commission.

Consumer Rights Act

Under the Consumer Rights Act (2015) there is a duty to trade fairly and requirements not to engage in misleading and aggressive practices. The act also prohibits a specific range of practices.

The food service operator and members of staff need to follow good practice to ensure:

- all food, beverages and other services provided are fit for purpose and of satisfactory quality in relation to price and description
- food, beverages and other services are accurately described in terms of size, quality, composition, production, quantity and standard
- all statements of price, whether in an advertisement, brochure, leaflet, website or given by letter or orally in person or over the telephone, are clear and accurate
- pricing and the display of priced items complies with the Consumer Protection from Unfair Trading Regulations 2008 (see page 277) and the ABV (alcohol by volume) of alcoholic drinks is declared on the drinks list to comply with the Food Labelling Regulations 1996
- food, beverages and other services correspond to their description in brochures/promotional materials

- times, dates, locations and nature of service promised are adhered to
- customer billing is fair, transparent and reflects the prices quoted either orally or in writing.

The act also made some changes to rights to return faulty goods for refund, replacement or repair, and adds new rights on the purchase of digital content.

To ensure compliance with legislation, care must be taken when:

- wording menus and wine lists
- describing menu and beverage items to customers
- stating if prices include local and/or government taxes
- describing conditions such as cover charges, service charges or extras
- describing the service provision.

Providing services

Generally, food and beverage operators are under no specific requirement to serve anyone. However, it is important that the supervisor and staff are aware of:

- circumstances where there may be a mandatory requirement to provide services
- valid reasons for refusal.

Contracts

A contract is made when one party agrees to the terms of an offer made by another party; this can be written or verbal. In food and beverage service there are essentially two types of customer: those who pre-book and those who do not (often called chance or casual customers).

All food service establishments should be clear on how they will deal with these different types of customers, including:

- circumstances where the restaurant may seek compensation from the customer if they do not turn up or pay for their meals or services
- taking care when making contracts with minors (persons under 18).

Customer property and customer debt

Good practice usually means that supervisors need to ensure care is taken of customers' property to minimise potential loss or damage. Notices warning customers of 'no responsibility' may help in defence when a customer is seeking compensation in court, but they do not guarantee exemption from liability for the food and beverage operator.

Clear guidance must be given to staff on the procedures to follow if a customer is unable or unwilling to pay.

Health and safety regulations

The **Health and Safety at Work Act 1974**, the **Fire Safety Order 2006** and **Fire (Scotland) Act 2005** cover areas of safety within the workplace. Key responsibilities under the legislation include ensuring that:

- there is a written health and safety policy
- service standards comply with health, safety, environmental and food hygiene regulations

KEY TERMS

Risk assessment – identifying hazards and actions required to remove or reduce the risk involved.

Risk – the chance of somebody being harmed by a hazard.

Hazard or hazardous – anything that can cause harm.

- adequate arrangements are in place to ensure the safety, security and well-being of staff and customers
- periodic **risk assessments** are carried out and recorded
- emergency exits are clearly marked, and regular fire drills are carried out
- staff are trained in procedures to follow in the event of a fire and know how to use firefighting equipment
- staff are aware of evacuation procedures in the event of a fire or a security **risk** such as a bomb threat
- health and safety notices are displayed in working areas
- staff and customers are trained, as appropriate, on correct usage of equipment and facilities
- all food handlers are trained in safe and hygienic working practices.

In addition, the **Employers' Liability Act (1969)** and **Employers' Liability (Northern Ireland) Order (1972)** require employers to ensure that they have valid employer liability insurance cover at all times and that a notice is displayed to that effect.

The **Health and Safety at Work Act (1974)** covers all full-time and part-time workers as well as unpaid workers. The Health and Safety Executive (HSE) is responsible for enforcing health and safety in the workplace.

Under the terms of the Health and Safety at Work Act (1974), an employer must make sure that all staff are safe while at work. This means that the employer must:

- provide safe equipment and utensils, train staff in safe working practices, provide first aid equipment
- keep an accident book
- produce a policy document telling everyone how to work safely
- provide good welfare facilities for staff including rest facilities, drinking water, toilets, washing facilities, changing rooms and lockers.

Safety at work is a civil duty and negligence is a criminal offence. The legislation states that staff must:

- understand the food hygiene regulations and that it is their responsibility to act within the bounds of these regulations
- notify management of any serious or infectious illness
- perform duties in any area concerned with the handling of food in a hygienic manner, paying attention to food and hygiene regulations
- make themselves familiar with all escape routes and fire exits in the building
- ensure that fire exits remain clear at all times
- participate in fire evacuation drills and practices
- take reasonable care for the health and safety of themselves and of others, and ensure that health and safety regulations are followed
- report to heads of department or duty managers any **hazards** that may cause injury or ill-health to customers and/or staff.

Control of Substances Hazardous to Health

The **Control of Substances Hazardous to Health (COSHH) Regulations 2002** state that an employer must not carry out any work that might expose employees to any substances that are hazardous to health, unless the employer has assessed the risks of this work to employees. In food service establishments there are many chemicals and substances used for cleaning that can be harmful if not used correctly (see Table 2.6). The employer should make sure that measures are in place to control the use of chemical substances and monitor their use.

▲ **Figure 2.3** A potential hazard

▼ **Table 2.6** Work areas and the chemicals and substances likely to be found in them

Work area	Chemicals and substances
Kitchen	Cleaning chemicals including alkalis and acids, detergents, sanitisers and descalers
	Chemicals associated with burnishing; possibly some oils associated with machines
	Pest control chemicals, insecticides and rodenticides
Restaurant	Cleaning chemicals, polishes, fuel for flame lamps including methylated spirits, liquid petroleum gas (LPG)
Bar	Beer-line cleaner, glass-washing detergent and sanitisers
Housekeeping	Cleaning chemicals including detergents, sanitisers, descalers, polishes, carpet-cleaning products, floor-care products
Maintenance	Cleaning chemicals, adhesives, solvents, paint, LPG, salts for water softening, paint stripper, varnishes
Offices	Correction fluid, thinners, solvents, methylated spirits, toner for photocopier, duplicating fluids and chemicals, polishes

Substances that are dangerous to health are labelled as very toxic, toxic, harmful, irritant or corrosive. Figure 2.4 shows some hazardous substances symbols. People using these chemical substances must be trained to use them correctly. They must also wear protective clothing such as goggles, gloves and face masks. Hazardous substances can enter the body through the skin, eyes, nose (by inhaling) and mouth (by swallowing).

Guidelines for using chemical substances include:

- Inform, instruct and train all staff in their use and safety.
- Ensure the manufacturer's instructions are followed.
- Make sure the chemicals are always stored in their original containers, away from heat.
- Keep lids tightly closed.
- Do not expose chemicals to heat or naked flames.
- Read all the labels carefully.
- Never mix chemicals.
- Know the first aid procedure.
- Get rid of empty containers immediately.

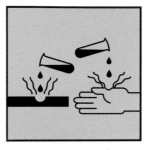

Corrosive

Flammable

Harmful

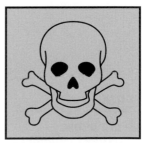

Toxic

▲ **Figure 2.4** Hazardous substances symbols

- Get rid of waste chemical solutions safely.
- Wear safety equipment and clothing.

Hazardous substance monitoring

To comply with legal obligations under the COSHH Regulations, all areas should be surveyed to ascertain which chemicals and substances are used. A COSHH register should be kept by the manager of all substances used in the establishment. Technical data sheets should be attached to the completed COSHH assessment sheet.

Reporting of Injuries, Diseases and Dangerous Occurrences Regulations (RIDDOR) 2013

The law says that all work-related accidents, diseases and dangerous occurrences must be recorded and reported. Employers must report the following injuries to the Incident Contact Centre at the HSE:

- fractures (apart from fractures to fingers, thumbs or toes)
- amputation (cutting off) of limbs
- dislocation of a hip, knee or spine
- temporary or permanent loss of sight (blindness)
- eye injuries from chemicals, hot metal burns or any penetration of the eye
- any injury from electric shock or burning that leads to unconsciousness, the need to resuscitate the person or send them to hospital for more than 24 hours
- any injury resulting in hypothermia (when someone gets too cold), or illness due to heat that leads to unconsciousness
- the need to resuscitate a person or send them to hospital for more than 24 hours – for example, a gas flame 'blown back' that causes burns
- unconsciousness caused by exposure to a harmful substance or biological agent (such as cleaning products and solvents)
- unconsciousness or illness requiring medical treatment caused by inhaling a harmful substance or absorbing it through the skin (for example, breathing in poisonous carbon monoxide leaking from a gas appliance)
- illness requiring medical treatment caused by a biological agent or its toxins or infected material (for instance, harmful bacteria used in laboratories).

Some diseases are also reportable under RIDDOR and these include:

- dermatitis
- skin cancer
- asthma
- hepatitis
- tuberculosis
- tetanus
- anthrax.

See Unit 203, page 82 for an example of an incident report form.

Personal protective equipment (PPE)

According to the **Personal Protective Equipment (PPE)** at Work Regulations (1992), employees must wear personal protective equipment and clothing (such as safety shoes or eye protection such as goggles) for tasks that may pose a risk or hazard.

KEY TERM

Personal protective equipment (PPE) – protective clothing and equipment used for tasks that may pose a risk or hazard.

▲ **Figure 2.5** Personal protective equipment

For more information on PPE see Unit 203, page 86.

Fire safety

Every employer has an explicit duty for the safety of his or her employees in the event of a fire. The Regulatory Fire Safety Order (2005) emphasises that fires should be prevented. It says that fire safety is the responsibility of the occupant of the premises and the people who might be affected by fire, so in catering this will usually be the employer (the occupant) and the employees (who will be affected by fire).

The responsible person must:

- make sure that the fire precautions, where reasonably practicable, ensure the safety of all employees and others in the building
- assess the risk of and from fire in the establishment; special consideration must be given to dangerous chemicals or substances and the risks that these pose if a fire occurs
- review the preventative and protective measures.

Procedure in case of fire

All employees should be given fire drill training as part of their induction programme. This initial training should then be followed up by regular training sessions on the procedures to be followed in the event of fire.

For more details on firefighting equipment see Unit 203, page 85, for fire detection see page 83 and for evacuation procedures see page 84.

Food Safety Regulations

Everyone consuming food prepared for them by others when they are away from home (for example, in canteens and restaurants) has the right and expectation to be served safe food that will not cause illness or harm them in any way.

Food safety means putting in place all of the measures needed to make sure that food and drinks are suitable, safe and wholesome throughout the whole process of food provision – from selecting suppliers and delivery of food, to serving the food to the customer.

Why is food safety important?

Food poisoning is an acute intestinal illness that is the result of eating food contaminated with pathogens and/or their toxins. Food poisoning may also be caused by eating poisonous fish or plants, chemicals or metals. Symptoms of food poisoning are often similar and may include diarrhoea, vomiting, nausea, fever, headache, dehydration and abdominal pain.

Eating 'contaminated' food can cause illness (food poisoning) and, in some cases, even death. The number of reported cases of food poisoning each year in England and Wales remains high, between 70,000 and 94,000 reported cases each year. However, as many food poisoning cases are not reported, no one really knows the actual number.

Food poisoning can be unpleasant for anyone but for some the illness can be very serious or even fatal. Extra care with food safety must be observed when providing food for these groups of people. High-risk groups include:

- babies and the very young
- elderly people
- pregnant women
- those with an impaired immune system who are already unwell.

The Food Hygiene (England) Regulations 2006 set out the basic food safety requirements for all aspects of a food business, from premises to personal hygiene of staff, with specific attention on temperatures relating to food. There is similar legislation for other parts of the UK.

Food safety standards and legislation are enforced by environmental health officers (EHOs) – also known as environmental health practitioners (EHPs). They may visit food premises as a matter of routine, after problems have occurred or after a complaint. The frequency of visits depends on the type of business, the food being handled and whether there is a history of problems.

EHOs can enter a food business at any reasonable time, usually when the business is open. The main purpose of inspections is to identify any possible risks from the food business to the consumer and to assess how well the food safety management systems are working.

Serving of notices

- **A Hygiene Improvement Notice** will be served if the EHO/EHP believes that a food business does not comply with regulations. The notice states the details of the business, what is wrong, why it is wrong, what needs to be put right and the time in which this must be completed (usually not less than 14 days). It is an offence if the work is not carried out in the specified time.

- **A Hygiene Emergency Prohibition Notice** is served if the EHO believes that the business poses an immediate risk to people's health. This includes serious issues such as sewage contamination, lack of water supply, or a rodent infestation. Serving this notice results in immediate closure of the business for three days, during which time the EHO must apply to a magistrate for a Hygiene Emergency Prohibition Order to keep the premises closed. A Hygiene Prohibition Order prohibits a person (the owner/manager of the premises) from working in a food business.

▲ **Figure 2.6** Rodent activity can cause a food business to be closed down

Fines and penalties for non-compliance

Magistrates' courts can impose fines of up to £5000, a six-month prison sentence or both. For serious offences, magistrates can impose fines of up to £20,000. In a Crown Court, unlimited fines can be imposed and/or two years' imprisonment.

Due diligence

'Due diligence' can be an important defence under food safety legislation. This means that if there is proof that a business took all reasonable care and did everything it could to prevent food safety problems, legal action may be avoided. Proof would need to be provided in the form of accurate written documents such as pest control reports, staff training records, fridge temperature records, etc.

Food businesses must ensure that all staff who handle food are supervised and instructed and/or trained in food hygiene appropriate to the work they do. Training can take place in-house or with a training provider. All records of staff training must be kept for possible inspection.

Food Standards Agency

The Food Standards Agency was set up in 2000 'to protect public health and to protect the interest of customers in relation to food'. The agency is committed to putting customers first, being open and accessible, and being an independent voice on food-related matters.

'Scores on the Doors' is a strategy that was introduced by the Food Standards Agency to raise food safety standards and reduce the incidence of food poisoning. On inspection, food premises can be awarded up to 5 stars (0 stars = very poor food safety; 5 stars = excellent food safety). The intention is that the star-rating certificate given will be placed in a prominent position on the door or window of a premises, but as yet it is not mandatory to do so.

It is expected that the Scores on the Doors scheme will have a positive impact on food safety standards. No matter how good the food in a particular establishment, few people will want to eat there if the food safety score is low!

Food safety management systems

It is good practice for all food businesses to have a food safety management system in place. In line with the Food Standards Agency's commitment to reduce food poisoning cases, it became a legal requirement from January 2006 for all food businesses to operate such a system. When environmental health officers/practitioners inspect the premises of these businesses they will also check that food safety management systems are in place and are working well.

For information on the Hazard Analysis and Critical Control Point (HACCP) food management system see Unit 203, page 104.

Pricing Act

The Consumer Protection from Unfair Trading Regulations 2008

Under these regulations, there is an obligation to give sufficient information to customers at the point of sale, so that they are not misled on prices. Providing the nature of prices in a manner which is unclear or failing to provide the price in a timely fashion before a transactional decision is made may amount to a misleading omission.

If customers are not informed about prices prior to placing an order they may have the right to refuse to accept and pay for food and drinks, for example where they have purchased food and drinks and the price charged is excessively more than the customer would reasonably expect to have to pay.

Menus and price lists must include all material information required by an average consumer to make an informed choice. This may include:

- accurate description of the name
- stating the brand of the drink
- including alcoholic strengths where appropriate
- prices shown inclusive of VAT
- stating if there is a compulsory service charge, a cover charge or a minimum charge per customer.

How or where you display the information required is not prescribed but it should be clear and easily readable by the average consumer. The best way to ensure that customers are given the required information is using detailed menus and beverages lists or clearly displayed price lists, so there is sufficient information to enable a consumer to make an informed decision before they are committed to a purchase.

Bars should show the price list at the bar where orders are taken. In cafés and restaurants, the prices can be marked in menus or price lists. So that customers are informed from the outset, prices should be displayed in a window or entrance to the service area. For takeaways and fast food operations, prices should be displayed where the purchase is to take place.

To fail to show all or part of the information necessary, or to provide misleading information, is regarded as an unfair trading practice and constitutes an offence.

Data Protection Act

Under the terms of the General Data Protection Regulation (GDPR) (Regulation (EU) (2016/679)), which has replaced the Data Protection Act (1998), customers have a right to expect that data about them is secure and is used only for the published business purposes. The general requirements for businesses are to ensure that:

- the company is registered with the Data Protection Registrar
- information on customers is kept up to date, fairly, lawfully and securely

- customer information is not passed on to third parties without prior consent from the customer
- staff are aware of the importance of the protection of customer information and the procedures to follow to ensure it is held securely.

GDPR applies to all personal data, including any information collected automatically online, for example when a customer makes a booking through an online reservation system. The data includes any details that may identify a person online, such as their IP address. GDPR also includes 'special categories of personal data', such as biometric and genetic information. Failure to comply with the legislation can lead to large fines and imprisonment.

The Licensing Act (2003)

This act covers all licensed premises in England and Wales and is written around the four Licensing Objectives:

1 The prevention of crime and disorder.
2 Public safety.
3 The prevention of public nuisance.
4 The protection of children from harm.

It applies to any premises that carries out any of the four Licensable Activities:

1 Sale of alcohol by retail.
2 Sale of alcohol in club premises.
3 Provision of regulated entertainment.
4 Late night refreshment.

To sell alcohol, the business must have a Premises Licence, a Designated Premises Supervisor (DPS) and every shift should ideally be supervised by at least one Personal Licence Holder. Without these licence holders the business is in contravention of Licensing Law and will not be able to retail alcohol until the correct licences are in place. These licences are applied for through the Local Licensing Authority and can take several weeks to obtain.

The Operating Schedule shows which of the Licensable Activities are allowed on the premises and between which hours. Being open outside these hours or carrying out one of these activities without a licence would be a criminal offence and the DPS could face a fine, prison and possible forfeiture of their Personal Licence if they had the power to prevent such activities and failed to do so.

The act also includes late night refreshment, where hot food or drink may be sold to members of the public whether for consumption on or off the premises between the hours of 11 p.m. and 5 a.m. The premises may not serve any alcohol at all, but would still require a Premises Licence.

The act requires a food service operation to:

- display a summary of the Premises' Licence, including the days and times of opening, the name of the Registered Licence Holder, the licence number and a valid date

- display a price list of drinks
- enforce restrictions on under-aged persons being served alcohol or employed to serve alcohol
- ensure an authorised person (or the Personal Licence Holder) is on site at all times.

Weights and Measures Act (1995)

All sales of goods by weight or measure should be in accordance with the legislative requirements of the **Weights and Measures Act (1985)** and the **Weights and Measures (Packaged Goods) Regulations 1986**. This usually requires:

- a display of the prices and the measures used for all spirits, wines, beers, ciders and any other alcohol served
- the food and beverage items for sale to be of the quantity and quality demanded by the customer
- the use of officially stamped measures.

Because of the updated Mandatory Conditions on all Premises Licences, if sold or supplied on the premises drinks must be available in the following measures:

- **beer or cider** – ½ or ⅓ pint or multiples thereof
- **gin, rum, vodka or whisky** – 25 ml or 35 ml or multiples thereof. You are only permitted to serve measures of either 25 ml or 35 ml as standard. Only one or the other size may be used, not both
- **still wine in a glass** – 125 ml, 175 ml or multiples thereof
- **wine in a carafe or jug** is sold in measures of 25 cl, 50 cl, 75 cl and 1 litre.

Customers must be made aware of the availability of these measures – for example, by making their availability clear on menus and price lists, and ensuring that these are displayed in a prominent place in the relevant premises (such as at the bar).

Customers must also be informed verbally of the availability of these smaller measures when, for example, the customer asks for 'a beer', 'a whisky' or 'a glass of wine'. However, this does not apply if the drinks in question are sold or supplied having been made up in advance ready for sale or supply in a securely closed container.

Equality Act (2010)

The **Equality Act (2010)** sets out requirements that the food service operator and staff should be aware of relating to discrimination on grounds of ethnic origin, race, creed, sex or disability.

Both the food service operator and staff must take steps to ensure that discrimination does not occur. There are potentially three ways in which discrimination can take place:

1 **Direct discrimination** – for example, refusing service to customers of particular ethnic origin, race, creed, sex or disability.

2 **Indirect discrimination** – for example, denying consumer services by imposing unjustifiable conditions or requirements that have ethnic origin, sex or disability implications.

3 **Discrimination through victimisation** – for example, by:
(a) refusal of provision, that is refusal of admission on the basis of ethnic origin, sex or disability; or
(b) omission of provision, that is providing services to ethnic or disabled customers that are markedly inferior to those available to the public in general or which may only be available at a price premium.

It is the responsibility of the business and members of staff to ensure that no such discrimination occurs.

Under the legislation there are requirements to ensure:

- a commitment to providing consistently high levels of service to all internal and external customers to ensure they are not discriminated against on the grounds of race, sex, age, disability, sexual orientation, religion or belief
- an equal opportunities policy is available
- job adverts use wording that indicates equal opportunities
- a diversity of staff is employed or considered for employment, including mixed sexes, ages and races, and people with disabilities
- reasonable adjustments are made to the way services are delivered to make it easier for disabled customers to use them, including easy wheelchair access for disabled customers and staff, disabled toilet facilities, elevator facilities as an alternative to stairs for disabled customers and staff, and assistance being given to any disabled customer on request.

It is an offence under the Asylum and Immigration Act (1996) to employ a foreign national subject to immigration control (a person who needs a visa or work permit) who does not have the right to enter or remain in the UK or to take up employment while in the UK. Job application forms should caution future employees that they will be required, if shortlisted, to produce documents confirming their right to be in, and to take up employment in, the UK.

2 CUSTOMER SERVICE DELIVERY
2.1 TEAM WORKING

Staff must be able to work as part of a team, both within and between departments. The people in a team depend on each other to be successful. Each team will have targets and deadlines and to meet these there must be good communication and planning. All members of the team need to understand what is expected of them.

Structure of teams
Individual roles
It is important that you:

- do your job in a professional way
- are punctual for work

▲ **Figure 2.7** Staff working as a team

- inform your employer, ideally your line manager, if you are ill
- are reliable and courteous because other people depend on you
- manage your time and deadlines well and are able to prioritise
- can communicate well, listen carefully and understand facial expressions, gestures and body language. (Also see Unit 201, page 23 for more information on verbal and non-verbal communication.)

Collective roles

Usually there will be a work plan developed for every day of the week. Your manager will discuss duty rotas and work schedules with team members to determine who will be covering what duties.

The manager will also discuss targets and required outcomes with team members, and will be responsible for evaluating your performance and the team's performance.

- In smaller organisations, some employees have to become multi-skilled so that they can carry out a variety of duties. Managers may have to take on a supervisory role at certain times.
- Large hospitality companies need a structure for their staff in order for the business to run efficiently and effectively. Different members of staff have different jobs and roles to perform, and the team consists of operational staff, supervisory staff, management staff and, in large organisations, senior management. All these roles are explained in more detail on page 16 in Unit 201.

Levels of responsibility of self and others

Employees must:

- work in the way that has been agreed in their contract and job description
- follow all the organisation's policies and practices.

Employers must provide each employee with:

- a detailed job description (see Figure 2.8)
- a contract of employment that gives details of the job itself, working hours, the amount of annual holiday the employee will have and the required notice period.

An essential feature of a contract of employment is the mutuality of obligation. This means that the employer will provide the employee with work on specified days of the week for specified hours and, if employed under a limited term contract, for an agreed number of weeks or months. In return, the employee agrees to carry out the work for an agreed wage or salary.

Employers must adhere to laws relating to employment of staff, health and safety, and food safety.

JOB DESCRIPTION

Title of job: Restaurant waiter

Purpose of job: To provide a quality food and beverage service to meet our customers' expectations and to enhance and maintain the reputation of the company.

Reporting to: Restaurant supervisor

Skills, experience and qualifications required:
- Good communication, presentation, time management and social skills
- One year's similar experience
- Wine knowledge useful but not essential as training will be given
- Current Food Handler's Certificate desirable but full training will be provided

Main duties:
- Preparation of the restaurant area ready for service in accordance with the establishment daily duties list.
- Service of food and beverages to customers in accordance with the service specification.
- Ensuring correct charges are made and payment received.
- Clearing of restaurant area in accordance with service specification.
- Ensuring compliance with control procedures for equipment and other stock.
- Following correct health and safety procedures to ensure welfare of both staff and customers.
- Explaining to customers the content, preparation and presentation of all menu and beverage items, and promoting sales through positive selling techniques.
- Additional food and beverage service duties as required in order to meet business demands.

Training requirements
- Induction and company policy as contained in the Staff Handbook
- Menu and beverage list content and updates as required
- Customer care programme
- Basic food hygiene
- Basic fire training at induction and further training every six months
- Basic health and safety at induction and full COSHH every six months
- Manual handling at induction

Performance measures
- Customer feedback
- Management feedback
- Regular knowledge test on foods, wine and other services offered
- Six-monthly appraisals with restaurant supervisor

▲ **Figure 2.8** Example of a job description

Working relationships with other teams and departments

Working with other departments will be inevitable. It is important that all staff are treated with respect – everyone has a role to play in the smooth running of the operation so cooperating and communicating with each other builds a strong team overall.

Importance of working as a team and supporting others

Meet/exceed customer requirements

Staff must have sufficient knowledge of all the items on the menu and wine and drinks lists in order to advise and offer suggestions to customers. They must also know how to serve correctly each dish on the menu, what its accompaniments are, the correct cover, the make-up of the dish and its garnish.

For beverage service, staff should know how to serve several types of wine and drink, in the correct containers (such as glasses, cups) and at the right temperature.

Staff need to be accurate in the information they give to customers. This is especially important when related to knowledge about the ingredients in a particular dish as some customers may have allergies or intolerances.

Present a professional image

Staff need to be aware of how they look – the first impression they create reflects the hygiene standards of the establishment and the quality of service to come. See Unit 205, page 158 for a list of tips on maintaining a professional appearance.

Meet standards and deadlines

An establishment needs to be profitable and generate the maximum amount of business over the service period, therefore staff must develop a sense of urgency in their work.

Deadlines for reaching targets must also be observed, as there will be other members of staff working to achieve results within the same timeframes who may be relying on your results to move their contribution on.

Maintain staff morale

This is the main way to have a good, cohesive team. All team members will have good and bad days, but it is important to maintain an even, professional, cheerful temperament while on duty. Showing your support for colleagues through team working, being punctual and reliable, and assisting them when their workload is higher than yours will help maintain morale within the team.

Management will also play a large part in maintaining staff morale by monitoring the team and intervening when morale is low, rewarding hard work and offering incentives for team effort and supporting staff with training, briefings and clear instructions and assisting staff when there are high volumes of business. This will benefit customers as staff who are happy in their work will perform better and offer a level of service above the customer's expectations.

2.2 MEETING AND EXCEEDING CUSTOMER EXPECTATIONS

To achieve customer satisfaction, it is important to be able to interpret customers' perceptions of excellent service.

Value for money

Customers make choices by considering the relationship between price, cost, worth and value:

- Price is the amount of money required to purchase the product.
- Cost includes, in addition to price, the cost of not going somewhere else, the cost of transport and time, the cost of potential embarrassment if things go wrong, the cost of having to look and behave in a required manner and the cost in terms of effort at work to earn the money to pay the required price.

- Worth is a perception of the desirability of a particular product over another in order to satisfy a set of established goals.
- Value is a perception of the balance between worth and cost.

Excellent value for a food and beverage operation is where the worth is perceived as greater than the costs, and poor value is where the costs are perceived as greater than the worth. Customers have expectations of the food, beverage and service they will receive relative to the price paid and the level of service expected. For example, customers visiting a fast food outlet will be expecting a low cost and have low service expectations, whereas for a visit to a 5-star restaurant they will expect high costs and a high level of service. Customers will expect the quality of the food, beverages and decor to match their expectation, an hygienic environment and good service. Also see notes on meal experience on page 72 in this chapter.

Proactive approach to anticipating needs and customer dissatisfaction/anxiety

Staff need to be aware of customers' needs. Good preparation of the service area before service will alleviate many issues. During service, a careful watch must be kept on customers to check the progress of the meal; this allows service staff to anticipate customer needs with minimal intrusion. Communicating with colleagues and having a good sense of timing will keep customers satisfied.

Staff also need to have attributes such as:

- **A good memory**: it may help if they know the likes and dislikes of regular customers, where they like to sit in the food service area, what their favourite drinks are, and so on.
- **Honesty**: trust and respect among staff, customers and management leads to an atmosphere at work that encourages efficiency and a good team spirit. Staff also deal with confidential information and personal possessions and therefore honesty is paramount.
- **Loyalty**: the obligations and loyalty of staff are first to the establishment in which they are employed and its management.
- **Conduct**: staff conduct should be impeccable at all times, especially in front of customers.

Recording information accurately

Food and beverage staff deal with a lot of information daily. Recording this information is vital to ensure smooth service, customer satisfaction and profitability. The variety of information includes:

- Reservations – customer details, special requests and times.
- Food and beverage orders – customers' choices from the menu and special requests should be repeated back to the customer before placing the order with the kitchen and bar. The order should also show table number, date, number of covers (place settings) and server's name.
- Specific requirements – allergens, alterations to standard menu choices, portion size.

65

- Billing – ensure the bill is accurate and easy to follow.
- Lost property – any items left should be recorded and securely stored.
- Complaints – these should be recorded and followed up with action.
- Allergens – updates to menu items require staff to be fully briefed on the changes to inform the customers.

Information, advice and help

Members of staff will feel more confident about selling if they have information about the products on offer – if staff can 'tell well' they can then 'sell well'. Examples of the type of information staff will need to know include:

- a description of what the item is (food, wine or other drink) and an explanation of how it is prepared and served
- where the produce comes from, what the local animals are fed on, where the fish are caught
- where the local fruit and vegetables are grown
- how the produce is delivered
- where and how the local drinks are made
- what the specialities of the establishment are and their origin
- any allergens present in dishes on the menu.

There are various ways of enhancing the product knowledge of staff, such as:

- arranging for staff visits to suppliers
- arranging visits to other establishments that use local produce
- seeking out supplier information
- allowing staff to taste products
- arranging for staff to visit local trade fairs
- organising training and briefing sessions for staff.

Problems and complaints

Staff should never show their displeasure, even during a difficult situation. They should never argue with a customer and, if they are unable to resolve a situation, they should refer immediately to a senior member of the team. They should be able to reassure the customer and put right any fault, as delays dealing with complaints only make the situation worse.

Dealing with incidents during service

During service there can be unexpected situations. However, a well-managed operation will have procedures in place to deal with such incidents promptly and efficiently without causing more disturbance than is necessary to the other customers. Quick action will usually soothe an irate customer and maintain a good impression of the waiting staff and the establishment.

In the case of accidents, a report of the incident must be recorded and signed by those involved.

Spillages

If, during the service, a few drops of sauce or gravy fall on to the tablecloth, the following steps might be taken:

1 Check immediately that none has fallen on the customer being served. Apologise to the customer.

2 If some sauce *has* fallen on the customer's clothing, allow the customer to rub over the dirtied area with a clean damp cloth. This will remove the worst of the spillage.

3 If it is necessary for the customer to retire to the cloakroom to remove the spillage then the meal should be placed on the hotplate until he or she returns.

4 Depending on the nature of the spillage the establishment may offer to have the garment cleaned.

5 If the spillage has gone on the tablecloth, the waiter should first of all remove any items of equipment that may be dirtied or in the way.

6 The waiter should then mop or scrape up the spillage with either a clean damp cloth or a knife.

7 An old menu card should then be placed on top of the table but under the tablecloth beneath the damaged area.

8 A second menu should be placed on the tablecloth over the damaged area.

9 A clean rolled napkin should then be brought to the table and rolled completely over the damaged area. The menu will prevent any damp from soaking into the clean napkin.

10 Any items of equipment removed should be returned to their correct position on the table top.

11 Any meals taken to the hotplate should be returned and fresh covers put down where necessary.

12 Again, apologies should be made to the customer for any inconvenience caused.

▲ **Figure 2.9** Example process for covering spillages

Accidents

1 As a more serious spillage usually involves changing the tablecloth, the party of customers should be seated at another table and allowed to continue their meal without delay.
2 If the customers cannot be moved to another table then they should be seated slightly back from the table, so the waiter can carry out the necessary procedures to rectify the fault speedily and efficiently.
3 The customers' meals should be placed on the hotplate to keep warm.
4 All dirty items must be removed on a tray to the waiter's sideboard ready to go to the wash-up area.
5 All clean items must be removed and kept on the waiter's sideboard for relaying.
6 The tablecloth should be mopped with a clean absorbent cloth to remove as much of the liquid as possible (Figure 2.9a).
7 A number of old menus should be placed on the tabletop but underneath the spillage area of the soiled tablecloth (Figure 2.9b).
8 A clean napkin should be placed over the spillage (Figure 2.9c).
9 The cover is re-laid (Figure 2.9d).
10 If the spillage is more severe then a clean tablecloth of the correct size should be brought to the table. It should be opened out and held in the correct manner as if one were laying a tablecloth during the pre-service preparation period. The table should then be 'clothed up' in the usual manner except that when the clean tablecloth is being drawn across the table towards the waiter, he or she is at the same time removing the soiled tablecloth. The soiled tablecloth is removed at the same time that the clean tablecloth is being laid to ensure the customers do not see the bare tabletop at any time. The old menus will prevent any dampness penetrating to the clean tablecloth.
11 When the table has its clean tablecloth on it should be re-laid as quickly as possible.
12 The customers should then be re-seated at the table and the meals returned to them from the hotplate.

Returned food

If, for example, a customer suggests that their chicken dish is not cooked, then the following steps might be taken:

1 Apologise to the customer.
2 The dish should be removed and returned to the kitchen.
3 The customer should be asked if he or she would like another portion of the same dish or would prefer to choose an alternative.
4 The new dish should be collected as soon as possible and served to the customer.
5 Apologies should be made for any inconvenience caused.
6 The policy of the establishment will dictate whether or not the customer is charged for the alternative dish.

Lost property

If a waiter finds lost property in a service area that has recently been vacated by a customer, the steps listed below might be taken:

1 Immediately check to make sure the customer has definitely left the service area. If they are still in the area, the property may be returned to them.

2 If the customer has left the service area, the waiter should hand the item to the head waiter or supervisor in charge.

3 The supervisor or head waiter should check with reception and the hall porter to see if the customer has left the building.

4 If the customer concerned is a resident, then reception may ring their room, stating the property has been found and can be collected at a convenient time.

5 If the customer is a regular customer, it is possible that the head waiter or receptionist may know where to contact them to arrange for them to collect the property.

6 If the customer is a regular customer but cannot be contacted, the property should be kept in the lost property office until the customer's next visit.

7 If the owner has not been found or contacted immediately, the head waiter or supervisor should list the items found, including the contents if appropriate, with the waiter who found the property. The 'lost property record sheet' (see Figure 2.10) should then be signed by both the head waiter or supervisor and the finder. This record sheet must be dated and also indicate where the property was found and at what time.

8 A copy of this list should go with the property to the lost property office, where the contents of the property must be checked against the list before it is accepted. The details of the found item are then entered in a lost property register.

9 Another copy of the list should go to the hall porter in case any enquiries are received concerning the property. Anyone claiming lost property should be passed on to the lost property office.

10 Before the lost property office hands over any lost property, a description of the article concerned and its contents should be requested to ensure as far as possible that it is being returned to the genuine owner. The office should also see proof of identity of the person claiming ownership.

11 In the case of all lost property, the steps mentioned above should be carried out as quickly as possible as this is in the best interests of the establishment and causes the customer minimum inconvenience. On receipt of lost property, the customer should be asked to sign for the article concerned and to give their address and telephone number.

12 Any lost property unclaimed after three months may become the property of the finder, who should claim it through the head waiter or supervisor.

Lost property record sheet	
Date:	Establishment:
Item description:	
Found by:	
Checked by:	
Where stored:	
Claimed by:	Date:
Contact details :	
Proof of identity seen:	

▲ **Figure 2.10** Example of a lost property record sheet

Overconsumption of alcohol

The Licensing Act 2003 states that you cannot serve a person who appears to be drunk or their companion if you think the drink is for the drunken person's consumption. This places a responsibility on serving staff to be aware when customers have consumed too much alcohol.

If a customer is suspected of having had too much to drink the following steps might be taken:

1 If a prospective customer asks for a table and staff believe the client is under the influence of drink, they may refuse them a table, even though there may be one available. It is not always possible, however, to recognise a customer who may prove objectionable later on.
2 If difficulty is found in handling this type of person then assistance in removing the person from the eating area may come from other members of staff (depending on establishment policy; physical contact should be avoided).
3 If a customer is suspected of being drunk this must first of all be ascertained by the head waiter or supervisor.
4 The customer should then be asked to leave rather than be allowed to become objectionable to other customers.
5 If the customer has already consumed part of the meal ordered but is not being objectionable then the remainder of the meal should be served in the normal fashion, but the head waiter or supervisor must ensure no more alcoholic beverage is offered.
6 On finishing, the customer should be watched until he or she has left the premises.
7 It is always advisable to make out a report of all such incidents. They should also be brought to the immediate attention of the restaurant manager in case of any claim at a later date concerning a particular incident.

Other problems during service

See Unit 205, page 166 for guidelines on what to do if a customer falls ill.

See Unit 205, page 167 for guidelines on what to do if a customer's appearance does not comply with the dress code of the establishment.

Recording incidents

It is advisable that when any incident occurs a report is made out immediately. The basic information that should be found in the report is as follows:

- place
- date
- time
- nature of the incident
- individual, signed reports from those concerned

- action taken
- name, address and phone number of the customer involved
- names of the staff involved.

All reports should be kept in case similar incidents occur at a later date. Such reports also provide a record if there is a subsequent complaint from a customer and can be used when looking at new procedures for dealing with various incidents.

Health, safety and security

The Health and Safety at Work Regulations now require employers to conduct a risk assessment regarding the safety of staff in the catering business.

General procedures

Depending upon the nature of the establishment, the security measures that are laid down may vary considerably. As employees, staff should be aware of all such measures as they relate to their own work environment. Consideration needs to be given to the aspects of security outlined below.

- The importance of wearing some form of recognised identity badge.
- Being observant and reporting 'suspicious' persons and/or packages.
- Not discussing work duties with customers or outside of the workplace.
- Allowing bags, packages and one's person to be searched upon request when either entering or leaving the workplace.
- Being aware of the security procedures for the establishment, should sudden and urgent action need to be taken.
- Ensuring external fire doors are kept shut but not locked, and not left ajar in error.
- Ensuring that all areas have been vacated when responsible for 'locking up' duties.
  - All toilets/cloakrooms must be carefully checked and, at the same time, all windows and doors should be checked to ensure they are locked.
- Keys should only be handled by someone in authority. A signing-out book should be available when staff request keys.
- Ensuring keys are never left unattended.
- When handling cash, all large denomination notes should be checked carefully as well as all cheque and credit card payments, to prevent fraud, the passing of illegal notes and the acceptance of altered credit cards.
- Being alert and observant at all times, and not hesitating in reporting anything suspicious to the immediate superior.

The meal experience

Customers' needs vary, so food and beverage operators should be aware of any factors that might affect the customer's meal experience. Much research has been carried out in recent years identifying these factors. They range from location to the acceptance of credit cards, and from attitudes of staff to the behaviour of other customers. These factors are summarised in Table 2.7

▼ **Table 2.7** Meal experience factors

Factor	Description
1. Food and beverages on offer	Includes the range of food and beverages, choice, availability, flexibility for special orders and the quality of the food and beverages
2. Level of service	The level of service sought will depend on the needs people have at a particular time. For example, a romantic night out may require a quiet table in a top-class restaurant, whereas a group of young friends might seek a more informal service. This also takes into account the importance to the customer of other services such as booking and account facilities, acceptance of credit cards and the reliability of the operation's product
3. Level of cleanliness and hygiene	This relates to the premises, equipment and staff. This factor has increased in importance in customers' minds due to media focus on food production and the risks involved in buying food increasing customer awareness of health and hygiene
4. Perceived value for money and price	Customers have perceptions of the amount they are prepared to spend and relate this to differing types of establishments and operations
5. Atmosphere of the establishment	This factor takes account of issues such as design, decor, lighting, heating, furnishings, acoustics and noise levels, other customers, the smartness of the staff and the attitude of the staff

The five experience factors influence both the customers' choice of a food and beverage operation and the potential enjoyment of a meal. Although the five factors are found in all operations, the relative importance of them to the customer is not the same for all occasions or all operations. For example, for a fast food operation customers are likely to be more concerned with value for money and the speed of service. In a first-class restaurant customers are more likely to be concerned about the quality of the food and beverages and a high level of personal service.

It is worth remembering that service staff also contribute to the customers' perception of value for money, hygiene and cleanliness, the level of service and the atmosphere that the customer experiences.

2.3 MEASURING EFFECTIVE CUSTOMER SERVICE

It is important to establish if customers are satisfied with the service they have received. Feedback enables adjustments to be made to service styles, levels and reducing complaints. Careful monitoring of feedback will establish if there are patterns to issues and where and when training should be given to rectify or improve service.

This can be done in the following ways:

- **Customer comment cards** – usually a quick-response format to avoid inconveniencing customers too much, leave space for contact details to be able to follow up the comments, both positive and negative. See Figure 2.11.
- **Mystery shopper visits** – these are usually carried out by an independent person or organisation to give honest and accurate feedback. Several areas of service are measured, including atmosphere, ambience, hygiene, level of occupancy, time of service, as well as length of service times.
- **Audits and inspections through in-house auditors, external rating inspectors** – external rating inspections are carried out by organisations such as the AA (The Automobile Association), Michelin or The Tourist Board to determine if the business offers services that meet set criteria of service and quality standards. Audits are usually measuring against Standard Operating Procedures (SOPs) to ensure consistency across a chain or brand. Points are scored for compliance and lost for non-compliance. Scores are measured across the brand/chain and ratings given.
- **Verbal feedback from check backs** – asking every customer if they are satisfied should be done, but be careful not to become intrusive by repeatedly asking. Gauge the level of interaction you have with customers based on body language and the purpose of their visit.
- **Website feedback from evaluation surveys, reviews and social media** – care must be taken when handling online feedback. Never respond to a negative review/feedback negatively. Apologise to the customer if they were not happy with their experience and request they either contact the business directly or provide their details for the business to contact them, then deal with their issues offline and work to resolve their issues.
- **Organisational reflections and feedback to employees through debriefs** – this is essential in order to communicate both positive and negative issues to all staff at the end of each service session. This enables clear communication and resolves issues as and when they have occurred. Further investigations can then be carried out where necessary and revisions to service procedures and standards can be assessed if required.

THE EXAMPLE RESTAURANT

We strive to provide the best experience for all our customers.
We also welcome feedback on how we met your expectations today.

Table number: _____   Date: _____   Time: _____

	Excellent	Good	Average	Poor
Welcome				
Menu and wine list				
Quality of food and beverages				
Friendliness of staff				
Quality of service				
Speed of service				
Value for money				
Atmosphere				
Overall meal experience				

What did you most like about your visit? _____

Was there anything that you didn't like? _____

Do you have any other comments/suggestions? _____

Where did you hear about the restaurant? _____

Optional

Name _____

Telephone _____

Email address _____

Please tick here if you would like to be added to our mailing list. ☐

▲ **Figure 2.11** A customer comment card

2.4 IMPACT OF CUSTOMER SERVICE ON THE BUSINESS

Good customer service helps to:

- **Create a positive image of the business** – the impact of customer service should not be underestimated. Good service should always be given, although often not remembered by the customers. Poor service will be noticed and commented on, often not directly. Ultimately this will damage a business's reputation and cause a loss in revenue.
- **Enhance the business's reputation** – in order to retain and gain market share, businesses should always give customer service their top priority as this can make or break a business. This creates a positive image to customers.
- **Increase sales/repeat business** – good service skills, attention to detail and a desire to get to know customers' likes and dislikes enhances a business's reputation and ultimately increases footfall, repeat business and revenue.
- **Increase customers' confidence in the consistency of service standards** – having consistent service standards and methods will enable staff to know their job roles thoroughly and put customers at ease. SOPs will assist staff with their training and they can refer to them again when procedures need revising and refreshing. This applies to all service methods and all additional items introduced into the business. A SOP review/compilation is essential to ensure brand standards are followed. (SOPs have photographs to assist in explaining appearance, style and layout of areas, items, equipment, food, drink and accompaniments.)
- **Encourage customer loyalty/brand protection** – following a brand standard is vital when operating as part of a chain. This ensures the customer experience is the same on every occasion, at every service and in every venue. This in turn enhances the business's reputation. Chains invest heavily in getting their brand recognised and in their marketing collateral. This in turn requires all venues to follow brand standards to maintain reputation and achieve consistency of service and production. Customers give their loyalty and repeat business to organisations that consistently deliver value for money; the customer has an expectation of the brand, product and service and this needs to be maintained on every occasion to retain that loyalty to the brand.

Test your learning

To complete these questions, you may also need to refer to other chapters in this book.

1 Identify and briefly describe **three** characteristics of excellent service.

2 Define the difference between internal and external customers.

3 Give **three** examples of customers with specific needs.

4 Identify **three** of the possible customer incidents that could occur when serving customers.

5 Briefly describe the steps that can be taken if a customer makes a complaint.

6 Give **three** examples of how poor customer service can affect the business.

7 There are a wide variety of legal requirements for food service operations. Name **three** enforcement bodies.

8 State **one** of the objectives of the Licensing Act 2003.

9 Identify **one** piece of legislation that governs the sale of goods.

10 Name **one** act that governs the way alcohol and other goods are measured and sold.

11 Identify the **three** types of discrimination that can take place in the workplace.

12 Identify **one** provision that a restaurant should make for wheelchair users in order to adhere to the Disability Discrimination Act 1995.

13 What are the **three** benefits of good health and safety?

14 What does COSHH stand for?

15 State **four** potential costs of accidents in the workplace.

16 What is the main act that covers the health and safety of people in their workplaces?

17 State **three** responsibilities an employer has under health and safety law.

18 In relation to health and safety, what does PPE mean?

19 Suggest **two** ways to make premises more secure.

20 Give **three** examples of measures that can help to ensure personal safety at work.

SAFE WORKING PRACTICES

INTRODUCTION

The purpose of this chapter is to help you gain the knowledge required to work safely and legally within a hospitality service environment, with an emphasis on personal responsibilities and actions within the hospitality front of house area.

This unit will help you to learn about:

- health and safety, your responsibilities, and how your actions impact on the business and other people
- how you can help to ensure that food is safe
- the hazards related to food safety and what you can do to reduce the risk of these hazards
- how the bacteria which cause food poisoning multiply and survive
- what food allergies are and what you must do if a customer has one.

1 PERSONAL RESPONSIBILITIES

1.1 HEALTH AND SAFETY RESPONSIBILITIES

You have the responsibility to know about health and safety legislation so that you can maintain a safe workplace environment. An establishment has a common law duty to care for all staff and lawful visitors. In addition, an establishment must not:

- sell (or keep for sale) food and beverages that are unfit for people to eat
- cause food or beverages to be dangerous to health
- sell food or beverages that are not what the customer is entitled to expect, in terms of content or quality
- describe or present food in a way that is false or misleading.

All people employed by an establishment have the responsibility to ensure working practices are maintained.

Safety of self and others – duty of care

It is important to be safe and avoid injuries to you or your work colleagues. Food service operations can be dangerous places, so it is important to work in a safe and systematic way. Over 200 people die in accidents at work each year; accidents can happen in any workplace.

Stress and accidents are currently the two biggest causes of absence from work. According to the http://hse.gov.uk/statistics 2016 survey, absence due to sickness costs the UK economy approximately £14.1 billion each year and the average number of sick days taken each year in the UK is approximately 30.4 million.

▼ **Table 3.1** Safety in the workplace

Potential benefits of good health and safety practices	Potential costs of accidents in the workplace
<ul><li>reduction in accidents and ill-health</li><li>motivated workers</li><li>enhanced company reputation</li><li>increased productivity</li><li>improved profitability</li></ul>	<ul><li>employees absent from work due to illness and stress</li><li>compensation claims</li><li>prosecution</li><li>fines</li><li>legal costs</li><li>damage to the business's reputation</li><li>high staff turnover</li></ul>

See Unit 202, page 51 for full details of the requirements of the **Health and Safety at Work Act (1974)** which covers areas of safety within the workplace.

Who is responsible for health and safety?

The simple answer is that everyone is responsible for health and safety. More specifically:

- employers/employees
- people in control of work premises
- the self-employed
- designers
- manufacturers
- suppliers

- local authorities
- the Health and Safety Executive (HSE)
- enforcement officers
- environmental health officers
- health and safety inspectors.

See Unit 202, page 52 for a full list of the employer's responsibilities to make sure that all staff are safe while at work under the terms of the **Health and Safety at Work Act (1974)**.

Identify and report/record potential hazards

Staff have a duty to report potential hazards. If they see a hazard that they are allowed to deal with they must do so to ensure the safety of others. If the hazard requires specialist attention then a safety sign should be placed near the hazard, any power source should be switched off and the hazard reported to a superior. The hazard should also be recorded. The use of risk assessment will increase awareness of hazards and reduce likelihood of occurrence and severity.

See Unit 202, page 54 for full details of the requirements of the Reporting of Injuries, Diseases and Dangerous Occurrences Regulations (RIDDOR) 2013.

Risk assessment

A risk is the chance of somebody being harmed by a hazard. There may be a high risk or a low risk of harm.

There are five steps to assessing risk:

1. Look for hazards (things that can cause harm).
2. Identify who could be harmed and how.
3. Work out the risks and decide if the existing precautions are good enough or whether more should be done to prevent harm being caused.
4. Write down what the hazard is and what the risk is and keep this as a record.
5. Re-check the hazard and the risk at regular intervals and go back and change the risk assessment (the written record) if necessary.

▼ **Table 3.2** Common risks and hazards and ways to minimise them

Common risks and hazards	Ways to minimise risk
Poor design and structure of building	Refurbishment of buildings and safer design of new buildings in line with current legislation
Poor signage	Correct and clear/visible signage should be used throughout the establishment to assist both staff and customers find their way around
Poor housekeeping standards	Good housekeeping is essential in maintaining a safe and hygienic business
Poor lighting and ventilation	Well-lit areas to ensure staff and customers can see hazards and act accordingly, and ventilation to ensure clean air
Dangerous working practices	Employ well-trained staff to follow correct health and safety practice and procedures at all times
Distraction and lack of attention	Staff should always concentrate on their work and avoid distractions to ensure they reduce the likelihood of accidents and injuries in the workplace
Working too quickly	Don't rush and ask for help if you need it. Work methodically and efficiently with attention to detail to avoid accidents and missing out vital steps in risk prevention.
Not wearing protective clothing	Wear correct personal protective clothing (PPE) as this will protect vulnerable body parts from injury in the event of an accident

Avoiding hazards

A hazard is anything that can cause harm, such as:

- uneven floors
- excessive noise
- chemicals
- electricity
- working using ladders
- moving parts and machinery
- dust and fumes.

Health and safety policy

This is the statement of general policy and arrangements for: ⬚ (Name of company)		
(Name of employer/senior manager)	has overall and final responsibility for health and safety	
(Member of staff)	has day-to-day responsibility for ensuring this policy is put into practice	
Statement of general policy	Responsibility of: name/title	Action/arrangements (What are you going to do?)
Prevent accidents and cases of work-related ill-health by managing the health and safety risks in the workplace		
Provide clear instructions and information, and adequate training, to ensure employees are competent to do their work		
Engage and consult with employees on day-to-day health and safety conditions		
Implement emergency procedures – evacuation in case of fire or other significant incident. You can find help with your fire risk assessment at: www.gov.uk/workplace-fire-safety-your-responsibilities		
Maintain safe and healthy working conditions, provide and maintain plant, equipment and machinery, and ensure safe storage/use of substances		

Signed: * (Employer)	Date:

You should review your policy if you think it might no longer be valid, e.g. if circumstances change.
If you have fewer than five employees, you don't have to write down your policy.

Health and safety law poster is displayed at (location):
First-aid box is located:
Accident book is located:

Accidents and ill-health at work reported under RIDDOR (Reporting of Injuries, Diseases and Dangerous Occurrences Regulations) www.hse.gov.uk/riddor
To get an interactive version of this template go to www.hse.gov.uk/risk/risk-assessment-and-policy-template.doc
Combined risk assessment and policy template published by the Health and Safety Executive 08/14

Risk assessment

All employers must conduct a risk assessment. If you have fewer than five employees you don't have to write anything down.

We have started off the risk assessment for you by including a sample entry for a common hazard to illustrate what is expected (the sample entry is taken from an office-based business). Look at how this might apply to your business, continue by identifying the hazards that are the real priorities in your case and complete the table to suit. You can print and save this template so you can easily review and update the information as and when required. You may find our example risk assessments a useful guide (www.hse.gov.uk/risk/casestudies). Simply choose the example closest to your business.

Company name: **Date of risk assessment:**

What are the hazards?	Who might be harmed and how?	What are you already doing?	Do you need to do anything else to control this risk?	Action by who?	Action by when?	Done
Slips and trips	Staff and visitors may be injured if they trip over objects or slip on spillages.	General good housekeeping is carried out. All areas well lit, including stairs. No trailing leads or cables. Staff keep work areas clear, e.g. no boxes left in walkways, deliveries stored immediately.	Better housekeeping needed in staff kitchen, e.g. on spills. Arrange for loose carpet tile on second floor to be repaired/replaced.	All staff, supervisor to monitor Manager	From now on xx/xx/xx	xx/xx/xx xx/xx/xx
						Hint: tab here for new row

You should review your risk assessment if you think it might no longer be valid (e.g. following an accident in the workplace or if there are any significant changes to hazards, such as new work equipment or work activities).
For information specific to your industry please go to www.hse.gov.uk
For further information and to view our example risk assessments go to www.hse.gov.uk/risk/casestudies
Combined risk assessment and policy template published by the Health and Safety Executive 08/14

▲ **Figure 3.1** Health and safety risk assessment forms

Source: hse.gov.uk

The following aspects of the food service environment have the potential to give rise to hazards:

- equipment: liquidisers, food processors, mixers, mincers
- substances: cleaning chemicals, detergents, sanitisers
- work methods: carrying knives and equipment incorrectly and not following a logical sequence
- work areas: spillages not cleaned up, overcrowded work areas, insufficient work space, uncomfortable working conditions due to extreme heat or cold.

Employees have a responsibility to themselves, work colleagues and customers to be aware of hazards that may arise when working. Many accidents occur through carelessness or through lack of thought, for example:

- not having the correct protective clothing such as an apron
- not wearing sensible (stable and properly fitted) shoes
- delay in clearing spillages or picking up items of equipment that have fallen on the floor
- not being aware of customers' bags placed on the floor
- items of equipment not stored correctly
- broken glass or crockery not wrapped up sufficiently before being placed in the bin
- forgetting to unplug electrical appliances prior to cleaning
- putting ashtray debris into rubbish bins containing paper (a fire hazard)
- forgetting to switch off and unplug an appliance after use, or at the end of the service
- not being observant with table lamps or lit candles on a buffet
- over-filling coffee pots, soup tureens, glasses
- using cups, glasses, soup bowls for storing cleaning agents
- stacking trays incorrectly
- carrying a mix of equipment on a tray, such as cutlery, crockery and glassware
- carpet edges turned up
- faulty wheels on trolleys or castors on sideboards
- being unaware of customers' walking sticks and crutches
- lack of adequate space for the safe service of food and drink due to bad planning
- lack of knowledge in carrying out certain tasks, for example opening a bottle of sparkling wine.

Report/record accidents or incidents

Health and safety has to be monitored regularly in the workplace by the designated health and safety officer. Any incidents or near misses must be recorded, even if no one is injured.

All accidents should be reported to your line manager, chef or a supervisor. Each accident is recorded in an accident book, which must be provided in every business. Figure 3.2 shows an example of an incident report form showing all the details required.

Full name of injured person:			
Occupation:		Supervisor:	
Time of accident:	Date of accident:	Time of report:	Date of report:
Name of injury or condition:			
Details of hospitalisation:			
Extent of injury (after medical attention):			
Place of accident or dangerous occurrence:			
Injured person's evidence of what happened (include equipment/items and/or other persons):			
Witness evidence (1):		Witness evidence (2):	
Supervisor's recommendations:			
Date:		Supervisor's signature:	

▲ **Figure 3.2** An incident report form

Training

All staff are required to receive regular training to ensure their safety and the safety of others. Organisations should show commitment to health and safety training so the people being trained recognise the importance of the training. Employees or their representatives should be consulted on the planning and organisation of the training to make sure that it is properly prioritised and planned for the business.

Training for health and safety

Training for health and safety awareness is mandatory. Training should be recorded and reviewed at set intervals specified by the company.

Manual handling training

Picking up and carrying heavy or difficult loads can lead to accidents if not done properly.

Training staff to lift correctly will reduce accidents, time off work and costly medical bills. Ensuring all staff know how to lift heavy objects safely using equipment provided when appropriate will also reduce injuries and accidents in the workplace. Also see Manual handling using equipment on page 86 of this chapter.

The safest way to lift objects is to have your feet slightly apart and to bend your knees rather than your back (see Figure 3.3). This will help to prevent straining and damage to your back.

For heavy items it is better if two people lift the object together, rather than one person trying to do it on their own.

▲ **Figure 3.3** How to lift correctly

Control of Substances Hazardous to Health (COSHH)

See Unit 202, page 53 for details of the Control of Substances Hazardous to Health (COSHH) Regulations 2002, and how they relate to your individual role. Also see notes on page 106.

Fire evacuation

Evacuation drills

New staff must be trained in fire drills and all employees must be told about any new fire risks. The establishment where you work should organise at least one fire drill per year and record the results. You must keep the results as part of your fire safety and evacuation plan. For more on the employer's responsibility for fire safety, see Unit 202, page 55.

Fire detection and fire warning

It is important that there is an effective way of detecting a fire and warning people about it quickly enough to allow them to escape before the fire spreads.

- In small workplaces, such as small restaurants, a fire will be detected easily and quickly and is unlikely to cut off the escape routes. In this case, if people can see the exits clearly, shout 'FIRE!' and direct everyone to leave immediately via the nearest fire exit.

- In large establishments fire warning systems are needed. Manually operated call points are likely to be the minimum that is needed. These are the type of fire alarm where you break glass to set off the alarm.

How a fire is caused

A fire requires heat, fuel and oxygen – known as 'the fire triangle' (see Figure 3.4). Without any one of these elements there is no fire, so taking precautions to avoid the three coming together will reduce the chances of a fire starting.

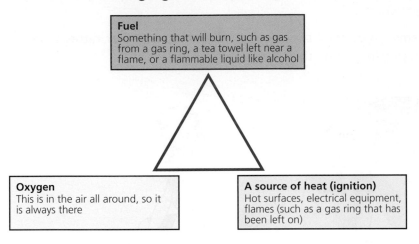

Fuel
Something that will burn, such as gas from a gas ring, a tea towel left near a flame, or a flammable liquid like alcohol

Oxygen
This is in the air all around, so it is always there

A source of heat (ignition)
Hot surfaces, electrical equipment, flames (such as a gas ring that has been left on)

▲ **Figure 3.4** The fire triangle

Fire evacuation procedures

All employees should be given fire drill training as part of their induction programme. This should then be followed up by regular training sessions on the procedures to be followed in the event of fire. This training should include:

- fire procedures in employees' own specific areas of work
- fire drill instructions for both customers and staff
- the location of fire points (safe places where staff and customers should assemble after an evacuation) nearest to own particular area of work
- the location of the fire exits
- the correct type of fire extinguisher to be used in relation to the type of fire
- identification of the employee's own specific responsibilities in the event of fire.

In the event of the fire alarm ringing employees must:

- follow the fire instructions as laid down for the establishment
- usher all customers and staff out of the work area promptly and calmly
- pay special attention to customers with special needs such as those with mobility problems
- walk quickly but not run. Display a sense of urgency
- not panic; remain calm as composure will be imitated by others
- proceed as promptly as possible to the nearest assembly point
- ensure that someone watches to see that there are no stragglers

- follow the exit route as laid down in the establishment fire instructions
- never use a lift
- not re-enter the building until told it is safe to do so by the fire service
- not waste time attempting to collect personal items.

Employees have a responsibility to assist in fire prevention, control and safety. They must therefore ensure that:

- fire exits are not obstructed
- firefighting equipment is not damaged or misused
- no smoking rules are observed at all times
- as far as possible, all electrical and gas equipment is switched off when not in use
- all doors and windows are closed when not being used for evacuation purposes
- fire doors are not locked or wedged open
- sufficient ashtrays/stands are available for the disposal of cigarette ends and used matches
- the procedure for calling the fire brigade is known.

Firefighting equipment

Methods of extinguishing fires concentrate on cooling (as in a water extinguisher or fire hose) or depriving the fire of oxygen (as in an extinguisher that uses foam or powder to smother the fire). Portable fire extinguishers enable people to tackle a fire in its early stages. Staff should be trained to use the extinguishers – and should only use them if they can do so without putting themselves in danger.

Fires are classified in accordance with British Standard EN2 as follows:

- **Class A**: fires involving solid materials where combustion (burning) normally forms glowing embers (e.g. wood).
- **Class B**: fires involving liquids (such as methylated spirits) or liquefiable solids (any kind of flammable gel used under a burner).
- **Class C**: fires involving gases.
- **Class D**: fires involving metals.
- **Class F**: fires involving cooking oils or fats.

Different types of fire extinguishers are suitable for different types of fire. Portable extinguishers all contain a substance that will put out a fire. See Table 3.3 for details of the different types of fire extinguishers.

▼ **Table 3.3** Fire extinguishers and their uses

Content of fire extinguisher:	Water	Foam	Carbon dioxide	Dry powder	Wet chemical
Label colour:	White on red	Cream on red	Black on red	Blue on red	Yellow on red
Electrical suitability:	Dangerous (electrically conductive)		Safe (non-electrically conductive)		
Suitable for:	Solids	Some liquids	Electrical – do not use in a confined space	Liquid	Liquid, especially cooking fats and oils
Unsuitable for:	Oil	Electrical	Solids	Very little	Solids

Safe use of equipment

All staff should be trained to use equipment. Some equipment requires specific training, such as some fire extinguishers (see page 113) or electric food processing equipment. Training should also be in place for manual handling of equipment and goods (see page 83).

Personal protective equipment (PPE)

According to the Personal Protective Equipment (PPE) at Work Regulations 1992, PPE must be supplied by employers to protect their staff in the workplace. Staff need to be trained how to put it on, and how to wear it or use it correctly to ensure their safety. PPE is provided to help to prevent injuries to:

- **the lungs** – for example, from breathing in contaminated air
- **the head and feet** – for example, from falling materials
- **the eyes** – for example, from flying particles or splashes of corrosive liquids
- **the skin** – for example, from contact with corrosive materials
- **the body** – for example, from extremes of heat or cold.

Employees must make proper use of PPE and report its loss or destruction or any fault in it.

If staff are seen not wearing or using PPE while carrying out their work then they should be stopped immediately, questioned as to what they are doing and why they are not working safely. If necessary disciplinary procedures should be followed to enforce compliance.

Service equipment

Before service takes place, staff need to ensure that there is sufficient service equipment ready in order to meet the volume of customers expected. For example, making sure that there are enough serving utensils of the appropriate size and style for the dishes to be served will reduce the risk of equipment being used in several dishes, preventing cross-contamination. This will also reduce waiting time and inefficiency of service.

Manual handling using equipment

- When you move goods on trolleys, trucks or other wheeled vehicles:
  - load them carefully
  - do not overload them
  - load them in a way that allows you to see where you are going.
- In stores, stack heavy items at the bottom.
- If a stepladder is needed to reach higher items, use it with care.
- Take particular care when moving large pots of liquid, especially if the liquid is hot.
- Do not fill pots to the brim.
- Use a warning sign to let people know if equipment handles, lids and so on might be hot. This is traditionally done by sprinkling a small amount of flour, or something similar, on to the part of the equipment that might be hot.
- Take extra care when removing a tray from the oven or salamander to avoid burning someone else.

Also see notes on manual handling on page 83.

Follow your manager's instructions

During an incident supervisors or managers will need to give instructions and these need to be followed to reduce the impact of the incident.

Most establishments will have an incident manual where instructions on incident procedures are stored but also where incidents can be recorded for future reference and evidence.

This needs to be kept centrally so it can be accessed quickly if required.

1.2 FOOD SAFETY RESPONSIBILITIES

Everyone consuming food prepared for them by others when they are away from home (for example, in canteens and restaurants) has the right and expectation to be served safe food that will not cause illness or harm them in any way. See Unit 202, page 55 for more details on **food safety** legislation and the responsibilities of staff for ensuring food safety.

Report/record incidents/malpractice relating to times, temperatures, storage

All food items will undergo Hazard Analysis Critical Control Point (HACCP) analysis. This should be recorded and logged in a central system. This information is used to highlight where potential risk of food spoilage/contamination could occur and the necessary precautions that need to be taken to prevent any incidents of food poisoning occurring.

Records must be kept on all stages of food processes. This includes details of times, temperature and storage. For details of the HACCP system please see 2.3 Reducing the risk from food safety hazards on page 104.

Temperatures of cooked food are taken to ensure it is thoroughly cooked, and if required rapidly cooled or held for service. These temperatures will be different depending on what the food has been prepared for and the time it is to be kept at that temperature.

Records must be kept for all stages from delivery to service. This is also evidence of '**due diligence**', which can be used as part of the defence if a case of malpractice is alleged against the business.

Any potential food safety risks must be reported to line managers immediately the occurrence has been discovered. The food should be removed and destroyed to avoid it being consumed by anyone if it is considered to have become a risk to health. Again, records must be kept to show 'due diligence'.

These records may be requested by the **environmental health officer** when carrying out a premises inspection.

Illness reporting

People who are suffering from certain infections (mainly from bacteria and viruses) can contaminate the food or surfaces that they come into contact with. This can spread infection to other people through the food. Managers and staff must work to prevent the spread of infection by knowing which illnesses and symptoms staff should report and what managers should do in response.

KEY TERMS

Food safety – putting in place all of the measures needed to make sure that food and drinks are suitable, safe and wholesome through all of the processes of food provision.

Due diligence – ensuring that a business has taken reasonable care, followed legal requirements and generally done everything it can to prevent food safety problems.

Environmental health officer (EHO) – responsible for food safety standards and enforcement. Sometimes called an environmental health practitioner (EHP).

- Diarrhoea and/or vomiting are the main symptoms of illnesses that can be transmitted through food.
- Staff handling food or working in a food-handling area must report these symptoms to management immediately.
- Staff with infected wounds, skin infections or sores must seek medical advice and treatment before coming into any food-handling area.
- Managers must exclude staff with these symptoms from working with or around open food, normally for 48 hours from when symptoms stop naturally.

The legal requirement also extends to managing the risk from contamination by other infected workers and visitors to rooms and areas where open food is stored or handled – for example managers, maintenance contractors, inspectors. Therefore, use of the terms 'food handlers', 'staff' and 'workers' should be taken to include these additional people.

Keep food safe at all times

Some foods pose a greater risk to food safety than others and are called high-risk foods. They are usually ready to eat, so do not need to be cooked to the high temperatures that would kill bacteria. Such foods are usually moist, contain protein and need to be stored in the fridge. Examples of high-risk foods include:

- soups, stocks, sauces, gravies
- eggs and egg products
- milk and milk products
- cooked meat and fish, and meat and fish products
- any foods that need to be handled or reheated.

▲ **Figure 3.5** Milk and eggs are high-risk foods

See page 56 for more information on food safety and avoiding food poisoning.

Keep the work environment clean

Premises

Suitable buildings with well-planned fittings, layout and equipment allow for good food safety practices. Certain basics need to be available if a building is to be used for food production:

- electricity and ideally gas supplies
- drinking water and good drainage
- suitable road access for deliveries and refuse collection
- no risk of contamination from surrounding areas and buildings – for example chemicals, smoke, odours or dust.

Layout

When planning food premises, a linear workflow should be in place. See Figure 3.6. This type of workflow means there will be no crossover of activities that could result in cross-contamination.

- There must be adequate storage areas – refrigerated storage is especially important.
- Staff hand-washing/drying facilities suitable for the work being carried out must be provided.

▲ **Figure 3.6** A linear workflow

- Clean and dirty (raw and cooked) processes should be kept apart.
- Cleaning and disinfection should be planned with separate storage for cleaning materials and chemicals.
- All areas should allow for good cleaning, disinfection and pest control.
- Personal hygiene facilities must be provided for staff, as well as changing facilities and storage for personal clothing and belongings.

Cleaning programmes

Maintaining clean work areas plays an essential part in the production of safe food and the team must plan, record and check all cleaning tasks as part of a cleaning schedule. Clean premises, work areas and equipment are important to:

- control the bacteria that cause food poisoning
- reduce the possibility of physical and chemical contamination
- reduce the possibility of accidents (for example, slips on a wet or greasy floor)
- create a positive image for customers, visitors and employees
- comply with the law
- avoid attracting pests to the kitchen.

The cleaning schedule needs to include the following information:

- What is to be cleaned.
- Who should do it (name if possible).
- How it is to be done and how long it should take.
- When it is to be done (time of day).
- Materials to be used, including chemicals and their dilution, cleaning equipment and protective clothing to be worn.
- Safety precautions that must be taken.

Signatures of the cleaner and the supervisor checking the work, along with the date and time.

Cleaning products

Different cleaning products are designed for different tasks:

- **Detergent** is designed to remove grease and dirt. It may be in the form of liquid, powder, gel or foam, and usually needs to be added to water before use. Detergent will not kill pathogens (bacteria), although the hot water it is mixed with may help to do this. Detergent will clean and degrease surfaces so that disinfectant can work properly. Detergents usually work best with hot water.
- **Disinfectant** is designed to destroy bacteria when used properly. Make sure you only use a disinfectant intended for kitchen use. Disinfectants must be left on a clean, grease-free surface for the required amount of time (contact time) to be effective.
- **Heat** may also be used to disinfect – for example, using steam cleaners or the hot rinse cycle of a dishwasher. Items that should be both cleaned and disinfected include all items in direct contact with food, all hand contact surfaces, hand-wash basins and cleaning equipment.

- **Sanitiser** cleans and disinfects. It usually comes in spray form. Sanitiser is very useful for work surfaces and equipment, especially when cleaning them between tasks.

All food and beverage service staff should be made aware of the importance of cleaning programmes to reduce and minimise the build-up of dust, bacteria and other forms of debris. Full attention needs to be paid by all concerned to cleaning tasks and when they should be carried out. Regular maintenance will make the service area look attractive and will project a positive image for the establishment.

A cleaning programme should be set up for any cleaning tasks that must be done in a particular area. Some tasks are done daily, even twice daily, for instance the washing and polishing of crockery before each service period. Other tasks might be done weekly, monthly or every six months. Certain items of equipment need cleaning immediately after each service period is finished.

Storage of cleaning products

All cleaning products should be stored correctly, kept out of direct sunlight in their original containers and, if necessary, in a lockable cupboard away from heat sources and naked flames. Always follow the manufacturers' instructions for the product's use and dilution. Never mix chemicals together unless you have followed the manufacturer's instructions explicitly. Always wear personal protective safety wear when using cleaning products and ensure all cleaning products are recorded in the COSHH manual. This will need to be updated at regular intervals and when a new product is purchased.

See Unit 202, page 53 for full details of the Control of Substances Hazardous to Health (COSHH) Regulations 2002.

Good personal hygiene

Because humans are a source of food poisoning bacteria it is very important for all food handlers to take care with personal hygiene and to adopt good practices when working with food. These include:

- Arrive at work clean (bathe or shower daily) and ensure hair is clean.
- Wear approved, clean kitchen clothing and only wear it in the kitchen. This must completely cover any personal clothing.
- Keep hair neatly contained in a suitable hat/hairnet.
- Keep nails short and clean, and do not wear nail varnish or false nails.
- Do not wear jewellery or watches when handling food (a plain wedding band is permissible but could still trap bacteria).
- Avoid wearing cosmetics and strong perfumes.
- Smoking should not be allowed in or near food preparation areas (ash, smoke and bacteria from touching the mouth area could get into food).
- Do not eat food or sweets or chew gum when handling food as this may also transfer bacteria to food.
- Cover any cuts, burns or grazes with a blue waterproof dressing, then wash hands.

- Report any illness to the supervisor as soon as possible. Symptoms such as diarrhoea and/or vomiting, infected cuts, burns or spots, bad cold or flu symptoms, or if an illness was experienced while away from work, must be reported.

Hand-washing

Hands are constantly in use in the kitchen and touch numerous materials, foods, surfaces and equipment. Contamination from hands can happen very easily so you must take care with hand-washing to avoid this.

A basin should be provided that is used *only* for hand-washing. Hands should be washed as follows:

- Wet your hands under warm running water.
- Apply liquid soap.
- Rub your hands together and rub each hand with the fingers and thumb of the other.
- Remember to include your fingertips, nails and wrists.
- Rinse off the soap under the warm running water.
- Dry your hands on a paper towel and use the paper towel to turn off the tap before throwing it away.

You should always wash your hands:

- when you enter the kitchen, before starting work and handling any food
- after a break (particularly if you have used the toilet)
- between different tasks, but especially between handling raw and cooked food
- if you touch your hair, nose, mouth or use a tissue for a sneeze or cough
- after you apply or change a dressing on a cut or burn
- after cleaning preparation areas, equipment or contaminated surfaces
- after handling kitchen waste, external food packaging, money or flowers.

▲ **Figure 3.7** Wash hands thoroughly

Use of personal protective equipment (PPE)

PPE should be worn when handling and serving foods, especially when serving high-risk categories of customers to reduce the risk of cross-contamination. Disposable gloves, hairnets and aprons should be worn in addition to freshly laundered uniforms. The disposable items can then be replaced when moving from raw to cooked ingredients or if service happens between departments (for example, hospital wards).

Goggles, gloves and aprons should also be worn when using chemicals to clean beer lines, clean washroom and toilet facilities, and when adding chemicals to machinery for cleaning equipment or floors.

You can read more about the use of PPE on page 86.

▼ **Table 3.4** Types of PPE you can use

Body part	Hazards	Options	Note
Eyes	Chemical or metal splash, dust, projectiles, gas and vapour, oils and acids	Safety spectacles, goggles, face screens, face shields, visors	Make sure the eye protection chosen has the right combination of impact/dust/splash/eye protection for the task and fits the user properly
Head and neck	Impact from falling or flying objects, risk of head bumping, hair getting tangled in machinery, chemical drips or splash, climate or temperature	Caps and hairnets	Some safety helmets incorporate or can be fitted with specially designed eye or hearing protection Don't forget neck protection, e.g. scarves for use during welding Replace head protection if it is damaged
Ears	Noise – a combination of sound level and duration of exposure, very high-level sounds are a hazard even with short duration	Earplugs, earmuffs, semi-insert/canal caps	Provide the right hearing protectors for the type of work, and make sure workers know how to fit them Choose protectors that reduce noise to an acceptable level, while allowing for safety and communication
Hands and arms	Abrasion, temperature extremes, cuts and punctures, impact, chemicals, electric shock, radiation, vibration, biological agents and prolonged immersion in water	Gloves, gloves with a cuff, gauntlets and sleeving that covers part or all of the arm	Avoid gloves when operating machines where the gloves might get caught Some materials are quickly penetrated by chemicals – take care in selection Barrier creams are unreliable and are no substitute for proper PPE Wearing gloves for long periods can make the skin hot and sweaty, leading to skin problems. Using separate cotton inner gloves can help prevent this
Feet and legs	Wet, hot and cold conditions, electrostatic build-up, slipping, cuts and punctures, falling objects, heavy loads, metal and chemical splash, vehicles	Safety boots and shoes with protective toecaps and penetration-resistant, mid-sole wellington boots and specific footwear, e.g. foundry boots and chainsaw boots	Footwear can have a variety of sole patterns and materials to help prevent slips in different conditions, including oil- or chemical-resistant soles. It can also be anti-static, electrically conductive or thermally insulating Appropriate footwear should be selected for the risks identified

Follow your manager's instructions when using PPE

To avoid confusion and to ensure procedures are followed instructions are provided either in writing or verbally. These instructions need to be followed to avoid incidents and reduce the likelihood of contamination occurring.

1.3 MAINTAINING A SAFE WORKING ENVIRONMENT

Follow risk assessments

See page 79 earlier in this chapter for information on risk assessments.

Report all incidents

Incidents that affect the safety of the working environment and which must be reported to a supervisor include the following.

- **Threats** – such as discovering a suspicious package (a bomb threat).
- **Security** – such as finding that doors are unlocked or noticing unauthorised people entering the establishment and back of house areas.

- **Inappropriate behaviour** – such as someone using equipment incorrectly (not how they were trained), ignoring safety requirements (not wearing their PPE), or exhibiting threatening behaviour (colleagues or customers).

Dealing with a suspicious item or package

All employees should be constantly on the alert for suspicious items or packages.

- If an object is found then it must immediately be reported to the security officer, manager or supervisor.
- Do not touch or attempt to move the object.
- If there are customers in the immediate vicinity, discreetly attempt to establish ownership of the object.
- If the ownership is established, then ask the customer to keep the object with them, or to hand it in for safe keeping.
- If no immediate ownership is established, then the area should be cleared, and the authorities notified without delay.

Dealing with a bomb threat

Immediate action needs to be taken as a bomb could go off at any moment. As a result, staff should:

- be aware of and follow establishment policy with regard to bomb threats and evacuation procedures
- evacuate the immediate work area
- search the work area to ensure it is cleared, if this is part of their own responsibility
- evacuate the premises and usher all customers/staff through the nearest usable exits to specified assembly areas
- count all persons present to determine their safety and minimise the risk of fatal accidents.

Security

Security is a major concern. Staff need to be aware of the type of incidents that can occur at a premises and when to report them to a supervisor.

The main security risks in the hospitality industry are:

- **Theft**: where customers' property or employers' property (particularly food, drink and equipment) is stolen.
- **Burglary**: where a person comes on to the premises (trespasses) and steals customers' property or employers' property.
- **Robbery**: theft with assault (for example, when staff are banking or collecting cash).
- **Fraud**: such as false insurance claims, counterfeit money, stolen credit cards.
- **Assault**: this can be fights between customers, assaults on staff by customers (for example, if a customer is not happy with the service and/or is drunk, they may become violent towards staff) and attacks on staff while they are transferring cash to and from the bank.
- **Vandalism**: damage to property can be caused by customers, intruders or employees.
- **Arson**: deliberately setting fire to the property.

- **Undesirables**: when people such as drug dealers and prostitutes attempt to operate their business on the premises.
- **Terrorism**: suspect packages/containers (bombs), telephone bomb threats.

Staff should be trained to be vigilant at all times and if they see anything that could be a security risk to immediately report it to a supervisor who will make the decision as to what should happen next.

All staff should be aware of evacuation and 'lock down' procedures, and there should be regular training on these in place at their establishment.

Reporting hazards to a supervisor

When hazards are identified a supervisor should be notified as soon as possible to assess the risk and appropriate action. If appropriate a safety warning sign should be placed to warn others of the danger and if necessary prevent other people from coming into the area where the hazard is present until the risk has been removed or made safe.

Recording information

Temperature readings

Temperature readings must be taken every session of:

- fridges
- freezers
- cooked food
- cooled food
- core temperatures of large joints of meat to assess thorough cooking.

The temperature at which the fridge and freezer are operating should be taken at least once a day. This is an example of monitoring. These temperature readings should be kept with other kitchen records.

Using temperature probes

Using a temperature probe is the most effective way of ensuring that food is served at the correct temperatures. The core temperature is taken at the thickest part of the dish or joint as this is the slowest part to absorb heat. The probe needs to be disinfected before and after each insertion to avoid cross-contamination and should be calibrated regularly following the manufacturer's instructions to ensure the temperature readings are accurate.

There are three main methods for checking temperatures:

1 **Comparison method**: this is carried out by comparing the readings of the device against a device that is known to be accurate.
2 **The ice method**: the probe is inserted into a small container of crushed ice topped up with cold water. When the indicator has stabilised, the calibration may be set to show 0°C.
3 **The boiling point method**: the probe is inserted into a small container of boiling water. When the indicator has stabilised, the calibration may be set to show 100°C (at normal altitude).

▲ **Figure 3.8** Temperature probe

Food deliveries

Food must be delivered in suitable packaging, properly date coded and at the correct temperature. On arrival deliveries should be checked to ensure the delivery note matches the purchase order. All items should be counted and checked for quality, freshness and quantity. They are then accepted into the premises and the delivery note is signed, date stamped, and the top copy retained and attached to the purchase order.

The stock is then placed in the appropriate storage area and the paperwork is passed to the stores controller to enter the stock into the food control system. This paper trail can be retraced in case of any stock discrepancies.

Food displays

There are certain circumstances where it may not be practical to keep foods at the required temperatures. The Food Safety and Hygiene (England) Regulations 2013 allow you to keep food out of temperature control for limited periods of time.

Food displayed in restaurants or cafés, put out on buffets, or served in shops, can be kept out of temperature control for a limited time. However, you must take care not to exceed the maximum display times, because otherwise you could cause a risk to health.

Foods that normally need to be kept chilled can be kept un-chilled for up to four hours, to allow them to be served or displayed. Foods can only be kept un-chilled for one period of service or display. After this, any food that is left must be thrown away or chilled until final use.

Food that will be served hot can be kept below 63°C for two hours, for serving or display. After this time, the food must be thrown away or cooled as quickly as possible and then chilled until final use. It must not be kept out of temperature control for more than two hours and must not be reheated more than once.

Also see notes on the safety growth curve, page 102, and Danger Zone, page 103.

Accurate records need to be kept showing when the foods were placed on display and when they must be removed from display and destroyed to prevent any risk to health. These records must be kept in the kitchen log as evidence of good food control on the food displays.

Identify and communicate information about allergies and food safety hazards

Staff must be briefed prior to every service on the allergens in dishes and if there are any food safety hazards they should be aware of. Using symbols on menus, displays and signage will assist both staff and customers when making their choices.

Preparing a folder containing all the allergen and food hazards will assist staff in giving accurate information to customers. This folder may be electronic and linked via the EPOS system to the kitchen system; this can be easily updated by the chef when altering menus, suppliers and recipes.

Refer to chemical information sheets (COSHH)

All controlled substances must be recorded in the Control of Substances Hazardous to Health (COSHH) register and regularly reviewed. Staff must receive training in the use of these substances and each chemical must have an information sheet that gives instruction on handling, the requirements for PPE and action to be taken in case of accidents when handling.

See Unit 202, page 53 for details of the Control of Substances Hazardous to Health (COSHH) Regulations 2002, and how they relate to your individual role.

Follow business standard operating procedures (SOPs)

An overall SOP that covers all aspects of the business, from meeting and greeting to taking orders and processing payments, can be a means to satisfy customers on time, the same way, every time. It removes employee guesswork about how tasks are to be performed, improving productivity, efficiency and teamwork while providing a base for evaluating performance and making improvements.

SOPs can also cover incident handling such as evacuation procedures, security alerts and lock downs, hazard handling, and accident procedures. This will ensure all staff have a process to follow in line with company standards and are able to make informed decisions within the law. Having these procedures written down and combined with training will give staff more confidence when handling stressful and possibly life-threatening situations.

Follow your manager's instructions when following standard operating procedures

If staff are instructed how to carry out their roles and responsibilities within their working environment, this will reduce incidents and require minimal supervision. Staff will be able to carry out their duties safely and be updated regularly when procedures, regulations or materials and equipment changes.

Staff will need to be aware of the purpose and relevance of these instructions to their and others' safety and well-being. This will reinforce the information given and the importance of following procedures.

Maintain personal hygiene

See page 105 for guidelines on maintaining your own personal hygiene. Staff should also wash themselves thoroughly before every shift using deodorant. If make-up is allowed this should be kept to a minimum, as should perfumes and aftershave, as otherwise this can cause an overpowering smell that may interfere with the smells and aromas of the food and wine being served to customers.

Uniform

All staff have a duty to ensure that they arrive on duty in clean uniform and to the organisation's dress code standards. If the organisation does not launder staff uniforms then sufficient sets should be provided for staff to be able to wash, dry and iron their own uniform. They will usually need a minimum of three sets. Uniforms are expensive and so should be easy to wash, dry and keep looking smart. Spare uniforms should be available for when staff need to change mid shift (due to the nature of food service, liquids and food will leak, spill and splash).

Staff should change into their clean uniforms once they arrive at their place of work and not commute to work in them. This is to avoid external dirt getting on to uniforms and reduce the potential for spreading germs and contamination.

Where necessary hairnets, aprons and disposable gloves should be worn and replaced frequently as necessary between tasks.

Regular workplace cleaning and immediate cleaning when necessary

All food and beverage service staff should be made aware of the importance of cleaning programmes to reduce and minimise the build-up of dust, bacteria and other forms of debris. See page 106 in this chapter for details of what should be included in a cleaning programme and the use of cleaning products.

Regular hand-washing

Frequent hand-washing should also be carried out, especially between handling raw and cooked foods, when handling food deliveries, after taking toilet and smoking breaks and after coughing or sneezing.

Use correct hazard signage

All staff need to be aware that when carrying out cleaning (which might be hazardous to others) the appropriate signage should be displayed.

Safety signs are used to control a hazard and they should not replace other methods of controlling risks. See Table 3.5.

Use correct PPE

According to the Personal Protective Equipment (PPE) at Work Regulations 1992, employees must wear personal protective equipment and clothing (for example, safety shoes, goggles for eye protection) for tasks that may pose a risk or hazard.

See more about PPE on pages 86 and 91.

Correct manual handling

See page 83 earlier in this chapter for information on manual handling.

Review and update own training

All staff should regularly review their own safety training and seek further training where necessary. The Health and Safety at Work Act states that we all have a duty of care and therefore the safety of others as well as ourselves is everyone's responsibility. Therefore, training and its importance should not be dismissed as 'not my job'. An accurate record of training taken and updated should be kept, usually with HR in staff personnel records. This should be reviewed as part of staff reviews and gaps in training should be scheduled into each staff member's training for the coming period.

▼ **Table 3.5** the different types of signage used in food service

Type of sign	Use	
Yellow warning signs	These are warning signs to alert people to various dangers, such as slippery floors, hot oil or hot water. They also warn people about hazards such as a corrosive material	 ▲ **Figure 3.9** Yellow warning sign
Blue mandatory signs	These signs inform people about precautions they must take. They tell people how to progress safely through a certain area. They must be used whenever special precautions need to be taken, such as wearing protective clothing	 ▲ **Figure 3.10** Blue mandatory signs
Red prohibition signs – firefighting signs	Red signs tell people that they should not enter. They are used to stop people from doing certain tasks in a hazardous area. Red signs are also used for fire-fighting equipment	 ▲ **Figure 3.11** Red prohibition signs
Green safe signs	These are route signs designed to show people where fire exits and emergency exits are. Green is also used for first aid equipment	 ▲ **Figure 3.12** Green safe signs

2 FOOD SAFETY HAZARDS
2.1 FOOD SAFETY HAZARDS AND KEY SOURCES OF CONTAMINATION
Chemical hazards

Chemicals can sometimes get into food accidentally and can make the consumer ill. The kinds of chemicals that may get into food include:

- cleaning materials – such as disinfectants and sanitisers
- pesticides – these are substances to control pests. These include substances such as insecticides, insect repellent and fungicides
- veterinary residue – this is another name for the medication given to animals which is then left in food products from animals
- rodenticides – poisons used to control rats and mice.

Allergenic hazards

Food businesses are required to provide allergy information on food sold unpackaged, for example in restaurants and cafés, deli counters, bakeries and sandwich bars. Table 3.6 shows the 14 **allergens** that must be tracked and displayed.

▼ **Table 3.6** The 14 allergens

Allergens		
1 Celery	6 Lupin	11 Peanuts
2 Crustaceans	7 Milk	12 Sesame
3 Eggs	8 Molluscs	13 Soybeans (also, soya bean)
4 Fish	9 Mustard	14 Sulphur dioxide and sulphites
5 Gluten	10 Nuts	

Allergen information can be supplied on the menu, on chalk boards, tickets or provided verbally by service staff as well as in other formats made available to the consumer. It must be clear and conspicuous, easily seen and read. If the information is to be provided by asking a member of staff then this must be made clear on a notice, menu, ticket or label that can easily be seen by customers.

It will not be enough for a food business operator to say that they do not know whether or not a food contains an allergen. It will also not be enough to say that all their foods may contain allergens. Allergen information must be specific to the food and complete and accurate. This also applies to food pre-packed for direct sale, such as from takeaways, deli counters, bakeries or sandwich bars.

Food poisoning bacteria

Bacteria are microscopic organisms (often referred to as germs), which are found everywhere. Most bacteria are harmless and some are essential – for example, in food manufacturing processes like cheese and yoghurt. However, a small number of bacteria cause foods to perish. Other bacteria – such as food poisoning bacteria, are known as **pathogens**. If pathogens get into food, they make people ill. A summary of food poisoning bacteria is given in Table 3.7.

KEY TERMS

Chemicals – include cleaning fluids, disinfectants, machine oil, insecticides and pesticides.

Allergens – food items that cause allergic reactions in some people. There are 14 allergens that customers should be notified of.

KEY TERMS

Bacteria – organisms harmful to humans.

Pathogens – harmful bacteria.

▼ Table 3.7 Food poisoning bacteria

Bacteria	Sources	Onset period	Typical symptoms and duration of illness
Salmonella	Raw meat, raw milk, raw eggs, raw poultry, pets, rodents, flies and sewage	Usually 12 to 36 hours	Abdominal pain, diarrhoea, vomiting and fever (1 to 7 days)
Clostridium perfringens	Animal and human excreta, soil (on vegetables), dust, insects and raw meat	Usually 8 to 12 hours	Abdominal pain and diarrhoea. Vomiting is rare (12 to 48 hours)
Staphylococcus aureus	Human nose, mouth, skin, boils and cuts Raw milk from cows or goats	1 to 7 hours	Abdominal pain, mainly vomiting, some diarrhoea, low temperature (6 to 24 hours)
Clostridium botulinum	Soil, fish, meat and vegetables	Usually 12 to 36 hours	Difficulties in swallowing, talking and breathing. Double vision and paralysis of nerves. Fatalities are common. Recovery of survivor may take months
Bacillus cereus	Soil, fish, meat and vegetables	1 to 6 hours	Vomiting, abdominal pain and some diarrhoea (12 to 24 hours)

Food-borne diseases

Food-borne illnesses are caused by pathogenic bacteria and/or their toxins, and also viruses. Pathogens do not need to multiply in the food, they just need to get into the intestine where they start to multiply. Only tiny amounts are needed and may be transmitted person to person, in water or airborne, as well as through food. Symptoms of food-borne illness vary and include severe abdominal pain, diarrhoea, vomiting, headaches, blurred vision, flu symptoms, septicaemia and miscarriage.

▼ Table 3.8 Food-borne diseases

Mirco-organism	Sources	Onset period	Typical symptoms
Campylobacter (most common cause of diarrhoea from bacteria)	Raw poultry, meat, milk, farm animals, pets, birds, sewage and untreated water	2 to 5 days	Diarrhoea (often bloody), abdominal pain, nausea and fever
E. coli O157 (often fatal for elderly and young children)	Intestines of people and animals, sewage and untreated water	Usually 3 to 4 days	Nausea, diarrhoea (often bloody), abdominal cramps. Kidney failure (especially in children)
Listeria (multiplies in refrigerated foods)	Soil, sewage, water, vegetation, people, animals and birds	1 to 70 days	Flu-like symptoms. Vomiting, diarrhoea and fever. Miscarriage in pregnant women
Norovirus (only multiplies in the body)	The environment and sewage (airborne and person to person)	Usually 24 to 48 hours	Vomiting, diarrhoea, abdominal pain and fever
Typhoid	Carriers, sewage, manure and water	Usually 8 to 14 days	Fever, nausea, headache, slow pulse, poor appetite, constipation and sometimes diarrhoea

Viruses

Viruses infect the cells of living organisms from plants to people. Some infections are so mild they usually go unrecognised. Other viruses can rapidly cause death. Viruses cause a broad array of human diseases. These microscopic particles spread easily, typically via person-to-person contact or touching contaminated surfaces.

Illnesses include influenza, common colds, gastroenteritis and skin infections.

Moulds

Moulds are essential components of a number of food products, such as cheeses. Some are responsible for spoilage of food, especially baked products and fruit, mostly due to the age of the product and/or prolonged unsatisfactory storage.

Parasites

Parasites are organisms that pass on diseases. For example, malaria is passed on by the malarial parasite. Another example is tapeworm, which can be found in pork. Making sure that food is fully cooked and following rules of hygiene can reduce the risk from parasites.

Food handlers

Food handlers must wash their hands thoroughly after using the toilet, after coughing or sneezing, after breaks (especially if they have been smoking) and after handling raw or high-risk foods. Wearing a clean uniform that has been washed at a high temperature will reduce the risk of cross-contamination and outdoor footwear must not be worn in the food preparation area (only wear shoes that are not worn outside the building).

If a food handler has any symptoms of food poisoning or diarrhoea then they must not come into work, they must notify their manager and should stay away from the workplace for 48 hours after the symptoms have gone. If a food handler returns to work too quickly they may spread infection (even though they have recovered from their symptoms). This person is known as a convalescent carrier.

Food handlers must also be aware that they may become infected and carry diseases without having any symptoms. In this case, they would be known as a healthy carrier.

Physical contamination

Physical contamination is caused when something gets into food that should not be there. This could be anything that a person should not eat – such as glass, pen tops, paperclips, blue plasters, hair or fingernails.

To reduce physical contamination the following should be done on a daily basis:

- packaging should be removed away from the food preparation area to reduce the risk of cross-contamination
- regular checks should be made of machinery to ensure it is well maintained
- toughened safety glass should be used for 'sneeze guards' and shelving
- staff should not be allowed to use pens with a separate top and should be issued with click retract pens; this reduces the risk of tops being dropped into food

KEY TERM

Physical contamination – when something gets into food that should not be there.

101

- paperclips should not be used to secure papers; use staples or bulldog clips
- cuts and scratches should be covered with blue plasters for ease of identification
- hair and beard nets should be worn to reduce the risk of hair falling into food
- fingernails should be cut short, scrubbed clean before work and throughout the shift; coloured nail varnish or false nails are not acceptable in the food and beverage department
- protective guards should be left in place while machines are in use.

2.2 CHARACTERISTICS OF PATHOGENIC BACTERIAL GROWTH

Food poisoning bacteria are tiny bugs which are present in the air, soil, water and sometimes in people and food. Bacteria can cause harmful illnesses; these are known as pathogenic bacteria. Most of these bacteria can rot and decay food. These types of bacteria are known as spoilage bacteria.

Growth curve

The best temperature for the multiplication of most food poisoning bacteria is around 37°C (body temperature), although they can multiply quickly between 20°C and 50°C. Figure 3.13 illustrates how bacteria multiply.

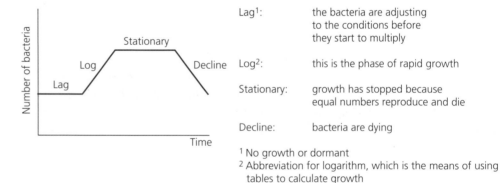

Lag[1]: the bacteria are adjusting to the conditions before they start to multiply

Log[2]: this is the phase of rapid growth

Stationary: growth has stopped because equal numbers reproduce and die

Decline: bacteria are dying

[1] No growth or dormant
[2] Abbreviation for logarithm, which is the means of using tables to calculate growth

▲ **Figure 3.13** How bacteria multiply

Danger Zone

Temperatures between 8°C and 63°C are called the Danger Zone because it is possible for bacteria to multiply between these temperatures, with most rapid multiplication at around body temperature (37°C). Best practice is to keep the temperature of the food below 5°C or above 63°C.

- Thorough cooking is one of the best methods available to control bacteria. Cooking to 75°C and holding that temperature for at least two minutes will kill most pathogens (but not spores and toxins).
- When reheating foods bring the core temperature up to 70°C as quickly as possible and hold this temperature for a minimum of 2 minutes (in Scotland this is 82°C).
- Never put hot or warm food into a fridge or freezer as this will raise the temperature in the fridge or freezer and potentially put food into the Danger Zone.

Protein, moisture, time, warmth

- Protein: high protein foods are preferred by bacteria, especially raw or cooked meat, poultry and dairy produce.
- Moisture: many foods contain the nutrients and moisture required by bacteria. Foods such as gravy, milk powder or dried egg do not provide the moisture necessary for bacteria to grow.
- Time: given the right conditions of food, moisture and warmth, some bacteria can divide into two every ten to twenty minutes. This process is known as binary fission.
- Warmth: the best temperature for the multiplication of most food poisoning bacteria is around 37°C (body temperature).

Binary fission – vegetative reproduction

Bacteria grow by splitting in half. They can do this approximately every twenty minutes. This process of reproduction is called binary fission.

Spore formers

The bacteria form spores when the conditions surrounding them become hostile, for example as temperatures rise or in the presence of chemicals such as disinfectant. A **spore** forms a protective 'shell' inside the bacteria, protecting the essential parts from the high temperatures of normal cooking, disinfection or dehydration. Once spores are formed the cells cannot divide and multiply as before but simply survive until conditions improve, for example the high temperatures drop to a level where multiplication can start again.

Toxin producers

Other bacteria produce **toxins** (poisons) outside their cells as they multiply in food. These mix with the food, making it poisonous, and symptoms of food poisoning follow. Toxins in food are resistant to heat, thus causing illness even if the food is heated to boiling point. Different toxins can be released by some pathogens as they multiply in the human body.

Contamination

Cross-contamination

Cross-contamination is when bacteria are transferred from contaminated food (usually raw food), equipment or surfaces to ready-to-eat food. Cross-contamination is the cause of significant amounts of food poisoning and care must be taken to avoid it. Cross-contamination is caused by:

- foods touching each other, such as raw and cooked meat
- soil from dirty vegetables coming into contact with high-risk foods
- dirty cloths or dirty equipment

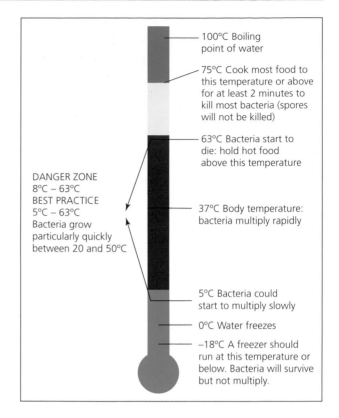

DANGER ZONE
8°C – 63°C
BEST PRACTICE
5°C – 63°C
Bacteria grow particularly quickly between 20 and 50°C

- 100°C Boiling point of water
- 75°C Cook most food to this temperature or above for at least 2 minutes to kill most bacteria (spores will not be killed)
- 63°C Bacteria start to die: hold hot food above this temperature
- 37°C Body temperature: bacteria multiply rapidly
- 5°C Bacteria could start to multiply slowly
- 0°C Water freezes
- –18°C A freezer should run at this temperature or below. Bacteria will survive but not multiply.

▲ **Figure 3.14** Important food safety temperatures

KEY TERMS

Spore – protective shell which allows cells to protect themselves from heat or freezing.

Toxin – poison.

Cross-contamination – when bacteria are transferred from contaminated food (usually raw food), equipment or surfaces to ready-to-eat food.

- equipment (such as chopping boards or knives) used to prepare raw food and then cooked food
- hands touching raw food and then cooked food, without hand-washing between tasks
- pests depositing bacteria from their own bodies around the kitchen.

Drip contamination

Drip contamination can happen when raw meat or poultry drips on to high-risk foods. Raw foods should be placed in containers big enough to contain the item and any liquid that may seep from it. Fresh foods should always be placed on a shelf below cooked foods and ideally in a separate fridge.

Routes and vehicles

Delivery vehicles must have storage systems to ensure foods are kept away from any contaminants. They must also be refrigerated, especially when transporting meat and fish. Travelling time should be the minimum safe time limit required and the route of the delivery vehicles planned accordingly. See Delivery procedures on page 107 later on in this chapter.

2.3 REDUCING THE RISK FROM FOOD SAFETY HAZARDS

Hazard Analysis and Critical Control Point (HACCP) system

In line with the Food Standards Agency's commitment to reduce food poisoning cases, it is a legal requirement for all food businesses to operate a food safety management system. When environmental health officers/practitioners inspect these businesses they will always check that food safety management systems are in place and are working well.

All food safety management systems must be based on the Hazard Analysis and Critical Control Point (HACCP) system. This is an internationally recognised food safety management system that aims to identify the critical points or stages in any process. The system must provide a documented record of the stages all food will go through right up to the time it is eaten. Once the hazards have been identified, measures are put in place to control the hazards and keep the food safe.

The HACCP system involves seven stages:

1 Identify hazards – what could go wrong.
2 Identify CCP (critical control points), that is, the important points where things could go wrong.
3 Set critical limits for each CCP, for example the temperature that fresh chicken should be at when it is delivered.
4 Monitor CCPs and put checks in place to stop problems from occurring.
5 Identify corrective action – what will be done if something goes wrong.
6 Verification – check that the HACCP plan is working.
7 Documentation – record all of the above.

The system must be updated regularly, especially when the menu or systems change (for instance, when a new piece of equipment is introduced to the kitchen). Specific new controls must be put in place to include any changes.

'Safer food, better business' and 'CookSafe'

The HACCP system may seem complicated and difficult to set up for a small business. With this in mind, the Food Standards Agency launched its 'Safer food, better business' system for England and Wales. This is based on the principles of HACCP but is in a format that is easy to understand, with pre-printed pages and charts in which to enter the relevant information, such as temperatures for individual dishes. It is divided into two parts.

1　The first part is about safe methods – for example, avoiding cross-contamination, personal hygiene, cleaning, chilling and cooking.
2　The second part covers opening and closing checks. These are checks that procedures are in place and being followed on a daily basis – for example, safe methods of working, cleaning areas and surfaces, temperature checks, removal of waste, etc; recording of safe methods; training records; supervision; stock control; and the selection of suppliers and contractors. This will ensure that the operation is working to the standards required to produce safe food.

A similar system called 'CookSafe' has been developed by the Food Standards Agency (Scotland). Details of both schemes can be found at

www.food.gov.uk

Risk assessments

Knowing what a risk or hazard is and how to control it should form part of staff induction training and be regularly updated. With good training and reinforcement of how and why to avoid risks and hazards, a culture of prevention will be embedded into a company's daily practice.

See the 'five steps to assessing risk' listed earlier in this chapter on page 79.

Personal hygiene

Everyone carries bacteria in their mouths, gut and on their skin, so practising good personal hygiene will reduce the risk of cross-contamination. However, personal standards will vary compared with what is considered to be the standard required for an organisation, therefore staff training will help reduce risk and encourage good practice. Personal hygiene training will include:

- **the use of protective clothing** – issued to reduce cross-contamination and protect skin from burns, scalds, exposure to chemicals and bacteria
- **wearing gloves** – issued to reduce cross-contamination and protect from chemicals and heat
- **wearing a hair net** – to reduce the risk of hair falling into food and therefore cross-contamination of food
- **regular hand-washing** – to remove bacteria and chemicals and reduce the risk of cross-contamination

- **sickness reporting** – it is the responsibility of all staff to report to their supervisor if they are suffering from sickness or diarrhoea and they must not return to work for 48 hours from when the symptoms cease.

Cleaning

Regular and thorough cleaning will reduce the risk of contamination to others and will also extend the life of equipment and reduce costs to a business from loss of reputation and possible legal action. The following areas should be considered:

- **A cleaning schedule** – this will cover the frequency of cleaning and the depth to which it should be done.
- **'Clean as you go'** – all staff should clean down their work area as they work to avoid hazards and risks being created. This will also give a professional image to customers and increase efficient and safe working practices.
- **Equipment cleaning methods** – all equipment should be cleaned regularly, especially when working between different foods and especially raw and cooked foods. Staff must be trained how to clean equipment safely in order to protect both themselves and others from any risks – and always follow the manufacturer's instructions.

Control of substances hazardous to health (COSHH)

Staff should be made fully aware of how their use and handling of COSHH items.

- **Storage** – chemicals should be stored in their original containers (the ones designed for them and their use) with their original labels and instructions intact. They should be stored in a secure area that is away from direct sunlight and naked flames and kept cool. Certain chemicals can be corrosive and also react if mixed with other chemicals, therefore they should be checked to ensure what they should be kept away from.
- **Handling** – all chemicals carry a risk if they come into contact with the skin, eyes, polished surfaces and other chemicals. Therefore careful handling of all chemicals must be practised. If there is damage to a container or there is a leak or spillage, the supervisor should be notified and the correct procedures taken to deal with the situation.
- **Use of correct chemicals such as detergent, disinfectant** – detergents break down grease and dirt to assist in their removal, and disinfectant is designed to destroy bacteria. They are best used according to the manufacturer's instructions but will only be effective if used correctly.
- **Chemical contact time** – in order for a product to do the job it is designed for it will require to be used correctly and the contact time followed; failure to do so reduces the impact of the chemical, and overexposure due to excessive amounts of chemical or increased contact time could result in damage to the surface.
- **Materials** – materials are selected for their properties; during manufacture additional benefits can be built into materials to make them more effective in reducing risks or in extending the product's life – such as anti-bacterial

properties for fridges, chopping boards, work surfaces, flooring, etc. All materials are classified as being either porous or non-porous and this will have an effect on their suitability for selection in their use and application.

Always wear personal protective safety wear when using cleaning products and ensure all cleaning products are recorded in the COSHH manual. This will need to be updated at regular intervals and when a new product is purchased.

See Unit 202, page 53 for details of the Control of Substances Hazardous to Health (COSHH) Regulations 2002.

Delivery procedures

The risk to a business can be reduced if all goods are checked when entering a premise. There is always a chance that the delivery could be contaminated and therefore the establishment's policy for the receipt of stock should always be followed. Key points to remember when receiving goods are listed here.

- Reputable suppliers – checking suppliers' premises and delivery vehicles comply with food safety regulations should be carried out regularly to ensure compliance at source.
- The maximum allowable time between delivery and storage – reducing the time food items are kept in the Danger Zone should be paramount. Good design of the goods receiving area at the premises enables items to go from refrigerated vehicles to chilled stores and fridges/freezers in the shortest possible time.
- Acceptance or rejection – on delivery the person receiving a delivery should check for damage to the boxes and containers, that the dates on the packaging are within acceptable limits and, if necessary, take temperatures using a clean food probe (to check that the core temperature is within the acceptable range). The refrigeration temperature of the delivery vehicle may also be checked and recorded. If there is any cause for concern regarding the quality and safety of goods, then the delivery should be refused and returned to the supplier.

Storage

Use-by, best-before and sell-by dates can be explained as follows.

- **Use-by dates** – these appear on perishable foods with a short life. Legally, the food must be used by this date and not stored or used after it.
- **Best-before dates** – these apply to foods that are expected to have a longer life, for example dry products or canned food. A best-before date advises that food is at its best before this date; using it after this date is legal but not advised.
- **Sell-by dates** – indicate how long the food should remain on sale.

Temperatures for foods

- Chilled temperature – a chill room is not the same as a walk-in refrigerator. It keeps food cold without freezing and is particularly suitable for those foods requiring a consistent, cold temperature – such as dessert fruits, salads and cheese, which requires differing temperatures depending on the type of cheese. Fresh fruit, salads and vegetables are best stored at a temperature of 4–6°C. Dairy products should be stored at 2°C. Fats and oils are best stored at 4–7°C.

- Frozen temperature – frozen foods are required to be kept at -18 to -22°C. Frozen food increases the variety of products an operation can offer and retains its nutritional content for a long period.
- Ambient temperature – this is the temperature of the surrounding environment. This suits dry goods – such as biscuits, flour, bread, sugar, cordial, loose and bagged tea, coffee grounds, beans, etc.
- Temperature probes – a temperature probe measures the core temperature of an item. They must be wiped clean with an anti-bacterial wipe before and after use to avoid cross-contamination. More details of how to use a temperature probe can be found on page 94.

Preparation and service

Preparation of food products

- Worktops and chopping boards will come into contact with the food being prepared, so need special attention. Colour-coded chopping boards are a good way to keep different types of food separate. Make sure that chopping boards are in good condition (cracks and splits trap bacteria that can be transferred to food).

    - As well as colour-coded chopping boards, some kitchens also provide colour-coded knives, cloths, cleaning equipment, storage trays, bowls and even staff uniforms to help prevent cross-contamination.
    - Date labelling, covering foods and keeping raw and cooked foods separate during preparation of foods prior to service is vital in ensuring food safety.
    - Food should be cooked through properly to kill off any bacteria. If it is to be held for service the cooking time should be reduced to the minimum amount, and if it is to be reheated then the food should be rapidly cooled, then chilled and brought back to service temperature quickly and thoroughly checked in different places to ensure the correct temperature has been reached throughout the dish.
    - Cook-chill dishes require food to be kept at 0–3°C and then when regenerated to reach 70°C for a minimum of two minutes.

Use of correct service equipment
See Unit 204, page 141 for details of the correct service equipment for different tasks.

Use of personal protective clothing (PPE)
PPE should be replaced or cleaned in readiness for service. This presents a professional image and increases customer satisfaction. See notes on PPE on page 86.

▲ **Figure 3.15** Colour code chart for chopping boards

Avoid cross-contamination

Using separate utensils, having clean and fresh PPE and a clean serving environment will reduce the risk of cross-contamination. Keeping cooked and raw ingredients separate and ensuring high-risk foods are carefully controlled will also reduce service risks to customers.

Hot and cold holding

If food is to be held (stored ready for service) then it should be kept either below 5°C or above 63°C. Between these temperatures the growth of pathogenic micro-organisms or the formation of toxins will occur. Hot food being held for service should not be allowed to fall below 63°C. Cold food held in refrigeration/display cabinets should be discarded after four hours, including preparation time.

Temperature probing

Regular temperature probing should be carried out before, during and again after service. This will ensure food is held at correct temperatures to reduce the time bacteria have to multiply.

Record keeping

Record keeping ensures compliance with food safety legislation. These records should be signed by the person taking the readings and kept as part of an establishment's due diligence procedure.

- Delivery records – these record what has come into a business, when it arrived, in what condition and, if necessary, its delivery temperature. These records can be valuable when tracing a product's journey with regard to HACCP if required.
- Temperature checks should be recorded for hot and cold food, and for equipment – such as fridges, chill display cabinets and hot buffets.

Maintenance

A well-maintained premises is the first line of defence in the fight against the contamination of food and drink.

Buildings

Having a regular maintenance programme and investment in keeping the building in good order will reduce the risk of bacteria and infestations being harboured in the fabric of the building.

Ensuring drains and water supplies and air conditioning units are regularly checked for their physical condition and also checking for bacteria (such as legionella) is essential in the prevention of contamination and risk to customers and staff.

Pest control

Pests can be a serious source of contamination and disease. Allowing them near food is not permitted and is against the law. Pests carry food poisoning bacteria into food premises in their fur/feathers, feet/paws, saliva, urine and droppings. Other problems caused by pests include damage to food stocks and packaging, as well as damage to buildings, equipment and wiring. They can cause blockages in equipment and in pipe networks.

▼ **Table 3.9** Signs of pest presence and how to keep them out

Pest	Signs that they are present	Ways to keep pests out or eliminate them
Rats and mice	Sightings of rodents or their droppings; gnawed wires; greasy marks on lower walls; damaged food stock; paw prints; an unpleasant smell	• Block entry to building by making sure there are no holes around the pipe work • Fill all gaps and cavities where pests can get in • Use sealed drain covers • Damage to the building or fixtures and fittings should be repaired quickly • Use window/door screening/netting • Check packaging of deliveries for pests • Use baits and traps • Use an electronic fly killer • Used sealed containers and ensure no open food is left out • Do not allow a build-up of waste in the kitchen • Do not keep outside waste too close to the kitchen • Arrange professional and organised pest management control, surveys and reports
Flies and wasps	Sightings of flies and wasps; hearing them; signs of dead insects; sightings of maggots	
Cockroaches	Sightings (dead or alive), usually at night; unpleasant smell	
Ants	Sightings, including in food; tiny pale-coloured pharaoh ants are difficult to spot but can still be the source of a variety of pathogens	
Weevils	Sightings of weevils in stored products, e.g. flour, cornflour; they are very difficult to see but can be spotted by their movement in flour, etc.	
Birds	Sightings; droppings in outside storage areas and around refuse	
Domestic pets	These must be kept out of food areas as they carry pathogens in fur, whiskers, saliva, urine, etc.	

Pest control measures can also introduce food safety hazards. The bodies of dead insects or even rodents may remain in the kitchen (causing a bacterial contamination). Pesticides, insecticides and baits can introduce a chemical contamination if not managed properly. Pest treatment and disposal is best managed by professionals.

Equipment

All equipment should be cleaned regularly and have a safety check carried out on it periodically. A visual check can be done every time it is used to check for wear and tear, cracks, fraying cords, splinters and chips. If the equipment is not fit for use then it should either be removed (to a safe place), disposed of, or repaired. If it must remain in situ then a warning notice should be placed on it to stop anyone using it.

Visual inspection of food at all times

A visual check of food is often the quickest way to identify food spoilage; if this is noticed the food should be removed from display or from storage and preparation areas and replaced with fresh items.

Waste

The production of waste is costly for the business but inevitable in the food and beverage industry.

- **Storage of waste products** should be controlled to reduce the attraction to pests and the multiplication of bacteria. The waste storage area should be washed down daily using strong disinfectant, bins should be washed daily after emptying, and bins in kitchen and service areas should also have bin liners and lids to reduce infestations.

- **Handling waste** should be done wearing PPE because hazards are often hidden in waste – for example, broken glass or sharp plastic or metal items. PPE is essential to reduce the risk of injury. Any cleaning products should be returned to their original containers and disposed of in accordance with the manufacturer's and the local authority's recommendations.
  - Oils and fats: cool to room temperature before decanting them into suitable containers prior to removal. Do not dispose of fat and oil down a drain or into the watercourse as this can contaminate water supplies or block drains.
- **Recycling waste** is an effective way of reducing waste and can earn income for the business. Glass, metal, paper, cardboard, oil, fat and food waste all have a commercial value and therefore it makes both environmental and business sense to source companies willing to remove recyclable waste from a business. Items to be recycled should be carefully stored, away from the building, and frequent collections arranged to reduce storage times.

Allergens

Allergens are very common in food and drink service and it is a legal requirement that staff are able to identify allergens and communicate this information to customers when required. See the list of allergenic hazards on page 99. In order to do this with confidence the following will assist staff:

- **Information sheets**. These list the items for sale, their ingredients and highlight any known allergens. These can be either printed sheets or held electronically in the EPOS system. These lists are available on some companies' websites, especially where they are part of a national chain.
- **Menus**. These can list allergens or may use symbols to denote allergens, however this is not a universal system and therefore needs to be clearly explained.
- **Procedures for dealing with allergen notification**. If a customer has notified a member of staff that they have an allergy this should be written down in the booking diary/EPOS system and highlighted for all staff to see, especially the kitchen staff who will be producing the food. Additionally, staff should try to mention food allergens when asked or individually flag up relevant items by annotating the customer's menu card or by display on a general menu highlighting the allergens in the dishes. Note that this is not a fail-safe way of avoiding cross-contamination, and if a customer has a severe allergy then a separate dish will have to be prepared using a separate preparation area, equipment and fresh ingredients.
  Customers with a severe allergy must be listened to and their needs checked very precisely with both the customer and the most senior chef in charge of the kitchen. If their safety cannot be guaranteed, the customer should be informed of this; if they still wish to order, good advice would be to obtain written consent from them, stating that they have been informed of the inability to guarantee that the food/drink served in the business may not be free of their specific allergen. Also see Unit 205, page 166 for more information on handling customer illness.

③ MAINTAINING A SAFE AND SECURE SERVICE AREA

3.1 MAINTAINING A SAFE WORKING ENVIRONMENT

Many factors contribute to the maintenance of a safe working environment.

Participation in and application of training

All staff must receive, and sign to say they have received, health and safety, manual handling and fire safety training as part of their initial induction training. The level will depend on the job role and experience. This should be renewed at mandatory intervals or sooner if additional training needs are identified.

Identify and remove hazards

All staff play a part in ensuring a safe working environment is maintained.

▲ **Figure 3.16** Emergency exit clear of obstructions

- Clutter should be cleared from work stations, corridors and store rooms regularly to avoid incidents occurring.
- Floors need to be kept clean, grease-free and dry, and dust mats and carpets should be well maintained and smooth to reduce the likelihood of slips and trips in the workplace.
- Emergency exit routes should be kept clear – furniture and materials should not be placed or stored in corridors, or obstruct emergency exits, because this will hinder the evacuation during an emergency. Storing items in areas not designed for storage also poses a fire risk and therefore should not be permitted at any time.

Report and record

Keeping accurate records such as an accident book, near misses and faulty equipment log will highlight patterns of incidents. These can be completed by anyone and countersigned by a supervisor or manager to ensure they are dealt with. This enables action to remove or repair items of equipment or identify where retraining of staff is required. This will form part of the establishment's due diligence policy.

Follow safety instructions

Staff should always follow safety instructions, health and safety policies, and chemical and equipment usage procedures. These should be contained within the SOPs manual for the department and are there to protect both staff and customers and maintain standards.

Use of appropriate PPE

The use of PPE as supplied by the business, appropriate to the tasks to be carried out, is the responsibility of the staff member. Failure to use PPE supplied by the business would be at the staff member's own risk and could result in personal injury and possible disciplinary procedures.

Correct use of safety equipment

Proper training in the use of fire extinguishers, warning signs and machinery guards should be carried out before any member of staff can use them. This ensures staff can safely use the equipment for the purpose intended and not increase the risk of danger to themselves or others when using the equipment.

3.2 MAINTAINING A SECURE WORKING ENVIRONMENT

Many factors contribute to the maintenance of a secure working environment.

Handling situations and incidents

Threatening behaviour and violence

No staff member should have to deal with threatening behaviour or violence. Staff should remain calm and if possible try to create a space between themselves and the customer.

- Stand behind the bar, a counter or a table to create a safe space – do not shout. Speak slowly and clearly to try and calm the customer down.
- Report the behaviour to a senior member of staff – if security staff are employed then they should be summoned to assist. The customer should then be asked to leave, and be escorted away from the premises.
- Record the incident as per the establishment's procedure. Any witnesses' statements should be included.

Threatening behaviour or violence within the workforce is a grave disciplinary matter and should be treated with the upmost importance as it cannot be tolerated. This could result in disciplinary proceedings and even dismissal.

Terrorism

This is a real threat in modern society. The establishment's policy including the training procedure must be agreed in advance to ensure staff understand how to react – to protect themselves and customers. The decision to evacuate or to 'lock down' an establishment should also be discussed, policy formulated and additional training put in place on how to follow instructions from the security services and the police if an incident occurs.

Training will help staff prepare and give them more confidence to deal with a terrorist attack situation if necessary.

Dealing with a suspicious item or package or people

All employees should be constantly on the alert for suspicious items or packages. See page 93 in this chapter for advice how to deal with suspicious items or bomb threats.

All employees must be on the alert for suspicious-looking people.

- If a person is identified as potentially suspicious (has no reason to be there) this must immediately be reported to the security officer, manager or supervisor.
- Unless authorised to do so, do not approach a suspicious person but try and monitor their activities.

Robbery

This is a real threat to any business. Knowing how to stay safe should be part of the training and discussed with staff. Staff should never put themselves or others in danger and following company safety and security procedures will reduce the likelihood of injury and loss.

Use of stock control systems

KEY TERMS

Costs – of materials and providing the service.
Revenue – the amount of money taken (sales).
Profit – the difference between revenue and cost.

Stock control is vital in ensuring profitability in a business. All purchases, sales and expenses are recorded and stock issues to departments are recorded and apportioned to those departments as **cost** of sales. The **revenue** taken through sales is then recorded and the **profit** can be calculated.

More commonly electronic systems now record all orders, stock movements and sales. This calculates the profit/loss and a manual stock count is carried out monthly to establish the accuracy of the electronic system.

All commodities are valuable and many have a limited shelf life. Use-by dates must be carefully observed and managed (to avoid unnecessary waste/cost to the business). Regular stocktaking will ensure the correct level of stock for the business is maintained and will provide a check against inaccuracies and theft. Businesses will conduct stocktakes on a weekly or monthly basis depending on their policy. Spot checks can also take place at other times. If you are responsible for completing a stocktake, always report any discrepancies to your manager.

Internal and external theft

Good stock control systems and secure cash and stock-handling policies are vital to reduce theft. Internal audits may be carried out by the Food and Beverage Controller, Head Chef or Food and Beverage Manager. These audits will highlight discrepancies in stock, which can be investigated and rectified. An independent external auditor can also be used to confirm whether good control procedures have been followed.

All staff should be briefed to not bring cash on to the work floor in their pockets and that their bags can be searched as they exit the building. Any items found in their possession without proof of ownership will be considered as theft and dealt with accordingly.

Theft of food and drink not authorised for consumption also constitutes theft and staff need to be explained this during their induction. Supervisors should also remind staff of this periodically.

Secure payment points

This is covered in detail in Unit 205, 2.4 Customer bills and payments, page 206. Also see Unit 208, 2.1 Securing financial information, page 328.

Card fraud

Training on accepting cards for payment should be given. Check the card is in date. Most cards are now Chip and PIN; this means that the customer enters their PIN (personal identification number) into a keypad when they use a credit, debit or charge card for face-to-face transactions.

For more information on accepting debit and credit cards, and the chip and PIN system, see Unit 205, page 207.

Data protection

All information held on customers must be kept secure and private. The business has a responsibility under the General Data Protection Regulations (GDPR) (May 2018) to keep this information secure and to report any breaches as soon as they are discovered. For more on the effects of GDPR, see Unit 202, page 58.

Secure building

Keep doors and windows secure

If the premises is open for business, then fire exits must not be chained or locked. Doors to other areas may be operated by using swipe cards or keys for entry/exit to increase security between public and restricted areas. Outside trading hours, external exits should be alarmed and checked to ensure they are secure. Windows should be closed and locked as appropriate. Keys should be signed in and out for this purpose to ensure these duties are carried out by a designated responsible person.

Stock rooms

Stock rooms should be secure at all times. Stock is valuable, and access should be limited only to those with the authority to enter them. A 'requisition form' for stock items should be countersigned by a senior member of the department and stock should only be issued to an authorised staff member on production of the appropriate requisition form. A copy of the requisition form should be retained by the stockroom manager and reconciled with stock movement when a stock count is made. This will reduce the potential for theft and require staff to plan their stock ordering and the issuing of stock at appropriate times.

Fire exits

Fire exits should be kept clear at all times as obstructions could cost lives and waste time when a rapid exit is required. Checks both internally and externally should be made to ensure the outward-opening fire exit door is not obstructed.

3.3 CONSEQUENCES OF NON-COMPLIANCE WITH LEGISLATION

The consequences of non-compliance are far-reaching and could ultimately result in the death of a customer or member or staff. It is therefore critical that staff are trained and understand the consequences of not following legislation which is put in place to protect them and the public from harm. Consequences are shown in Table 3.10.

▼ **Table 3.10** The importance of following legislation

Consequence	Explanation
Harm to self, colleagues or customers – this is a real risk when procedures are not followed	**Food poisoning**: can happen very easily through incorrect storage, poor temperature and stock control and cross-contamination of foods. Control measures are designed to reduce this risk and therefore are the responsibility of everyone involved in the process
	Risk of physical injury or death: health and safety is the responsibility of all staff and following safety instructions and guidance to avoid the risk of injury to self and others is a basic requirement of all food handlers and service staff
Internal discipline	Failure to follow procedures and the law could result in an internal procedure being carried out; this could then require further training and could result in dismissal for a serious breach
Risk of prosecution	The employer, employee or both could face **criminal proceedings** if a case brought against them was severe, i.e. if serious physical injury, harm or **death** has occurred because of not following procedures
	This could lead to **civil compensation** claims which, if many people were affected and a class action was brought against the business or individual, could result in pay-outs reaching into millions of pounds and damage to business reputation
Damage to the reputation of the business	Non-compliance with health and safety legislation not only puts a business at risk of injuring someone but can lead to a loss of reputation and subsequently a loss of business
Loss of customers, leading to loss of jobs and income	Customers are easily influenced by the media – bad publicity about breaches of health and safety procedures at a premises may lead to customers choosing to take their custom elsewhere. This then reduces the need for staff and job losses can then occur

Test your learning

1 Name **three** benefits of following good health and safety procedures.

2 State **four** of the potential costs of accidents in the workplace.

3 What does COSHH stand for?

4 A hazard is anything that can cause harm. Identify **four** examples of potential hazards in the workplace.

5 List **three** measures that could help minimise the risk of accidents in food service operations.

6 In relation to health and safety, what does PPE mean?

7 Briefly describe the procedure for lifting a box that is not too heavy for you to lift.

8 Which fire extinguisher can you use on electrical equipment fires?

9 What colour are the mandatory health and safety signs?

10 If you see a security risk, whom should you immediately inform?

11 Identify **two** of the high-risk food groups.

12 Give **one** example of each of the following:

   a. Chemical contamination

   b. Microbiological contamination

   c. Physical contamination

13 What are the **four** conditions needed for bacteria to multiply?

14 Give **two** examples of the typical symptoms of food poisoning.

15 What is a food allergy?

16 State **three** ways that cross-contamination could occur.

17 What is the range of temperature referred to as the 'Danger Zone' for multiplication of bacteria?

18 Briefly define what is meant by:

   a. Use-by date

   b. Best-before date

19 What is meant by HACCP?

20 What is a disinfectant?

MENU KNOWLEDGE

INTRODUCTION

The purpose of this chapter is to help you gain knowledge of various menu styles, food product knowledge and service methods. It also covers the customer's dietary needs and lifestyle choices.

This chapter will help you to:
- identify types of menus
- describe service methods and service styles
- increase your knowledge of foods and cooking methods
- identify what drinks can be served with different types of food.

1 MENU STYLES AND SERVICE METHODS

1.1 DIFFERENT MENU STYLES

The menu is primarily a selling aid. The design of the menu should be appealing and interesting to the customer, so it encourages them to view its contents. Information that is clear and found easily will make the customer feel more at home and will assist in selling the food on your menu.

Cooked to order

À la carte menu

À la carte means 'from the card'. The key characteristics of the **à la carte** menu are:

- **the choice** – the choice is generally more extensive
- **cooked to order** – so there may be longer waiting times as some dishes are finished
- **individually priced** – each dish is priced separately.

KEY TERM

À la carte – offers a selection of dishes to choose from, where the food is cooked to order and each dish is individually priced on the menu.

Tapas

This is an example of *à la carte* where all items are ordered separately and priced individually. Traditional Spanish savoury dishes served in bar, a **tapas** menu can consist of an extensive selection of snack-size, individual dishes that when ordered together can make a substantial meal.

The dishes are shared with the table rather than an individual plate being served to each customer. Tapas are often served when cooked – so may not arrive at the table at the same time as all the other tapas items. Some examples of tapas are included in 2.1 Menu terminology later in this chapter.

Meze

With its Turkish, Greek and Middle Eastern origins, **meze** are similar in size to tapas and similarly served hot or cold with alcoholic or non-alcoholic beverages. Examples of meze dishes are included in 2.1 Menu terminology later in this chapter.

Limited choice, fixed price

Table d'hôte menu

The key characteristics of the **table d'hôte** (table of the host) menu are:

- the menu has a fixed number of courses
- there is a limited choice within each course
- the selling price is fixed
- the food is usually available at a set time.

Some menus offer combinations of both table d'hôte and à la carte, with a number of menu items being offered together at a set price and other menu items being priced separately.

Sometimes the term 'menu du jour' is used instead of the term table d'hôte menu.

No choice, set price

Prix fixe

Another menu term used is 'carte du jour' (literally 'card of the day') or 'menu of the day', which can also be a fixed meal with one or more courses for a set price.

A '**prix fixe**' (fixed price) menu is similar.

Tasting menu

A 'tasting menu' (menu degustation) is a set meal with a range of courses (often between 6 and 10). The tasting menu can also be offered with a flight of wines (a selection of wines also for tasting) and beverages. Sometimes a different wine or liqueur is served with each course.

For all classes of menu, the price of the meal may or may not also include wine or other drinks.

KEY TERMS

Tapas – a type of à la carte menu traditionally eaten in Spain, with snack-size dishes that are ordered together to make a meal.

Meze – a type of à la carte menu, Turkish, Greek and Middle Eastern in origin and with small dishes that are ordered together.

Table d'hôte – a menu with a limited choice of dishes for a fixed price.

Prix fixe (menu of the day) menus – have one dish on offer (there's no choice) for a set price.

1.2 FOOD SERVICE METHODS

The service of food and beverages may be carried out in many ways, depending on factors such as:

- type of establishment
- time available for the meal
- type of menu presented
- location of the establishment
- type of customer to be served
- turnover of custom expected
- cost of the meal served.

All modern food and beverage service methods can be categorised into four main groups, as shown in Table 4.1.

▼ **Table 4.1** Food and beverage service methods

1. Table service	
Service to customers at a laid cover. This type of service, which includes plated service, silver service and family service, is found in many types of restaurant, cafés and in banqueting.	
Plated	Service of pre-plated foods to customers. Now also widely used for banqueting
Family	Main courses plated (but may be silver served) with vegetables placed in multi-portion dishes on tables for customers to help themselves; sauces offered separately
Silver/English	Presentation and service of food by waiting staff, using a spoon and fork, on to a customer's plate, from food flats or dishes
Butler/French	Presentation of food individually to customers by food service staff for customers to serve themselves
Guéridon	Food served on to customer's plate at a side table or trolley; may also include carving, jointing and fish filleting, the preparation of foods such as salads and dressings, and flambage for dishes such as *Crêpes Suzette*
2. Counter service	
Self-service of customers. This type of service can be found in cafeterias and canteens. Other forms of counter service include where the customer orders, pays and receives the food and beverages, for instance at a counter in a fast food operation or at a bar in licensed premises.	
Counter	Customers queue in line formation past a service counter or a range of counters and choose their menu requirements in stages before loading them on to a tray
3. Assisted service	
Combination of table service and self-service. The customer is served part of the meal at a table and is required to obtain part through self-service from some form of display or buffet. This type of service is found in carvery-type operations and is often used for meals such as breakfast in hotels. It may also be used for functions.	
Buffets	Customers select food and drink from displays or offered from trays; consumption is either at a table, standing or in a service area
Carvery	Some parts of the meal are served to seated customers; other parts are collected by the customers. Also used for breakfast service and for banqueting
4. In situ	
Service to customers in areas not primarily designed for service. The food and drink is taken to the customer. This includes tray service in hospitals or on aircraft, trolley service on a train, home delivery, lounge and room service.	
Tray	Method of service of whole or part of meal on a tray to the customer *in situ*, e.g. at hospital beds, aircraft seats and train seats; also used in outdoor catering
Trolley	Service of food and beverages from a trolley, away from dining areas, e.g. for office workers at their desks; for customers at aircraft seats; at train seats

Note: The terms 'banqueting' or 'function' are used to describe catering operations for specific numbers of people at specific times – often in a variety of dining layouts and styles. The service methods will vary and banquet catering refers to the organisation of the service rather than a specific service method.

1.3 IMPACT OF MENU STYLES

Mise en place

A number of tasks and duties are undertaken both prior to service through **mise en place** – the preparation and setting up for service – and during the actual service of food and beverages. Each of the four groups of service method given in Table 4.1 will have different setting up procedures.

Flexibility, timings and order of service

- Service will need to be **flexible** to accommodate the needs of the customers.
- Service timings will vary according to needs and demands of each service style.
- The traditional order of service may not apply in some service styles, with some customers choosing to eat out of sequence or even having all courses at the same time, such as with tapas menus.

Staff requirements – customer-to-staff ratio

The level of complexity of food and beverage service, and the level of staffing needed, depends on the type of service being provided.

- **Table service** is the most complex. For full silver service a staff-to-customer ratio can be about 1:10, whereas with plated service this can increase to 1:20.
- For **assisted service** the staff-to-customer ratio could be 1:3.
- For **counter service** the ratio could be reduced to 1:50.
- **In situ** service contains a range of specialised forms of service which require additional service skills. Staff ratios for each of these situations can follow the general examples given above but the staff may have other duties such as aircraft safety and security.

When determining **customer-to-staff ratios**, it is also necessary to take into account the size (maximum capacity) of the operation and the likely level of business at any particular time.

Daily duty rota

The object of a **duty rota** is to ensure that all the necessary duties are covered in order that efficient service may be carried out. The exact nature of the duty rota will vary according to the type of establishment, the duties to be performed, the number of staff, staff time off and whether a split/straight shift is worked. Figure 4.1 gives an example of a daily duty rota for pre-service duties for a table service operation and shows how they may be allocated.

KEY TERMS

Mise en place – preparation for service.

Table service – service to customers at a laid cover.

Assisted service – a combination of table service and self-service.

Counter service – self-service by customers from a buffet or counter in cafeterias. Also includes counter service in fast food operations or at a bar in licensed premises.

In situ – usually service to customers in areas not primarily designed for service.

Customer-to-staff ratio – the number of staff required to serve a specific number of customers.

Duty rota – allocation of days and hours on duty for members of staff.

Waiter	3.6.18	4.6.18	5	6	7	8	9	10	11	12	13	14	15	16.6.18	Task No.
A	1	11	10	9	8	7		6	5	4	3	2	1		1. Menus
B	2	1	11	10	9	8		7	6	5	4	3	2		2. Restaurant cleaning
C	3	2	1	11	10	9		8	7	6	5	4	3		3. Linen
D	4	3	2	1	11	10		9	8	7	6	5	4		4. Hot plate
E	5	4	3	2	1	11	CLOSED	10	9	8	7	6	5	CLOSED	5. Silver
F	6	5	4	3	2	1		11	10	9	8	7	6		6. Accompaniments
G	7	6	5	4	3	2		1	11	10	9	8	7		7. Sideboard
H	8	7	6	5	4	3		2	1	11	10	9	8		8. Dispense bar
I	9	8	7	6	5	4		3	2	1	11	10	9		9. Stillroom
J	19	9	8	7	6	5		4	3	2	1	11	10		10. Miscellaneous
K	11	10	9	8	7	6		5	4	3	2	1	11		11. Day off

▲ **Figure 4.1** Example of a daily duty rota

A duty rota also provides the basis for staff training. Detailed lists are drawn up for all the tasks and duties that must be covered. These task and duty lists will also identify the standards that are to be achieved for the operation.

Working practices

Different types of food and beverage service will require different working practices:

1 **Service level**: as the level of personal service increases, the number of staff required and the labour costs will also increase, as will the level of professional staff. Mealtimes are likely to become longer and therefore the potential capacity of the operation will reduce.
2 **Availability of service**: increasing the availability of the service will potentially increase labour and material costs and will reduce the efficiency of the facilities used. In these cases, it is necessary to try to match the labour and materials being used to the expected volume of business, which will vary over a given period.
3 **Level of standards**: increasing standards in the food and beverage operation will increase the cost of materials as better grade materials are used. The cost of labour will increase as the level of professional staff will need to be higher.
4 **Reliability of the service**: to make the provision of the service more reliable, labour and material costs will increase because it will be necessary to have a higher proportion of equipment, labour and materials available.
5 **Flexibility of the service**: moving away from a limited range of products and services will increase material and labour costs and will reduce the efficiency of the facilities being used.

1.4 BUSINESS IMPACT OF MENU STYLES

Stock levels, staff skills and levels, food and service costs

Compilation of the menu is one of the food service operator's most important jobs. The menu is a key document that directs and controls the food service operation. It establishes what is going to be purchased, the cost, what staff and other resources are required, and the types of service needed. In addition, the beverage offers, the decor, atmosphere, theme or logo and service system, all revolve around the provision of the menu. The advantages and disadvantages of using different menu styles are outlined in Table 4.2.

▼ **Table 4.2** Advantages and disadvantages of menu styles

Menu styles	Advantages	Disadvantages
Cooked to order		
À la carte, individually priced such as tapas or meze	Provides a high business image which may attract a wider target market and increased sales Food costs can be controlled, and food waste can be minimised Items can be cooked to meet customer requirements Increased skills level to produce cook-to-order dishes Customers have a greater selection and more flexibility in what they can order Menus can be extensive and reflect the theme of the establishment, using specific language, fonts and imagery The menu can be designed around the specific target market The establishment theme can be more closely met with these styles of menus Sales can be maximised as additional items such as 'sides', sauces and accompaniments can be offered, along with beverages to match	Higher stock levels can lead to high wastage if stock level is not matched to demand and items are left unsold Food costs are harder to control due to the wider range of ingredients and therefore profit margins must take these unpredictable aspects into consideration Staff skills and levels required may not be available due to staff shortages, recruitment problems and business location Additional equipment costs may be incurred due to the range of dishes to be served and their respective accompaniments Service costs may be higher due to additional equipment costs and service skills level
Limited choice		
Fixed price – *table d'hôte*	Stock levels more easily controlled due to the limited range of items and the predictability of sales Better buying power for bulk purchases of food can save money on food costs Food stocks can be more closely managed and monitored, and wastage can be minimised Staff skills can be more focused on delivering a service around the menu items, and the levels of service can be lower due to the reduced range of items. This can also help reduce the staff wage costs due to the lower level of skills Customers will see this style as a more cost-effective way of dining and target markets can be more easily identified and accommodated in the theming of the food Menus can more closely reflect the theme of the restaurant and the printing costs can be minimised as imagery and styling are limited Sales can be more predictable allowing for better budgeting, staff wage control, energy savings and greater profit-margin monitoring Tables can be turned quicker allowing for a greater number of customers to be served Staff can focus on promoting additional beverages	Limited stock levels will not allow for flexibility in food production Lower staff skills levels may result in lower service standards There may be a greater impact on profits if mistakes and wastage occur Customers may be put off by the limited choice and inflexibility of the menu Regular menu change will be needed to ensure customer return and satisfaction

No choice		
Set price – *prix fixe*, taster menu	Stock levels can be better predicted, and food orders can be more accurate	Inflexibility of the menu may disappoint customers
	Faster production and service allowing for greater turnover of tables	Customers may get bored or put off by the limited choice
	Food costs are dramatically lowered as stock holding can be kept to the absolute minimum	Regular menu change will be needed to ensure customer return and satisfaction
	Staff skills and levels will be lower as the speed of service is increased	Lower staff skills levels may result in lower service standards
	Staff costs can be predicted and managed more accurately	
	Customers get better value for money	
	Menu printing costs will be reduced due to limited imagery and paper size	
	Sales of additional items such as beverages can be made	
	More predictable profit margins and budgeting.	
	Greater food buying power and control	

Customer expectations

Customer expectations are linked to the price paid and the perception of value for money – the higher the price, the higher the expectations and conversely the lower the price, the lower the expectations. The aim is always to provide the best possible service and product to meet the expectation of the customer within the price and cost band in which the business operates.

The design of the menu should encourage the customer to view its contents. Clear information that is easy to read will make the customer feel more relaxed and will assist in selling the food on the menu. Customers will expect:

- accurate descriptions of the dishes
- clear indications of pricing, including whether a service charge or any other charge is included
- dietary information, such as identification of low fat dishes, details of allergen content, as well as offering to cook foods plainly
- items or groups of items having names that customers recognise and understand.

Menu language

Carefully devised descriptions can help to promote an individual dish, the menu generally and in turn the establishment. However, descriptions should describe the item realistically and not mislead the customer as this has legal implications. Care should be taken therefore in the use of terms such as 'fresh', 'British' or 'organic'. Also cooking terms such as 'fried', 'roasted', etc. The description should always be a true one. If using the term 'home-made' this indicates that the dish has been made at the premises; in the case of the term 'organic', only the food item can be described as organic.

Being able to write interesting descriptive menu copy is a skill; a good menu designer can highlight menu terms or specific culinary terms and in doing so draw attention to them. Simplicity in menu copy enhances the communication process and enables better understanding. Always check the spelling and the descriptions; if using words from other languages have a policy on accents: use either none or all.

Style

Nowadays, menus are presented in a wide variety of styles. These include:

- traditional book-style
- single laminated cards
- fold-out cards with inserts of various sizes
- iPads and other forms of tablets, which can also allow customers to explore the ingredients offered in the dishes and the drinks
- chalk boards or white boards
- printed signs, sometimes illuminated from behind
- projections on to table tops.

Design considerations of the menu include:

- Size and shape
- Artwork/colour
- Ease of handling
- Logical flow of information.

Use of symbols and images

Symbols can be used to indicate, for example, allergens; dishes accredited by the Vegetarian Society or Heart Foundation; or other standards such as Fairtrade.

The menu can be enhanced with images of the dishes or of the establishment. Images will often help sell a product but are not always suitable, for example a fine dining menu would not typically have images of the food but might have, for example, subtle watermarked paper containing the company crest.

Font

Menu copy should be set in a style of print and font size that is easy to read and surrounded by space. Mixing fonts is often done to achieve emphasis, but if overdone the overall concept is likely to look a mess and therefore unattractive to the eye.

Business image

Compiling and presenting the menu is one of the food service operator's most important jobs. The menu presents a business's image, whether in house, online or via advertising outlets, and needs to reflect the requirements of the sector that the business is operating in.

Theming

The design, presentation and theme of the menu have to reflect and match with the beverage offers, the decor, atmosphere, logo and service style. The menu also has to reflect the image the business wants to convey.

▲ **Figure 4.2** The Vegetarian Society logo and the Fairtrade Mark

Marketing

The presentation and the format of a menu has to reflect the intended target markets of the business. For example, fast food operations will have large, colourful backlit boards, whereas a full-service restaurant will have individual menus printed to a high standard.

Sales

The regular sale of products is key to a business's sustained success. The promotion of temporary sales must be encouraged to increase business during off-peak periods in business, such as Mondays, early evenings and during January/February.

Examples of off-peak promotions include:

- offering meal 'packages', for example a free glass of wine with a main course, a 'buy one get a second free' deal, or offering a free soup or starter as part of the meal package
- developing customer loyalty schemes.

Special sales promotions, including custom menus, may also be used to increase sales by promoting particular products, such as:

- festival promotions or links with local, regional or national celebrations (such as St Patrick's Day, royal events and so on)
- wine and spirit or food promotions (possibly in association with suppliers)
- children's menus
- menus that meet a range of dietary requirements
- 'Taste of the Country' menus
- products to complement specific calendar dates – for example Valentine's Day, Christmas, Diwali, Eid, Easter, Mother's Day.

Four types of sales promotion are particularly useful for food service operations:

1 **Sales promotion through advertising**: concerned with contacting and informing the existing or potential market of a business, providing information on the products available and encouraging purchase.
2 **Sales promotion through internet presence and social media**: such as using advertising with the potential to cover a far wider than intended market. This has the advantage of information being available to customers on demand, but is not so easy to target specific customers and to control as the medium is also interactive and volatile. Careful monitoring of a business's online presence is required due to the changing trends in food, beverage and eating habits along with styling and accessibility. Getting the online presence right can greatly enhance the success of the business.
3 **Sales promotion through merchandising**: related mainly to point-of-sale promotion. Its main role is to improve the average spend per head of the customer. However, it is also used to promote particular services or goods.
4 **Sales promotion through personal selling**: refers to the ability of the staff in a food and beverage operation to actively contribute to the promotion of sales.

2 MENU PRODUCT KNOWLEDGE

2.1 MENU TERMINOLOGY

Over the last hundred years the European menu has used the same classic format to present the order of dishes. A summary of this sequence is shown in Table 4.3.

▼ **Table 4.3** Summary of different menu items

Course	Description
Canapés and *amuse bouche*	Canapés may be served pre-dinner to stimulate the appetite or as an alternative to a finger buffet; they are designed to be a light, tasty, one bite snack. Often offered in fine dining establishments, an *amuse bouche* is a small appetiser. It does not count as a course in the menu
Hors d'oeuvres and other appetisers	These first three sets of dishes are usually grouped together as 'starters'. Sometimes separately presented as 'cold starters' and 'hot starters'
Soup	
Egg dishes	
Pasta and rice	A starter or main course. Also known as farinaceous dishes
Fish	A starter or main course. May also be a middle course in, for example, a four-course meal
Meats, poultry and game	Often listed just as main courses. Sometimes meats such as steaks are listed separately under grills
Potatoes, vegetables and salads	If not included with a main course, these dishes are now often listed as 'sides' (meaning side order) for which there is an additional charge
Cheese	Cheese is shown here after the main course and before the sweet course. However, the sweet course is still sometimes offered before the cheese course
Sweets / desserts	Usually listed as a separate category and refers to both hot and cold dishes
Savoury	Simple savoury dishes served at the end of the meal
Fruit (dessert)	Fresh fruit, nuts and sometimes candied fruits

Note: Beverages (hot or cold) are not counted as a course and should not be included when stating the number of courses for a meal. For example, if a meal is stated as having four courses, this means that there are four food courses and that the beverages at the end are in addition to these.

Knowledge about the product is at the core of successful food and beverage service. This knowledge enables the server to advise the customer of:

- the content of dishes
- the methods used in making the dishes
- the correct accompaniments to be offered with a selected dish.

The rest of this chapter provides information on the foods, accompaniments and service for a range of menu items by course.

Pre-starters and appetisers

Canapés

These are often slices of bread with the crusts removed, cut into a variety of shapes, then toasted or fried in oil or butter and garnished. Garnishes can include smoked salmon, foie gras, prawns, cheese, asparagus tips, tomato, egg, capers, gherkins, salami and other meats.

Amuse bouche

An *amuse bouche* (translated as 'please the mouth') is a small, one-bite or spoonful pre-starter. It is designed to stimulate the taste buds. They are usually savoury and served on a spoon, in a shot glass or on a small plate.

Starters

Starters can be separated into hot and cold starters:

- **Cold starters**: salads, cured/smoked fish, oysters, seafood cocktails, eggs, charcuterie, cured hams, pâtés, antipasti and hors d'oeuvres
- **Hot starters**: vegetables, eggs, pasta, fish, seafood and snails.

A selection of starters is given in Table 4.4.

▼ **Table 4.4** Examples of starters

Antipasti	Traditional antipasto include cured meats, olives, pepperoncini, mushrooms, anchovies, artichoke hearts, various cheeses (such as provolone or mozzarella), pickled meats, and vegetables in oil or vinegar
Asparagus	Fresh asparagus may be eaten hot with, for example, melted butter or Hollandaise sauce or cold with vinaigrette or mayonnaise
Caesar salad	Salad of cos (or Romaine) lettuce, dressed with vinaigrette or other similar dressing (originally containing near-raw egg), garlic, croutons and grated (or shaved) parmesan cheese. There are a number of variations to these ingredients
Charcuterie, cured hams, pâtés	This can include a range of meat (mainly pork) items including Bayonne ham, salamis, smoked ham, Parma ham and also pâtés and terrines. Accompaniments are freshly ground pepper and cayenne pepper, gherkins and sometimes onions. Occasionally a small portion of potato salad is offered. Bread is usually offered but brown bread and butter is now less common
Crustaceans	Crabs or lobsters served hot or cold. With or without the shell. Dressed with sauce or plain. Accompaniments include half a lemon and cayenne pepper, ground pepper, mayonnaise, malt vinegar. Traditionally brown bread and butter is also offered
Eggs	These can be poached, presented in aspic or mayonnaise, or hard-boiled, cut in two and garnished or stuffed with various fillings, which include the yolk
Globe artichokes (Artichaut)	This vegetable is usually served whole as a starter. The edible portion of the leaves is 'sucked off' between the teeth after being dipped in a dressing (for example, vinaigrette if served cold or melted butter or Hollandaise sauce if served hot). A side knife and sweet fork are laid to enable the 'heart' of the globe artichoke to be eaten. A finger bowl containing lukewarm water and a slice of lemon and a spare napkin are essential as the 'leaves' are eaten using the fingers
Gravlax (Gravadlax)	Salmon pickled with salt, sugar and dill. Traditional accompaniments are a slightly sweetened sauce of mustard and dill and often half a lemon (which may be wrapped in muslin to prevent the juice squirting on to the customer when the lemon is squeezed). A variety of unbuttered breads may be offered, with butter and alternatives served separately
Hors d'oeuvres	A selection of salads, fish and meats, often now plated
Mousses and pâtés	Hot, unbuttered breakfast toast or bread is offered. Butter or alternatives may be offered and other accompaniments appropriate to the dish itself, for example, lemon segments with fish mousses, although lemon is also often offered with meat-based pâtés
Niçoise salad	There are a number of versions of this salad. Generally, it includes boiled potatoes, whole French beans, tomatoes, hard-boiled eggs (quartered or sliced), stoned black olives, flakes of tuna fish and anchovy fillets. This salad is usually made up and plated. Vinaigrette is often offered
Oysters	Cold oysters are usually served in one half of the shell on a bed of crushed ice in a soup plate on an underplate. An oyster fork is usually offered but a small sweet fork can also be used. These are placed on the right-hand side of the cover. Oysters are usually eaten by holding the shell in one hand and the fork in the other. Therefore, a finger bowl on an underplate and containing lukewarm water and a slice of lemon together with an extra napkin may be offered. Accompaniments include half a lemon and the oyster cruet (cayenne pepper, ground pepper, chilli vinegar and Tabasco sauce)

Pasta and rice dishes	These dishes, which are also referred to as farinaceous dishes, include all pastas such as: spaghetti, macaroni, ravioli and gnocchi, as well as rice dishes such as pilaff or risotto. Grated Parmesan cheese is normally offered with all these dishes
Potted shrimps	Accompaniments include hot, unbuttered, breakfast toast (there is plenty of butter already in this dish), cayenne pepper, freshly ground pepper and segments of lemon
Seafood cocktails	The traditional accompaniments are a lemon segment, ground pepper, sometimes cayenne pepper and traditionally brown bread and butter, although this is less common now
Smoked salmon	Traditional accompaniments are half a lemon (which may be wrapped in muslin to prevent the juice squirting on to the customer when the lemon is squeezed), cayenne pepper, freshly ground pepper and brown bread and butter. Nowadays a variety of unbuttered bread may be offered with butter and alternatives served separately. Oil is sometimes offered and also chopped onions and capers
Other smoked fish	As well as the accompaniments offered with smoked salmon, creamed horseradish has become a standard offering with all other smoked fish including trout, mackerel, cod, halibut and tuna

Tapas

Tapas can be served hot or cold. They are little dishes from Spain which are normally served with a drink and can vary from a simple bowl of olives to more complex dishes such as stuffed mussels. In some parts of northern Spain, they are known as *pincho* or *pintxos* in Basque.

The type and style of tapas is a reflection of the various regions of Spain and the list of tapas is extensive. Examples are:

▲ **Figure 4.3** An example of plated hors d'oeuvres

- **Gambas al Ajillo**: fresh prawns in sizzling olive oil with garlic and chili peppers.
- **Bacalao**: salt cod, breaded and fried or stewed in tomato sauce.
- **Calamares**: fried squid rings.
- **Espinacas con garbanzos**: spinach and chick peas with olive oil and garlic.
- **Patatas bravas**: fried potato wedges served with a spicy aioli sauce.
- **Ensaladilla**: a potato salad with mayonnaise and either tuna or prawns.
- **Calamares del Campo**: breaded and fried onions and peppers.
- **Tortilla**: a potato omelette.
- **Montaditos**: small filled buns, often served toasted.
- **Jamón Iberico**: thinly sliced salt cured ham from free range pata negra pigs.
- **Albóndigas**: meatballs – most often pork, but also beef or seafood.

Meze

With their Turkish, Greek and Middle Eastern origins, meze are similar in size to tapas and similarly served hot or cold with alcoholic or non-alcoholic beverages. Meze reflect their origins' food styles:

- **Greek** – roasted red peppers, stuffed grape leaves, marinated feta, pita breads, tomatoes, taramasalata, grilled octopus, meatballs, fried potatoes, cured meats, sausages
- **Turkish** – in addition to the Greek styles, grilled aubergine, mussels, stuffed courgette flowers, pinto beans, pickles and stuffed jalapeños

▲ **Figure 4.4** Meze

- **Middle Eastern** – hummus with tahini (sesame seed paste), artichoke, lamb kebab, baba ghanoush.

Soups

Soups are divided into a number of categories, including consommés, veloutés, crèmes, purées, potages, bisques (shellfish soups) and broths. Examples of these are shown in Table 4.5. There are also various national soups and examples of these are shown in Table 4.6.

▼ **Table 4.5** Types of soup

Consommé	Clarified soup made from poultry, beef, game or vegetable bouillon. There are no traditional accompaniments to consommé
Veloutés, crèmes and purées	Soups made from stock and vegetables with some including meats. They are all sieved and are finalised slightly differently, with veloutés being refined, and crèmes more so
	Traditionally croutons were only offered with purées and cream of tomato soup, but they are now commonly offered with a range of soups
Potages and broths	Soups made from stock and vegetables with some including meats. They are not sieved
Bisques	Bisques are soups made with a shellfish base

▼ **Table 4.6** National soups

Poland	
Bortsch	Duck-flavoured consommé garnished with duck, diced beef and turned root vegetables. The accompaniments are sour cream, beetroot juice and bouchées filled with duck pâté
France	
Bouillabaisse	This is really a form of fish stew. Although a soup plate on its underplate and a soup spoon are used, it is common for a side knife and sweet fork to also be laid as part of the cover. Thin slices of French bread dipped in oil and grilled (sippets) are offered as well as rouille
Soupe à l'oignon	French onion soup. May be served with grilled flûtes and grated (shaved) Parmesan cheese but is often topped with a slice of French bread gratinated with cheese
USA	
Chowder	Chowders are thick soups usually containing seafood, potatoes and cream or milk. The most well known is New England clam chowder made with potatoes, onion, bacon or salt pork, flour and clams. Served with clam cakes, which are deep fried balls of buttery dough with chopped clam inside
Spain	
Gazpacho	A cold, tomato-based soup. It contains tomatoes, onions, breadcrumbs, peppers, cucumber, garlic, ice water, sugar and spices. Croutons, diced cucumber, peppers, tomato and onion may all be offered as accompaniments
Italy	
Minestrone	Simple vegetable soup with pasta. Traditional accompaniments are grated (shaved) Parmesan cheese and grilled flutes
Japan	
Miso	Miso is a paste made from fermented soya beans. The soup is made by adding this paste to dashi soup stock. The stock itself is made from bonito flakes and konbu (kelp seaweed). Ingredients that provide contrasts such as spring onion and the delicate tofu, and those that float and sink such as potatoes and seaweed, may be paired together and offered as a garnish at the last moment

Fish course

For menus which offer a separate fish course, the fish is often served as a complete dish. Fish as a separate course can include cod, seabass, plaice, salmon, shellfish and whiting.

For more information on fish generally see Fish on page 132.

Main course

For examples of meat, fish and game dishes see: *Practical Cookery for the Level 2 Technical Certificate in Professional Cookery* by David Foskett, Patricia Paskins, Steve Thorpe, Neil Rippington, published by Hodder Education, 2017. You can also find examples of dishes by looking at restaurant menus or online recipes.

Red meat

Beef and lamb are red meats. These meats are prepared in a variety of ways. The methods used for cooking are related to the cut of the meat. Steaks, for example, are grilled or fried whereas beef joints are mostly roasted. Silverside of beef is often boiled. There are a wide range of other dishes including, for example, casseroles and burgers. There are traditional accompaniments for most dishes listed in the tables below.

▼ **Table 4.7** Accompaniments for plain roast meats

Dish	Accompaniments
Roast beef	Horseradish sauce, French and English mustards and Yorkshire pudding
Roast lamb	Traditionally mint sauce, although redcurrant jelly is sometimes also offered
All meats	Gravy is offered in all cases

▲ **Figure 4.5** A selection of roast meats and accompaniments offered in a carvery-style establishment

▲ **Figure 4.6** Grilled steak

▼ **Table 4.8** Accompaniments for boiled meats

Dish	Accompaniments
Salt beef (silverside)	Turned root vegetables, dumplings and the natural cooking liquor
Boiled fresh beef	Turned root vegetables, natural cooking liquor, rock salt and gherkins

▼ **Table 4.9** Accompaniments for other meat dishes

Dish	Accompaniments
Irish stew	Worcestershire sauce and pickled red cabbage
Curry	Poppadum (crisp, highly seasoned pancakes) and mango chutney. Also offered is a curry tray, which will have items such as diced apple, sultanas, sliced bananas, yoghurt and desiccated coconut
Mixed grill and other grills	These dishes may be garnished with cress, tomato, straw potatoes and parsley butter. Various mustards (French and English) and sometimes proprietary sauces (tomato ketchup and brown sauce) are offered as accompaniments
Steaks	As for mixed grill. Sauce Béarnaise is offered with Chateaubriand (double fillet) and sometimes with other grilled steaks

White meats

Chicken (poulet), turkey (dinde), pork (porc) and veal (veau) are white meats. These meats are also prepared in a variety of ways which include all cooking methods. There are traditional accompaniments for a number of dishes and these are given below.

▼ **Table 4.10** Accompaniments for plain roast meats

Dish	Accompaniments
Roast chicken	Bread sauce, roast gravy, parsley and thyme stuffing, game chips, grilled bacon and watercress. Sage and onion stuffing is also used
Roast turkey	Cranberry sauce, chestnut stuffing, chipolata sausages, game chips, watercress and roast gravy are the usual accompaniments
Roast pork	Apple sauce and sage and onion stuffing
Roast veal	Thickened roast gravy, lemon, parsley and thyme stuffing
All meats	Gravy is offered in all cases

▼ **Table 4.11** Accompaniments for boiled meats

Dish	Accompaniments
Boiled mutton	Caper sauce is traditionally served
Boiled ham	Parsley sauce or white onion sauce

▲ **Figure 4.7** Roast chicken

Fish

A wide variety of fish and shellfish are available. They are divided into five main groups:

1 **Round white fish:** such as bass, bream, cod, coley, haddock, hake, John Dory, monkfish, red mullet and whiting.

2 **Flat white fish**: such as sole, lemon sole and turbot. Others are brill, dab, flounder, halibut, plaice and skate.

3 **Oily fish**: such as mackerel and tuna. Others are eels, herring, pilchards, salmon, salmon trout, sardines, trout, tuna and whitebait.

4 **Shellfish**: these are divided into two main groups:
   ● Crustaceans, such as crabs and lobster. Others under this category are crayfish, prawns, scampi and shrimps
   ● Molluscs, such as clams, cockles, mussels, oysters, scallops, snails and winkles.

5 **Cephalopods**: such as octopus and squid.

Cooking methods vary according to the type of fish and the particular cuts of fish. The general accompaniments for fish dishes are shown in Table 4.12.

▼ **Table 4.12** Accompaniments for fish dishes

Dish	Accompaniments
Hot fish dishes with a sauce	Usually no accompaniments
Hot fish dishes without a sauce	These often have Hollandaise or another hot butter-based sauce offered. Lemon segments may also be offered
Fried fish which has been bread crumbed	These dishes often have tartare sauce or another mayonnaise-based sauce offered, together with segments of lemon
Fried or grilled fish dishes (not bread crumbed)	These dishes are usually offered with lemon. Sometimes sauces such as Hollandaise or tartare are offered
Deep-fried fish which has been dipped in batter	A (kitchen-made) tomato sauce is sometimes offered together with segments of lemon. Proprietary sauces can also be offered, as can vinegar if chips are being served
Cold-poached fish dishes	Usually mayonnaise or another mayonnaise-based sauce, such as sauce verte, is offered, together with segments of lemon
Grilled herring	Usually served with a mustard sauce
Sushi and sashimi	Served with wasabi and soy sauce
Whitebait	Accompaniments are cayenne pepper, ground pepper, segments of lemon and brown bread offered with butter or alternatives
Mussels (moules marinière)	Served with brown bread and butter, or more commonly now a variety of breads offered with butter or alternatives. Cayenne pepper may be offered
Cold lobster	Lemon and mayonnaise are the usual accompaniments
Snails	Snails are usually served with garlic butter, brown bread and butter and can be placed in a special snail dish that has dimples in it to hold the snails

Game

Game is usually classified as being either furred or feathered.

● Furred game includes rabbit and venison.
● Feathered game refers to birds such as pheasant and grouse.

There are traditional accompaniments for a number of types of game (see Table 4.13).

▼ **Table 4.13** Accompaniments for furred and feathered game

Dish	Accompaniments
Furred game	
Rabbit (lapin)	Rabbit can be cooked in a number of ways, e.g. roasted or casseroled. There are no particular accompaniments
Venison (venaison)	When roasted the traditional accompaniments are Cumberland sauce, redcurrant jelly and roast gravy. Sauce poivrade might also be offered
Feathered game	
• **partridge (perdreau)** • **grouse (lagopède)** • **woodcock (bécasse)** • **quail (caille)** • **pheasant (faisan)**	When roasted the accompaniments for all feathered game are fried breadcrumbs, hot liver pâté spread on a croûte on which the meat sits, bread sauce, game chips, watercress and roast gravy

Specialist dishes

Specific dietary requirements will require specialist dishes that accommodate the individual choice, allergy or medical need. Customers will need to know about the ingredients used in a dish since eating certain ingredients may make them ill and may even be fatal.

Vegetarian diets

Vegetarianism can be either a choice or form part of a cultural or religious influence. The needs of vegetarians can be diverse and complicated, and it is often a tricky balance to accommodate all vegetarian types as key ingredients in a range of foods can contain meat extracts or be linked to animal life.

Examples of common ingredients that contain animal content are:

- Gelatine – used as a setting agent for many mousse-based dishes and glazes for flans and hors d'oeuvres. Agar agar is often used a suitable alternative as it is derived from algae.
- Cheese – rennet is used to separate the curds and whey. Traditional animal rennet is an enzyme derived from the stomachs of calves, lambs or goats but vegetable rennets are becoming more widely used.
- Worcester sauce – made using anchovy.
- Hollandaise and mayonnaise – egg-based sauces.

See Unit 202, Table 2.4 for details of different vegetarian diets.

Gluten-free diets

Gluten is a protein found primarily in wheat, barley and rye. If a person has a gluten intolerance, this protein can cause digestive problems such as gassiness, abdominal pain or diarrhoea.

A gluten intolerance is different to coeliac disease. When people with coeliac disease eat gluten, their body mounts an immune response that attacks the small intestine. This causes damage to the digestion system, resulting in the inability to absorb nutrients from foods and beverages.

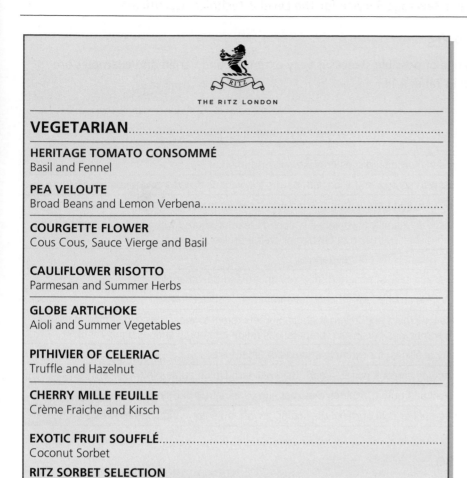

THE RITZ LONDON

VEGETARIAN

HERITAGE TOMATO CONSOMMÉ
Basil and Fennel

PEA VELOUTE
Broad Beans and Lemon Verbena

COURGETTE FLOWER
Cous Cous, Sauce Vierge and Basil

CAULIFLOWER RISOTTO
Parmesan and Summer Herbs

GLOBE ARTICHOKE
Aioli and Summer Vegetables

PITHIVIER OF CELERIAC
Truffle and Hazelnut

CHERRY MILLE FEUILLE
Crème Fraiche and Kirsch

EXOTIC FRUIT SOUFFLÉ
Coconut Sorbet

RITZ SORBET SELECTION

▲ **Figure 4.8** Sample vegetarian menu

Ingredients to avoid are:

- wheat starch
- wheat bran
- wheat germ
- couscous
- cracked wheat
- durum
- einkorn
- emmer
- farina
- faro
- fu (common in Asian foods)
- gliadin
- graham flour
- kamut
- matzo
- semolina
- spelt

In addition the following must also be avoided:

- barley
- bulgur
- oats (oats themselves don't contain gluten, but they are often processed in facilities that produce gluten-containing grains and may be contaminated)
- rye
- seitan
- triticale and mir (a cross between wheat and rye).

Dietary needs

Customers may have a range of dietary requirements based on medical, cultural and religious reasons and on lifestyle choices. See 3.2 Customer choices, page 150 and also Dietary requirements in Unit 202, page 46.

Desserts

The range of possible sweets is very extensive and varied and examples are shown in Table 4.14.

▼ **Table 4.14** Examples of types of sweet dishes

Bavarois, mousses, syllabubs	Either served in individual dishes or glassware or portioned and served. Various fruit flavours
Charlottes	Moulds lined with sponge and filled with bavarois in various flavours and sometimes with fruits
Coupes and sundaes	Usually ice cream and various fruit combinations, served in coupe dishes or sundae dishes
Creams	Examples include Chantilly (sweetened whipped cream flavoured with vanilla), custard (Sauce Anglaise) and dishes such as egg custard or crème brûlée
Fritters (beignets)	For example, Beignets de pomme (apple)
Fruit dishes	Examples are fruit salads, poached fruits (compôte) and baked apples
Gâteaux	Examples include au chocolat (chocolate) and forêt noir (black forest)
Ices and sorbets	Ices refers to ice cream and frozen yoghurt. Sorbets refers to water ices. Presented in various forms, including bombs (ice cream preparations made into bomb shapes using moulds)
Pancakes	With a variety of fillings, for example cherries or other fruits
Pies, flans and other pastries	Examples include flan aux poires (pear), Bakewell tart, Dutch apple pie
Puddings	Includes bread and butter, cabinet, diplomat and various fruit puddings
Soufflés	Can be served hot or cold and include soufflé au citron (lemon) and soufflé au café (coffee)

Cheese

Cheeses are distinguished by flavour and categorised according to their texture. They differ from each other in a number of ways, mainly because of variations in the making process. Differences occur in the rind and how it is formed, in the paste and the cooking process (both time and temperature at which it is cooked). Cheeses also vary because the milk used comes from different animals such as cows, sheep and goats. The texture of a cheese depends largely on the period of maturation. Cheese is often categorised as soft, semi-hard, hard and blue.

▲ **Figure 4.9** Mille-feuiles are an example of a sweet

▲ **Figure 4.10** Cheeses

Table 4.15 below shows different kinds of soft and hard cheese.

▼ **Table 4.15** Examples of soft and hard cheeses

Soft cheese	
Bel Paese	This light and creamy Italian cheese has a name that means 'beautiful country' and was first produced in 1929
Brie	Famous French cheese made since the eighth century. Other countries now make this style of cheese, distinguishing it from the original French brie by the addition of the name of the country or county of origin, e.g. German brie, Somerset brie
Camembert	Famous French cheese which is stronger and often more pungent than French brie
Mozzarella	Italian cheese made from buffalo milk. May now also be made from cow's milk
Ricotta	Italian cheese made from the whey of cow's milk. Other Italian varieties made from sheep's milk are available
Semi-hard cheese	
Caerphilly	Buttermilk-flavoured cheese with a soft paste. Some people find it almost soapy. Originally a Welsh cheese but now manufactured all over Britain
Cheddar	Classic British cheese now made all over the world and referred to as, for example, Scottish cheddar, Canadian cheddar
Cheshire	Crumbly, slightly salty cheese, available as either white or red. It was originally made during the twelfth century in Cheshire but is now made all over Britain
Edam	A Dutch cheese that is similar to, but harder than, Gouda. It has a fairly bland, buttery taste and a yellow or red wax-coated rind. It is sometimes flavoured with cumin
Emmenthal	The name of this Swiss cheese refers to the Emme Valley. It is similar to Gruyère, although it is softer and slightly less tasty
Gloucester/Double Gloucester	Full-cream, classic English cheeses originally made only from the milk of Gloucestershire cows
Gouda	Buttery textured, soft and mild-flavoured well known Dutch cheese with a yellow or red rind
Gruyère	Mainly known as a Swiss cheese, but both the French and Swiss varieties can legally be called by this name. It has small pea-size holes and a smooth, relatively hard texture. The French varieties may have larger holes
Leicester	Mild-flavoured and orange-coloured English cheese
Port Salut	Mild-flavoured cheese with a name meaning 'Port of Salvation', referring to the abbey where exiled Trappist monks returned after the French Revolution
Wensleydale	An English cheese from Yorkshire originally made from sheep's or goat's milk but now made from cow's milk. This cheese is the traditional accompaniment to apple pie
Hard cheese	
Parmesan	Classic Italian hard cheese, more correctly called Parmigiano Reggiano. It is also known as the grated cheese used in and for sprinkling over Italian dishes, especially pasta, and also minestrone
Provolone	Smoked cheese made in America, Australia and Italy. Now made from cow's milk but originally from buffalo milk. Younger versions are softer and milder than the longer-kept and more mature varieties
Blue cheese	
Gorgonzola	Soft, sharp-flavoured, classic Italian cheese with greenish veining, which is developed with the addition of mould culture
Roquefort	Classic sheep's milk cheese from the southern Massif Central in France. The maturing takes place in caves, which provide a unique humid environment that contributes to the development of the veining
Stilton	Famous and classic English cheese made from cow's milk. White Stilton has also become popular and is slightly less flavoursome than the blue variety

2.2 PREPARATION AND COOKING METHODS

Influence of different preparation and cooking methods on dishes

Food production (cooking) may be carried out in a variety of ways. Each of these can have an effect on:

- colour – for example, roasting will brown meat
- flavour – for example, seasonings increase the intensity of the taste of foods
- texture – for example, boiling softens vegetables
- appearance – for example, grilling bacon makes it darker in colour and it shrinks
- moisture – for example, grilling reduces the moisture in burgers, causing them to shrink
- aroma – for example, seasoning, and cooking in general, increase the intensity of smell of foods
- cooking timings – for example, the sous vide process takes longer than boiling
- service style and equipment – depending on the foods, they can be presented on flats, in dishes or tureens for service at a table, or in bowls or on plates for plated service.

Cooking methods

The main cooking methods are shown in Table 4.16.

▼ **Table 4.16** Cooking methods

Method	Explanation
Roasting	Cooking with dry convection heat in the oven
Barbecuing	Can refer to: • cooking slowly over low, indirect heat with the food being flavoured by the smoking process, or • similar to grilling, cooked quickly over direct heat that produces little smoke
Grilling	Quick and dry method of cooking food by radiant heat, either over heated charcoal or under electric or gas salamanders
Rotisserie	Cooking on a device equipped with a spit on which food is roasted
Griddling	Cooking on a solid heated surface which can be smooth or corrugated
Baking	Cooking in either a fan oven or conventional oven. Often referred to as 'dry' cooking
Boiling	Cooking food in a simmering liquid
Poaching	Cooking in a minimum amount of liquid held at simmering point
Steaming	Cooked in the steam produced by a boiling liquid, preserving the nutrients in the food
Braising	Slow cooking in minimum liquid in a casserole dish with a lid
Sous vide	Food is sealed in airtight plastic pouches then cooked using steam or by placing it in a hot water bath
Deep frying	Cooking by placing into deep fat held at a temperature of about 175–190°C (350–375°F)
Shallow frying	Cooking in the minimum amount of heated fat or oil
Smoking	The process of flavouring, browning, cooking or preserving food by exposing it to smoke from a burning or smouldering material (most often wood) • Cold-smoking imparts a smoky flavour, usually for foods that need to be cooked later such as salmon • Hot-smoking adds flavour to food and cooks them at the same time
Curing	Preserving by various combinations of fermentation, pickling or smoking

2.3 SERVICE EQUIPMENT

The range of service equipment includes:

- crockery
- linen
- tableware
- trays for silver, plated and family service
- chafing dishes and portable hot plates for buffet carvery service
- specialist trolleys and lamps for guéridon/flambé
- flats, liners and service spoons and forks for silver service
- specialist items such as lobster picks, cheese knives and finger bowls.

Plated service

Crockery

The crockery must blend in with the general decor of the establishment and with the rest of the items on the table. An establishment generally uses one design and pattern of crockery, but when an establishment has a number of different service areas it is easier, from a control point of view, to have a different design in each service area.

Food service crockery

There are various classifications of food service crockery. Although referred to as crockery throughout this book, all glazed tableware is traditionally referred to as china. Items include:

- **flatware** – for example plates, saucers and serving flats
- **cups and bowls** – for example tea and coffee cups, soup and sweet bowls, and serving dishes
- **hollow-ware** – for example pots and vases.

Types of crockery

There are four main types of crockery used in food service operations: bone china, earthenware, stoneware and porcelain. Contemporary styles now include other materials such as glass, slate, plastic or wood.

A whole range of crockery items is available (see Table 4.17) and their exact sizes will vary according to the manufacturer and the design produced.

▼ **Table 4.17** Types of crockery

• side plate	• salad crescent
• sweet plate	• egg cup
• fish plate	• butter dish
• soup plate	• ashtray
• joint plate	• teapot
• cereal/sweet bowl	• hot water jug
• breakfast cup and saucer	• coffee pot
• teacup and saucer	• milk jug
• coffee cup and saucer (demi-tasse)	• cream jug
• consommé cup and saucer	• hot milk jug
• soup bowl/cup	• sugar basin
• platter (oval plate)	• salt and pepper pots

▲ **Figure 4.11** Selection of crockery: traditional style

▲ **Figure 4.12** Selection of tableware as an alternative to crockery: contemporary style

Linen

The type of linen used will depend on the class of establishment, type of clientele and cost involved, and the style of menu and service to be offered. The main items of linen normally to be found are shown in Table 4.18.

▼ **Table 4.18** Linen items used in food and beverage service

Linen items	Uses
Tablecloths	Various sizes are available to cover different table shapes and sizes
Slip cloths	Can be used to cover a slightly soiled tablecloth
Napkins (or serviettes)	Can be linen or paper
Buffet cloths	Various sizes are available; longer cloths will be used for longer tables
Waiters cloths (or services cloths)	Servers use these as protection against heat and to help keep uniforms clean
Tea and glass cloths	These are used for drying items after washing; tea cloths should be used for crockery and glass cloths for glassware

A range of disposable linen, including napkins, place mats and tablecloths, are available in varying colours and qualities.

Tableware (flatware, cutlery and hollow-ware)

Traditionally flatware included spoons and forks, and cutlery referred only to knives. The modern usage of these terms has changed. All spoons, forks and knives used as eating implements are now referred to as cutlery. The term 'cutlery' is therefore used throughout this book.

Hollow-ware consists of other items such as teapots, milk jugs, sugar basins and serving dishes.

▲ **Figure 4.13** Examples of cutlery

Service equipment that may be used includes serving tongs, fish slices and gâteaux slices, serving spoons, scoops, small sauce ladles and larger soup ladles, as shown in Figure 4.14.

▲ **Figure 4.14** Examples of service equipment

Trays

Service salver (round tray)

A service salver is a round, often silver or stainless steel, tray (wood or plastic may also be used). A napkin (folded flat) or non-slip mat is placed on the tray to help prevent items slipping on it as they are being carried. Some trays are made with non-slip surfaces. The service salver is often used to:

- carry clean glasses to, and remove dirty glasses from, a customer's table
- carry clean cutlery to and from a customer's table
- place clean cutlery on the table
- place clean cups and saucers on the table
- provide an underflat when silver serving vegetables.

▲ **Figure 4.15** Cutlery positions when carrying on a service salver

A service plate

A service plate is a joint plate with a napkin on it. During the meal service it can be used for:

- placing clean cutlery on and removing it from the table
- clearing side plates and side knives
- crumbing down after the main course or any other stage of the meal if necessary
- clearing accompaniments from the table.

Carrying and using large trays

Trays are used for:

- carrying food from the kitchen to the restaurant
- service in rooms and lounges
- clearing from sideboards/workstations
- clearing from tables at functions or when the customer is not seated at the table in the restaurant
- carrying equipment.

A safe way of holding and carrying an oblong tray is to position the tray lengthways on to the forearm and to support it by holding the tray with the other hand (see Figure 4.16). Note that the tray is organised so that the heaviest items are nearest the carrier. This helps to balance the tray. Also note that one hand is placed underneath the tray and the other at the side.

▲ **Figure 4.16** Carrying a loaded oblong tray

Family service

Traditionally, family service has all the customers at one table. Plates are placed in front of each customer by the waiting staff, and the customers eat and share the food in serving dishes or sharing platters that are placed in the centre of the table, with service spoons and forks placed in them. The customers help themselves to the food.

The range of crockery, linen, tableware and trays used for plated service are also used for family service and buffet and carvery service.

Buffet/carvery service

Buffet and carvery styles of service may also use portable methods of keeping food warm where full buffet stations cannot be used, e.g. in event catering. Here **chafing dishes or portable hot plates** may be used. These can keep food hot for short periods of time, sufficient for a short service period, without affecting the quality of the food.

▲ **Figure 4.17** Chafing dishes used for buffets

- Chafing dish – the food is placed in a dish that sits in a frame over hot water. Below the water bath is a heat source, which can be a gel burner or an internally insulated electric element. A lid is placed over the top of the food, which helps retain the moist heat inside. Caution should be taken to avoid scalds from the escaping steam when the lid is lifted.
- The shallower pans, which are used for lamp cookery, are called Suzette pans. They resemble frying pans in shape and size and have a diameter of 23–30 cm (9–12 in), with or without a lip. The lip is usually found on the left-hand side. The pans are generally made of silver-plated copper as this gives an even distribution of heat.

- A portable hotplate gives off dry heat through a metal underplate and the food-serving dishes are placed directly on to the metal plate. The plates can be heated with either a gel burner or be connected to mains electricity where possible. This works well but overheating due to little control over the heat source can lead to food drying out at the bottom and going cold on top.

Guéridon service

Guéridon service usually indicates serving foods on to the customers' plates at the guéridon. Guéridon service is also often used to refer to other enhanced service techniques – for example, the use of a drinks trolley, a carving trolley, a cheese trolley or a sweet trolley.

Further enhancements to the basic guéridon service include:

- **preparing** and serving foods in the service area such as salads and dressings
- **carving**, jointing or filleting foods in a service area
- **flambage** (the preparation and finishing, or cooking, of foods in the restaurant, which are also flambéed).

Specialist trolleys

Guéridon trolley

A guéridon is a movable service table or trolley from which food may be served. In effect the guéridon is a movable sideboard or service station carrying sufficient equipment for the service requirements, together with any spare equipment that may be necessary.

In many establishments where guéridon service is carried out, the basic layout is standardised. This is to ensure that the required standards of service are met and that safety is a prime consideration of all the service staff. There are many designs of guéridon available, a good example is shown in Figure 4.18.

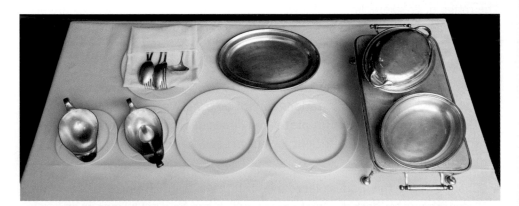

▲ **Figure 4.18** Example of a basic guéridon lay-up. From left to right on the back row: service plate with the service gear in a napkin; place for the food dish which is to be serviced and hot plate showing places for vegetable and potato dishes. On the front row are places for sauce dishes and the two plates on to which the food is to be served.

Flambé trolley

A flambé trolley is used for the preparation, cooking and finishing of foods which are also flambéed. A measure of spirit is added which is ignited. See Unit 205, page 206 for an example of a flambé dish.

The top of the trolley is stainless steel, which allows for easy cleaning. The guéridon will normally also have a control switch for the gas lamp, a drawer for surplus service equipment, a cutting board for use when cooking dishes at the table, a bracket on the lower shelf used for holding bottles of spirit and liqueurs, and an indentation in the top to hold accompaniments.

▲ **Figure 4.20** Carving trolley

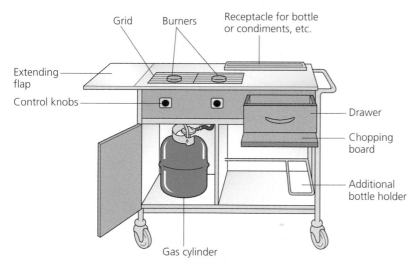

▲ **Figure 4.19** Example of a flambé trolley: gas-fuelled flambé trolley

Carving trolley

The purpose of the carving trolley is to display foods that are to be carved at the table. They act as an aid to selling and provide space for the equipment that is necessary to complete the service.

Sweet and cheese trolleys

When the customer makes a selection from the sweet or cheese trolley, a plate should be positioned near the item to be served. Then, using the service equipment (one in each hand) the food should be portioned and transferred neatly to the plate. The plate should then be placed in front of the customer from the right. For larger parties, two people will be required – one to take the orders and place the plate with food in front of the customer, the other to stand at the trolley and portion and plate the foods.

▲ **Figure 4.21** A cheese trolley

Flare lamps

The main types of lamp used today are fuelled in one of three ways (see Figure 4.24):

1 **Methylated spirits**: these have a good flame (heat) but care must be taken to trim the wick, to help avoid fumes. The use of these lamps is on the decline.
2 **Flammable gel**: this is very clean and safe to refill as the gel either comes in individual lamp-size containers which fit directly into the lamp or in a large container with a dispenser. However, the flame can be fairly weak.
3 **Calor gas**: these lamps are very popular and replacement canisters can be obtained that fit directly into the lamp. The gas is odourless and excellent control of the flame can be achieved. These lamps are often used in purpose-built trolleys where the lamp is incorporated into the structure, thus giving the same working height all along the trolley top, reducing the chance of accidents.

▲ **Figure 4.22** A sweet trolley

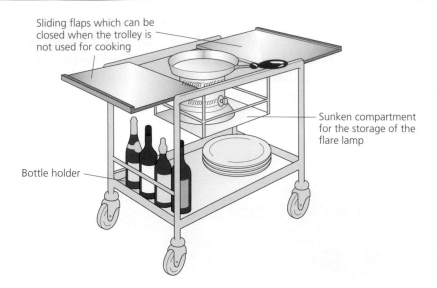

▲ **Figure 4.23** Flambé trolley with flare lamp

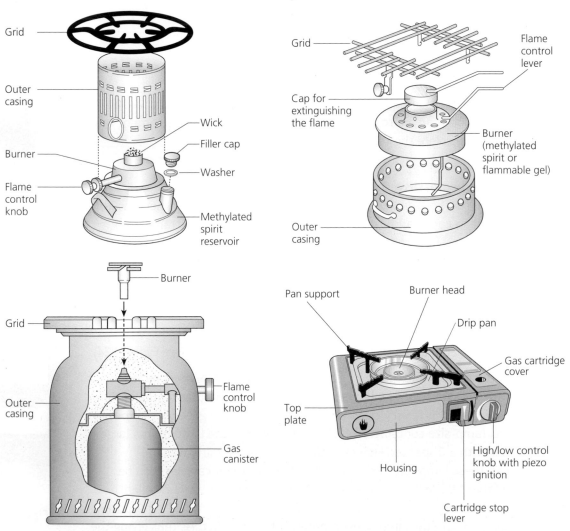

▲ **Figure 4.24** Four types of Guéridon lamp: (a) Traditional methylated spirit lamp; (b) Modern methylated spirit gel lamp; (c) Gas lamp; (d) Gas stove

Portable gas stoves, which were first produced as camping stoves, have begun to be used for cooking purposes on the guéridon trolley. These are lightweight, self-contained, portable stoves with their own carry case. They have an automatic push button ignition and built-in safety features. These stoves are considerably less expensive than the average flare lamp.

Silver service

Silver service (or English service) is a higher technical level of service which is not as widely used as it once was but is still used in a wide variety of establishments. Expertise in this technique can only be achieved with practice. It requires presentation and service of food by waiting staff on to customers' plates from food flats or dishes, using a spoon and fork.

For silver service of courses, the plates will be laid in front of each customer, the dishes to be served will be presented to the table and an explanation of the dishes given. The course(s) will then be silver served to the customers from their left-hand side and any accompaniments will be offered. Plated foods will be offered from the right-hand side.

The range of crockery, linen, tableware and trays used for plated service are also used for silver service.

Flat

Foods are presented for silver service on what is known as a service flat. This is a large, usually oval, service platter made of metal – silver or stainless steel. The flat is held next to the customer at the left-hand side and the food is served to the customer's plate using a spoon and fork.

A service cloth is folded neatly and placed on the palm of the hand as protection against heat from the serving flat. This also makes it easier to turn the dish on the cloth to serve the food from either end.

Liners

When silver serving from food dishes at the table, such as for potatoes or vegetables, a liner should be used. A liner is also called an underflat. It is a cold, usually oval, silver or stainless-steel dish used by waiters to carry and serve hot dishes at the table. A service salver or service plate can also be used.

The liner can be used to hold either one large vegetable dish or a number of smaller ones, depending on the customer's order. The uses of the underflat or liner are to:

- add to the presentation of the food being served
- give the waiter more control when using the service spoon and fork to serve from the food dishes on to the customer's plate
- provide greater protection in case of spillage, therefore not detracting from the presentation of the food on the plate or the overall table presentation
- give the waiter added protection against heat and possible spillage on the uniform.

Service spoon and fork

The purpose of the service spoon and fork is to enable the waiter to serve food from a flat or dish on to the customer's plate quickly and to present the food on the plate well.

- The service fork should be positioned above, or on top of, the service spoon.
- The key to developing this skill is the locking of the ends of the service spoon and fork with the small finger and the third finger, as illustrated in Figure 4.25a;
- The spoon and fork are manoeuvred with the thumb and the index and second fingers (see Figure 4.25b). Using this method food items may be picked up from the serving dish in between the service spoon and service fork.
- Alternatively, the service fork may be turned to mould to the shape of the items being served, for example when serving bread rolls (see Figure 4.25c).

▲ **Figure 4.25** Hand positions for holding a service spoon and fork

There are occasions where two service forks may be used, for example when serving fillets of fish, as this makes the service of this food item easier.

When using a service spoon and fork for serving at a sweet or cheese trolley, or at a buffet or guéridon, the spoon and fork are held one in each hand.

Specialised service equipment

There is an almost unlimited range of flatware, cutlery and hollow-ware in use in the catering industry today. There are also a number of specialist items of equipment such as finger bowls and lobster picks, and service items such as cheese knives.

Finger bowls

A finger bowl is given to a customer to clean their fingers after they have consumed food that required them to use their fingers to break, disassemble or extract the food from a shell or bone in order to consume it.

The finger bowl should be sufficiently large that hot, not boiling water, can be placed in it. A slice of fresh lemon, to break up any grease on the fingers, should be added to the water. The bowl should be placed on a napkin that sits on a side plate. This is placed to the side of the customer's cover within easy reach, and an additional napkin is placed next to the finger bowl for the customer to dry their fingers on once they have dipped them in the water. This should all be cleared away when the course is being cleared.

3 DIETARY REQUIREMENTS
3.1 NUTRIENTS FOR BALANCED DIETS

The key issue in the relationship between health and eating is a healthy diet. This means eating a **balanced diet** rather than viewing individual foods as healthier or less healthy. Customers are increasingly looking for the availability of choices that will enable them to achieve a balanced diet. They also require more specific information on the methods of cooking used, for example low fat or low salt methods.

General consensus suggests that a normal diet should consist of around one-third bread, cereals, rice and potatoes; one-third fruit and vegetables and the remainder should be dairy foods, including low-fat milk, low-fat meats and fish, and small amounts of fatty and sugary food. Figure 4.26 indicates the recommended daily intake for the different food groups.

There is now a greater emphasis on alternatives such as low-fat milks (for example, skimmed or semi-skimmed), non-dairy creamers for beverages, alternatives to sugar such as sweeteners, and polyunsaturated fat and non-animal fats as alternatives to butter. Cooking ingredients and methods are also affected, with the development of lower fat dishes, lighter cuisine and attractive and decent alternatives for non-meat eaters, including the greater use of animal protein substitutes such as Quorn and tofu.

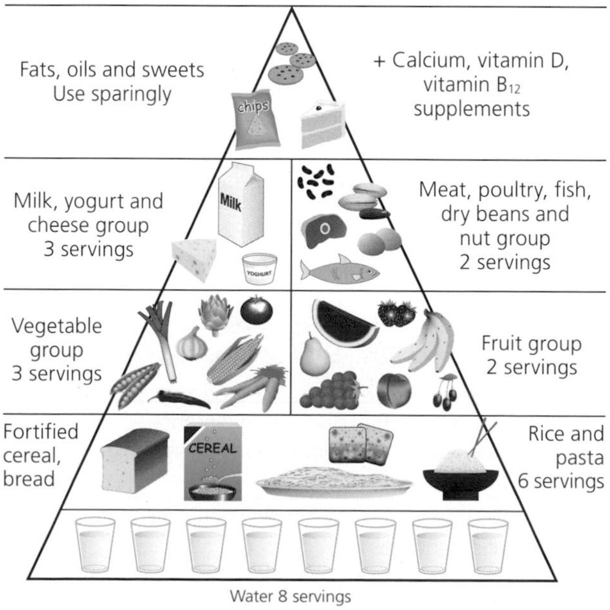

KEY TERM

Balanced diet – a diet which contains the correct amounts of all of the food groups.

Fats, oils and sweets
Use sparingly
chips

+ Calcium, vitamin D, vitamin B_{12} supplements

Milk, yogurt and cheese group
3 servings
Milk
YOGHURT

Meat, poultry, fish, dry beans and nut group
2 servings

Vegetable group
3 servings

Fruit group
2 servings

Fortified cereal, bread
CEREAL

Rice and pasta
6 servings

Water 8 servings

▲ **Figure 4.26** Recommended daily intake for different food groups

149

▼ **Table 4.19** Key nutrients and their purpose in maintaining a healthy diet

Nutrient	Purpose
Carbohydrates	• This is the main energy source for the brain. Without carbohydrates, the body could not function properly • Sources include fruits, breads and grains, starchy vegetables and sugars • Whole grains and fruit are full of fibre, which reduces the risk of coronary heart disease and helps maintain normal blood glucose levels. Make at least half of the grains you consume whole grains
Protein	• This is the major structural component of cells and is responsible for the building and repair of body tissues • Protein is broken down into amino acids, which are building blocks of protein • 9 of the 20 amino acids, known as essential amino acids, must be provided in the diet as they cannot be synthesised in the body • 10–35 per cent of your daily calories should come from lean protein sources such as low-fat meat, dairy, beans or eggs
Fat	• Fat is an energy source that when consumed increases the absorption of fat-soluble vitamins including vitamins A, D, E and K • 20–35 per cent of your daily intake should come from fat • Choose options such as omega-3-rich foods like fish, walnuts and vegetable-based oils. Omega-3s help with development and growth. Limit intake of saturated fats such as high-fat meats and full-fat dairy. Other smart choices include nuts, seeds and avocado

3.2 CUSTOMER CHOICES

Customer dietary requirements

Customers may have a range of dietary requirements, as outlined in Unit 202, page 46. Such customers will need to know about every ingredient used in a dish, since eating certain ingredients may make them very ill and may even be fatal.

To aid the customer in making the appropriate choice, menu items that are suitable for a vegetarian diet can be identified with 'V', while menu items containing nuts can be identified with 'N' next to their description. Nevertheless, it is important that the server is able to accurately describe the dishes so that the customer can make an appropriate choice. The server should never guess and, if in doubt, should seek further information. Some examples of dietary requirements are given in Table 4.20.

▼ **Table 4.20** Examples of dietary requirements

Low fat/low cholesterol	Diets will include polyunsaturated fats and may include limited quantities of animal fats. Other items eaten may include lean poached or grilled meats and fish, fruit and vegetables and low-fat milk, cheese and yoghurt
Low sodium/salt	This requires a reduction in the amount of sodium or salt consumed. Diets will include low sodium/salt foods and cooking with very limited or no salt
Diabetic	This refers to the inability of the body to control the level of insulin within the blood. An appropriate diet for type 2 diabetes may include foods listed in the low cholesterol section and the avoidance of dishes with high sugar content
Low carbohydrate	A low-carb diet limits carbohydrates – such as those found in grains, starchy vegetables and fruit – and emphasises foods high in protein and fat. Many types of low-carb diet exist. Each diet has varying restrictions on the types and amounts of carbohydrates that can be eaten
Gluten intolerance	Gluten is a protein found primarily in wheat, barley and rye. If a person has a gluten intolerance, this protein can cause digestive problems such as gassiness, abdominal pain or diarrhoea. Gluten intolerance is sometimes confused with coeliac disease, or thought of as a food allergy
Lactose intolerance	The basis for lactose intolerance is the lack of an enzyme called lactase in the small intestine. The most common symptoms of lactose intolerance are diarrhoea, bloating and gas

See page 134 earlier in this chapter for information on vegetarianism.

Impact of customer choices on menus

Cultural influences

Celebration days, weddings and festivals have food associated with them — for example:

- Turkey at Christmas, Simnel cake at Easter for Christians.
- Diwali, the 'Festival of Lights', was traditionally a Hindu celebration but is now also celebrated by Sikhs, Buddhists and Jains, particularly in India and Nepal. Mithai is eaten – this is a name for all of the Indian sweets and desserts. Samosas are also traditional; these are small pockets of pastry, usually shaped into a triangle, stuffed with minced meat, peas, lentils and other vegetables.

Religious influences

Different religious faiths have differing requirements with regard to the dishes/ingredients that may be consumed, and these requirements often also cover preparation methods, cooking procedures and the equipment used. See Table 2.2 on page 42 for dietary requirements according to the various faiths.

Lifestyle dietary choices

- **Health and weight loss.** Healthy lifestyle and weight loss regimes may determine what a customer can and/or wishes to consume and should be seen as a **dietary requirement**. Consumers are more aware of the benefits and impact of a range of ingredients that can cause weight gain or encourage weight loss.
- **Pregnancy.** There are no special diets required during pregnancy but it is important to get the right balance of nutrients. Folic acid is often taken as a supplement. It is recommended that some foods are avoided. These include: soft and blue cheeses, raw or partially cooked eggs (unless Lion branded), all types of pâté, raw or undercooked meats, liver and game.
- **Allergens.** See Unit 203, Table 3.6 on page 99 for more information on the 14 allergens that must be tracked.

KEY TERM

Dietary requirements – customers may have a range of dietary choices based on vegetarianism, medical requirements (including food intolerance and the prevention of allergic reactions), ethical considerations or lifestyle choices.

4 FOOD AND BEVERAGE MATCHING

4.1 CONSIDERATIONS FOR FOOD AND BEVERAGE MATCHING

Food and its accompanying wine/drink should harmonise well together, with each enhancing the other's performance. However, the combinations that prove most successful are those that please the individual. Considerations to be taken into account are given below.

Occasions and service stage

Special events

The type of occasion will be influential for the selection of beverages offered and the style of service offered. Often, the customer budget will dictate the quality and range offered and the style of service provided. Some examples are given in Table 4.21.

▼ Table 4.21 Examples of beverage provision for different events

Event	Range of beverages to be offered and style of service
Wedding reception	<ul><li>Bar drinks service – either an open bar or guests pay for their own orders</li><li>Arrival drinks – hosts may pre-order champagne, sparkling wines, soft drinks which are often given while guests wait to be seated for the wedding breakfast</li><li>Wines and soft drinks – pre-ordered by the hosts and will usually follow the traditions above</li></ul>
Business dinner	<ul><li>Bar drinks service – guests pay for their own orders</li><li>Arrival drinks – hosts may pre-order sparkling or still wines, soft drinks which are often given as a reception drink</li><li>Wines and soft drinks – pre-ordered by the hosts and will usually follow the traditions above</li><li>Other alcoholic beverages may be requested – beers, ciders, ports or other fortified wines</li></ul>
Award ceremony	<ul><li>Bar drinks service – guests pay for their own orders</li><li>Arrival drinks – hosts may pre-order champagne and soft drinks which are often given as a reception drink</li><li>Wines and soft drinks – pre-ordered by the hosts and will usually follow the traditions above</li></ul>

Tasting menus

There is an ever-increasing trend and demand for tasting menus (sometimes called menu degustation) that consist of a number of set dishes specially prepared to give the customer smaller, taster-size portions of the chef's menu. The sommelier or restaurant manager will create a wine recommendation for each dish (a flight of wines) that can be incorporated into the menu price or offered at an additional charge.

Drinks on arrival

Arrival drinks are often referred to as aperitifs. These can be alcoholic or non-alcoholic. Sparkling wine, such as champagne or prosecco, or wine-based drinks such as dry and medium dry sherries and dry vermouths are often served. Cocktails are also popular as well as some beers. Non-alcoholic drinks can include various juices, mineral water, aerated waters such as cola or tonic, and also non-alcoholic cocktails (called mocktails).

Religious and cultural influences

It is essential that your beverage recommendations are sympathetic to the clients' religious and cultural requirements and as such do not contravene or undermine these – see Unit 202, page 42 for more information on religious and cultural influences.

Customer preference

Customers may have some preferences for the type and style of beverage served, for example a customer may prefer wines from specific regions or containing specific grape varieties. They may also wish to order brand or artisan products or support local, national or international causes such as Fairtrade.

Customer budget

The amount the customer is willing to pay will have an impact on the range, quality and selection of beverages supplied. Customers may wish to impress their guests by ordering an expensive or rare range. Others may be on a budget.

Cooking method

A big influence on the beverage selection is the way the food is cooked. If a meal is produced predominantly on a barbeque then it may be worth offering ranges of heavy beers or dry ciders along with sweeter wines which will complement and/or stand out from the smoky flavours and nose.

Sauces used

The base ingredients to a dish must be known when choosing wine to accompany a dish. It is better to match the wine with the sauce than with the meat or fish.

- A cream-based sauce will need a more acidic wine that can cut through the fat.
- A tomato-based sauce will be acidic, and the wine will need to be more acidic.
- A reduction will have very concentrated flavours and could be very complex, so the wine should have the same flavour intensity as the food.

Contrasting and compatible flavours

Matching wine with food

Food pairing has many options. Some pairings are obvious, for example a fish dish goes best with a light wine like Sauvignon Blanc while a grilled steak would pair well with a spicy red wine made from the Shiraz grape. But fruits, herbs, spices, starches and dairy products are a little harder to pinpoint.

When considering a possible food and wine partnership there are no precise rules. However, general guidelines on matching wine and food are summarised in Table 4.22.

▼ Table 4.22 General guidelines for matching wine and food

Characteristic	Food considerations
Acidity	Can be used to match, or to contrast, acidity in foods, for example crisp wines to match lemon or tomato, or to cut through creamy flavours
Age/maturity	As wine ages and develops it can become delicate with complex and intricate flavours. More simple foods, such as grills or roasts, work better with older wines than do stronger-tasting foods, which can overpower the wines
Oak	The more oaked the wine then the more robust and flavoursome the foods need to be. Heavily oaked wines can overpower more delicate foods
Sweetness	Generally, the wine should be sweeter than the foods or it will taste flat or thin. Sweet dishes need contrast for them to match well with sweeter wines, for example acids in sweeter foods can harmonise with the sweetness in the wines. Savoury foods with sweetness (e.g. carrots or onions) can match well with ripe fruity wines. Blue cheeses can go well with sweet wines. Also, sweeter wines can go well with salty foods
Tannin	Tannic wines match well with red meats and semi-hard cheeses (e.g. cheddar). Tannic wines are not good with egg dishes, and wines with high tannin content do not work well with salty foods
Weight	Big, rich wines go well with robust (flavoursome) meat dishes, but can overpower lighter-flavoured foods

Matching beers, ciders and perries with food

Recently there has been an increasing trend to offer beers, ciders and perries with food, either alongside or as an alternative to wines. As with wines it is a question of trial and error to achieve harmony between particular beers, ciders and perries and foods. Generally, the considerations for the pairing of beers and foods are similar to those for matching wines with foods.

Relationship between regional food and types of beverages

National dishes should normally be complemented by the national wines of that country, for example Italian red wine with pasta dishes.

4.2 TRADITIONAL FOOD AND BEVERAGE MATCHING

A few general pointers are set out below that may be followed when customers are making their choices or when advising the customer on which beverage to choose to accompany a meal. However, customers should always be given freedom in their selection of wines or other drinks. A summary of traditional matches is given in Table 4.23.

▼ Table 4.23 Summary of traditional food and beverage matching

Food	Traditional matching suggestions
Starters and light dishes such as fish or pasta	• These are often best accompanied by light dry white wines, for example Pinot Gris or Sauvignon Blanc grapes or dry rosé wine, or light beers • Fish and shellfish dishes are often most suited to well-chilled dry white wines such as Chablis, Muscadet, Soave and also dry and medium sherries and lagers and beers
Chicken and pork	• White meats such as chicken, veal and pork can be paired with medium white wines or lighter reds such as Beaujolais, New Zealand Pinot Noir, Californian Zinfandel, Burgundy and Corbières, or medium strength beers

Food	Traditional matching suggestions
Red meat	• Red meats such as beef and lamb will harmonise well with full-bodied red wines such as Medoc, Saint-Emilion, Pomerol and any of the Cabernet Sauvignons and most beers. • Alternatives include big red Burgundies, Rioja, Barolo, Dão and flavoured beers (e.g. heather or honeydew)
Game	• Best served with red wines with distinctive flavour. These include: Côte Rôtie, Bourgeuil, Rioja, Chianti, Australian Shiraz, Californian Cabernet Sauvignon, Chilean Cabernet Sauvignon, and also fine red Burgundies and Bordeaux reds and Belgian Abbey-style and Trappist beers
Foods that come with rich cream sauces	• These require wines with high acidity. Sauvignon Blanc would complement these foods well
Sweets and desserts	• Sweet wines such as the luscious Muscats (de Beaumes-de-Venise, de Setúbal, de Frontignan, Samos), Sainte-Croix-du-Mont, Sauternes, Banyuls, Monbazillac and Tokay wines made from late-gathered individual grapes in Germany • Sparkling wines such as brut or demi-sec Champagne and Cava also work well with desserts • Fruit beers (which can also be especially good with chocolate), porters, and Belgian-style strong golden ales can all pair well with various sweets and puddings
Spicy foods	• These can be paired with dry white aromatic wines such as Gewürztraminer, Rieslings, Albariños, Vinho Verde and also rosé wines • Fruit-flavoured beers, IPA, ciders and perries also match well with mild, and most lagers with hot spicy foods
Cheese	The majority of cheeses blend well with port and other dry robust red wines. However, cheese can also be served with sweet whites

Test your learning

1 Briefly describe the two key differences between an à la carte and a table d'hôte menu.

2 What are the main differences between 'menu du jour' and 'prix fixe'?

3 Give one example of the service style used in table service.

4 What is the object of a duty rota?

5 Identify **two** impacts on the business that different menu styles can have.

6 What is the main purpose of a menu?

7 List **three** special dietary needs that should be considered when planning a menu.

8 What is gluten intolerance?

9 What is the definition of guéridon?

10 State the three key nutrients.

11 What type of wine is suited to starter dishes?

12 What type of wine is suitable for roasted red meats?

13 What type of wine is suited to foods with rich cream sauces?

14 What type of wine is suited to sweets and desserts?

15 What type of wine is suited to spicy foods?

FOOD SERVICE

INTRODUCTION

The purpose of this chapter is to help you to develop and implement interpersonal and technical skills for a range of food service styles found within the hospitality industry.

This chapter will help you to:
- identify how your personal presentation affects the reputation of the organisation.
- know the importance of teamwork in the food service industry and how you can contribute to it.
- display a professional attitude.
- contribute to providing a memorable meal experience.

1 INTERACTION WITH CUSTOMERS

1.1 PERSONAL PRESENTATION

Food and beverage service is the essential link between customers and the menu on offer in an establishment. The server is the main point of contact between customers and the establishment and therefore plays an important role. The skills and knowledge of the food and beverage service are transferable between establishments and different sectors all over the world.

To be successful in food and beverage service members of staff must have:
- sound product knowledge
- well-developed interpersonal skills
- a range of technical skills
- an ability to work as part of a team.

KEY TERM

Personal presentation – includes all aspects of how an employee appears to the customer, including hygiene, grooming, dress, body language, posture and attitude.

How staff look and the first impression they create are a reflection of the hygiene standards of the establishment and the quality of service to come. All staff should be aware of the factors listed below and it is their individual responsibility to ensure that these are practised in the workplace.

Hygiene

- Staff should be clean and use subtle-smelling deodorants.
- Hands must always be clean and free of nicotine stains, with clean, well-trimmed nails. Hands must be washed immediately after using the toilet, smoking or dealing with refuse.
- Teeth should be brushed immediately before coming on duty and the breath should be fresh smelling.
- Cuts and burns must be covered with waterproof dressings. These should be coloured to be easily seen if they fall off.
- If a member of staff is suffering from a cold or other possible infection this must be reported immediately.

Dress

Dress must be as per establishment requirements.

- Uniforms must be clean, starched as appropriate, neatly pressed and in good repair. All buttons must be present.
- Shoes must be comfortable and clean and of a plain, neat design. Fashion is less important than safety and comfort.

Grooming

- Men should normally be clean-shaven or with moustache or beard neatly trimmed.
- Women should only wear light make-up. If nail varnish is worn, then it should be clear.
- Hair must be clean and well groomed. Long hair should be tied up or back to avoid hair falling into food and drink and to avoid repeated handling of the hair.
- Earrings should not be worn except for studs/sleepers.
- Excessive jewellery should not be worn – the establishment policy should be followed.

Body language and posture

Body language is often unconscious and can tell us what people really think and feel. It is a non-verbal method of communication but is key to the success of any hospitality business. Think about how you approach people and what body language you use. For example, when in the role of host your initial non-verbal contact can have a positive or negative impact on the first impressions of the customers and the meal experience. In addition to these first impressions, the customer is also set the scene of what to expect, which once

▲ **Figure 5.1** Waiter in correct uniform

again can impact on the total meal experience. Everyone uses body language, but it can mean different things in different cultures and to different people.

- Staff should try to avoid any mannerisms they may have, such as running their fingers through their hair, chewing gum or scratching their face.
- Standing tall will give the appearance of confidence which will give both staff and customers a good impression.
- Staff should be made aware not to fold their arms as this will convey boredom or a defensive attitude.
- Staff should ensure they have sufficient sleep, an adequate and healthy intake of food and regular exercise to maintain good health and the ability to cope with the pressures and stress of work.
- See Unit 207, page 287 for more information on body language.

Attitude

Having the right attitude includes:

- Being tactful, courteous, good humoured and of an even temper. Staff must converse with the customer in a pleasing and well-spoken manner and the ability to smile at the right times is helpful.
- Being supportive of colleagues and knowing your job will show that you have a good, professional attitude.
- Anticipating customer needs and being discrete when checking the progress of the meal allows service staff to anticipate customer needs with minimal intrusion.
- Maintaining loyalty to the establishment in which you are employed and its management.
- Contributing to maintaining trust and respect among staff, customers and management leads to an atmosphere at work that encourages efficiency and a good team spirit.

1.2 TRANSFER OF INFORMATION
Importance of transferring relevant information accurately

Accurate communication is vital to ensure the food service is carried out smoothly. Information needs to be recorded, checked and then transferred on to the relevant people or departments as soon as is possible. This will enable all parties to know what is happening, when it is required and what is required. This will then give time to resolve any issues and give better customer service.

Passing on information about food and beverage orders to the payment point should be done as soon as the order is placed to ensure all items are charged to the customer and will avoid loss of revenue and increase accuracy of billing.

Bookings

Care must be taken with information relating to bookings. If bookings are taken over the telephone the information should be written directly into the booking diary, this should then be repeated back to the customer. The information should include:

- customer's name
- telephone number
- date of reservation
- time of reservation
- number of customers
- any dietary needs
- any special requests.

The same information is needed for online/email bookings and a confirmation email must be sent to inform the customer that the booking is confirmed.

This information forms the basis for compiling rotas, stock ordering and preparation for both the restaurant and kitchen for service.

Orders and special requests

Orders and special requests for service should be communicated as soon as they are received to the relevant departments to allow decisions to be made as to what needs to be ordered, when and if unavailable to seek an alternative item and if necessary inform the customer of this. This is especially important if the request is for an allergy, a specialist item or something that may not usually be available on the premises – for example a birthday cake – as this will take time to either make or order and would disappoint the customer if not there when they come for their booking.

Briefings

Clear communication during a briefing will ensure staff have all the correct information to run a smooth service. This will also give them confidence to be able to communicate clearly with customers regarding the menu, drinks list and any allergens.

Briefings will also inform staff as to low or unavailable stock and the spread and number of bookings expected for the service period, any special customers expected and any additional information to assist them for the service.

Product knowledge

All staff members need to have a thorough knowledge of the products available. Training should cover information regarding:

- the opening times of the restaurants, bars, lounges and any other services within the business
- what other facilities are available – for example, spa, leisure, beauty
- the menu, and especially 'specials'
- the prices.

Knowing the above will mean that staff can assist customers with relevant and accurate information when customers are making their menu choices. This not only conveys professionalism but reduces waste, refunds and complaints.

Billing

Communicating orders to the payment point as soon as the order is taken will ensure all items are charged for and that the bill can be compiled swiftly and presented to the customer without delay. The bill can be processed efficiently and the customers thanked without them needing to query any mistakes or discrepancies. This ensures that the customer leaves the establishment with a good impression.

Stock levels

All stock issued must be recorded accurately and requisition information recorded and placed in time for the next shift. This will reduce the risk of stock being unavailable and also informs the store/cellar staff when replacement stock needs to be ordered. Also see Unit 208, page 321 on requisition forms procedure.

If there is an event booked that requires additional stock, care must be taken to ensure this is communicated to the relevant department so that the stock can be ordered and delivered in time.

Waste and breakages

- Waste food and beverages should be monitored. The kitchen should be looking at plate waste and food service staff should communicate customer feedback, especially if there is a consistent comment regarding quality or over-sized portions.
- Beverage waste due to improper use of equipment or wrongly dispensed drinks and breakages should all be recorded in the wastage book and signed off by a supervisor or manager.
- The wastage is then allowed for in the stocktake and will highlight if there is a need to replace items, repair equipment and/or retrain staff.
- Breakages to glassware, crockery and equipment should be communicated to supervisors and managers to enable them to reorder or repair these items. They should also be recorded in a breakages book.

Types of communication used to transfer information

See Unit 201, pages 22 and 23 for information on body language and listening.

Written communication

Letters, emails, memos and reports will be received and handled on a daily basis. Written communication is necessary when a formal response is required. The operation will issue guidelines for staff on when and how to use written communication. It is essential that spelling, grammar and tone are checked before any correspondence is sent out to ensure it is accurate and sets a professional tone.

Verbal communication

This is a valuable tool in selling products and services. Having knowledge of what is available and being able to describe it in a way that makes customers want to order it, is a skill that all service staff should have. The use of persuasive language to promote products will increase sales, help with customer satisfaction and job satisfaction. See Unit 207, page 287 on Transfer of information, including staff briefings.

Visual communication

Some gestures are open and positive. For example, leaning forwards with the palms of your hands open and facing upwards shows interest, acceptance and a welcoming attitude. On the other hand, leaning backwards with your arms folded and head down might show that you are feeling closed, uninterested, defensive and negative or rejected.

If someone uses plenty of gestures this may indicate that they are warm, enthusiastic and emotional. If someone does not use many gestures this may indicate that they are cold, reserved and logical.

However, one gesture does not always reveal exactly what a person is thinking. For example, if someone has his or her arms folded this may mean that they are:

- being defensive about something
- feeling the cold
- relaxed and comfortable.

Electronic

Good training in the use of electronic communications and accurate recording of information will reduce errors and increase efficiency across all departments.

▼ **Table 5.1** Forms of electronic communication

Form of communication	Description
Email	• Emails are now the most common form of communication. It is important to check all emails for accuracy, spelling and grammar, and often a business will have standard templates for staff to use when corresponding with customers to ensure accuracy and keeping to a standard that represents the business • As this is an instant form of communication that can easily be shared care must be taken to ensure that the email is factual, does not offend anyone and is legally compliant • A disclaimer is often part of the footer for all emails in an attempt to protect the business if things go wrong. However, in this digital age information can easily be taken out of context and shared in a way that may misrepresent the business
EPOS	The electronic point of sale system allows information about orders to be sent to departments for preparation, for billing and for reordering of stock. Staff should be fully trained as to how to input as well as extract information relevant to their job role
Hand-held service equipment	Hand-held systems have in many establishments taken over from written check pads; they can increase efficiency as orders are sent directly to the preparation and dispensing areas, but care must be taken to: • ensure the accuracy of information being input • highlight special requests so that all relevant staff can respond accordingly

1.3 CUSTOMER INTERACTION
Communicate with customers, team members and other departments

In person – meet and greet

When interacting with customers in person good communication will show professionalism. Staff should be trained to address customers with 'Sir' or 'Madam' when the customer's name is not known. If the name is known, then the member of staff should also address the customer as 'Mr Smith' or 'Miss Jones', for example. First names should only be used in less-formal operations and where the customer has explicitly indicated that this is acceptable.

Greetings such as 'good morning' and 'good evening' should be used upon receiving customers, or when the member of staff first comes into contact with the customer.

When dealing with colleagues and other departments the same courtesy as shown to customers also applies.

In person – through briefings

Face-to-face briefings for staff are always preferred as this ensures an up-to-date understanding of the situation can be gauged. Questions can be asked and answered and any grey areas clarified straightaway. When a briefing or handover is written in the diary, often the 'bigger picture' cannot be conveyed and details may be forgotten.

Via the telephone – enquiries and reservations

When interacting with customers via the telephone (taking enquiries and reservations) staff should always speak clearly, repeat information as often as necessary and stay calm. The caller may have a lot of questions and each one should be carefully listened to and answered as fully as possible.

A smile while speaking will give a friendly and confident tone to your voice; this will convey to the customer that this is a pleasant place to be and enhance the customer expectation that they will have a good experience in a friendly establishment.

Most establishments will have a standard greeting and closing to all telephone calls which will help identify the business to the caller – this confirms who has answered the call and that the call is welcome. This will also provide a professional image of the business to the caller.

When taking a booking by telephone the procedure shown below might be used.

- When the telephone rings, lift the receiver and say either: 'Good morning', 'good afternoon' or 'good evening' (then state the name of the establishment). 'How may I help you?'
- If the customer is making the booking in person, say either: 'Good morning', 'good afternoon' or 'good evening' and address the caller as 'Sir' or 'Madam', then ask, 'How may I help you?'
- When taking the booking the essential information required is as listed on page 160.

- When you have received this information from the customer and made your notes, the full details of the booking should be repeated back to the customer to check that you have understood the customer's requirements properly and to give the customer the opportunity to confirm the details.
- At the end of a telephone call for a booking you should say: 'Thank you for your booking, we shall look forward to seeing you on (then confirm the date and time).'

Written – recording orders, bookings

All written communication between the business and customers or suppliers should be carried out within the establishment's guidelines. Standard templates should be used where information is inserted; this aids clarity, avoids mistakes and confusion and reduces errors in spelling and grammar, which in turn reflects a professional image of the business to the customer or supplier.

Respond to customers during service

Requests

Customers will often have requests during service, which should be dealt with politely and efficiently. If you are unable to satisfy their request either explain why or seek assistance from your supervisor or manager.

Questions

Customers always have questions; staff should remember that for the customer it may be the first time they have asked this question – no matter how many times the staff members have heard or answered the question. Deal with the questions politely and give honest answers. If staff are unable to answer the question they should seek advice from a supervisor or manager and get back to the customer with the answer as soon as possible.

Compliments

Throughout a service, customers may offer compliments for the following reasons:

- The quality of the food and drink
- The food and drink have exceeded their expectations
- The service staff have provided excellent service
- The customer's needs have been acted upon
- The customer has received an unexpected level of courtesy
- Staff have gone out of their way to help.

It is important that the staff member acknowledges compliments, thanks the customer and then passes on the comments to the relevant person or department. It may be appropriate to suggest that the customers show their appreciation – either by filling in the customer feedback form online or on another online rating site such as TripAdvisor or OpenTable – perhaps requesting that the staff member's name is used. It is now more common for a business to recognise customer compliments as an incentive and reward their staff accordingly in the form of a staff bonus or a promotion.

Complaints

Valid complaints provide important feedback for a food service operation and can be used as valuable learning opportunities to improve service.

When a problem arises, a customer may make a complaint because, for example:

- service is slow
- food is cold when served
- wine is served at the incorrect temperature
- their reservation is not recorded in the booking diary
- the server has been inattentive
- the wrong dish is brought to the table
- explanation of the menu is inaccurate
- poor attitude of staff.

Level of responsibility

Most customer complaints can be handled by the waiting staff but it is always advisable to inform your supervisor immediately and make them aware of the issue raised and what you have done so far to deal with it. This will allow the manager to be proactive – should he or she wish to deal with the customer directly or to follow up on the complaint.

There are occasions where the customer complaint must be referred to the supervisor or manager. The reasons can include:

- complaints about specific members of staff
- complaints about poor levels of service
- ongoing issues that have failed to be resolved by the service staff
- confidential issues that require a level of discretion
- requests for refunds, reimbursement or compensation
- customers or staff requesting that items not be charged for
- customers who become argumentative or aggressive.

Procedure for dealing with complaints

Staff should never show their displeasure or argue with a customer, even during a difficult situation. If they are unable to resolve a situation, they should refer immediately to a senior member of the team. They should be able to reassure the customer and put right any fault quickly, as time spent dealing with complaints only makes the situation worse.

The following steps should be taken when dealing with a complaint:

- Do not interrupt the customer – let them have their say and make their point.
- Apologise – but only for the specific problem or complaint.
- Restate the details of the complaint briefly back to the customer to show you have listened and understood.
- Agree with the customer, by thanking the customer for bringing the matter to your attention. This shows you are looking at the problem from the customer's perspective.
- Act quickly, quietly and professionally and follow the establishment's procedures for handling complaints.

Never:

- lose your temper
- take it personally
- argue
- lie
- blame another member of staff or another department.

Also see Unit 202, 1.4 Impact of poor customer service on page 48.

Building customer rapport

Food service team members must be able to build a rapport with customers. The development of an understanding and harmonious relationship between the customers and service staff can have the following benefits:

- An improved meal experience for the customer
- Increased revenues and sales
- Increased tips
- Loyalty and repeat business
- Customer referrals
- Business reputation
- Improved staff motivation
- Improved atmosphere.

Building rapport with new customers can be very rewarding, it puts the customer at ease and adds to their experience. Asking about their day, their experiences, likes and dislikes about food and drink can also assist you in helping the customer make an informed choice from the food and beverages on offer.

To help build a rapport with customers, staff should have a reasonable knowledge of the local area in which they work so they may be able to advise customers on the various forms of entertainment offered, the best means of transport to take to places of interest, parking and so on.

Dealing with incidents during service

During service there can be unexpected situations. A well-managed operation will have procedures in place to deal with such incidents. It is important to deal with incidents promptly and efficiently without causing more disturbance than is necessary to the other customers.

Quick action will usually soothe an irate customer and enable a good impression of the waiting staff and the establishment to be maintained. Complaints, of whatever nature, should be referred immediately to the supervisor – any delay will only cause confusion and very often the situation may be interpreted wrongly if it is not dealt with straightaway. In the case of accidents, a report of the incident must be kept and signed by those involved.

Customer illness

If a customer falls ill in your establishment then the steps below might be taken.

1   As soon as it is noticed that a customer is feeling unwell, a senior staff member should be called immediately.

2 If the customer is a woman then a female member of staff should attend her.

3 The senior staff member must enquire if the customer needs assistance. At the same time, she or he must try to judge whether the illness is of a serious nature. If in any doubt it is always better to call for medical assistance.

4 It is often advisable to offer to take the customer to another room to see if they are able to recover in a few minutes. If this happens, their meal should be placed on the hotplate until their return.

5 If the illness appears to be of a serious nature, a doctor, nurse or someone qualified in first aid should be called immediately. The customer should not be moved until a doctor has examined him/her.

6 If necessary, the area should be screened off.

7 Although this is a difficult situation to deal with in front of the general public, minimum fuss should be made and service to the rest of the customers should carry on as normal.

8 The medical person will advise whether an ambulance should be called.

9 The customer may have had a sudden stomach upset and wish to leave without finishing the meal. Assistance should be offered in helping the customer leave the restaurant.

10 Payment for the part of the meal consumed and any ensuing travel costs would be according to the policy of the establishment.

11 It is most important that for all accidents (minor or serious) all details are recorded in an accident book. This is in case of a claim against the establishment at a later date.

12 If after a short period of time the customer returns and continues with the meal, a fresh cover should be laid and the meal returned from the hotplate or a new meal served.

Dress code

If a customer's appearance does not meet the dress code policy of the establishment, the following steps might be taken.

1 The customer should be asked to correct their dress to the approved fashion required by the establishment – or so that it does not cause offence to others.

2 Staff should be made aware of the need for sensitivity towards cultural dress.

3 If the customer will not comply with the request, he or she should be asked to leave.

4 If they have partly consumed a meal, then whether they will be charged or not depends on the policy of the house and the discretion of the head waiter or supervisor.

5 A report of this incident must be made and signed by the staff concerned.

Supporting customers with additional needs

See Unit 202, page 43 for guidelines on supporting customers with additional needs relating to mobility, sight and communication difficulties.

2 FOOD SERVICE SKILLS

Developing good technical skills is essential for three main reasons:

1 It helps to develop greater confidence in undertaking technical service tasks.
2 It allows servers to concentrate on their social skills and increases their contribution to achieving excellence in the service.
3 It increases efficiency and reduces the risks of accidents.

There are six basic technical food and beverage service skills. These are identified in Table 5.2 below, together with examples of their application.

▼ **Table 5.2** Technical service skills and their application

Technical skill	Examples of application
1 Holding and using a service spoon and fork	For the service of food at a customer's table, especially for silver service, and for serving at a buffet or from a trolley
2 Carrying plates	When placing and clearing plates from a customer's table
3 Using a service salver (round tray)	For carrying glasses, carrying tea and coffee services, as an under liner for entrée dishes and for potato and vegetable dishes
4 Using a service plate	For carrying items to and from a table, including clean cutlery, clearing side plates and knives, crumbing down and clearing accompaniments
5 Carrying glasses	Carrying clean glasses by hand or on a salver and for clearing dirty glasses from a service area
6 Carrying and using large trays	For bringing equipment or food and beverage items to the service area and for clearing used equipment from the service area

2.1 PREPARE AND SET UP FOR SERVICE

The success of all types of service is determined by the preparation that goes into setting up the service areas. Successful preparation helps staff to provide efficient service and create an ambiance that is attractive and pleasant for the customers.

The three main table service styles are silver service, plated service and family service. In all cases the service is by service staff to customers seated at tables. The set-up tasks and duties are similar for the three different service styles.

The term 'mise en place' (literally 'put in place' but also meaning preparation for service) is the traditional term used for all the duties carried out in order to prepare the area for service. The supervisor will draw up a duty rota showing the tasks and duties to be completed before service and the members of staff responsible for them. When all duties are completed, then the service area is referred to as **'en place'**.

The duties to be carried out before the service begins will vary according to the particular food and beverage service area concerned. A list of the possible tasks and duties is shown below, but not all of these are applicable to every situation and there may be some jobs not listed which are specific to a particular establishment.

The duties should proceed in a certain order so that they may be carried out effectively and efficiently. The duties involved in bar preparation may be included within the duty rota depending upon the type of establishment.

KEY TERM

En place – the traditional term used when all the preparatory duties have been completed.

A suggested order of work might be as follows:

1 dusting
2 stacking chairs on tables
3 vacuuming
4 polishing
5 arrange tables and chairs according to the table plan
6 linen
7 accompaniments
8 hotplate
9 still room
10 sideboards/workstations
11 silver cleaning
12 other duties such as preparing trolleys.

Some of these duties will be carried out at the same time and the supervisor must ensure they are all completed efficiently.

As the necessary preparatory work is completed the staff report back to the supervisor, who will check that the work has been carried out in a satisfactory manner. The supervisor will then re-allocate the member of staff to other work involved in the setting up of the service areas.

The duties to be carried out before the service commences will vary according to the particular food and beverage service area concerned. Duties will include:

- Checking that a full team of staff is present and that all duties on the duty rota are covered.
- Checking the booking diary for reservations.
- Making the seating plan for the meal service to come and allocating customers accordingly.
- Making a plan of the various stations and showing where each member of staff will be working.
- Going over the menu with staff immediately before service is due to commence.

There are several service preparation principles that should be followed. These are listed in Table 5.3 together with the rationale for them.

▼ **Table 5.3** Service preparation principles

Principle	Rationale
Use checklists for preparation tasks	Ensures that all members of staff complete all preparatory tasks in the same way
Prepare service areas in sequence	Ensures service areas are laid out and housekeeping duties have been completed before the preparation for service begins. This can save time and unnecessary duplication of effort afterwards
Use a model lay-up	Lay one initial full place setting (cover) to use as a model for all staff to measure against. A place setting is usually about 60 cm wide
Hold glasses or cups at the base or by the handle	This is hygienic practice. Service staff should not hold glasses or cups, etc., by the rim
Hold cutlery in the middle at the sides between the thumb and forefinger	This is safer, makes for more accurate placing of items on the table and also helps to prevent finger marking on the clean cutlery items
Lay table place settings (covers) from the inside out	This makes table-laying easier. Place a centre to the cover (a table mat or side plate, for instance) then lay tableware in order from the inside of the cover outwards. When laying a number of covers it is more efficient to lay each piece of tableware for all covers in sequence, i.e. all side plates, then all side knives, etc.
Place items on the table consistently	Make sure that any crested or patterned crockery or glassware is always placed the same way around on the table, i.e. crests or badges at the head of the cover, and that it is evenly spaced.

Still room

Duties might include:

- the ordering of stores requirements (including bar and accompaniment requirements), to hold over the coming service period
- checking with the supervisor/head waiter the number of accompaniments and sets of cruets to prepare and the number of sideboards/workstations and tables that will be in use during the service period
- the preparation of:
  - beverage service items – for example teapots, coffee pots, cold milk jugs
  - butter scrolls/butter pats and alternatives
  - bread items – for example brioche, croissants, wholemeal rolls, breadsticks and grissini
- polishing and refilling oil and vinegar stands, sugar basins and caster sugar dredgers, peppermills and cayenne pepper pots
- preparing all accompaniments such as tomato ketchup, French and English mustard, ground ginger, horseradish sauce, mint sauce, Worcestershire sauce and Parmesan cheese (grated), oils
- distributing the accompaniments to the sideboards.

Sideboards/workstations

After ensuring that the sideboard/workstation is clean and polished it can be stocked up. Figure 5.2 gives an example of a sideboard lay-up including these items:

1 Water jug	8 Fish knives and forks	13 Service salver/plate
2 Butter dish	9 Soup spoons, tea and coffee spoons	14 Underflats
3 Check pad on service plate	10 Sweet spoons and forks	15 Coffee saucers
4 Assorted condiments	11 Service spoons and forks	16 Side plates
5 Hotplate	12 Bread basket	17 Sweet/fish plates
6 Side knives		18 Joint plates
7 Joint knives		19 Trays

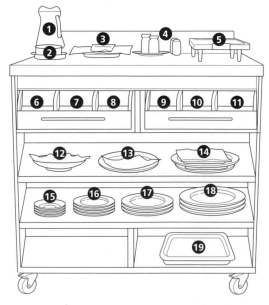

▲ **Figure 5.2** Example of a sideboard lay-up

▲ **Figure 5.3** The laid sideboard

Prepare the area for service

The duties should proceed in a certain order so that they may be carried out effectively and efficiently. For example, dusting should be done before the tables are laid, and vacuuming should be completed before the tables and chairs are put in place. The duties involved in bar preparation may be included within the duty rota depending upon the type of establishment.

The waiting/reception area

Duties may also include the reception area and might involve:

- vacuuming the carpet and brushing surrounds daily
- cleaning and polishing doors and glass
- emptying waste bins
- performing the daily tasks as indicated on the duty rota, for example:
  - Monday: brush and dust tables and chairs
  - Tuesday: polish all sideboards, window ledges and cash desk
- every day, on completion of all duties, line up tables and chairs for laying up.

If drinks and snacks are served in the waiting area, then these should be prepared and covered in readiness for the customers' arrival. Menus and drinks lists should be placed on the tables and if fresh flowers are to be placed on tables these should be checked for freshness (including replacing the water if necessary).

Cloakrooms

These should be swept and tidied ready to receive coats and belongings. Tickets/receipts should be re-stocked and coat hangers tidied. If the toilets are situated in this area they should be checked for cleanliness and re-stocked in readiness for the customers' arrival.

Table plans

These should be checked against the booking diary to accommodate any special requests and large bookings.

Table settings

One of the technical terms often used in the food service industry is a 'cover' (couvert). The term cover has two definitions, according to the context in which it is being used:

- When discussing how many customers a restaurant or dining room will seat, or how many customers will be attending a cocktail party, we refer to the total number of customers concerned as 'so many' covers. For example, a restaurant or dining room will seat a maximum of 85 covers (85 customers); there will be 250 covers (250 customers) at a cocktail party; this table will seat a party of 6 covers (6 customers).
- When laying a table in readiness for service there are a variety of place settings that may be laid according to the type of meal and service being offered. We refer to this place setting as a certain type of cover being laid. In other words, a cover refers to all the necessary cutlery, crockery, glassware and linen required to lay a certain type of place setting for a specific dish or meal.

When deciding on the laying of covers there are two basic service considerations:

1   When cutlery for the meal is to be laid before each course is served – *à la carte* cover.
2   When the cutlery for the meal is to be laid prior to the start of that meal and for all the courses that are to be served – *table d'hôte* cover.

Laying the tablecloth

Before laying the tablecloth, the table and chairs should be in their correct position. The table top should be clean and the table level, with care being taken to ensure that it does not wobble. If the table wobbles slightly, a disc sliced from a cork, a small wedge or an old menu folded neatly can be used to correct the problem. Next, the correct size of tablecloth should be collected. Most tablecloths are folded in what is known as a screen fold.

The waiter should stand between the legs of the table while the tablecloth is being laid, as this ensures that the corners of the cloth cover the legs of the table once the clothing-up has been completed.

The screen fold should be opened out across the table in front of the waiter with the inverted and two single folds facing him, ensuring that the inverted fold is on top.

The tablecloth should then be laid in the manner shown in Figure 5.4.

1   Place the thumb on top of the inverted fold with the index and third fingers either side of the middle fold.

2   Spread out your arms as close to the width of the table as is possible and lift the tablecloth so that the bottom fold falls free. This should be positioned over the edge of the opposite side of the table from where you are standing.

3   Now let go of the middle fold and open the tablecloth out, by drawing it towards you until the table is covered with the tablecloth. Check that the fall of the cloth is even on all sides.

4   Adjustments may be made by pulling from the edge of the cloth.

▶ **Figure 5.4** Laying the tablecloth

If the tablecloth is laid correctly the following should be apparent:

- the corners of the tablecloth should be over (cover) the legs of the table
- the overlap should be even all round the table: 30–45 cm (12–18 in)
- the creases of all tablecloths laid should run the same way in the room.

If two tablecloths are necessary to cover a table for a larger party, then the overlap of the two tablecloths should face away from the entrance to the room. This is for presentation purposes of both the room and the table.

À la carte cover

The *à la carte* cover follows the principle that the cutlery for each course will be laid just before each course is served. The traditional cover, given below (shown in Figure 5.5) represents the cover for hors d'oeuvre, which is the first course in the classic menu sequence. The traditional cover is made up as follows:

- fish plate (centre of cover)
- fish knife
- fish fork
- side plate
- side knife
- napkin
- water glass
- wine glass.

▲ **Figure 5.5** *À la carte* cover

Where an *à la carte* cover has been laid, the cutlery required by the customer for the dishes he or she has chosen will be laid course by course. There should not, at any time during the meal, be more cutlery on the table than is required by the customer at that given moment in time.

Classic or basic lay-up

There are a variety of approaches to what is laid for the *à la carte* form of service. This can include using large decorative cover plates and a side plate and side knife only or replacing the fish knife and fork with a joint knife and fork. This is known as a classic or basic lay-up. An example of this type of lay-up is shown in Figure 5.6.

▲ **Figure 5.6** Classic or basic cover

If decorative cover plates are used for an *à la carte* cover, it is common for the first course plates to be placed on this plate. The first course and the cover plate are then removed when the first course is cleared.

Table d'hôte cover

The *table d'hôte* cover follows the principle that the cutlery for the whole meal will be laid before the first course is served. The traditional cover is made up as follows:

- joint knife
- fish knife
- soup spoon
- joint fork
- fish fork
- sweet fork

- sweet spoon
- side plate
- side knife
- napkin
- water glass
- wine glass.

Again, there are some variations to this approach. The sweet spoon and fork may be omitted, for example, or the fish knife and fork replaced with a side knife and small/sweet fork.

▲ **Figure 5.7** Table *d'hôte* cover

Where a *table d'hôte* cover has been laid the waiter should remove, after the order has been taken, any unnecessary cutlery and relay any extra items that may be required. This means that before the customer commences the meal he or she should have the entire cutlery.

Equipment

▼ **Table 5.4** Equipment

Item	Explanation
Crockery	Service staff should spend time and care getting the crockery ready for service. This task may be allocated to a few members of the team if the quantities are large due to volume of business Duties might include: ● checking and polishing side plates ready for lay-up ● checking and polishing crockery for the hotplate according to the menu and service requirements ● preparation of service plates for sideboards/workstations ● preparation of finger bowls for still room to be used during service for finger foods such as mussels, asparagus, lobster, etc. ● preparation of stocks of crockery for sideboards/workstations, such as fish plates, side plates and saucers
Hotplate	The hotplate is not just for passing food through from the kitchen to the restaurant. Crockery is stored here for the kitchen to access to place food on to and for service staff to retrieve crockery for service in the restaurant. One or more service staff may be allocated the task of getting the hotplate ready for service. Duties might include: ● switching on the hotplate and checking that all doors are closed ● placing items in the hotplate according to the menu offered ● stocking up the hotplate after each service with clean and polished crockery in readiness for the next meal service
Bread baskets	Depending on the service style and price point of the establishment bread is commonly offered to customers from a bread basket. This should be lined with a fresh napkin, either paper or linen ● The bread should be served warm and so placed into the basket for each order ● Staff should be able to silver serve the bread on to the side plate when the customer has made their choice from the basket, and place butter in a dish on to the table for customers to help themselves to ● In some establishments, bread is placed either in the bread basket or on a wooden board with a bread knife, or on to the table for customers to help themselves throughout the service

Accompaniments

Many dishes are normally served with traditional accompaniments, such as:

● Proprietary sauces: ketchup, brown sauce, Worcestershire sauce, Tabasco
● Mustards – such as English, French or Dijon
● Sauces – such as mayonnaise, apple, mint, horseradish, tartare, French dressing or wasabi
● Oils and vinegars
● Salt and pepper
● Sugars and sugar alternatives, such as sweeteners
● Accompaniments for bread – butter and alternatives such as spreads, olive oil and balsamic vinegar
● Other accompaniments may include Parmesan cheese and croutons for soups.

Ambiance

When setting up the service area staff are working towards creating an ambience – this relates to the decor, the lay-up and the atmosphere, temperature, lighting, music and how that makes the customers feel. In addition to the physical elements, the ambience will also be influenced by the attitude of staff towards the customers.

Prepare items required for service

Menus

Menus should be checked prior to service to ensure they are up to date, clean, presentable and replaced where necessary.

Daily specials, menu prix fixe and table d'hôte menus will all need checking too. It is important to ensure there is a sufficient number available to ensure customers have them available when needed.

Menus will need to be easily accessible throughout service and must be continually checked throughout service to ensure they are presentable and removed where necessary.

Cutlery

Service staff will need to prepare sufficient stocks of cutlery to last the whole or a large part of the service period. Sometimes it will be necessary to wash and polish additional cutlery during the service period when demand is high.

Duties might include collection of cutlery from the storage area (sometimes called a silver room) and polishing and sorting on to trays some or all of the following items, in quantities agreed with the supervisor, and in readiness for laying up the tables and setting up the sideboards:

- service spoons
- joint/service forks
- soup spoons
- fish knives
- fish forks
- joint knives
- side knives
- sweet spoons
- sweet forks
- tea/coffee spoons
- specialist service equipment as required, for example soup and sauce ladles
- identifying broken items or those in need of replacing.

Crockery

Please see Table 5.4 on page 175.

Glassware

Duties might include:

- collection of the required glassware from the glass pantry (store)
- checking and polishing glassware needed for the general lay-up
- checking and polishing glassware needed for any special events
- checking and polishing glassware required for any special menu dishes – for example goblets for prawn cocktails, tulip glasses for sorbets, and liqueur, port and brandy glasses for the liqueur trolley
- stacking the cleaned and polished glassware on to trays or placing into glass racks in readiness for setting up or movement to the point of service.

Polishing glassware

The following equipment is required to carry out this technique:

- a container of near-boiling water (sometimes a little vinegar is added as it helps to remove grease)

- a clean, dry tea cloth
- the required glassware.

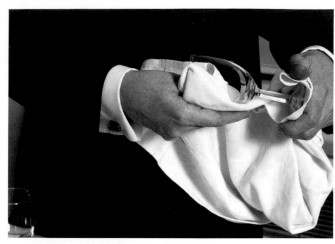

1   Hold the wine goblet over the steam from the boiling water so that the steam enters the bowl of the glass. Rotate the wine goblet to allow the steam to circulate fully within the bowl of the glass and then hold the base of the glass over the steam. Now hold the base of the wine goblet in the clean, dry teacloth. Place the other hand underneath the tea cloth in readiness to polish the bowl of the glass.

2   Place the thumb of the polishing hand inside the bowl of the glass and the fingers on the outside, holding the bowl of the wine goblet gently but firmly. Rotate the wine goblet with the hand holding the base of the glass. When fully polished, hold the wine goblet up to the light to check that it is clean. Ensure that the base of the glass is also clean.

▲ **Figure 5.8** Polishing glassware

The process described here is for single glasses. Larger quantities of glassware may be polished by placing a glass rack full of inverted glasses over a sink of very hot water in order to steam the glasses. A number of people would then work together to polish the glassware.

Linen

Nothing is more attractive in the room than tables clothed-up with clean, crisp and well starched linen tablecloths and napkins. The tablecloths and napkins should be handled as little as possible, which will be ensured by laying the tablecloths quickly and properly first time and folding napkins in the more simple folds, upon a clean surface, and with clean hands.

Linen refers to table, buffet and slip cloths, and glass and waiter cloths. There are also paper slip cloths and napkins plus dish papers and doilies. Duties might include:

- collecting clean linen from the housekeeping department, checking items against list and distributing them to the various service points. Spare linen should be folded neatly into the linen basket
- ensuring that stocks are sufficient to meet needs
- laying tablecloths
- folding napkins
- ensuring that glass cloths and waiter cloths are available
- providing dish papers and doilies as required
- the preparation of the dirty linen basket for return to the linen room.

Laying of cloths is detailed on page 172.

Napkins

The considerations for napkins are the same as for linen above. Napkins may be made of linen or paper. Staff should be reminded that napkins are expensive to buy and launder and should not be used to clean up spillages unless at the customer's table.

There are many forms of napkin (or serviette) fold. Some are intricate in their detail while others are simpler. The simpler folds are used in everyday service and some of the more complex and difficult folds may only be used on special occasions, such as luncheons, dinners and weddings.

The simple folds are better than the more complex ones because:

1 The napkin, if folded correctly, will add to the general appearance of the room, whether it is a simple or complex fold.
2 A simpler fold is more hygienic as the more complex fold involves greater handling to complete. In addition, its appearance, when unfolded to spread over the customer's lap, is poor as it often has many creases.
3 The complex fold takes much more time to complete properly.

Many of the napkin folds have special names, for example:

- Cone
- Bishop's mitre
- Rose
- Cockscomb

- Triple wave (French fold)
- Fan
- Candle.

The four napkin folds shown in Figure 5.9 are some of the more common folds used. These are simpler folds that may be completed more quickly and require less handling by the operator and are therefore more hygienic.

The rose fold of a napkin is one in which rolls or Melba toast may be presented for the table. It is not often used for a place setting. The triple wave is an attractive fold that may also be used to hold the menu and a name card.

Condiments

Table numbers and cruets need to be placed on the tables and this duty will be carried out by the person responsible for condiments.

Duties might include:

- collection of cruets, table numbers and butter dishes from the silver room
- polishing, checking and filling the cruet sets (salt cellars, pepper and mustard pots)
- laying on tables of cruet sets, table numbers and butter dishes with butter knives, according to the establishment standards.

Table decorations

Tables can be decorated in a variety of ways. These include:

- flower decoration such as stems in small vases
- ornamental, such as silver statues or ornaments made of other materials
- lighting, such as candles or tealights
- preparing a floral table decoration.

▲ **Figure 5.9 (a)** Bishop's mitre

▲ **Figure 5.9 (b)** Rose

▲ **Figure 5.9 (c)** Cockscomb

▲ **Figure 5.9 (d)** Triple wave (French fold)

A simple centre table display (posy arrangement) can be made in small shallow bowls, with oasis in the bowl to hold the flowers. Oasis is a green-coloured sponge-like material that holds moisture and is soft enough for greenery and flower stems to be pushed into it to hold them secure.

The oasis should be kept moist to maximise the life of the flowers. Moisture content can be checked by lightly pressing the oasis – it should feel wet. The flowers may also be kept moist by lightly spraying them from time to time with a water gun.

As an alternative, many establishments purchase blooms, often single stem, on a daily basis or as required. These are presented in a single stem vase on the table. This approach is cheaper, less time-consuming and equally effective in providing floral decor for tables.

▲ **Figure 5.10** Centre table posy arrangement

2.2 TAKE AND PROCESS ORDERS
Communicate product knowledge to customers when taking orders

Service staff contribute to the customers' perception of value for money, hygiene and cleanliness, and to the level of service and the atmosphere that the customer experiences – their contribution to the meal experience is therefore vital.

Good food and beverage service staff must have a detailed knowledge of the food and beverages on offer, be technically competent, have well-developed interpersonal skills and be able to work as part of a team.

All members of staff reflect the image of the establishment. They are sales people and must therefore have a complete knowledge of all forms of food and drink and their correct service.

To help customers, staff should be able to:

- describe the **dish content** of food dishes and the wines and drinks on offer in an informative and appealing way that makes the product sound interesting and desirable
- convey **allergen information** and offer advice on **special dietary requirements** and ensure customer preferences are noted
- describe key **cooking methods** used for a dish, such as boiled, grilled, poached, fried, etc.
- inform customers of **timings** for service and how long things will take
- provide information on the **accompaniments** that will be offered with dishes
- give information on **portion sizes** that will also include the weights and measures of food items and beverages, such as 8oz (225 g) fillet steak, 125 ml wine
- provide information on **provenance and ethically sourced products** – for example, know where the food and beverage are produced, grown or manufactured
- give accurate information on **pricing** and additional charges.

Types of information required for orders

When taking the food order it is written from top to bottom of the food check pad.

- Initially, the customers order their first and main courses.
- A second new food check is written out for the sweet course, this order being taken after the main course is finished.
- A third new check will then be completed if any beverages such as coffee, tea or tisanes are required.
- Should the food order be taken from the *à la carte* menu similar procedures are followed except that customers may order course by course according to their needs.

All orders should be recorded correctly. Abbreviations may be used when taking the order as long as everyone understands them, so that the correct order is completed.

To ensure efficient control the server must fill in the following information on the check:

- table number (or room number if the order is for room service in a hotel)
- number of covers
- dishes ordered
- special requests including cooking times and information on dietary requirements and allergens

- portion size – such as large, medium, small
- time and date of order
- customer seating information – when taking orders, a note should be taken of who is having what order. This ensures that specific orders are identified and that they are served to the correct customer. A system for ensuring that the right customer receives the correct food is to identify on the order which customer is having which dish. A check pad design that might be used for this is shown in Figure 5.11
- waiter/service identifier – this can be as simple as a signature or can be a code number.

Take and process orders using different types of equipment

There are four main methods of taking food and beverage orders from customers. These are summarised in Table 5.5.

▼ **Table 5.5** Main methods of taking food and beverage orders

Method	Description
Triplicate	Order is taken: ● top copy goes to the supply point ● second copy is sent to the cashier for billing ● third copy is retained by the server as a means of reference during service
Duplicate	Order is taken: ● top copy goes to the supply point ● second copy is retained for service and billing purposes
Service with order	Order is taken: ● customer is served ● payment is received according to that order, for example bar service or takeaway methods
Pre-ordered	● Individually – for example, room service breakfast ● Hospital tray system ● Events

▲ **Figure 5.11** Check pad design enabling the waiter to identify specific orders

All order-taking methods are based upon these four basic concepts. Even the most sophisticated electronic system is based upon either the triplicate or duplicate method.

- Checks can be written by staff on check pads or keyed in on hand-held terminals.
- Customers can also hand write orders (as in some bar operations) or use electronic systems. There are systems where the menu is projected on to table tops, enabling the seated customers to select their order from these interactive displays.
- The written order is then either communicated by hand to the food production or beverage provision areas, or, for computer-based systems, electronically to visual display units (VDUs) or printout terminals in those areas. The main billing systems used are described in 2.4 Customer bills and payments in this chapter, page 206.

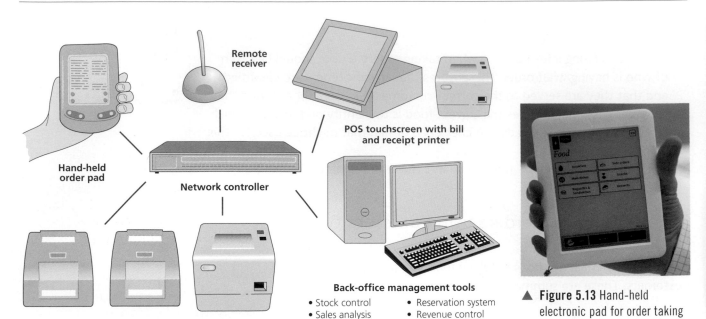

▲ **Figure 5.12** Electronic system for order taking and communication to food production and bar areas

▲ **Figure 5.13** Hand-held electronic pad for order taking

Single order sheet

This is a simple way of checking used in cafés and quick turnover restaurants. It is a simple type of ordering where the order is written on one form and this is handed to the dispense point. Before leaving, the customers pay at the payment point, which is next to the dispense.

Customer self-complete order

A more modern trend is to ask customers to take their own food and drink order. This method is often found in bar operations and it allows staff to concentrate on the service of food (plate service) and on accepting payments. An example of a customer order form is shown in Figure 5.14.

The order for the food and drink requirements, once complete, is taken by the customer to the food till and sent electronically by a member of staff to the kitchen where a printed copy is processed for the kitchen staff to produce the dishes required.

Please note down your table number and choice of meals on this slip. Take it with you and place your order and pay at the food till	TABLE NUMBER	Main meals	
Starters			
Children's meals		Side orders	Drinks
		Desserts, coffees and teas may be ordered at the food till at the end of your meal	

▲ **Figure 5.14** Example of a customer self-complete order sheet

2.3 SERVE DISHES AND ACCOMPANIMENTS
Serve and clear menu items

There are a range of traditional service principles. Examples are given in Tables 5.6, 5.7 and 5.8.

▼ **Table 5.6** Personal service principles

Principle	Rationale
Always work as part of a team	All members of the team should know and be able to do their own job well, to ensure a smooth, well-organised and disciplined operation
Work hygienically and safely	For the protection of other staff and customers from harm and to avoid accidents
Pass other members of staff by moving to the right	Having an establishment rule about each member of staff always moving to the right (or left) when passing each other avoids confusion and accidents
Avoid contact between fingers and mouth or hair	If contact between fingers and mouth or hair, etc., is unavoidable, then hands must be washed before continuing with service. Always wash hands after using the toilet
Cover cuts and sores	Covering cuts and sores with waterproof plasters or dressings is an essential health and safety practice

▼ **Table 5.7** General service principles

Principle	Rationale
Avoid leaning over customers	This shows courtesy and respect for personal physical space. Remember that no matter how clean service staff members are, food and beverage smells do tend to cling to service uniforms. If you are having to stretch across a customer always use the arm furthest away from the customer
Use underplates (liners)	These are used (cold): • to improve presentation on the table • to make carrying of soup plates, bowls and other bowl-shaped dishes easier • to isolate the hand from hot dishes • to allow cutlery to be carried along with the item
Use service salvers or service plates (with napkins or mats on them to prevent items slipping)	Service salvers or service plates are used: • to improve presentation of items to be served • to make carrying of bowl-shaped serving dishes easier and more secure (also avoids the thumb of the server being inside a service dish) • to allow for more than one serving dish to be carried at a time • to isolate the hand from hot dishes • to allow service gear to be carried along with the item(s)
Hold flats, food dishes and round trays on the palm of the hand	This is safer and ensures that the food items are best presented for the customer. It also makes for easier carrying and avoids the server's thumb or service cloth being seen on the edge of flats, dishes and round trays. If the flats or dishes are hot then the service cloth can be underneath, folded and laid flat on to the palm to protect the hand

▼ **Table 5.8** Principles when serving

Principle	Rationale
Serve cold food before hot food	When the hot food is served the service is complete and customers can enjoy the meal without waiting for additional items to be served. For the same reason, accompaniments should be automatically offered and served at the same time as the food item
Serve wine before food	Similar to above. Customers will wish to enjoy the wine with their meal. They will not want to wait for the wine service, as their hot food will go cold
Serve women first	Often done if it does not slow the service. Particular care needs to be taken so as not to confuse things when the host is a woman. A host of either gender is still the host and should always be served last
Serve plated foods from the right-hand side of a customer	Plates can be placed in front of the customer with the right hand and the stack of other plated food is then behind the customer's chair in the left hand. If there is an accident, the plates held in the left hand will go on to the floor rather than over the customer. Plated foods should be placed so that the food items are consistently in the same position for all customers
Silver serve food from the left-hand side of a customer	Ensures that the service dish is nearer the plate for ease of service and to prevent food being spilt on to the person. Customers can more easily see the food being served and make choices if necessary, and members of the service staff are also able to see and control what they are doing
Use separate service gear for different food items	This should be standard. It avoids different food items or sauces being transferred from one dish or plate to another and avoids messy presentation of foods on the customers' plates
Serve foods on to plates consistently	For silver service of the whole main course on to a joint plate, place the main item at the six o'clock position with potatoes served next at the ten past two position and vegetables last at the ten to two position. For main courses with potatoes and vegetables and/or salads served on a separate plate or crescent, the main item is placed in the centre of the main plate with the separate plate or crescent of potatoes and vegetables and/or side salad to the left of this
Serve all beverages from the right-hand side of a customer	Glasses are placed on the right-hand side of a cover and the service of beverages follows from this. For individual drinks and other beverages, the tray is held behind a customer's seat in the server's left hand. Other beverages such as coffee and tea are also served from the right. All beverages should also be cleared from the right
Clear from the right-hand side of a customer	Plates can be removed from in front of the customer with the right hand and the stack of plates is then behind the customer's chair, in the server's left hand. If there is an accident, the plates held in the left hand will go on to the floor rather than over the customer. The exception to this is for side plates, which are on the left-hand side of the cover. These are more easily cleared from the left, thus avoiding stretching in front of the customer

When carrying pre-plated foods and when clearing plates from a customer's table, a single hand is used to hold the plates (usually the left hand) and the right hand is used to place plates on and remove plates from, the customer's table. Special hand positions are used as follows.

1 Illustrates the initial hand position for the first plate. Care must be taken to ensure that the first plate is held firmly as succeeding plates are built up from here. The second plate will rest firmly on the forearm and the third and fourth fingers.

2 Shows the second plate positioned on the left (holding) hand.

▲ **Figure 5.15** Hand positions when clearing plates and carrying plates of pre-plated food and for clearing plates

Order of service of a meal

In the example for the order of service given below, customers are having a starter, intermediate course, main course and dessert, to be accompanied by aperitifs (a pre-meal drink, for example gin and tonic), wine with the meal and then liqueurs. The service in this example is plated service.

1 Greet customers and check to see if they have a reservation.
2 Assist with the customers' coats as required.
3 Offer an aperitif in the lounge or reception area, or if preferred one at their table.
4 If they are to have the aperitif at their table, lead the customers to their table.
5 Assist customers with their seats and place their napkin over their lap (see Figure 5.16a).
6 The order for any aperitifs is taken and the order is then served.

For silver service see page 190 and for clearing while serving see page 193.

The number of customers in a party can be less than the table is laid for. The spare cover(s) laid on the table and the spare chair(s) should be removed. Where there is an uneven number of customers each side of a table, the covers should be positioned so that the full length of the table is used for both sides by making the space even between the covers on each side. This ensures that one customer is not left facing an empty space on the other side of the table.

▲ **Figure 5.16 (a)** Laid table with napkins being placed on to customer's laps and **(b)** menus being presented

Taking orders and adjusting covers

1 Present open menus to each customer, the host last. Bread is offered, butter and alternatives are placed on the table and any chilled water ordered is poured. At this point all the customers at the table will have something to read, drink and eat, so they can be left for a while to allow them time to make their selection.
2 If required explain the menu items and take the food order, usually from the host but each customer may be asked separately. Confirm all the items ordered – together with the style of cooking and sauces ordered.

3   Immediately after the food order has been taken, ask the host if wine is required to accompany the meal. Then adjust the glassware for the wine to be served.
4   Adjust the cover for the first course. In more casual establishments the covers are laid for the first and main course at the beginning of the meal.
5   The wine ordered will be presented to the host to confirm that the correct bottle of wine is about to be opened.
6   The wine or other beverages are always served before the food. Offer the host (or whoever ordered the wine) the wine to taste to assess the quality of the contents and that the serving temperature is correct. The person tasting the wine always has their glass topped up last.

Starters and first course

1   Serve the plated first course(s), cold before hot, and the accompaniments are then offered. Once all plates are on the table, explanations of the dishes are given to the customers.
2   The server will now check the table to ensure everything is satisfactory and the customers have all they require.
3   Wine and water glasses will be topped up as necessary. Remove used or empty glasses.
4   When all the customers have finished their first courses, clear the first course plates using the correct stacking techniques and remove any accompaniments.
5   If not already laid, the covers should be laid or adjusted for the next course.
6   If a different wine is to be served with the next course, the correct glasses should be placed on the table and the wine then served before the food, in the same way as the previous wine. If a new bottle of the same wine is to be served, then this is normally offered with a clean glass for tasting the new wine.

▲ **Figure 5.17** Plated first course being served

▲ **Figure 5.18** Wine glasses being topped up

▲ **Figure 5.19** Plated first course being removed

Intermediate – fish course, soup course

The service of the intermediate course will follow the same procedure as the service of the first course as detailed above.

Main course

1 The plated main course(s) are served from the right-hand side of the customer, cold before hot, and accompaniments offered. When all plates are on the table, explain the dishes to the customers.
2 The server will now check to ensure everything is satisfactory and the customers have all they require.
3 Wine and water glasses will be topped up as necessary.
4 When customers have finished eating their main courses, clear the main course plates and cutlery, side plates and knives, all accompaniments, butter dish and the cruet set using the correct clearing techniques.
5 The table is then crumbed down.

▲ **Figure 5.20** Plated main course being served from the right

▲ **Figure 5.21** Plated main course being cleared

▲ **Figure 5.22** Side plates being cleared

▲ **Figure 5.23** Crumbing down with a 'crumber'

Desserts and cheese

The service of dessert is shown below. For the service of cheese please see page 197.

1 Present the dessert or sweet menu. Advise customers on the dishes as necessary. Take the order and confirm the order back to check it is correct.
2 Covers for the sweet course are laid.
3 Empty or used wine glasses and bottles are cleared away.
4 If wine is to be served with the sweet course, the correct glasses should be placed on the table and then served before the food.
5 The plated sweet course(s) will now be served from the right-hand side of the customer, cold before hot, and accompaniments offered. Once all plates are on the table, explain the dishes to the customers.
6 Offer any appropriate accompaniments such as caster sugar, custard or cream with the sweet course.

▲ **Figure 5.24** Sweet cutlery being put into position

▲ **Figure 5.25** Plated sweet course being served from the right

7 Clear the sweet course and remove accompaniments.
8 The server will now take the hot beverage order for tea, coffee or other beverages if not taken with the sweet order.
9 While the hot beverages are being prepared a drink order for digestifs, such as liqueurs, brandy or port will be taken.
10 Tea and coffee or other beverages will be served. (For further information on the service of tea, coffee and other hot beverages, see Unit 206, page 250 and Unit 207, page 306.)
11 If petits fours (sometimes called friandises) are to be served, then these are offered to the customers or placed on the table.
12 When required the bill will be presented to the host. The server will receive payment from the host. (For billing see 2.4 Customer bills and payment on page 206.)
13 The server will see the customers out, assisting with their coats if required.
14 The table is cleared down and then re-laid if required.

▲ **Figure 5.26** Service of coffee

Silver service

The order of service for silver service is similar to the one given for plated service on page 185. The key difference is in the way the food is served at the table.

First and intermediate courses

For silver service of the first and intermediate courses the plates will be laid in front of each customer, the dishes to be served will be presented to the table and an explanation of the dishes given. The first course(s) will then be silver served to the customers from their left-hand side and any accompaniments will be offered. Some dishes may be served plated, such as soup.

Main courses

- The main course(s) will be silver served to the customer from their left-hand side, and accompaniments will also be offered from the left.
- The correct cover is laid prior to the food item ordered being served.
- Dishes to be served will be presented to the table and explanations given.
- The service cloth is folded neatly and placed on the palm of the hand as a protection against heat from the serving dish.
- The fold of the cloth should be on the tips of the fingers.
- The dish is presented to the customer, so they may see the complete dish as it has come from the kitchen. This is to show off the chef's artistry in presentation.
- The serving dish should be held a little above the hot joint plate with the front edge slightly overlapping the rim of the hot joint plate.
- The portion of food is placed in the six o'clock position (i.e. nearest to the customer) on the hot joint plate.
- When moving to serve the second portion, the flat should be rotated on the service cloth so the next meat portion to be served will be nearest the hot main course plate.
- Note that the portion of food served, on the plate nearest to the customer, allows ample room on the plate to serve and present the potatoes and other vegetables attractively.
- If vegetables are being served on to separate plates, then the main food item (meat or fish) is placed in the middle of the hot main course plate.

▲ **Figure 5.27** Silver service of main course

Potatoes and vegetables

- The general rule is for potatoes to be served before vegetables.
- When serving either potatoes or vegetables, the vegetable dish itself should always be placed on an underflat with a napkin on it. This is for presentation purposes.

- The purpose of the napkin is also to prevent the vegetable dish slipping about on the underflat while the service is being carried out.
- A separate service spoon and fork should be used for each different type of potato and vegetable dish to be served.
- Note again the use of the service cloth as protection against heat and to allow the easier rotation of the vegetable dish on its underflat. This ensures the items to be served are nearest the hot main course plate.
- With the serving dish in its correct position the potato dish nearest the hot joint plate should be served.
- The potato dish served is placed on the hot joint plate on the far side, in the two o'clock position, allowing the server to work towards themselves as they serve the remaining food items ordered and making it easier to present the food attractively. Any vegetables to be served are therefore placed on the hot joint plate nearer to the server and in the ten o'clock position.
- Creamed potato is served by placing the service fork into the service spoon and then taking a scoop of the creamed potato from the vegetable dish. This is then carried to the hot main course plate and the fork moved slightly. The potato should then fall off on to the plate.

▲ **Figure 5.28** Silver service of potatoes and vegetables

Figure 5.28 shows the use of an underflat under the potato and vegetable dishes. It also indicates:

- how a variety of potatoes and vegetables can be served at one time by using a large underflat
- the use of a service cloth for protection from heat and to prevent the underflat from slipping
- the correct handling of the service spoon and fork
- the separate service spoon and fork for each different potato and vegetable dish to be served
- service from the left-hand side of the customer.

Sauces

The sauce should be presented in a sauceboat on an underplate, with a sauce ladle.

A ladleful of sauce should be lifted clear of the sauceboat.

The underside of the sauce ladle should then be run over the edge of the sauceboat to avoid any drips falling on the tablecloth or over the edge of the customer's plate.

The sauce should be napped over the portion of meat already served or at the side of the meat, depending on the customer's preference.

Clearing during service

All clearing techniques stem from the two main hand positions shown in Figure 5.15 on page 184.

Clearing soup plates

- The server, having positioned themselves correctly, will pick up the first dirty soup plate on its underplate. This stance allows the waiter to pass the dirty soup service from the clearing hand to the holding hand.
- Using this procedure ensures the dirty plates are held away from the table and customers, reducing the likelihood of accidents.
- Figure 5.29 (step 1) shows one of the two main hand positions, and the first dirty soup plate cleared.
- This dirty soup plate should be held firmly on its underplate with the latter pushed up firmly between the thumb and the first and second fingers.
- It is important that this first dirty soup plate is held firmly as succeeding used plates are built up on this one, meaning there is a considerable weight to be held.
- The third dirty soup plate with its underplate is now cleared from the right and placed on the upper underplate on the holding hand. The above procedure is then repeated each time a dirty soup plate on its underplate is cleared.

1 First soup plate is cleared.

2 The second dirty soup plate on its underplate cleared and positioned on the holding hand.

3 The soup spoon is taken from the lower soup plate to be placed in the upper soup plate.

4 The upper soup plate with its two soup spoons is now placed in the lower soup plate, leaving the upper underplate behind.

▲ **Figure 5.29** Clearing soup plates

Clearing starter and joint plates

- Figure 5.30 shows one of the two main hand positions previously shown in Figure 5.15 (page 184), and the first dirty joint plate cleared.
- The dirty plate should be held firmly pushed up to the joint between the thumb and the first and second finger.
- Note the position of the cutlery: the fork held firmly with the thumb over the end of its handle and the blade of the joint knife placed under the arch in the handle of the fork.
- Any debris or crumbs will be pushed into the triangle formed by the handles of the joint knife and joint fork and the rim of the plate. This is nearest the holding hand.
- Figure 5.30(b) shows the second dirty joint plate cleared and positioned on the holding hand.

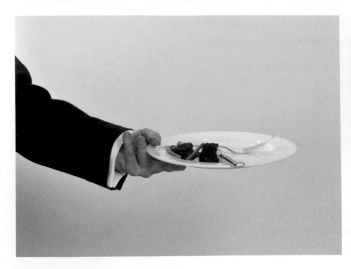

▲ **Figure 5.30 (a)** First joint plate is cleared

▲ **Figure 5.30 (b)** Second joint plate is cleared

Figure 5.31 shows the second dirty joint knife positioned correctly and debris being cleared from the upper joint plate on to the lower joint plate using the second dirty joint fork cleared. This procedure is carried out as the waiter moves on to his next position in readiness to clear the third dirty joint plate.

▲ **Figure 5.31** Clearing debris from the upper plate

▲ **Figure 5.32** Preparing to clear the next dirty plate

Figure 5.32 shows the holding hand with the already cleared items held correctly and ready to receive the next dirty joint plate to be cleared.

Clearing side plates

- Side plates are cleared using a service salver or service plate. The reason for this is to allow a larger working surface on which to clear the dirty side knives and any debris remaining.
- Figure 5.33 illustrates the method of clearing debris from the upper dirty side plate and on to the service salver/plate.

▲ **Figure 5.33** Clearing debris from the side plate to the service plate

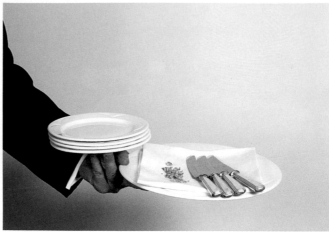

▲ **Figure 5.34** Hand position having cleared four side plates

Figure 5.34 shows the holding hand having cleared four place settings, with the dirty items and debris stacked correctly and safely.

This method generally allows the waiter to clear more dirty side plates and side knives in one journey between sideboard/workstation and table and is especially useful when working in a banqueting situation.

Figure 5.35 shows the dirty joint plates and cutlery correctly stacked, and with the side plates and side knives also being cleared in one journey to the table. This is an alternative to clearing the joint plates and then the side plates in two phases.

Clearing accompaniments

The service plate is also used to clear such items as the cruet, pepper mill or other accompaniments, which may not already be set on an underplate.

Crumbing down

Crumbing down usually takes place after the main course has been cleared and before the sweet order is taken and served. The purpose is to remove any crumbs or debris left on the tablecloth at this stage of the meal.

The items of equipment used are:

▲ **Figure 5.35** Clearing joint and side plates together

- a service plate (a joint plate with a napkin on it)
- a service cloth or napkin, a metal crumber or a crumber brush and pan.

Crumbing down is done from both sides of a customer. The process usually commences from the left-hand side of the first customer. The service plate is placed just beneath the lip (edge) of the table. Crumbs are brushed towards the plate using a folded napkin, a specialist crumber brush or a metal crumber. Then crumbing down is done for the customer to the left.

▲ **Figure 5.36** Crumbing down with a neatly folded napkin

▲ **Figure 5.37** Crumbing down using a metal crumber

▲ **Figure 5.38** Sweet/dessert cutlery in place after crumbing down

Figure 5.37 also shows sweet/dessert cutlery on the table. When crumbing down at each side of the customer the cutlery is moved down. When crumbing between two customers, the fork will be brought down for the customer on your left and the knife brought down for the customer on your right.

Accompaniments

Throughout the meal accompaniments are offered. These can include, for example, sauces, freshly ground pepper from a pepper mill, Parmesan cheese and bread. In all cases accompaniments should be offered and served. Sometimes accompaniments such as bottled proprietary sauces are placed on the table for the customer to help themselves. (See also examples of accompaniments on page 175.)

KEY TERMS

Service enhancements – food and beverages are served from trolleys such as cheese, sweet, carving or drinks trolleys.

Table theatre – sometimes used to refer to service enhancements, such as service from trolleys or guéridon service.

Guéridon – a movable service table or trolley from which food may be served.

Prepare and serve dishes at the table

Service enhancements – sometimes referred to as '**table theatre**' – include service from trolleys. These can include cheese, sweet, carving or drinks trolleys and also **guéridon** service. The various trolleys provide opportunities to use them as selling aids as they display the items on offer to the customers. These service enhancements are, however, costlier to provide as they:

● take longer than plated or silver service
● require a higher level of service skills
● use more expensive and elaborate equipment
● require larger service areas to allow for the movement of the trolleys.

When serving from a trolley, the trolley should always be positioned between the staff and customer as if it were in a shop. Sweet, cheese and drinks trolleys should be attractively presented from the customer's point of view and well laid out from behind for the server. Plates for dirty service equipment should therefore be to the back of the trolley. Staff should explain food or beverage items to customers, either from behind the trolley, to the side of the trolley or standing by the table, but not in front of the trolley. For larger parties the server can go to the customers at the table and then explain the items from there, ensuring that the customers can see the trolley.

When working at a trolley food is not usually served by the spoon and fork technique. Instead, service is with one implement in one hand and another in the other hand, with the service on to plates on the trolley. This is more accurate and quicker.

Always remember to push trolleys and not to pull them. This enables a trolley to be controlled when steering and to ensure it is moved safely to avoid accidents.

Sweet and cheese trolleys

Serving cheese

On a traditional menu the cheese course is served before the sweet/dessert course, but cheese may also be chosen instead of a sweet/dessert course. Cheese is often served pre-plated. The cover is a side knife and small/sweet fork. Cheese may also be served from a selection presented on a cheese board or a cheese trolley.

For service of cheese from a selection the procedure would be as shown in Table 5.9.

▼ **Table 5.9** Service of cheese from a selection

Equipment	<ul><li>Cheese board or cheese trolley</li><li>Sufficient cheese knives for cutting and portioning the different cheeses</li><li>Plates for the service of cheese – often a fish or sweet plate</li></ul>
Cover	<ul><li>Fish or sweet-size plate</li><li>Side knife and sometimes a small/sweet fork</li></ul>
Accompaniments	Accompaniments set on the table may include:<ul><li>cruet (salt, pepper and mustard)</li><li>butter or alternative</li><li>celery served in a celery glass part-filled with crushed ice, on an underplate</li><li>radishes (when in season) placed in a glass bowl on an underplate with teaspoon</li><li>caster sugar for cream cheeses</li><li>assorted cheese biscuits (cream crackers, Ryvita, sweet digestive, water biscuits) or various breads</li></ul>
Method	<ul><li>Ensure the entire 'mise-en-place' (term meaning 'put in place' but also meaning preparation for service) is complete before commencing</li><li>Check that all the cheeses on the trolley are known in order to be able to explain them to the customer</li><li>Check cheeses are properly presented. If cheese is wrapped in foil this must be removed by the waiter before serving. The waiter should remove the cheese rind if it is not palatable (edible). This is not necessary in the case of camembert and brie as the rind of these two French cheeses is palatable</li><li>Present the cheese board or trolley at the table</li><li>Explain the cheeses available to the customer</li><li>Cut or portion the cheeses and present on plates as required; Figure 5.39 gives examples of the methods for cutting, portioning and presenting cheeses</li><li>Present in front of the customer and offer further accompaniments at the table as required</li></ul>

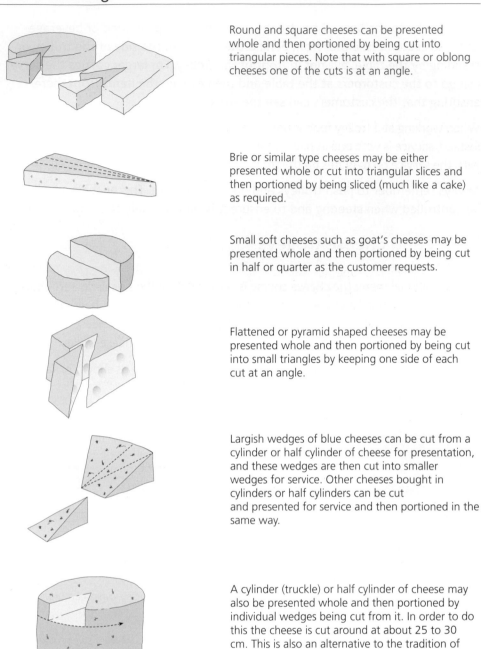

Round and square cheeses can be presented whole and then portioned by being cut into triangular pieces. Note that with square or oblong cheeses one of the cuts is at an angle.

Brie or similar type cheeses may be either presented whole or cut into triangular slices and then portioned by being sliced (much like a cake) as required.

Small soft cheeses such as goat's cheeses may be presented whole and then portioned by being cut in half or quarter as the customer requests.

Flattened or pyramid shaped cheeses may be presented whole and then portioned by being cut into small triangles by keeping one side of each cut at an angle.

Largish wedges of blue cheeses can be cut from a cylinder or half cylinder of cheese for presentation, and these wedges are then cut into smaller wedges for service. Other cheeses bought in cylinders or half cylinders can be cut and presented for service and then portioned in the same way.

A cylinder (truckle) or half cylinder of cheese may also be presented whole and then portioned by individual wedges being cut from it. In order to do this the cheese is cut around at about 25 to 30 cm. This is also an alternative to the tradition of Stilton being portioned by scooping the cheese out from the top of the cylinder after removing the top rind.

▲ **Figure 5.39** Examples of methods for cutting, portioning and presenting cheeses

Serving sweets

Sweets are often served plated or presented in a sweet dish such as a sundae glass. If served from a trolley, then they are plated at the trolley. Cut portions of cakes or pies are normally put on the table so that the point is towards the customer (see Figure 5.40).

There are no particular accompaniments to sweets. The customer may require a sugar sifter or, depending on the nature of the sweet selected, sauces such as custard or sauce à l'Anglaise may be offered. Alternatives to this might be single cream or double whipped cream.

Serving savouries

On the lunch and dinner menu a savoury may generally be served as an alternative to a sweet. In a banquet, it may be a separate course served in addition to either a sweet or cheese course.

Savouries are usually pre-portioned by the kitchen and are served to the customer plated after the cover has been laid and the accompaniments placed on the table. The cover for a savoury is usually a side knife and a sweet fork.

The accompaniments are:

- salt and pepper
- cayenne pepper
- freshly ground pepper
- Worcestershire sauce (usually only with meat savouries).

▲ **Figure 5.40** A plated cake showing the point towards the customer

Serving fresh fruit and nuts as dessert

Dessert may include all types of fresh fruits and nuts according to season, although the majority of the more popular items are now available all the year round. Some of the more popular items are dessert apples, pears, bananas, oranges, mandarins, tangerines, black and white grapes, pineapple and assorted nuts such as Brazils. Sometimes a box of dates may appear with the fruit basket.

The following accompaniments should be set on the table:

- caster sugar holder on a side plate
- salt for nuts.

Service using a guéridon

Guéridon service is an enhanced form of table service. It is normally found in establishments with an *à la carte* menu and higher levels of service. A guéridon is a movable service table or trolley from which food may be served. It carries sufficient equipment for the service requirements, together with any spare equipment that may be necessary.

Guéridon service usually indicates serving foods on to the customers' plates. Guéridon service is also often used to refer to other enhanced service techniques such as service using a drinks trolley, carving trolley, cheese trolley or sweet trolley.

Approaches to guéridon service

When guéridon service is being undertaken all dishes must be presented to the customers at the table before the actual service of the food and especially before the portioning, filleting, jointing, carving or service of any dish. This is so that the customers can see the dishes as the kitchen has presented them before the dishes are served. Customers can also confirm that the orders are correct.

If hotplates or food warmers are used, then these are placed on the left-hand side on the top of the guéridon. These heaters may be gas, electric or methylated spirit.

Procedure for guéridon service

- Guéridon service is essentially a chef and commis service. There must therefore be complete liaison and teamwork between them and the other members of the team.
- Always push the guéridon, never pull it. This helps to control and steer the guéridon in the right direction and avoid accidents.
- The guéridon should be kept in one position for the service of a complete course and not moved from customer to customer.
- Unlike silver service, where the spoon and fork are used together in one hand, guéridon service requires that the spoon and fork are used one in each hand. This gives more control and makes the service quicker.
- The dish is first presented to the customer and the name of the dish is stated, for example, 'Your Dover sole, madam'. The dish is then returned to the guéridon.
- Hot serving plates are placed on the side of the trolley, with the dish for the food to be served placed on to the hotplate.
- The food dishes are then served on to the customers' plates. This may also include portioning, carving, jointing or filleting if necessary.
- When transferring foods and liquids from the service flats and dishes to the plate, always run the fork along the underside of the spoon to avoid drips marking the plate.
- The waiter may then serve the potatoes and vegetables on to the plate while the plates are still on the guéridon. The waiter also serves the sauces on to the plates. The plates are then placed in front of the customers.
- Alternatively, where more than two covers are being served from the guéridon, only the main dish of each customer would be served from the guéridon, with potatoes and vegetables, sauces and accompaniments being served to the customer once the main food items have been served on to the customers' plates and put in front of the customers.
- The commis must always keep the guéridon clear of any dirty or used equipment.
- When the service is finished at one table, wipe down the guéridon and move on to the next table immediately. It will then be ready for the commis coming from the kitchen with a loaded tray.

Carving, jointing and filleting

Carving techniques are craft skills of real value to the food service trade. They are required in restaurants using a carving trolley, in carvery-type operations, for serving at a buffet and for special occasions. In some establishments these tasks are carried out by service staff as part of their usual service duties, especially for guéridon service. In other establishments there may be a specialist carver (trancheur). Carving, filleting and jointing skills are also necessary for counter or buffet assistants.

Never carve on silver or stainless-steel flats or dishes as a knife can ruin them. Use either a carving board or a hot joint plate.

▲ **Figure 5.41** Carving trolley

Carving, jointing and filleting are skilled arts only perfected by continual practice. General considerations are as follows:

- Always use a very sharp knife, making sure it is sharpened beforehand and not in front of the customer. Remember you are going to carve a joint, not cut it to pieces.
- Carving is best achieved by pulling the knife back towards you and not by pushing the knife forwards.
- Use the whole length of the knife in order to let the knife cut the food properly.
- Cut economically and correctly to maximise the portions obtained and to keep wastage to a minimum.
- Work quickly and efficiently to avoid hold-ups in the room.
- Meat is carved across the grain, with the exception of saddle of mutton or lamb, which is sometimes cut at right angles to the ribs.
- The carving fork must hold the joint firmly to prevent accidents. For smaller joints use the fork with the prongs pointed down to hold the food. For larger joints use the fork to pierce the meat to hold it steady while carving.
- Practise as much as possible to acquire expertise in the art of carving and to develop confidence in front of the customer.

Selection of tools

- For most joints a knife with a blade 25–30 cm (10–12 in) long and about 2.5 cm (1 in) wide is required.
- For poultry or game, a knife with a blade 20 cm (8 in) long is more suitable.
- For ham a carving knife with a long flexible blade is preferred. This is often referred to as a ham knife.
- Serrated knives do not always cut better than a plain bladed knife, with the latter giving a cleaner cut.
- A carving fork is needed to hold the joint firmly in position when carving.
- Carve on a board, either wooden or plastic. Avoid carving on china plates or metal. Apart from the damage this can cause (especially with silver), small splinters of metal can become attached to the meat slices.

During service staff must be salespeople and be able to sell the dishes on the menu by giving a brief and accurate description. The carving trolley supplements this by being a visual aid to selling and should be at the table as the waiter takes the orders so that they may suggest and show particular items to the customer.

Presentation of the trolley

- The carver must always ensure that the carving trolley is correctly laid up before it is taken to the table.
- The plate rest for the hot joint plates should be extended and the two containers for gravy and sauces should be already filled. These two containers should always be placed at the end nearest the plate rest. This is for ease of service and also provides the shortest space between the containers and the plates.

- When being used the carving trolley should be placed next to the customer's table, in between the customer and the carver. This ensures that the customer can see every operation performed by the carver and appreciate the skills involved.
- The trolley should be positioned to ensure that the safety valve is on the side away from the carver. This is to ensure that the carver will not be scalded when using the trolley.
- The trolley should be positioned in such a way that the lid is drawn back from the trolley towards the carver so as to reveal the foods to the customer.

See Unit 204, page 144 for guidelines on the equipment required for guéridon service.

Examples of how to serve guéridon dishes

Smoked salmon

▼ **Table 5.10** Smoked salmon

Equipment	<ul><li>carving knife, usually a ham or long thin flat knife</li><li>joint fork</li><li>service spoon and fork</li><li>plate used for service gear</li></ul>
Ingredients	Side of smoked salmon on a board
Accompaniments	<ul><li>cayenne pepper</li><li>freshly ground pepper</li><li>half of lemon wrapped in muslin or segment of lemon</li><li>(traditionally) brown bread and butter</li><li>sometimes chopped shallots and capers are offered together with soured cream</li></ul>
Cover	A fish knife and fork A cold fish plate
Method	1 Ensure all ingredients and equipment are organised before commencing 2 Present the salmon on the board to the customer, or the trolley with the salmon and board on it 3 Ensure that the side of smoked salmon has been prepared for service with the skin being trimmed and any small bones removed using a small pair of fish pliers 4 Carve from the head towards the tail and start about halfway down so that slices will not be too long when laid on to the fish plate for service 5 Remove the black line in the middle of each slice by making a small V-shaped incision at the centre of the side of smoked salmon before carving each slice 6 Carve each slice wafer thin, giving 2–3 slices per portion 7 As each slice is made, use a joint fork to slide the edge of the slice of smoked salmon between the prongs of the joint fork and roll up. Lift over to the cold fish plate and unroll neatly on to the fish plate. Repeat for each slice 8 Serve and offer accompaniments

NOTE

Because of the size of a side of smoked salmon it is often carved on the buffet or on a dedicated service trolley.

Salad

Below is an example of how to serve Caesar salad at the customer's table.

▼ **Table 5.11** Caesar salad

Equipment	<ul><li>salad bowl</li><li>service spoons and forks</li><li>plates or bowls for numbers of covers to be served</li><li>garlic press if not using pre-crushed garlic</li></ul>
Ingredients	Fresh clean, dry salad leaves (cos or Romaine) on a separate joint plate Croutons Grated or shaved Parmesan cheese
Dressing	<ul><li>olive oil</li><li>white wine vinegar</li><li>Dijon mustard</li><li>raw egg yolk (some establishments may substitute pasteurised egg for fresh egg yolk)</li><li>Worcestershire sauce</li><li>salt and pepper</li><li>peeled garlic cloves or pre-crushed garlic</li><li>chopped anchovy fillets</li></ul>
Accompaniments	None
Cover	Small knife Cold plates or bowls with underplates
Method	1 Ensure all ingredients and equipment are organised before commencing 2 Present the guéridon at the table 3 Mix the ingredients for the dressing in the salad mixing bowl using a service fork. These include crushed garlic (depending on the customer's requirements), mustard, dash of Worcestershire sauce, vinegar and raw egg yolk 4 Drip in the oil from a small jug (as for making mayonnaise) and blend this in using a service fork. Two forks may be used as a whisk, in order to make a sauce of creamy consistency 5 Add chopped anchovies 6 Add seasonings to taste (according to the customer's requirements) and stir 7 Put the whole lettuce leaves into the mixing bowl and break into smaller pieces (largish fragments) using a spoon and fork (one in each hand) 8 Add the croutons and fold in 9 Move the salad in the bowl with the service spoon and fork to ensure that it is fully covered by the dressing 10 Present the salad on to the cold plates for service 11 Sprinkle with grated (or shaved) Parmesan 12 Serve

Here are some of the many variations to this salad:

- Replacing the egg that is incorporated into the dressing with a one-minute boiled egg broken over the salad just before serving.
- Making the dressing by incorporating two or three chopped anchovy fillets into basic vinaigrette that has been seasoned with garlic and some horseradish cream.
- Substituting English mustard for Dijon.
- Garlic is usually used but some variants involve rubbing this over the wooden bowl before making the salad, while others use chapons (garlic croutons).
- Other ingredients that might be used include Roquefort cheese and seasonings such as Tabasco.

- Some recipes keep the anchovy fillets separate and then decorate the salad with them rather than incorporating them, chopped, into the dressing.
- Some variations also include sprinkling with freshly ground pepper and lemon juice.

Steak Diane

▼ **Table 5.12** Steak Diane

Equipment	<ul><li>lamp</li><li>pan on an underplate</li><li>service spoons and forks in a napkin on a service plate</li><li>teaspoon for the parsley</li><li>plate for placing used service gear on</li></ul>
Ingredients	<ul><li>sirloin steak batted out thinly</li><li>olive oil</li><li>butter</li><li>French mustard</li><li>Worcestershire sauce</li><li>salt and pepper</li><li>chopped shallots</li><li>sliced mushrooms</li><li>chopped parsley</li><li>small jug of double cream</li><li>one measure of brandy</li></ul>
Accompaniments	None
Cover	Joint knife/steak knife and fork Hot joint plate
Method	1 Ensure the guéridon is correctly laid up with all the mise en place 2 Present the guéridon at the table 3 Ask the customer how they would like their steak cooked 4 Heat about one sweet spoon of olive oil in a pan 5 Add a knob of butter and melt, blending with the heated olive oil (Figure 5.42a) 6 Add the shallots and mushrooms and cook gently on a low heat (Figure 5.42b) 7 Season the steak and smear both sides with French mustard (Figure 5.42c) 8 Cook the shallots and mushrooms until part done 9 Move the shallots and mushrooms to the side of the pan 10 Raise the heat and add the steak to the pan, sealing and cooking on both sides (Figure 5.42d) 11 Flame the dish with the brandy (Figure 5.42e) 12 Now season the steak with Worcestershire sauce 13 Add double cream to enhance the sauce and mix in well (Figure 5.42f) 14 Taste the sauce and adjust seasoning if required 15 Serve from the pan on to a hot joint plate and use a teaspoon to sprinkle the chopped parsley on the steak

NOTE

There are many variations in the making of Steak Diane, each done to an establishment's traditional recipe or being a speciality of the waiter who is making the dish.

▲ **Figure 5.42 (a)** Blend in the butter with the heated oil,

▲ **Figure 5.42 (b)** Add the shallots and mushrooms

▲ **Figure 5.42 (c)** Smear both sides of the steak with French mustard

▲ **Figure 5.42 (d)** Add the steak to the pan

▲ **Figure 5.42 (e)** Flambé the dish with brandy

▲ **Figure 5.42 (f)** Add double cream to enhance the sauce

▲ **Figure 5.42 (g)** Serve the steak and sprinkle with chopped parsley

Banana flambé

▼ **Table 5.13** Banana flambé

Equipment	<ul><li>lamp</li><li>pan on an underplate</li><li>service spoons and forks</li><li>plate for used service gear</li><li>carving board</li><li>small carving knife (12.5 cm, 5 ins)</li></ul>
Ingredients	<ul><li>one banana</li><li>one measure of dark rum (or Pernod depending on the recipe/dish)</li><li>knob of butter</li><li>caster sugar (if preferred, Demerara sugar may be used)</li><li>fresh orange juice (optional)</li></ul>
Accompaniments	Caster sugar, and sometimes vanilla ice cream
Cover	Sweet spoon and fork Hot sweet plate
Method	1 Ensure the entire mise en place is complete before commencing 2 Present the guéridon at the table 3 Prepare the banana at the guéridon, as explained on page 144 4 Place the pan on a low heat and, sprinkling the base with caster sugar, melt until light golden in colour 5 Blend the melted sugar and butter together using the back of the service fork (Figure 5.43a) 6 Place the butter in the pan and allow to melt 7 Pierce the banana carefully with the prongs of the service fork; this will allow the heat to penetrate when in the pan. If care is not taken here the banana may break 8 Carefully place the banana rounded side down in the pan and heat (Figure 5.43b) 9 Baste with the butter and sugar mixture. Colour slightly and then turn the banana over 10 Be careful not to overheat the banana or to cook for too long, as it will become too soft 11 When the sauce is golden brown add a little fresh orange juice and blend well. This produces the sauce and removes the surplus fat from within the sauce 12 When heated sufficiently, flambé with the rum (Figure 5.43c) 13 Serve on a hot sweet plate at the flambé trolley or serve at the table from the pan on to the hot sweet plate (Figure 5.43d)

▲ **Figure 5.43 (a)** Blend melted sugar and butter together

▲ **Figure 5.43 (b)** Place the banana rounded side down into the pan

▲ **Figure 5.43 (c)** Flambé with rum

▲ **Figure 5.43 (d)** Service of banana

2.4 CUSTOMER BILLS AND PAYMENTS
Types of systems and equipment used for customer billing
Till and POS terminal

KEY TERM

Electronic point of sale (EPOS) – system that allows orders to be sent to departments for preparation, for billing and for reordering of stock.

- Customers may be required to pay at the point of service, at the till.
- Staff enter in the customer order and a bill is generated in the **electronic point of sale (EPOS)**.
- This is sometimes also referred to as simply a point of sale (POS) terminal.
- The customer will see displayed their total and may then pay in either cash or use a Chip and PIN machine or swipe their card.

The systems that are used to support the various order taking and billing methods are summarised in Table 5.14.

▼ **Table 5.14** Order taking and billing method control systems

Method	Description
Manual systems	Handwritten duplicate or triplicate checks for ordering from kitchen and bar and for informing the cashier. Often used with a cash till or cash register. Found in independent restaurants and cafés
Pre-checking system	Orders entered directly on to a keyboard; each order check is printed with a duplicate and retains a record of all transactions. Keyboard may be pre-set or pre-priced. Found in many full-service restaurants
Electronic cash registers	Allows for a wider range of functions including sales analysis. Installed as standalone or linked systems. Found in store restaurants, cafeterias and bars
Electronic point of sale (EPOS) control systems	Separate keyboard terminals in the various service areas, linked to remote printers or visual display units (VDUs) in the kitchen, bar. Terminals can be fixed or set in docking stations for hand-held use. In hotels this equipment may also be linked to the hotel accounting systems. More sophisticated systems (point-of-sale, computerised and satellite) provide for increasingly efficient service at the point of sale, as well as improving the flow and quality of information to management for control purposes
Computerised systems	Enable a number of serving terminals, intelligent tills and remote printers to be controlled by a master unit compatible with standard computer hardware. Functions may also include a variety of performance measures such as planning and costing, sales analysis, gross profit reporting, stock control, reordering and forecasting, VAT returns, payroll, staff scheduling and account information. Often found in hotels, fast food and chain restaurants
Satellite stations	Remote terminals linked by telephone to a central processor to enable sales performance to be analysed (usually overnight) and reported back. These systems are found in fast food and chain restaurant operations

Stationery

At the payment point the cashier should retain spare stock of till rolls, pens, manual check pads in case of EPOS till point failure and credit card run-off slips to manually record card details in the event of electronic card machine failure.

Chip and PIN machines

Chip and PIN means that the customer enters their PIN (personal identification number) into a keypad when they use a credit, debit or charge card for face-to-face transactions in shops, hotels or restaurants.

- The POS terminals provide step-by-step instructions on how to complete a transaction.
- Customers *must* enter their own PIN – it is not secure for a member of staff to do it and customers are required not to reveal their PIN to anyone.
- The prompts on the POS terminal screen are followed and the payment is processed.
- The card is then removed from the card reader.
- The receipt is issued, and the receipt and the card are returned to the customer.

For payments in restaurants there are two ways of dealing with payments:

- The customer may be asked to come to the cash desk or workstation to complete the payment transaction there – some customers may prefer this.
- A hand-held self-powered terminal is taken to the customer at their table.

Some establishments may limit how many cards can be used to pay one bill.

Contactless payment

Most card issuers now offer contactless payment built in to their credit/debit cards along with the introduction of contactless mobile phone payments. If the business has opted to accept this method of payment, then consideration of the £30 limit must be made.

If problems are experienced during the operation of the card Process Data Quickly (PDQ) machine and the operator is unable to process the transaction, then a backup manual card swipe system can be used.

Methods of payment

Cash

Customers may choose to pay all or part of the bill in cash. This payment is normally made in the currency of the country. When accepting cash, always check the notes to see if they are current. Some operations use an ultraviolet scanner to check if notes are genuine.

There may be instances where the customer may wish to use a foreign currency. If foreign currency is offered for payment, there will be agreed procedures to be followed by the establishment.

▲ **Figure 5.44** Electronic point of sale billing and payment system

▲ **Figure 5.45** Example of a hand-held credit/debit card payment terminal with printer

Cards

▼ **Table 5.15** Methods of payment by card

Type of card	Description
Credit cards	These allow customers to spend up to a pre-determined limit. The customer receives a statement of payments at the end of each month, which can then be paid off in full or in part. Interest is charged on any remaining balance
Debit cards	Used in a similar way to a credit card but the amount due is immediately deducted from the customer's bank account. Examples include the Maestro card
Charge cards	These work in a similar way to credit cards, but the customer is invoiced once a month. The account must then be paid up in full. Examples include the American Express and Diners Club cards

Cash equivalents

Deposits and prepayments

Customers may have already paid part or all of the amount billed. They may also have a prepaid gift card for a specific amount. The bill will be made up in the same way as other bills. The amount or deposit will be deducted from the total payable. If all the costs have been prepaid in full then the customer is given a bill showing that nothing is owing. If there have been additional charges, then the bill will be presented showing these separately.

Discounts

Customers may be entitled to a discount – for example, they may belong to a loyalty scheme.

Customers may also be allowed a discount at the discretion of the manager. Discounts can be a percentage of the total price, or a specific amount. The bill is made up in the normal way, the discount is deducted and the bill is then presented to the customer for payment.

Vouchers and tokens

Vouchers, such as luncheon vouchers, may be offered in exchange for food in those establishments that accept them. The vouchers have an expiry date. Should the food purchased be above the value of the voucher, the difference must be paid in cash.

Tokens might be exchanged for specific meals or for certain values. If the price of the food purchased is more than the value of the token, then the difference is again paid in cash. No change can be given for purchases valued at less than the token being exchanged.

Travellers cheques

These may be issued in sterling, US dollars, euros and other currencies. The travellers cheque must be signed once when issued and again when used as payment or when exchanging for cash. The rate of exchange will be that at the time of the transaction. All travellers cheques come in different values and this value is guaranteed as long as the two signatures match.

Additional charges

There may also additional charges:

- Service charge – usually an optional charge based on a percentage of the total bill, such as 10 or 15 per cent.
- Special requests such as flowers or a cake for a customer's celebration.
- Room hire for when the service has been provided in a private room.
- Corkage charge per bottle or per person for where a customer has been allowed to bring in their own wines or other beverages.

Although VAT is included in prices, it is often shown as a separate amount on customer bills. The bill will also have the VAT registration number of the operation. This then becomes what is known as a VAT receipt.

Prepare customer bills for payment with relevant information

In order to process a customer's bill quickly and efficiently care should be taken to ensure the correct information appears on the bill. The majority of this information will be automatically generated within the EPOS system or till. The bill should include the following information:

- Date of visit and time of payment
- Number of covers served at the table
- The table number or name of the customer
- Prices of the items ordered and the quantity
- Totals of all the items added together – this can be split into food and drink and show any pre- or post-meal drinks consumed at the bar.

The seven basic billing methods are described in Table 5.16.

▼ **Table 5.16** Billing methods

Method	Description
1 Bill as check	Second copy of order used as bill
2 Separate bill	Bill made up from duplicate check and presented to customer
3 Bill with order	Service to order and billing at same time, for example bar or takeaway service methods
4 Pre-paid	Customer purchases ticket or card in advance, either for specific meal or specific value
5 Voucher	Customer has credit issued by a third party for either a specific meal or specific value, for example, a luncheon voucher or tourist agency voucher
6 No charge	Customer not paying – credit transaction
7 Deferred	Refers to, for example, event catering where the bill is to be paid by the organiser, or customers who have an account

All billing methods are based upon these seven concepts. The main systems used to support these methods and the different payment methods are listed in Table 5.14 (see page 206).

PALM COURT RESTAURANT & LOUNGE
The Langham, London
VAT: 672331741

1014 No11   1

T15/1   1546   GST 2
10NOV'13 21:30

----

1 053 LP NV Half   40.00
1 Dec. Sp 750ml   5.00
1 Gravadlax   14.00
1 Scallops 3 pcs   14.00
2 Fillet Steak   56.00
2 Chips   7.50
  2 SAUV BLNC, 125ML
2 Open Beverage   16.00
3 GL Pinot Noir   46.50
1 SharingPetitFour   10.00
  SUBTOTAL   205.00
  12.5% SERV CHG   26.13
21:30 TOTAL DUE   GBP235.13
  39.19 VAT 20.0%   235.13

Gratuity:_____

Name:_____

Room:_____

Signature:_____
A discretionary (2.5% Svc Charge
has been added to your total.
VAT: 672331741

▲ **Figure 5.46** Example of a bill

Process customer payments in line with current legislation and procedures

Types of payment:

- **Cash**. When accepting cash, the amount of cash received by the operator should always be discreetly checked in front of the customer and when change is given it should be counted back to the customer. Any notes received by the operator should be checked to ensure they are not forgeries. An itemised and receipted bill should always accompany the change.
- **Cards**. On receipt of a credit, debit or charge card, the operator should check that it is still valid by looking at the dates on the card. Most credit/debit/charge cards are now verified using Chip and PIN but, in some instances, they may be signature-verified.

Table 5.17 details some of the issues that can arise when taking payment by card.

▼ **Table 5.17** Problems that can arise when taking payment by card

Problem	Explanation
Declined transactions	Procedures for declined transactions are the same for any credit card/debit/charge card payments, whether signature-verified or Chip and PIN. If a card is declined, always ask for an alternative method of payment ● Cards that have been declined may have a warning message appear on the EPOS or hand-held reader ● If this is the case the card should not be returned to the customer. Ask the customer to come to the payment point and call the card company, who may wish to talk to the customer to confirm they are the card holder and not using it fraudulently ● Once the card company is satisfied either way they will inform you as to what they wish to be done with the card and customer next. Always follow their instructions
Locked PIN	If the customer enters the wrong PIN three times in a row, the card will become temporarily unusable. ● Customers can unlock their PIN by contacting their card issuer ● Contact numbers are on the back of most cards and most cash machines have an unlock PIN facility
Signature verified	This is a manual system in which the validity of the card is checked, often through an online or dial-up connection to the card issuer, by passing it through an electronic card reader ● Once verified, the details of the transaction are printed in the form of an itemised bill, which the customer is asked to sign. A copy of this itemised bill is given as a receipt ● Some establishments also make out a sales voucher. The customer is requested to sign the voucher, after which the operator should check the signature with that on the card. The customer receives a copy of the voucher as a receipt

Taking payment from people with disabilities

The procedures for taking payment are generally the same as described above. However, some additional considerations are given below.

1 Offer to assist when needed and most importantly exercise patience to ensure that the customer has enough time to complete a stress-free transaction.
2 Make sure all customers, including those who use wheelchairs, can easily reach the desk or table to sign the bill or to access the PIN pad.
3 Follow the terminal prompts – some cardholders may have chip and signature cards instead of Chip and PIN cards. Chip and PIN terminals will recognise this type of card and automatically ask for a signature.
4 Encourage or help the customer to pick up the PIN pad from the cradle if appropriate.
5 Suggest that the customer shields the PIN pad from other customers as they enter their PIN.

Travellers cheques

When a payment is made by travellers cheque the customer must:

● date the cheque or cheques required
● make the cheque payable to the establishment concerned
● sign the cheque or cheques for a second time in the space indicated.

The cashier will then:

● match the two signatures
● ask for other identification to check the two signatures against, for example, the customer's passport
● give change where needed; most often this will be in the local currency.

Technical issues

While the technologies available for billing and processing payments are, in the main, very reliable, there may be occasions where internet connectivity is unavailable and therefore digital payments such as credit/debit cards and contactless payments cannot be taken. There are a number of solutions to ensure you can get payment from customers.

- Ask the customer for another form of payment – cash, cheque, vouchers.
- Request that the customer visits a nearby ATM and draws the money for payment.
- See if another member of the customer's party has cash payment.
- Take the customer's personal details and arrange a time to ring them and take an 'over the phone' payment – this is not always allowed by the processing bank of the business, so it is imperative that this is confirmed by the manager before doing so.
- Use the manual card swipe system to take payment and verify the funds are available by calling the card issuer.

Dealing with discrepancies

When dealing with cash, do not allow anyone to interrupt you during the transaction or to get involved with the counting of money as this will only lead to confusion.

- Always double-check cash received before placing it in the till and any change before giving it out.
- If you make a mistake always apologise and remain polite. If you feel you cannot deal with a situation, ask for assistance from your supervisor or manager.
- Banknotes should be checked for forgeries and if found to be fake then they must not be accepted. You should explain why you cannot accept them, advising the customer to take the note to the police station.
- If credit card fraud is suspected the credit card company may request that the card is retained. Suggest to the customer that they contact the company to discuss the matter. You may wish to offer the use of a telephone with some privacy.

Documentation

Record keeping is essential for food and beverage operators. This is to ensure the control of revenue, stock and financial accounting and also to be able to respond to any customer queries.

Sales summary sheets

At the end of a service period sales summary sheets are produced. These are also known as restaurant analysis sheets, bill summaries or records of restaurant sales.

The purpose of the sales summary sheet is to provide:

- a way of checking and ensuring the revenue receipts match the items sold
- the reconciliation of items with different gross profits
- sales mix information
- records of popular/unpopular items

- records for stock control
- details of any overcharges.

It may also include breakdowns of individual staff sales or specific till sales.

There are many different formats for sales summaries and these are often electronically produced. Depending on the needs of the establishment, the information may include:

- date
- address of food and beverage outlet (if more than one exists)
- period of service
- bill numbers
- table numbers
- number of covers per table
- bill totals
- analysis of sales, e.g. food and beverages, or more detailed, such as menu and wine and drinks list items
- various performance measures
- cashier's name.

Carry out security checks

When payments are made staff should check that the payment method is valid, check banknotes and coins to see that they are not forged or counterfeit, check holograms, on new UK banknotes check the see-through panel, check the serial numbers and quality of printing. If in doubt, refer the banknote to a supervisor.

2.5 CLEAR AREAS AT THE END OF SERVICE

At the end of service, a range of duties need to be completed. These duties are carried out with or without customers in the service or dining areas. Depending on the type of establishment these duties may be carried out after a meal period, towards the end of the working day or be ongoing throughout the day.

▼ Table 5.18 Clearing duties at the end of service

Item	Clearing duties
Tables	Tables should be stripped and either reclothed or wiped clean, dried and polished before being reset for the next service
Service stations	All service stations should be cleaned down and then restocked with all the cutlery, trays, check pads, etc., required for the next service
Service areas	<ul><li>Service areas should be tidied, any perishable foods should be checked for their use-by dates and disposed of if necessary or covered and date-labelled and placed in fridges</li><li>A stock-count should be carried out and from this a requisition should be made to replenish stock for the next service</li><li>Any dirty equipment should be cleaned/taken to be washed up</li><li>Equipment needed for the next service should be assembled and placed in the correct positions for the next service</li><li>Floors should be swept and mopped</li></ul>
Crockery	Crockery should be taken to be washed up. Where stocks of crockery are kept in the service area, bar or on stations, it should be restocked with clean and polished crockery
Cutlery	Cutlery should be cleared from tables for washing, stock levels in the sideboards should be restocked with freshly polished cutlery

Item	Clearing duties
Glassware	• Glassware should be checked on the tables • Care should be taken as customers often touch the majority of glasses even if they don't use them. It may be easier and safer to remove all glassware and wash, polish and replace them, upturned, on the cleaned tables
Linen	• If tablecloths have not been used they should be either left in situ or carefully refolded, so they can be reused • Soiled linen should be removed and loosely folded and placed in either the dirty linen trolley or directly into the dirty laundry bag • Napkins should be bundled into sets of ten and placed into the dirty linen trolley or dirty laundry bag. All linen should be counted and recorded in the laundry book to check over-charging by the laundry
Fridges	• Fridges need to be checked for out-of-date items. If necessary they should be washed down with hot soapy water and then dried before being restocked • Temperature readings should be taken and recorded • A requisition should be made for stock that is needed for the next service
Equipment	Display equipment, buffets, guéridon trolleys and service utensils should be wiped down and returned to their storage point. All electrical equipment that does not need to be kept running, e.g. hot plates, should be switched off and if necessary unplugged at the end of service
Accompaniments	Sauces, dressings and garnishes should be wiped down, put away in airtight containers, refrigerated as necessary or placed back in their service points
Waste	• Waste should be separated into food waste and other waste • All waste should be removed from the service area at the end of the shift • Bin bags should be tied and lifted from bins, then taken to the appropriate area for disposal • Bins and skips should be cleaned and rinsed daily to keep them clean; this may be performed by porters during the day shift • At all times consideration should be given to sustainability issues, including the recycling of used items, the management of waste and the control of energy

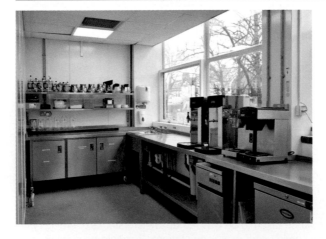

▲ **Figure 5.47** Still room area cleared at the end of service

Test your learning

1 Give **one** reason why it is important that staff create a good first impression.

2 List **three** of the factors contributing to professional appearance.

3 What does 'body language' mean and why is it important in food service?

4 Give **two** reasons why accurate communication is vital to a smooth service.

5 List **five** of the things to be recorded when taking a booking.

6 What is the main reason staff should be briefed before service?

7 List the steps that should be taken when dealing with a complaint.

8 What is the first thing you should do if a customer is unwell?

9 When taking an order, list **three** of the things that must be written on to a food check.

10 Identify and give a short description of **one** of the seven basic billing methods.

11 Give **one** example of an additional charge that might be made over and above the price of food and beverages.

12 List **four** different methods that can be used to pay a restaurant bill.

13 What does EPOS stand for?

14 Briefly describe the process for taking payment using the Chip and PIN system for a credit card, debit card or charge card.

15 Give **one** reason why it is important to carry out security checks.

BEVERAGE PRODUCT KNOWLEDGE

INTRODUCTION

The purpose of this chapter is to help you to gain knowledge of beverages, their characteristics, origins and different styles as well as developing knowledge about their production methods. This chapter also covers the legislation affecting the sale of alcoholic beverages and the consequences of non-compliance.

This chapter will help you to:

- know how different alcoholic and non-alcoholic beverages are made
- make different styles of cocktails
- make different types of coffees and teas
- know and apply the important legislation for serving beverages.

1 PRODUCTION METHODS AND CHARACTERISTICS OF ALCOHOLIC BEVERAGES

1.1 PRODUCTION METHODS AND CHARACTERISTICS OF BEERS

Methods of beer production

Beer is an alcoholic beverage found in most bars and areas dispensing alcoholic beverages. Beers are fermented drinks deriving their alcoholic content from the conversion of malt sugars into alcohol by brewer's yeast. The alcoholic content of beer varies according to type and is usually between 3.5% and 10% alcohol by volume.

Beer is made from four basic ingredients:

- Grains – such as barley, wheat and rye.
- Water – known as liquor.
- Hops – flowers of the hop plant.
- Yeast – known as brewer's yeast.

There are various stages to the beer-making process where sugars from grains (usually barley) are mixed together with the yeast, and through fermentation the liquid becomes alcoholic. Hops and other flavourings are added to provide flavouring and stability to the beer.

Malting

Raw grains are turned into malt. They are steeped in water then heated to allow the grains to germinate, which releases the sugars. They are then roasted at higher temperatures to further dry the grains. Depending on the length of this process, grains can be light roast (called light malt) through to a dark roast (called chocolate malt). The degree of roasting gives a different flavour to the beer. Barley that goes through this process is known as 'malted barley'.

Mashing

During mashing the grains are first milled to break them down to smaller pieces. Water (known as liquor) is added and the mixture (known as the mash) is heated in a 'mash tun'. This process is called steeping. During steeping the enzymes in the grains are activated, which causes them to break down and release sugars. Once this process is complete the water is drained from the mash, which is now full of sugar from the grains. The resulting sticky, sweet liquid is called 'wort'.

Flavouring

The wort is boiled in a large tank called a copper. This removes impurities from the wort. At the start of the boiling, hops are added. The hops are added to add bitterness to the beer. Hops and spices are added at other stages of the boiling process to add additional flavours and aromas to the beer.

Fermenting

Once the boiling is over the wort is cooled and then strained to remove any solids from the mixture. It's then put in a fermenting vessel containing yeast. During this time, the yeast will ferment the beer, creating alcohol and carbon dioxide. Some carbon dioxide is needed to carbonate the beer, the rest is allowed to escape through a vent.

Conditioning and maturing

The resulting liquid is usually transferred to another container to prepare for conditioning. This is also known as maturing or ageing. This process varies between types of beer. Ales are stored for about two weeks at room temperature, while lagers are stored for longer periods at cold temperatures.

The beer can also be conditioned in sealed tanks or bottles with additional wort added so that a secondary fermentation takes place. This makes the beer sparkling. Other beers are cask-conditioned with the secondary fermentation taking place in the cask. The beer is then allowed to mature. Some beers will take a few weeks to mature, while lagers may take up to six months.

Filtering

Some beers are filtered to give them a clear and bright appearance and to stabilise the flavour. This depends on the type of beer being produced – not all beer is filtered. Some are stored to allow the solids in the beer to form sediment at the bottom of the vessel.

Packaging

Cask

Cask-conditioned beer is fermented further in the cask (or barrel). Casks are usually made of oak and hooped with metal bands or metal, but some plastic casks are also available. The liquid absorbs flavours from the cask. Cask beer is not filtered or pasteurised and needs to be carefully handled so that the yeast sediment is not disturbed. Before the beer can be served the cask needs to be tapped, where the tap is added by hammering it into the cask. A shive, which is a round bung with a hole in the centre, is put into the top of the cask and then a small wooden peg called a spile is put into the hole to make it ready to be served. Cask-conditioned beer has a very short shelf life as it is 'live' beer and therefore should only be ordered in quantities that will be consumed within that time. Also see notes on cask beer on page 254.

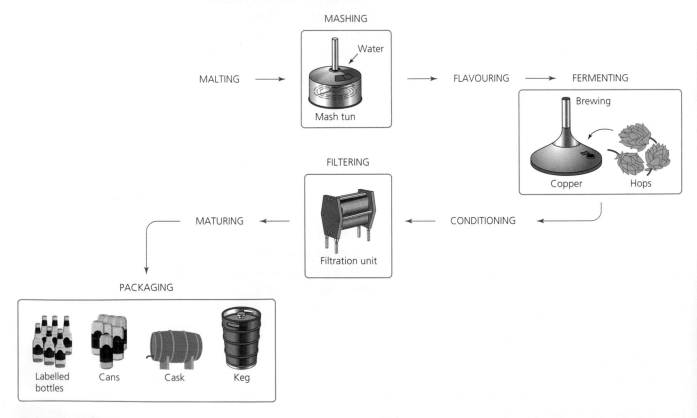

▲ **Figure 6.1** The beer-making process

Keg

To preserve beer for longer it may be put into kegs rather than casks. The beer is pasteurised or filtered to make it stable and filter out anything that might contaminate the beer. The keg is cold conditioned to maintain the flavour and prevent the beer becoming warm and foamy. To get beer out of the keg, gas pressure is applied to the top surface of the liquid, which presses the beer from the bottom of the keg up through a metal tube and out of a valve on top of the keg. The metal used is usually stainless steel which is impervious and therefore the beer arrives with the same flavour as when it left the brewery. Also see notes on keg beer on page 254.

Bottled

Also known as sediment beers, bottle-conditioned beers tend to throw a sediment in the bottle while fermenting and conditioning take place. These beers need careful storage, handling and pouring.

Cans

Draught beers in cans have an internal patented system that produces a pub-style, smooth creamy head when poured from the can. A range of beers are available in this format.

Non-draught beer in cans has carbon dioxide added to the liquid before the can is sealed. Beer packaged in this way often has a slightly different taste and texture than the same beer sold from kegs.

Difference between cask and keg beer

▼ **Table 6.1** Cask and keg beers

Cask	Keg
Not pasteurised or filtered	Pasteurised or sterile filtered
Continues to ferment in the cask	Fermentation is completed before the beer is put in the keg
Requires preparation prior to service (including tapping to serve)	Requires gas pressure to serve and a temperature-controlled chiller
Has a short shelf life so should only be ordered in quantities that will be consumed within that time	Needs to be kept chilled to prevent spoilage and maintain flavour
	Longer shelf life if kept correctly

Types of beer

There are many different types of beer which can be categorised according to the difference in appearance, taste and ingredients. Table 6.2 gives examples of different beer styles.

▼ **Table 6.2** Beer styles

Ales	Ales are usually hopped and are amber in colour
Abbey-style	Ale brewed in the monastic tradition of the Low Countries but also by secular brewers, often under licence from a religious establishment
Barley wine	Traditionally an all-malt ale. This beer is sweet and strong and sold in small bottles or nips (originally 1/3 of a pint, now 190 ml)
IPA (India Pale Ale)	Heavily hopped strong pale ale, originally brewed in the UK for shipping to British colonies. The modern style is a light-coloured, hoppy ale
Old ale	Brown, sweet and strong. Can also be mulled or spiced
Strong ale	Colour varies between pale and brown, and taste between dry and sweet. Alcoholic content also varies
Bitter	Pale, amber-coloured beer served on draught. May be sold as light bitter, ordinary bitter or best bitter. When bottled it is known as pale ale or light ale depending on alcoholic strength
Burton	Strong, dark, draught beer. This beer is popular in winter when it is mulled or spiced and offered as a winter warmer
Mild	Can be light or dark depending on the colour of the malt used in the brewing process. Generally sold on draught and has a sweeter and more complex flavour than bitter
Fruit beers and flavoured beers	Beers with additional flavourings such as heather or honeydew, or fruit beers, which have fresh fruits such as raspberry or strawberry introduced during the making process to add flavour
Wheat/white beer	These beers are pale in colour, lighter in body, have a tart flavour and often carry a sediment. They are traditional beers made with a high proportion of wheat
Lager	These beers are usually pale golden in colour, slightly sparkling and have a mild flavour. The beer is stored at low temperatures for up to six months and sometimes longer. Sold on draught, in a bottle or can
Pilsner	Clear, pale lagers (originally from Pilsen in the Czech Republic, hence the name). Modern styles are characterised by a zesty hop taste and bubbly body
Stout	These beers have a very malty flavour and creamy consistency. They are made from scorched, very dark malt and generously flavoured with hops. Sold on draught or in bottles and traditionally not chilled (although today it often is). Guinness is one example
Porter	Brewed from charred malt, highly flavoured and aromatic. Its name comes from its popularity with market porters working in Dublin and London

1.2 PRODUCTION METHODS AND CHARACTERISTICS OF CIDERS

Cider is an alcoholic beverage obtained through the fermentation of apple juice, or a mixture of apple juice and up to 25 per cent pear juice. Perry is an alcoholic beverage obtained through the fermentation of pear juice and up to 25 per cent apple juice.

Cider and perry are produced primarily in England and Normandy, but are also made in Italy, Spain, Germany, Switzerland, Canada, the USA, Australia and New Zealand. The main areas of production in the UK are the counties of Devon, Somerset, Gloucester, Hereford, Kent and Norfolk, where the best cider orchards are found.

Methods of cider production

Pressing

The apples are picked, left to mature and then milled to create a pulp called a pomace or pommy. The pulp is then pressed in a cider press to remove all of the juice.

Flavouring

Apple-based juice may also be combined with fruit, fruit purées or flavourings to create different flavours of cider. Fruits such as cherries, raspberries or cranberries are used. The fermenting process will also have an effect on the flavour of the cider.

Fermenting

The naturally sugar-rich apple juice is transferred into fermentation vessels. The juice can be fermented straight away or stored for later use. The natural wild, or cultured and introduced yeasts react with the sugar to create alcohol and carbon dioxide (CO_2). Some ciders, particularly from large commercial brewers, will have yeast added during fermentation, with the natural yeasts being removed so that they do not affect the flavour.

Conditioning and filtering

After fermentation is completed, the cider is given time to settle and develop flavours and aromas. This can take several months. Ciders are also blended with old and new ciders to try to achieve a particular flavour. Most commercial ciders are filtered to remove any yeast sediment, leaving a bright clear cider. Traditional ciders are not filtered and are drunk hazy or cloudy.

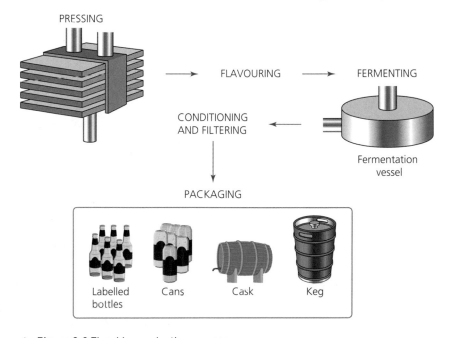

▲ **Figure 6.2** The cider production process

Packaging

Cider can be still or sparkling and can be packaged in different ways. Cider may be packed as a naturally conditioned cask cider, similar to real ale. Similar to beer, cider is also packaged and sold in kegs, bottles and cans.

▼ **Table 6.3** Differences between cask and keg ciders

Cask	Keg
Unfiltered and continues to ferment in the cask	Pasteurised or sterilised and filtered
Requires preparation prior to service including tapping to serve. The cask will need time to settle the sediment to the bottom of the cask, similar to cask beer	Usually carbonated by the injection of carbon dioxide gas, and will require gas pressure and chilling for serving

Characteristics of different ciders

Ciders can be categorised according to their difference in appearance, taste and ingredients.

Sweetness

The characteristics of keg and bottled ciders are:

- Medium sweet (carbonated): 4% ABV
- Medium dry (carbonated): 6% ABV
- Special (some carbonated): 8.3% ABV – some special ciders undergo a second fermentation to make them sparkle.

The characteristics of the apples that are required for making cider are:

- the sweetness of dessert apples
- the acidity of culinary apples
- the bitterness of tannin to balance the flavour and help preserve the cider.

Cloudiness/sediment

This comes from the yeasts used to activate the fermentation of the juice. In some ciders, such as scrumpy, the cloudiness is left in the cider. Other ciders are filtered to remove the cloudiness, giving the term 'star bright'. This also changes the texture of the cider to a cleaner finish on the mouth.

Fruit – apple cider, pear cider, use of other fruits

Traditionally cider is made from apples and perry from pears. It has become more common to find ciders from other countries made from a wide variety of fruits. These are made in the same way as apple cider but from other fruits and often blending flavours, for example fruits of the forest, strawberry and lime, or apple and blackcurrant.

Still or sparkling

Cider is naturally flat. To make it sparkling it is carbonated by having carbon dioxide pumped into the bottle or keg. It can also be made sparkling by the addition of yeast to create fermentation in the bottle, in the same way champagne is made.

1.3 PRODUCTION METHODS AND CHARACTERISTICS OF SPIRITS

Spirits such as brandy, whisky and rum are produced by distillation from wine or other fermented or brewed liquids.

Methods of spirit production

- **Mashing**. The process begins with mashing in a similar way to wine or beer. Different spirits use different substances in the mash. Some such as brandy will use fermented fruit or plant juice, while others such as whisky are made using various grains.
- **Fermenting**. This is a similar process to that for beer. Different ingredients will be added to the process at this stage depending on the spirit being made. For example, rum is created by fermenting sugarcane while vodka is created in various ways, including using potatoes, grains or molasses.
- **Distilling**. The difference between spirits and other alcoholic beverages is that they are distilled. The principle of distillation is that ethyl alcohol boils at a lower temperature (78°C) than water (100°C). If a liquid containing alcohol is heated above 78.5°C in an enclosed environment, the alcohol will form steam first and can be taken off, leaving the water and other ingredients behind. This process raises the alcoholic strength of the liquid resulting from the steam.

Types of still

Distillation takes place in a still. There are two main types of still.

- **The pot still method**. The pot still works by a process called batch distillation, where small amounts are produced and removed from the still before more mixture is added. The process allows much of the original flavour of the distillate to remain. The pot still method is used for full, heavy-flavoured spirits such as brandy. Irish and Scottish whiskies are legally required to be made in a pot still.

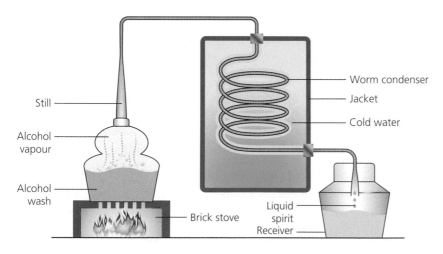

▲ **Figure 6.3** A pot still

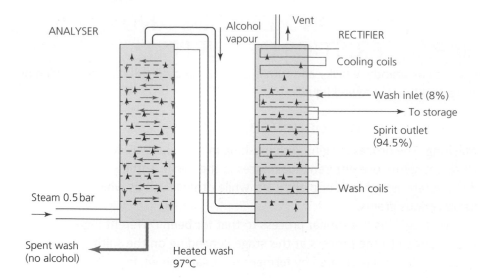

▲ **Figure 6.4** A patent still

- **The patent still method** (also referred to as the 'column still', 'continuous still' or 'Coffey still') is a continuous distillation process. The liquid is first passed through the analyser, which separates out the alcoholic vapour, and then the rectifier which purifies the spirit. Much of the original flavouring of the distillate is removed so the spirit is almost tasteless. This method is used to make lighter spirits such as vodka.

Finishing techniques

Containers

- **Stainless steel containers** are used for spirits which do not need to be matured – for example, vodka and gin. These are usually spirits produced by continuous distillation. They are stored in stainless steel vats and bottled shortly after they have been distilled.
- **Wooden containers** are used for products that are likely to be matured, such as whiskies and brandies. These are usually produced by the pot still method. Different types of wood have different effects on the flavour of the spirit.

Maturation

'Maturation' is the process of chemical change that occurs during storage. Whisky can be matured in new or reused wooden barrels. Rum is usually matured in reused oak containers. Brandy is also matured in oak containers. The maturation process adds flavours from the wood to the spirit.

There are some legal requirements regarding how long spirits should be allowed to mature. In Scotland and England they must be matured for at least three years, Ireland requires five years and the USA two years. Spirits such as vodka and gin do not usually require maturation.

The maturation procedure for brandies is similar to that of whisky, but the brandies are usually matured in fairly large casks or oak containers. Brandy has an age grading system:

- VS (Very Special) or *** (three stars) cognac – must age in wood for a minimum of two years.
- VSOP (Very Special Old Pale) cognac – must age in wood for three years.

In practice, most cognacs and Armagnacs are kept in wood longer than the minimum period. XO (Extra Old) or Napoléon brandy designates a blend in which the youngest brandy is stored for at least six years. Some remain for as long as 20 to 40 years, or even longer.

Blending

Different spirits or other ingredients can be blended together to create a particular flavour, For example, blended whisky may contain several different whiskies, a neutral grain spirit, colouring and additional flavours. There are some regulations on how whisky may be blended. A single malt whisky only comes from one distillery.

Flavouring

Clear or neutral spirits such as gin and vodka are in themselves flavourless. They can be flavoured with ingredients – such as botanicals, fruits and herbs.

Characteristics of spirits

The main types of spirits are listed in Table 6.4. This table provides a description of the flavours and identifies their base ingredients.

▼ **Table 6.4** The main types of spirits

Spirit	Flavours
Gin	Juniper is the main flavouring agent used in gin. Maize is the cereal used in gin production in the UK, but rye can also be used, for example, in Dutch gin. Malted barley and coriander seeds are alternative cereals used • **Fruit gins**: gins that may be produced from any fruit. The most popular are sloe, orange and lemon • **Geneva gin**: this is made in Holland by the pot still method alone and is generally known as 'Holland' gin • **London dry gin**: this is the most well-known and popular of all the gins. It is unsweetened • **Old Tom**: this is a sweet gin made in Scotland. The sweetening agent is sugar syrup. As the name implies, it was traditionally used in a Tom Collins cocktail • **Plymouth gin**: this has a stronger flavour than London dry and is manufactured by Coates in Devon. It is most well-known for its use in the cocktail Pink Gin, together with the addition of Angostura bitters
Whisky/ whiskey	Whisky, or whiskey, is a spirit made from cereals: 'Whisky' usually refers to the Scottish or Canadian drink and 'whiskey' to the Irish or American • Scottish whisky is primarily made from malted barley (hence the term 'malt whisky') then heated over a peat fire. Grain whiskies are made from other grains and are usually blended with malt whisky • Irish whiskey is made from barley but differs from Scotch in that hot air rather than a peat fire is used during malting, thus Irish whiskey does not gain the smoky quality of Scotch. It is also distilled three times (rather than two as in the making of Scotch) and is matured longer • Canadian whisky is usually a blend of flavoured and neutral whiskies made from grains such as rye, wheat and barley • American whiskey is made from various mixtures of barley, maize and rye. Bourbon is made from maize • Japanese whisky is made by the Scottish process and is blended
Vodka	A highly rectified (very pure) patent still spirit. It is purified by being passed through activated charcoal, which removes virtually all aroma and flavour. It is described as a colourless and flavourless spirit and can have either a grain or potato base

Spirit	Flavours
Rum	This is a spirit made from the fermented by-products of sugar cane. It is available in dark and light varieties and is produced in countries where sugar cane grows naturally – for example Jamaica, Cuba, Trinidad, Barbados, Guyana and the Bahamas. Molasses produces dark rum; sugar cane produces white rum
Brandy	Brandy may be defined as a spirit distilled from wine. The word 'brandy' is more usually linked with the names Cognac and Armagnac, but brandy is made in almost all wine-producing areas and is grape-based
Tequila/ Mescal	A Mexican spirit distilled from the fermented juice (pulque) of the agave plant/maguey plant. Traditionally drunk after a lick of salt and a squeeze of lime or lemon

1.4 PRODUCTION METHODS AND CHARACTERISTICS OF LIQUEURS

Liqueurs are defined as sweetened and flavoured spirits. They should not be confused with liqueur spirits, which may be whiskies or brandies of great age and quality. For instance, a brandy liqueur is a liqueur with brandy as a basic ingredient, while a liqueur brandy is usually defined as a brandy of great age and excellence.

Methods of liqueur production

There are two main methods for making liqueurs:

1 **Heat or infusion method**: best when herbs, peels, roots, etc., are being used, as heat can extract their oils, flavours and aromas. This method uses a pot still for distillation purposes.
2 **Cold or maceration method**: best when soft fruits are used to provide the flavours and aromas. This method allows the soft fruit to soak in the spirit in oak casks over a long period of time.

For all liqueurs a spirit base is necessary, and this may be brandy, rum or a neutral spirit. Many flavouring ingredients are used to make liqueurs.

Types of liqueurs

Table 6.5 lists some of the more popular liqueurs. The service of liqueurs is discussed in Unit 206, page 264.

▼ **Table 6.5** Popular liqueurs

Fruit liqueurs			
Liqueur	Colour	Flavour/spirit base	Country of origin
Abricotine	Red	Apricot/brandy	France
Archers	Clear	Peach/schnapps	UK
Cherry brandy	Deep red	Cherry/brandy	Denmark
Cointreau	Clear	Orange/neutral spirit	France
Crème de Cassis	Dark red	Blackcurrant	France
Grand Marnier	Amber	Orange/brandy	France
Maraschino	Clear	Maraschino cherry	Italy
Southern Comfort	Golden	Peach/orange/whisky	United States
Van Der Hum	Amber	Tangerine/brandy	South Africa

Cream liqueurs

Liqueur	Colour	Flavour/spirit base	Country of origin
Bailey's Irish Cream	Coffee	Honey/chocolate/cream/whiskey	Ireland

Herb liqueurs

Liqueur	Colour	Flavour/spirit base	Country of origin
Anisette	Clear	Aniseed/neutral spirit	France, Spain, Italy, Holland
Arrack	Clear	Herbs/sap of palm trees	Java, India, Sri Lanka, Jamaica
Bénédictine	Yellow/green	Herbs/various spirits	France
Chartreuse	Green (45% abv) Yellow (55% abv)	Herbs/plants/neutral spirit	France
Drambuie	Golden	Heather/honey/herbs/whisky	Scotland
Galliano	Golden	Herbs/berries/flowers/roots	Italy
Glayva	Golden	Herbs/spices/whisky	Scotland
Kümmel	Clear	Caraway seed/neutral spirit	East European countries
Pernod	Clear	Star anise	France
Sambuca	Clear	Liquorice/neutral spirit	Italy
Strega (The Witch)	Yellow	Herbs/bark/fruit	Italy

Bean liqueurs

Liqueur	Colour	Flavour/spirit base	Country of origin
Kahlúa	Pale chocolate	Coffee/rum	Mexico
Tia Maria	Brown	Coffee/rum	Jamaica

Nut liqueurs

Liqueur	Colour	Flavour/spirit base	Country of origin
Amaretto	Golden	Almonds	Italy
Disaronno	Amber	Almonds/herbs/fruits/apricot kernel oil	Italy
Frangelico	Golden	Hazelnut	Italy
Malibu	Clear	Coconut/white rum	Caribbean

Aniseed liqueurs

Liqueur	Colour	Flavour/spirit base	Country of origin
Pernod	Clear	Star anise	France
Sambuca	Clear	Liquorice/neutral spirit	Italy

Other liqueurs

Liqueur	Colour	Flavour/spirit base	Country of origin
Avocaat	Yellow	Egg/sugar/brandy	Holland

227

1.5 PRODUCTION METHODS AND CHARACTERISTICS OF WINE

Wine is the alcoholic beverage obtained from the fermentation of the juice of freshly gathered grapes. Only a few areas of the world are able to produce wine as particular conditions are needed:

- Enough sun to ripen the grapes.
- Winters that are moderate yet sufficiently cool to give the vine a chance to rest and restore its strength for the growing and fruiting season.

Three-quarters of the world's wine is produced in Europe (often referred to as Old World) and just under half of this is in the EU. France and Italy produce the most wine, followed by Spain, Germany and Portugal. Outside Europe (often referred to as New World), the largest producer is the USA followed by Australia, Argentina, Chile and South Africa.

Winemakers must ensure that their products conform to strict quality regulations – such as the location of the vineyards, the variety of grape used, how the wine is made and how long it is matured.

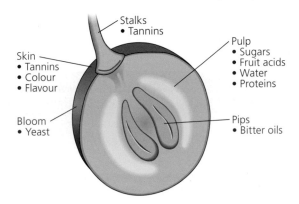

▲ **Figure 6.5** Wine-making grapes

Methods of wine production

The process of making wine (known as **vinification**) varies in different regions and produces different types of wine, but the basic method is similar for all types of wine.

Crushing and pressing

This process differs for different types of wine:

- **White wines** – most are processed without destemming or crushing and are put directly into the press. After pressing the juice goes into the fermentation vats.
- **Red wines** – stems of the grapes are usually removed before fermentation because the stems have a relatively high tannin content and can also give the wine a vegetable aroma. The grapes are then crushed. The juice and the skins are put into a fermentation vat. The juice is clear, as it is for white wines, but the skins give the red colour. After being in the fermentation vats the wine is then pressed.

- **Rosé wines** – the juice is run off after a few hours to separate the juice from the skins in order to keep a pink colour. It then goes into a fermentation vat.

Fermenting

The process of fermentation allows the yeast to react with the sugar in the juice to create alcohol and carbon dioxide. There are various techniques and technologies used during fermentation which have different effects on the flavour of the wine.

- For both red and white wines yeast is used to ferment the grape juice.
- For red wines, carbon dioxide is released during fermentation which causes the grape skins to rise to the surface. Winemakers must punch down or pump over the 'cap' several times a day to keep the skins in contact with the juice. This process is known as carbonic maceration. The grapes are pressed after fermentation is complete.

Maturing

Wine is matured in different ways, depending on the type of wine being produced and the flavour that the winemaker wants to achieve. Different factors in how wine is matured include:

- Time taken – wine can be matured for several years or for just a few months.
- Barrels used – wine can be aged in either steel vats or oak barrels. If using oak barrels, new barrels or barrels that have been previously used will have different effects on the wine.

Bottling

Once the wine has been aged sufficiently it can be bottled. Larger producers will have a fully automated bottling process, while smaller producers may do this by hand. Wines in bottles continue to develop (mature) and it can take years before the wine is ready to be enjoyed.

Different types of wine

Still (or light) wine

This is the largest category. The alcoholic strength may range from 9% to 15% by volume. The wines may be:

- **Red**: produced by being fermented in contact with grape skins (from which the wine gets its colour). Normally dry wines.
- **White**: usually produced from white grapes, but the grape juice (must) is usually fermented away from the skins. Can be dry to very sweet.
- **Rosé**: can be made in three ways – from black grapes fermented in the skins for up to 48 hours; by mixing red and white wines together; or by pressing grapes so that some colour is extracted. Rosé wines may be dry or semi-sweet. Rosé wines are called 'blush' wines in the USA when made wholly from red grapes.

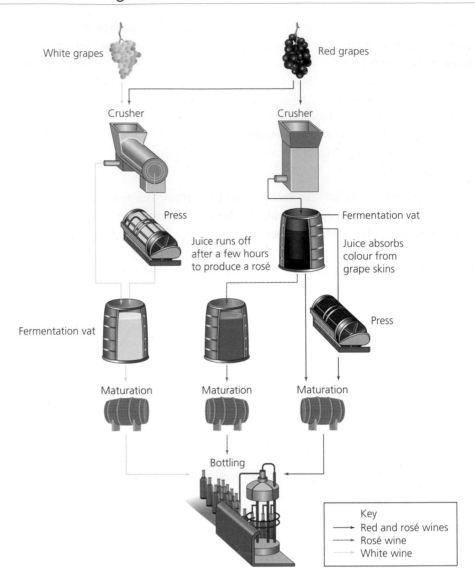

White grapes
Red grapes
Crusher
Crusher
Press
Fermentation vat
Juice runs off after a few hours to produce a rosé
Juice absorbs colour from grape skins
Fermentation vat
Press
Maturation
Maturation
Maturation
Bottling

Key
→ Red and rosé wines
→ Rosé wine
→ White wine

▲ **Figure 6.6** The wine-making process

Sparkling wines

Sparkling wines are available from France, Spain (cava), Italy (prosecco), Germany (sekt) and many other countries including England.

The most famous sparkling wine is champagne, which is made in an area of north-eastern France. It is created by the secondary fermentation in the bottle, known in Champagne as '*méthode champenoise*' and elsewhere as '*méthode traditionelle*' (or traditional method). Spanish cava is also made using the traditional method. Other sparkling wines are made with either secondary fermentation taking place in a sealed tank, or the wine being made to sparkle through carbonation.

Fortified (liqueur) wines

Fortified wines derive their name from the fact that they are wines to which a spirit (such as brandy) has been added – which increases their alcohol by volume and makes them stronger. Originally, this process was for preservation – to prevent further fermentation (which can lead to spoilage).

Fortified wines such as sherry, port and madeira have been strengthened by the addition of alcohol, usually a grape spirit. These are now known in the EU as liqueur wines or *vins de liqueur*. Their alcoholic strength may range from 15% to 22% by volume.

Examples are:

- **Sherry** (from Spain) 15–18% – Fino (dry), Amontillado (medium), Oloroso (sweet).
- **Port** (from Portugal) 18–22% – Ruby, Late Bottled Vintage, Tawny, Vintage.

Other fortified wines include vins doux naturels. These are wines made from sweet grapes to which a neutral grape spirit is added to stop the fermentation before it is complete. The wine then stays sweet. An example is Muscat de Beaumes de Venise.

Aromatised wines

These are flavoured and fortified wines, often referred to as 'vermouth'.

The main types of vermouth are:

- **Dry vermouth**: often called French vermouth or simply French (as in 'gin and French'). It is made from dry white wine that is flavoured and fortified.
- **Sweet vermouth**/bianco: made from dry white wine flavoured, fortified and sweetened with sugar or mistelle.
- **Rosé vermouth**: made in a similar way to bianco, but it is less sweet and is coloured with caramel.

Bitters

Bitters are a liquid extraction of seeds, herbs, bark, roots, flowers, leaves and fruit of various plants. Some bitters are highly concentrated and are used by the dash to flavour cocktails. Angostura and Peychaud's are the two most common bitters stocked in bars.

There are other bitters that are taken as drinks. The two main ones are:

- **Campari** is made from an infusion of herbs and fruit (including chinotto and cascarilla) in alcohol and water. It has a dark red colour and the alcohol content can vary from about 20 to 29% depending on in which country it is sold.
- **Aperol** has a lighter colour than Campari, is less bitter in taste and contains half the alcohol of Campari at 11%. It is an Italian apéritif made of bitter orange, gentian, rhubarb and cinchona, among other ingredients. Aperol is now produced by the Campari company.

KEY TERMS

Viticulture – cultivation of grape vines.

Vitis vinifera – main vine species for grapes used for wine making.

Varietal – the grape used to make a specific wine.

Vintage – the year the wine was made.

Factors affecting the taste and quality of wines

Grape varieties

The process of cultivating grapes is known as '**viticulture**'. The vine species that produces grapes suitable for wine production, and which stocks most of the vineyards of the world, is named **Vitis vinifera**. Most varieties now planted in Europe and elsewhere have evolved from this species through cross-breeding to suit local soils and climates. The grape used for a specific wine is known as the **varietal**. The same grape in different regions may be given a different name, for example Syrah in France is the same as Shiraz in Australia. There are many grapes that have become known for their distinctive characteristics. Examples of these principal grapes of the world, and their typical characteristics, are given in Table 6.6.

Modern vines come from stock that can be traced back many years. Modern vines will be grafted on to American root stocks to protect them from the Phylloxera vastatrix – a louse-type aphid which attacks the roots of the vine. The grape species or variety will be chosen according to the style of wine to be produced as well as chosen to grow well in the soil and climate of the area.

Other factors affecting taste and quality of wine

- **Tannin** – this is found in the pips and skin of the grape; it adds bitterness and astringency, as well as complexity, to wine.
- **Climate** and microclimate – each vineyard will have a different micro-climate which will affect how the vines grow and the grapes mature. The combination of factors that affect the quality of the grapes produced in a particular year is known as the 'luck of the year'. Wines made in a specific year are identified as '**vintage**' wines and this is stated on the bottle. Non-vintage wines are those where the bottle may contain wines from different years.
- **Nature of the soil and subsoil** – vines do not require rich soil to produce good grapes. The roots need to run deep into the soil to find moisture and carry back minerals and nutrients to the grapes, which will then influence the flavours in the juice.
- **Maturation** – process of maturing that helps to stabilise the wine, clarify it and encourage the creation of more complex aromas that increase the quality of the wine. Maturation can take place in steel tanks, barrels or glass bottles until the wine has reached the point where it is ready for selling in bottles, tanks, barrels, vacuum packs.

▼ **Table 6.6** Principal white and red grapes used for wine making

White grapes	Where grown	General characteristics of the wine
Chardonnay	Worldwide	The white grape of Burgundy, Champagne and the New World. Aromas associated with chardonnay include ripe melon and fresh pineapple. The fruity, oaky New World wines tend to be buttery and syrupy, with tropical fruits and richness. In Burgundy the wines are succulent but bone-dry, with a nutty intensity. Chablis, from the cooler northern Burgundy, produces wines that have a sharp, steely acidity that may also be countered by the richness of oak. Also one of the three grapes used to make champagne
Sauvignon Blanc	Worldwide	Common aroma association with gooseberries, the wines are green, tangy, fresh and pungent. When made with oak, it can be a different wine: tropical fruits in the Californian examples, while the classic Bordeaux wines are often blended with Sémillon and begin with nectarine hints and then become more nutty and creamy with age. May be called Blanc Fumé
Riesling	Alsace, Australia, Canada, Germany, New Zealand, South Africa, USA	Range of wines from the steely to the voluptuous; always well-perfumed with good ageing potential. Aromas tend towards apricots and peaches. Germany makes the greatest Riesling in all styles. Piercing acidity and flavours ranging from green apple and lime, to honeyed peaches, to stony and slate-like. Styles can range from bright and tangy to intensely sweet
Pinot Gris/Pinot Grigio/Ruländer/Tokay-Pinot Gris	Alsace, Canada, Germany, Hungary, Italy, New Zealand, Slovenia, USA	Generally full-bodied spicy white wines, often high in alcohol and low in acidity. Wines are crisp and neutral in Italy and aromatic and spicy in Alsace and elsewhere, with a hint of honey. Also used to make golden sweet wines, especially from Alsace
Chenin Blanc/Steen	Loire, California, South Africa	Variety of styles: bone-dry, medium-sweet, intensely sweet or sparkling wines, all with fairly high acidity making the wines very refreshing. Aroma association tends to be apples

Red grapes	Where grown	General characteristics of the wine
Cabernet Sauvignon	Worldwide	Principal grape of Bordeaux, especially in the Médoc. New World wines deliver big wines with upfront blackcurrant fruit; Bordeaux wines need time to mature. Generally, benefits from being blended, e.g. with Merlot, Cabernet Franc, Syrah, Tempranillo, Sangiovese. Also used to make aromatic rosé wines
Shiraz/Syrah	Worldwide	Warm, spicy, peppery wines with aromas of raspberries; French Syrah tends to be smoky, herby and packed with red fruits (raspberries, blackberries or blackcurrants); Australian Shiraz has sweeter black cherry fruit and often black chocolate or liquorice aromas. Very fruity rosé wines are also made
Merlot	Worldwide	Principal grape of Saint-Emilion and Pomerol in France. Aromas tend towards plums and damsons. The wines are low in harsh tannins and can be light and juicy, smooth and plummy or intensely blackcurrant
Pinot Noir/Spätburgunder/Pinot Nero	Worldwide	Principal grape of Burgundy's Côte d'Or. Aromas can be of strawberries, cherries and plums (depending on where grown). Silky and strawberry-like; simple wines have juicy fruit; the best mature wines, such as the great red wines of Burgundy, are well-perfumed. Loire and German wines are lighter. Also, one of the three grapes used to make champagne and used elsewhere (e.g. California and Australia) for making white, sparkling or red and very pale pink wines
Malbec	South-west France, Argentina	French wines tend to be plummy and tannic. In Bordeaux it is used for blending. The Argentinean wines tend to be rich and perfumed

Characteristics of wines

Wine can be categorised according to differences in appearance, nose (aroma) and taste. Table 6.7 summarises the terms and characteristics used to evaluate wine when tasting takes place.

▼ **Table 6.7** Examples of wine-tasting evaluation terms

Appearance	**Clarity**: clear, bright, brilliant, gleaming, sumptuous, dull, hazy, cloudy
	Colour intensity: pale, subdued, faded, deep, intense. Colour also includes the colour at the rim. In younger wines the colour of the wine is more even between the centre and the rim ● **White wine**: water clear, pale yellow, yellow with green tinges, straw, gold, deep yellow, brown or Maderised ● **Rosé wine**: pale pink, orange-pink, onion-skin, blue-pink, copper ● **Red wine**: purple, garnet, ruby, tawny, brick-red, mahogany
	Legs: mainly caused by alcohol in the wine – slow trickle indicates more body in the wine
Nose / aroma	**Intensity**: weak to pronounced
	Other aroma descriptors: fruity, flowery, perfumed, full, deep, oaky, spicy, vegetal, fine, rich, pleasant, weak, nondescript, flat, corky, herbal
Taste	**Sweetness/dryness**: bone dry, dry, medium dry, sweet, medium sweet, sweet, luscious
	Acidity: low to high
	Tannin: low to high
	Body: thin, light, medium, full-bodied
	Other flavour characteristics: fruity, bitter, spicy, hard, soft, silky, floral, vegetal, smooth, tart, piquant, flowery, oaky, herbal
	Length of finish: short to long

Labels on wines

The label on a bottle of wine can give a lot of useful information about that wine. The language used will normally be that of the country of origin. The information always includes:

● the name of the wine
● the country where the wine was made
● alcoholic strength in percentage by volume (% vol)
● volume in litres, cl or ml
● the name and address or trademark of the supplier.

It may also include:

● the varietal(s) (name of the grape(s) used to make the wine)
● the year the grapes were harvested, called the vintage, if the wine is sold as a vintage wine
● the region where the wine was made
● the property where the wine was made
● the quality category of the wine
● details of the bottler and distributor.

An example of the kind of information on a wine label is shown in Figure 6.7.

Domaine de Dionyses ———————— Winery name

2010 ———————————————— Vintage

CAIRANNE ————————— Village

CÔTES DU RHÔNE VILLAGES ⌐
APPELATION CÔTES DU RHÔNE VILLAGES CONTRÔLÉE ————— Appellation title

Grenache · Syrah · Mourvèdre · Vieux · Carignan ——— Grape varieties

Mis en bouteille au Domaine ——————— Bottled on the estate

14.5% PAR EARL DIONYSOS – 84100 UCHAUX – FRANCE 750ML —— Producer name and location

▲ **Figure 6.7** A guide to the French wine label

Source: wine-searcher.com

1.6 DEFINITIONS AND PREPARATION METHODS FOR COCKTAILS

Cocktails and mocktails

A modern cocktail is normally a short drink of up to about 10 cl (3½–4 fl oz), anything larger often being called a 'mixed drink' or 'long drink'. However, the term 'cocktail' is now generally recognised to mean all types of mixed drinks. Non-alcoholic cocktails are known as mocktails.

▲ **Figure 6.8** Cocktails

Methods of preparing classic cocktails

The art of making a good cocktail is to blend all the ingredients together so that upon tasting no one ingredient is predominant. The making of cocktails has become very popular and the professionalism of cocktail making is increasing. Cocktail making is often called **mixology** and cocktail makers are called **mixologists**.

The six main methods for making cocktails and mixed drinks are described in Table 6.8.

KEY TERMS

Mixology – cocktail making.
Mixologist – a person who makes cocktails.

235

▼ **Table 6.8** Methods for making cocktails and mixed drinks

Method	Example	Explanation
Shaken	Cosmopolitan, Daiquiri, Margarita, Whisky Sour	Ice is placed in a shaker together with the ingredients to combine them and chill them down. The lid is placed on the cocktail shaker, or Boston shaker, and then shaken hard until the outside is very cool and condensation has appeared. The mixture is then strained into the serving glass using a Hawthorne strainer to remove the ice and other solid ingredients
Stirred	Martini, Sidecar	The ice and ingredients are placed into a mixing glass and gently stirred with a bar spoon to mix the ingredients and chill them down. The mixture is then strained into the serving glass, using a Hawthorne strainer, to remove the ice and other solid ingredients
Muddled	Mojito	Some ingredients (for example fruit, leaves and sugar) are crushed at the bottom of the glass before other ingredients are added
Layered	B52	Liquids, which can be alcoholic and non-alcoholic, that have different specific densities are floated one on top of the other in the serving glass. These drinks can also be referred to as **poured** drinks
Built	Bellini	The drink is created in the serving glass by putting the ingredients and the ice into a service glass, one after the other. Drinks made in this way are often also muddled
Blended	Piña Colada	More recently smoothies have become popular and are often seen as healthy drinks. These are made in a blender. In addition to fresh fruit or vegetables, these drinks are sometimes sweetened. The recipe may also include crushed ice, frozen fruit, honey or frozen yogurt. Pre-made bottled or carton versions are also available

KEY TERMS

Shaken – the ingredients are placed in a cocktail shaker with ice and shaken.

Stirred – the ice and ingredients are placed into a mixing glass and stirred.

Muddled – some ingredients (for example fruit, leaves and sugar) are crushed at the bottom of the glass before other ingredients are added.

Layered – when liquids with different densities are floated one on top of the other.

Built – ingredients and ice are put into the glass one after the other.

Poured – another name for layered cocktails.

▲ **Figure 6.9 (a)** Whisky Sour ▲ **(b)** Dry Martini ▲ **(c)** Mojito ▲ **(d)** B52

In all cases, the presentation of a cocktail is paramount. Presentation should match the description of the cocktail. This is especially important if it is one of the classic and internationally known cocktails. The customer should also feel that the cocktail has been specially made for them.

For more information on the service of cocktails see Unit 206, page 265.

For examples of bar equipment see page 249.

2 PRODUCTION METHODS AND CHARACTERISTICS OF NON-ALCOHOLIC BEVERAGES

2.1 PROCESSING METHODS AND CHARACTERISTICS OF TYPES OF COFFEE

Methods of processing coffee and the effects on the final product

Roasting

The coffee beans are first roasted to give them their distinctive colour and aroma. While being roasted the beans are kept moving so that they do not get burnt. During the roasting process the beans release an oil called caffeol which gives the coffee its flavour. After roasting, the beans are immediately cooled either by air or water.

The common degrees of roasting are:

- Light or pale roasting: suitable for mild beans to preserve their delicate aroma.
- Medium roasting: gives a stronger flavour and often favoured for coffees with well-defined character.
- Full roasting: popular in many Latin countries; gives a bitter flavour.
- High roasted coffee: accentuates the strong bitter aspects of coffee, although much of the original flavour is lost.

Roasting is most often carried out in the country that imports the beans so that the consumer can obtain freshly roasted beans.

Blending

Most brands of coffee sold in shops are a blend of two or more batches of beans. Companies have their own blending experts who ensure that the quality and taste of their particular coffee brand is consistent, despite the fact that the beans will vary from shipment to shipment. The blending expert will roast beans from different shipments and test them before deciding which beans will be needed to make the required blend for a particular coffee. This ensures a consistent flavour and aroma for the blends across the brand.

Certain coffees also have flavourings added, either in the blend or added during the process of making them. Examples of these include:

- Turkish coffee – vanilla
- French coffee – chicory
- Viennese coffee – fig.

Grinding

Roasted coffee must be ground before it can be used to make the brew. The grinding process gets the flavour from the beans. Coffee is ground to different grades of fineness to suit the many different methods of brewing. The most suitable grinds for some common methods of brewing coffee are shown in Table 6.9.

▼ **Table 6.9** Grinds of coffee

Method	Grinding grade
Cafetière	Medium
Espresso	Very fine
Filter/pour and serve	Fine to medium
Jug	Coarse
Percolator	Medium
Turkish	Pulverised
Vacuum infusion	Medium-fine to fine

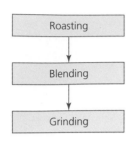

▲ **Figure 6.10** Coffee production

Instant coffee

This involves mixing soluble coffee solids with boiling water. This form of coffee is designed to be made very quickly, immediately before it is required, by pouring freshly boiled water on to a measured quantity of coffee powder and stirring.

Types of coffee bean

There are approximately 50 different species of shrub growing coffee beans, although only two of these are popularly sold. These are known as:

- Coffea **arabica** (lighter, citrus-flavoured)
- Coffea canephora, which is usually referred to as **robusta** (harsher, rounder flavour, bitter with more caffeine).
- Arabica accounts for around 75 per cent of world production.

Characteristics of good coffee

Coffee should have:

- good flavour
- good aroma
- good colour when milk or cream are added – not grey
- good body.

▲ **Figure 6.11** Coffee beans

Methods of production of different types of coffee

Espresso

This method is Italian in origin. Machines used to make this form of coffee can provide cups of coffee individually in a matter of seconds, with some machines being capable of making 300 to 400 cups of coffee per hour. The method involves passing steam through the finely ground coffee and infusing under pressure. Examples of different styles are given in Table 6.10.

Iced coffee/frappuccino

Strong black coffee should be made in the normal way. It is then strained, chilled well and stored in the refrigerator until required. It may be served mixed with an equal quantity of cold milk for a smooth beverage, or with cream. Often served in a glass tumbler set on a coaster, on an underplate and with a teaspoon.

▼ **Table 6.10** Different espresso-based coffee styles

Name of coffee	Description
Americano	Espresso with added hot water to create regular black coffee. May also be regular black coffee made using filter method
Cappuccino	Espresso coffee topped with steamed frothed milk, often finished with a sprinkling of chocolate (powdered or grated)
Caffè (or café) latte	Shot of espresso plus hot milk, with or without foam
Flat white	Double shot of espresso topped with frothed milk which has been stirred together with the flat milk from the bottom of the jug, to create a creamy rather than frothy texture
Caffè mocha (or mochaccino)	Chocolate compound (syrup or powder) followed by a shot of espresso. The cup or glass is then filled with freshly steamed milk topped with whipped cream and cocoa powder
Flavoured lattes	Flavoured syrups can be added to a latte to give it a different flavour – almond, ginger, toffee, chocolate, caramel, fruit flavours, spirit flavours, food flavours (cookies and cream, shortbread, etc.). These are high in sugar and care should be taken not to overpower the coffee with the flavoured syrup

Other methods of making coffee

Still-set

This method normally consists of a small central container into which the correct-sized filter paper is placed. A second, fine-meshed metal filter with a handle is then placed on the filter paper and the ground coffee placed on top of this. There is an urn on either side of varying capacities according to requirements. Boiling water is passed through the ground coffee and the coffee liquid then passes into the urn at the side. Infusion should be complete in 6 to 8 minutes for 4½ litres (1 gallon) of coffee when using medium-ground coffee. The milk is heated in a steam jacket container.

Filter

This method is used to make coffee individually in the cup or in bulk. Freshly boiled water is poured into a container with a very finely meshed bottom, which stands on a cup or pot. The infusion takes place and the coffee liquid falls into the cup/pot below. Filter papers may be used to avoid the grounds passing into the lower cup, but this will depend on how fine or coarse the ground coffee being used is. There are now many electronic units available of differing capacities. Cold water is poured into a reservoir and is brought to boiling point and then dripped on to the ground coffee.

Pour-through filter method

This is a different method of making filter coffee. When the measured quantity of freshly drawn cold water is poured into the top of the pour-through filter machine, this water displaces the hot water already in the machine. This hot water infuses with the ground coffee and runs into the serving container as a coffee liquid ready for immediate use. It takes approximately 3 to 4 minutes to make one brew.

▲ **Figure 6.12** Modern still set

Turkish or Egyptian coffees

These are made from darkly roasted mocha beans which are ground to a fine powder. The coffee is made in special copper pots, which are placed on top of a stove or lamp, and the water is then allowed to boil. The sugar should be put in at this stage to sweeten the coffee as it is never stirred once poured out. The finely ground coffee may be stirred in or the boiling water poured on to the grounds. The amount of coffee used is approximately one heaped teaspoonful per person. The coffee is served in small cups. While making the coffee it may also be flavoured with vanilla pods.

Cafetière (coffee maker)

The cafetière, or jug and plunger method, makes coffee by the infusion method. This ensures that the flavour and aroma are preserved. The cafetière is a glass container with a lip held in a black, gold or chrome-finished holder and sealed with a lid that also holds the plunger unit in position. The coffee is made by adding boiling water to the ground coffee, stirring and then placing the plunger unit and lid in position. Infusion time is from 3 to 5 minutes. During this time the coffee grains will rise to the top of the liquid. If the plunger is adjusted slightly, the coffee grains will fall to the bottom of the glass container. When the grains have fallen it is easier to push the plunger down.

▲ **Figure 6.13** Coffee-brewing methods (clockwise from top): pour and serve filter machine, single filter, Turkish/Greek/Arabic coffee, jug and plunger/cafetière

▲ **Figure 6.14** Tray laid for the service of Irish coffee

Liqueur coffees

Speciality coffees are coffees served with a spirit base and finished with cream floated on the top. These can also be referred to as floating coffees. Forms of speciality, or liqueur, coffees include:

- Irish coffee: Irish whiskey
- Calypso coffee: Tia Maria
- Café Royale or Café Parisienne: brandy
- Seville coffee: Cointreau
- Monk's coffee: Bénédictine
- Russian coffee: vodka

- Jamaican coffee or Caribbean coffee: rum
- Highland coffee: Scotch whisky
- Swiss coffee: kirsch.

Decaffeinated coffee

Coffee contains caffeine, a stimulant that reduces fatigue and drowsiness. At normal doses caffeine has variable effects on learning and memory, but it generally improves reaction time, concentration and task performance and it can also delay or prevent sleep. To reduce these effects, decaffeinated coffee is available.

In decaffeinated coffee, caffeine has been removed or at least reduced. It is often simply called 'decaff' and can be used instead of regular coffee in all of the methods identified above. Decaffeinated coffee usually has a milder flavour as caffeine is one of the components which gives coffee its bitter, acidic flavour.

2.2 PROCESSING METHODS AND CHARACTERISTICS OF TYPES OF TEA

Tea is prepared from the leaf bud and top leaves of a tropical evergreen bush called *Camellia sinensis*. It produces what is regarded as a healthy beverage, containing approximately only half the caffeine of coffee; at the same time, it aids muscle relaxation, stimulates the central nervous system and aids digestion.

The tea leaf itself contains a number of chemicals including amino acids, vitamins, caffeine and catechins. A catechin is a type of antioxidant which, in green tea, is thought to be effective in preventing certain cancers such as liver cancer. Green and black teas may also protect against cardiovascular disease.

Processing methods and characteristics of tea

Most teas are fermented (oxidised) during the process of manufacture, which gives them their black colour. The main exception is China green tea.

- **Black tea** – fully oxidised – has a strong malty taste, dark in colour.
- **Green tea** – steamed, rolled and dried. It has a lighter flavour and is green in colour because the tea is not fermented during manufacture.
- **White tea** – steamed, not rolled or oxidised, resulting in a flavour characterised as 'lighter' than green or traditional black teas. Only new shoots are used.

Tea should have good:

- flavour
- aroma
- colour when milk or cream are added – not grey
- body.

Different types of tea blend

Most teas are blended teas sold under proprietary brands or names. Other teas, sometimes called speciality or premium teas, are sold by the name of the specific tea (see Table 6.11). The word 'blend' indicates that a named tea may be composed of a variety of different teas to produce one marketable tea, which is acceptable to the average consumer taste. For instance, what is sometimes termed a standard tea may contain somewhere in the region of 15 different teas. These would almost certainly include Indian tea for strength, African tea for colour and China tea for flavour and delicacy.

▼ **Table 6.11** Characteristics and service of teas

Type of tea	Characteristic
English Breakfast	Often a blend of Assam and Kenya teas to make a bright, flavoursome and refreshing tea. Usually served as a breakfast tea but may be offered at any time. Usually served with milk but can also be taken with lemon. Sugar is offered separately
Assam	Rich, full and malty-flavoured tea, suitable for service at breakfast, usually with milk. Sugar is offered separately
Ceylon	Indian or Ceylon blend tea may be made in either china or metal teapots. These teas are usually offered with milk. Sugar is offered separately
Earl Grey	Blend of Darjeeling and China tea, flavoured with oil of bergamot. Usually served with lemon or milk. Sugar is offered separately
Oolong	This is the same plant that is also used to make black tea and green tea. The difference is in the processing. Oolong tea is partially fermented, black tea is fully fermented, and green tea is unfermented. Oolong tea is used to sharpen thinking skills and improve mental alertness
Lapsang Souchong	Smoky, pungent and perfumed tea, delicate to the palate and may be said to be an acquired taste. Usually served with lemon. Sugar is offered separately
Tisanes (herbal)	These are fruit-flavoured teas and herbal infusions that are often used for medicinal purposes and are gaining in popularity with trends towards healthier eating and drinking. Often these do not contain caffeine. Examples are: **Herbal teas:** ● camomile ● peppermint ● rosehip ● mint **Fruit teas:** ● cherry ● lemon ● blackcurrant ● mandarin orange These teas are usually made in china pots or can be made by the cup or glass. Sometimes served with sugar
Chai	A flavoured tea made by brewing black tea a mixture of aromatic Indian spices and herbs. Traditionally prepared by making an extract from green cardamom pods, cinnamon sticks, ground cloves, ground ginger and black peppercorn together with black tea leaves
Ice tea	This is strong tea that is made, strained and well chilled. The tea is then stored chilled until required. It is traditionally served in a glass, such as a tumbler. A slice of lemon may be placed in the glass and some additional lemon slices served separately on a side plate and with a sweet fork. Sugar may be offered
Decaffeinated	Decaffeinated tea has about a third of the amount of caffeine content of coffee

2.3 PROCESSING METHODS AND CHARACTERISTICS OF HOT CHOCOLATE

Hot chocolate may come sweetened or non-sweetened and as a powder or soluble granules. It may be mixed with hot water or hot milk. Whipped cream from a whipped cream dispenser, marshmallows or a sprinkling of powdered chocolate may be added upon request. There are also flavoured chocolates available such as ginger, hazelnut and chilli.

Continental-style chocolate is of a thicker consistency, while American-style chocolate is lighter. Usually offered as large, medium or small and served in a tall glass or mug.

Some products on the market only have to be mixed with hot water as dried skimmed milk and milk proteins are among the ingredients making up the product.

Drinking chocolate products may come in individual vacuum-sealed packs or pods for use with electronic beverage-making machines, or in containers of varying sizes to suit demand and turnover. These can contain chocolate powder, solid chocolate or liquid concentrate.

▲ **Figure 6.15** Hot chocolate served in a glass

2.4 TYPES OF NON-ALCOHOLIC SOFT DRINKS

Terms such as 'de-alcoholised' or 'alcohol free' do not actually mean that the drink has no alcohol in it. The various terms and definitions are included in Table 6.29 on page 273.

The drinks covered in this section are 'non-alcoholic' and contain no alcohol. These drinks are also often referred to as 'soft drinks', with alcoholic drinks sometimes being referred to as 'hard' drinks. Drinks described as 'low alcohol' have a very small percentage of alcohol in them.

Aerated waters

These beverages are charged (or aerated) with carbonic gas. Artificially aerated waters are by far the most common. The flavourings found in different aerated waters are obtained from various essences.

Examples of aerated waters are:

- cola: sweet clear brown colour with flavouring including cola nuts
- 'fizzy' lemonades
- orangeade: orange-coloured and made from orange juice, sugar and carbonated water
- tonic water: colourless and quinine-flavoured
- soda water: colourless and tasteless
- ginger beer: pale cloudy with ginger flavour
- ginger ale: golden straw-coloured with ginger flavour
- bitter lemon: pale, cloudy yellow-coloured with a sharp lemon flavour.

▲ **Figure 6.16** Aerated waters

243

Aerated waters are available in bottles and cans and many are also available as post mix (concentrated liquid syrup) for use in dispensers. (See Post mix dispensers on page 247.)

Sparkling and still water

The European Union has divided bottled water into two main types: mineral water and spring water.

- Mineral water has a mineral content (which is strictly controlled).
- Spring water has fewer regulations, apart from those concerning hygiene.

Flavoured waters are also widely available either as still or sparkling; these can contain high levels of sugar. Flavours such as fruit or botanicals are available.

Water can be still, naturally sparkling or carbonated during bottling.

▼ **Table 6.12** Examples of mineral waters

Brand name	Type	Country of origin
Appollinaris	Naturally sparkling	Germany
Badoit	Naturally sparkling	France
Buxton	Still or carbonated	England
Contrex	Still	France
Evian	Still	France
Perrier	Naturally sparkling and also fruit-flavoured	France
San Pellegrino	Carbonated	Italy
Spa	Still, naturally sparkling and also fruit-flavoured	Belgium
Vichy	Naturally sparkling	France
Vittel	Naturally sparkling	France
Volvic	Still	France

The potential medicinal value of these mineral waters has long been recognised by the medical profession.

Where natural spring waters are found, there is usually what is termed a spa, where the waters may be drunk or bathed in according to the cures they are supposed to effect. Many of the best-known waters are bottled at the spring (bottled at source).

▼ **Table 6.13** Examples of spring waters

Brand name	Type	Country of origin
Ashbourne	Still or carbonated	England
Ballygowan	Still or sparkling	Ireland
Highland Spring	Still or carbonated	Scotland
Llanllyr	Still or sparkling	Wales
Malvern	Still or carbonated	England
Strathmore	Still or sparkling	Scotland

Natural spring waters are obtained from natural springs in the ground, the waters themselves being impregnated with the natural minerals found in the soil and sometimes naturally charged with an aerating gas.

Bottle sizes for mineral and spring waters vary considerably from, for example, 200 ml to 2 l. Some brand names sell in both plastic and glass bottles, while other brands prefer either plastic or glass bottles depending on the market and the size of container preferred by that market.

Recently there has been a shift in consumer demand away from bottled waters. The reasons for this include:

- Environmental and sustainability concerns: in some cases, demand has reduced considerably. Regular tap water, from safe commercial supplies, has become more popular in food service operations and customers increasingly expect this to be available, chilled or served with ice.
- The emergence of commercial filter systems being used by food service operations: tap water is filtered at the establishment and then offered either as chilled still or sparkling water in branded carafes or bottles, for which the establishment makes a charge.

Squash, cordials and syrups

A squash may be served on its own, or diluted by water, soda water or lemonade. Squashes are also used as mixers for spirits and in cocktails or used as the base for drinks such as fruit cups. Examples are orange squash, lemon squash, grapefruit squash and lime cordial.

Syrups are concentrated, sweet, fruit flavourings. They are used as a base for cocktails, fruit cups or mixed with soda water as a long drink. The main ones used are:

- Cassis (blackcurrant)
- Cerise (cherry)
- Citronelle (lemon)
- Framboise (raspberry)
- Gomme (white sugar syrup)
- Grenadine (pomegranate)
- Orgeat (almond).

Syrups are also available as 'flavouring agents' for cold milk drinks such as milkshakes.

Information on the service of non-alcoholic bar beverages may be found on page 267.

Juices

Juices can be fruit, such as orange, pineapple, grapefruit or tomato, and vegetable, such as carrot or beetroot. They can be bottled, canned or sold in cartons. Apart from being served chilled on their own, these juices may also be used in cocktails and for mixing with spirits.

Pasteurised juices

The juice has been pasteurised (heat-treated) to preserve the juice. Pasteurisation deactivates the spoiling enzymes present in the liquids and can increase the shelf life of non-refrigerated beverages.

Fresh juices

These are natural products with limited shelf life.

Smoothies and milkshakes

Smoothies have become increasingly popular and are made in a blender. The ingredients required might include fresh fruit or vegetables (these are sweetened if necessary). Also frozen fruit, frozen yogurt, fruit juices, milk and honey may be used in a recipe. Crushed ice is often used to ensure the product is well chilled on serving. Pre-made bottled or carton versions are also available.

Milkshakes are made from:

- chilled milk
- syrups (concentrated flavourings)
- ice cream.

KEY TERM

Smoothies – drinks made using a blender.

▲ **Figure 6.17** Strawberry smoothie

③ PROCEDURES AND PRESENTATION FOR SERVING BEVERAGES

3.1 EQUIPMENT FOR SERVING BEVERAGES

Equipment and measures used to dispense cold beverages

Cask hand-pulled, electric keg

The main types of beer and cider glasses are:

- ½ pint/1 pint tankards for draught beer
- ⅓ pint (taster)
- 1 pint tumblers for draught beer
- tumblers for any bottled beer
- short-stemmed 34.08 cl (12 fl oz) beer glass for stouts
- ½ pint lager glass for lager
- wine goblets in various sizes including 22.72, 28.40 and 34.08 cl (8, 10 and 12 fl oz) for brown/pale/strong ales
- pitchers/jugs, usually 2- or 4-pint capacity.

Increasing sales of beers to be consumed with restaurant meals has encouraged changes in styles of glassware used. Generally, these beer glasses, although often based on the listing above, are more elegant in style and made of higher-quality glass; they may also be branded to match the product.

Optics and measures

Optics and measures are used to accurately measure:

- 25 ml/35 ml/50 ml for spirits, liqueurs and fortified wines
- 125 ml/175 ml/250 ml for still wines.

Optics are designed for clear spirits with a low sugar content. They should be washed regularly and checked to see that they are in good working order. A high sugar content would stop an optic working correctly and therefore a stamped measuring would be more suitable for dispensing the correct measure.

Strong-flavoured spirits such as Pernod should have a separate, bespoke optic as otherwise it would taint the next spirit used in the optic and spoil its flavour.

Carafes

Carafes can be used for the service of wine, and the legal measures for these are 250 ml, 500 ml, 750 ml, 1 litre. They can be made of glass, earthenware or metal.

Post mix dispensers

Post mix dispensers are widely used to produce soft aerated drinks such as cola, lemonade, tonic and soda water, especially where high volumes of mixers are required. Below the dispenser machine are boxes of post mix – concentrated liquid syrup. This is mixed with water to dilute the syrup and carbon dioxide is added to give the mix its aeration. This is a cheaper alternative to bottled or canned mixers and has a very high profit margin. Care must be taken to ensure the dilution is set at the correct mix (water/syrup/carbon dioxide) ratio to ensure a quality drink is dispensed.

Pre-packaged drinks

Bottles, cans and cartons are used for both alcoholic and non-alcoholic drinks. In this form, soft drinks are more expensive than post mix drinks but not all dispense bars are suitable for post mix drinks.

- Bottles, cans and cartons provide convenience and can offer a wider variety of choice to the customer.
- All bottles, cans and cartons should be wiped down before being placed into display fridges, with the label facing forward for ease of identification.

They also produce a lot of waste and should wherever possible be recycled.

Equipment required for serving cold beverages

All the equipment necessary for making cocktails, decanting wine, serving wine and preparing all other drinks ordered must be available at the bar to ensure correct and efficient service. The equipment will include the items described in Table 6.14 below.

▼ **Table 6.14** Equipment for serving cold beverages

Equipment	Description
Ice bucket and tongs	Plastic or metal buckets and tongs, often branded. The bucket may be double skinned to keep the ice cold and slow down the rate of melting
Ice machine	A good supply of ice will be needed, usually kept outside the bar as good ventilation is needed to ensure the machine can produce high volumes of ice. A plastic or metal scoop should be used to remove ice from the machine
Chilled unit	Drinks that are served chilled are stored within the chilled unit. For display all items should be 'faced up' with the labels facing the front of the unit so staff and customers can see what is on offer
Wine buckets and coolers	Either plastic or metal, they may require ice and cold water to be placed in them and may be double skinned so that a chilled bottle placed inside will remain cool
Bottle openers/waiters friend	A bottle opener is usually used for crown-capped bottles to remove the cap. This can be fixed to the wall/counter or be part of a tool kept on the bar. A waiters friend has a blade at one end to cut the foil on the bottle of wine, a corkscrew in the centre of the tool that is screwed into the cork, and a ratcheted mechanism that helps lever the cork from the bottle. It often has a bottle opener as part of the tool
Garnish trays	Sliced fruit and vegetable garnishes can be placed in trays and covered to keep them fresh and hygienic but easily accessible during service
Vending machine	A vending machine is an automated machine that provides items such as snacks, beverages, alcohol, hot beverages and confectionary to customers after money, a credit card, or a specially designed card is inserted into the machine
Bottle skip	Empty bottles are placed into the bottle skip to be wheeled out to the recycling container after the service period has finished. Usually made of heavy duty plastic and fixed to heavy duty wheels for ease of movement

Cocktail equipment

- Boston shaker: consists of two cones, one of which overlaps the other to seal in the mix. Made of stainless steel, glass or plated silver.
- Hawthorn strainer: used to strain the mix. This is a flat, spoon-shaped utensil with a spring coiled round its edge. It is used in conjunction with a cocktail shaker and mixing glass to hold back the ice after the drink is prepared. A special design is available for use with liquidisers and blenders.
- Drink mixer: used for drinks that do not need liquidising, especially those containing cream or ice cream. If ice is required, use only crushed ice.
- Blender: used for making drinks that require puréed fruit.
- Bar spoon: for use with a mixing glass when stirring cocktails. The flat 'muddler' end is used for crushing sugar and mint in certain drinks.

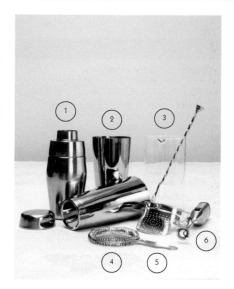 

▲ **Figure 6.18** Examples of cocktail bar equipment: (1) cocktail shaker, (2) Boston shaker, (3) mixing glass with bar spoon, (4) Hawthorn strainer, (5) jug strainer, (6) mini whisk, (7) straws, (8) ice crusher, (9) juice press, (10) ice bucket and tongs

▲ **Figure 6.19** Examples of bar equipment: (1) bottle coaster, (2) champagne star cork grip, (3) wine bottle holder, (4) vacu-pump, (5, 7, 9, 12) wine bottle openers, (6, 10) champagne bottle stoppers, (8) wine funnel, (11) wine bottle foil cutter, (13) champagne cork grip, (14) wine cork extractor, (15) appetiser bowls and cocktail stick holder, (16) measures on drip tray, (17) cutting board and knife, (18) cigar cutters, (19, 21) bottle stoppers, (20) bottle pourers, (22) crown cork opener, (23) mini juice press

Glassware

Glassware contributes to the appearance of the table and the overall attractiveness of the service area. All glassware should be clean and well-polished. Most manufacturers now supply hotel glassware in standard sizes for convenience of ordering, availability and quick delivery.

▼ **Table 6.15** Types of glassware

Type of glass	Use
Soda lime glass	For day-to-day use. Relatively inexpensive glassware
Lead crystal	Softer glass of high brilliance where the surface can be left plain or can be cut to produce prismatic effects and sparkle. Expensive
Borosilicate glass	Hard and heat-resistant glass used for flame ware
Tempered and toughened glass	Resistant to the effects of heat; this glass is mostly used as ovenware glass and can also withstand heavy usage

▼ **Table 6.16** Examples of sizes for glassware

Glass	Size
Beer	25–50 cl (½–1 pint)
Wine goblets	14.20, 18.93, 22.72, 28 cl (5, 6 ⅔, 8, 10 fl oz)
Champagne flute/tulip	18–23 cl (6–8 fl oz)
Shot	25 ml (1.5 fl oz)
Brandy balloon	23–28 cl (8–10 fl oz)
Cocktail glasses	4–7 cl (2–3 fl oz)

Equipment required when serving hot beverages

Hot water urns/vacuum flasks

Urns and vacuum flasks are a convenient way to have hot water available when a direct mains water supply is not possible. Urns can be powered by electricity via an extension cable if necessary or from transportable gas canisters. Where this is not possible, vacuum flasks/jugs are a suitable alternative but note that these will not maintain hot water at boiling point and therefore making quality tea and coffee may be compromised. It is recommended that flasks are marked as either 'tea' or 'coffee' or 'hot water' because tea and coffee made in the flask will taint the flavour and result in a very unappealing mix if the wrong flask is used.

▲ **Figure 6.20** Examples of insulated jugs and dispensers for coffee and tea service

Bean to cup machines

This machine produces a fresh cup of coffee each time. The coffee beans are stored in a hopper and ground specifically for the type of coffee selected, requiring little skill from the staff member to produce a high-quality beverage. The bulk of the rich flavour and aroma (which fades away the longer coffee grounds sit on store shelves) is retained during the extraction process without the need for paper filters, pods or loose coffee grounds.

Individual filters

Single cups of coffee can also be made with a disposable plastic individual filter, bought with the required amount of coffee already sealed in the base of the filter.

The filter is placed on to a cup. Freshly boiled water is then poured into the individual filter to the required level. The liquid infuses with the ground coffee within the individual filter and drips into the cup. A lid should be placed over the water in the filter to help retain the temperature. Time of making is approximately 3 to 4 minutes. Each individual filter is sufficient for one cup and, after use, the whole filter is thrown away.

▲ **Figure 6.21** Bean to cup machine

Pour and serve/filter machines

The principle behind this method is that when the measured quantity of fresh cold water is poured into the top of the pour-through filter machine, this water displaces the hot water already in the machine. This hot water infuses with the ground coffee and runs into the serving container as a coffee liquid ready for immediate use. It takes approximately 3 to 4 minutes to make one brew.

When coffee is made by this method, ensure that:

- the machine is plugged in and switched on at the mains
- the brew indicator light is on. This tells the operator that the water already held in the machine is at the correct temperature for use
- the correct quantity of freshly ground coffee, which will usually come in the form of a vacuum-sealed pack, is used. A fresh pack should be used for each new brew of filter coffee being made
- a new clean filter paper is used for each fresh brew.

Cafetière

The cafetière, or jug and plunger method, makes coffee simply and quickly by the infusion method and to order. This ensures that the flavour and aroma of the coffee are preserved. The cafetière is a glass container with a lip held in a black, gold or chrome-finished holder and sealed with a lid that also holds the plunger unit in position.

The method of making is completed simply by adding boiling water to the ground coffee, stirring and then placing the plunger unit and lid in position. A guideline to the quantity of coffee to be used might be:

- 2 level dessertspoonsful for the 3-cup size
- 6 level dessertspoonsful for the 8-cup size
- 9 level dessertspoonsful for the 12-cup size.

251

Infusion time is from 3 to 5 minutes. During this time the coffee grains will rise to the top of the liquid. After this if the plunger is moved slightly the coffee grains will fall to the bottom of the glass container. When the grains have fallen it is easier to push the plunger down.

▲ **Figure 6.22** Espresso machine

Espresso machine, bean grinders, tamper, knock out box

The espresso method is Italian in origin. Machines used to make this form of coffee can provide cups of coffee individually in a matter of seconds, with some machines being capable of making 300 to 400 cups of coffee per hour.

The method involves passing steam through the finely ground coffee and infusing under pressure. The advantage is that each cup is made freshly for the customer. Served black, the coffee is known as espresso and is served in a small cup. If milk is required, it is heated for each cup by a high-pressure steam injector. As an approximate guide, from ½ kg (1 lb) of coffee used, 80 cups of good-strength coffee may be produced. The general rules for making coffee apply here, but with this special and delicate type of equipment extra care should be taken in following any instructions.

The process for making espresso coffee can be summarised as follows:

1 Process sufficient coffee beans to the correct grind.
2 Insert correct dose into group handle.
3 Insert group handle into group head.
4 Use tamper to level and compact ground coffee.
5 Place cup under group head.
6 Select correct programme for hot water dispense.
7 Place cup on saucer with correct accompaniments.

Daily checks on espresso machines at the start of service include:

- steam valves opened
- steam wand(s) clean
- seals on group handles clean and undamaged
- steam pressure
- exterior of machine clean and polished.

Other equipment required to produce an espresso is listed in Table 6.17.

▼ **Table 6.17** Equipment used in making espresso

Equipment	Usage
Bean grinders	The bean grinders ideally should be made of ceramic disks which grind the roasted beans to the size of grain suitable for the type of coffee to be dispensed
Tamper	A tamper is used to level and lightly compress the grounds in the group handle; failure to do this will result in a poor-quality beverage lacking in flavour, aroma and possibly even grainy in texture
Knock out box	After each coffee is made the grounds need to be knocked out of the group head, into the knock out box; the group head should then be rinsed before the next lot of fresh grounds is dispensed and tamped down. The knocking box should be emptied regularly; the grounds can be taken away by companies specialising in recycling food waste for fuel, garden compost, etc.

Crockery and glassware

Equipment required for the tray service of coffee or tea is listed in Table 6.18.

▼ **Table 6.18** Crockery and glassware for serving coffee and tea

Tray	Equipment	
Coffee tray	tray or salver	
	tray cloth/napkin, teacup and saucer, teaspoon	
	sugar basin and tongs or a teaspoon according to the type of sugar offered	
	coffee pot	
	jug of cream or hot milk	
	stands for the coffee pot and hot milk jug	
Tea tray	tray or salver	tea strainer
	tray cloth/napkin	stands for teapot and hot water jug
	teapot	sugar basin and tongs
	hot water jug	teacup and saucer
	jug of cold milk	teaspoon
	slop basin	

Variations of this basic equipment will depend on the type of coffee or tea that is being served. For the various types of tea and their service see page 242.

For a list of modern by-the-cup coffee styles see page 239.

Thermometers

Thermometers measure temperature and are used in the preparation of hot beverages to ensure the correct temperature is reached. The most common type of thermometer is the hand-held wand thermometer. The bottom of the wand is inserted into the liquid and the temperature is read on the gauge which is fixed on the top end of the wand. Espresso machines and still sets usually have temperature gauges to indicate the temperature of the steam being used and the milk.

Methods of maintaining cellars to ensure optimum quality of beverages

Kegs/barrels

Keg beers have a typical maximum shelf life of 12 weeks. Keg beer should be consumed within three days of the container being opened, but this can be extended to up to seven days with correct temperature control and good hygiene practices.

▲ **Figure 6.23** Keg beers stored in a cellar

- It is good practice to turn off the supply of carbon dioxide to the keg between sessions, because the beer can absorb the carbon dioxide, making it difficult to dispense. To alleviate this problem, a mixed-gas system of carbon dioxide and nitrogen can be used.
- Before using the keg check the best-before date, that the new keg is full and that the gyle label is attached to the spear head.
- Turn off the gas supply to the keg.
- Release the broaching head correctly (there are two main types: lever-operated and pushdown, twist and lock).
- Remove the used keg and replace with the new keg.
- Remove the plastic gyle cap from the spear head and connect the broaching head to the keg.
- Turn on the gas supply and ensure the beer is flowing at the beer tap.

Cask/barrel

Cask/barrel-conditioned beers have a typical maximum shelf life of five weeks. Once the cask has been delivered to the cellar it needs to be stillaged by being placed on a stillage rack and secured in place using scotches. It can take between 12 and 36 hours for the yeast to settle and the beer to become clear and bright and ready for dispensing. The cask beer should be consumed within three days of the container being broached.

To prepare the cask for use a wooden peg is tapped into the cask closure to release the excess carbon dioxide. There are two types of pegs:

- Shive: soft pegs made of porous wood that allows the gas to vent naturally.
- Spile: hard pegs made of hard wood or plastic that is impervious to gas and keeps the natural condition of the cask when it is not being dispensed.

Finally, a tap is driven through the keystone of the cask, so the beer line can be connected.

Gases

▲ **Figure 6.24** Cask beer stored on a stillage rack with tap, shive and spile in place

A dispense gas is usually a mixture of two pressurised gases: carbon dioxide and nitrogen. These are used for dispensing both beer and post mix drinks. Care should be taken when storing and handling these gas canisters as if damaged they can leak the gases and could lead to asphyxiation. The cylinders should be kept in a separate, secured area when not in use. In the cellar, they should be securely chained to the wall to reduce the risk of them falling over or being knocked out of place. If any damage is noticed, the cylinder should not be used and should be discharged of gas in an open space, after securing to avoid it injuring anyone or causing damage to persons or property.

Post mixes

The syrups which are used as the base for post mix, such as cola, are contained in a bag or pouch which sits in a box. The dispense line is attached to the bag by a screw-fix mechanism. Care should be taken to ensure the connection is done correctly and the bag is not damaged, or the syrup will leak out and the product will be spoilt.

The mixes have a shelf life and therefore stock will need to be rotated to ensure the 'first in, first out' (FIFO) policy of the establishment. Keep the boxes in a dry environment off the floor. As they contain a high amount of sugar they are very attractive to pests and rodents, so ensuring the outer cardboard packaging is not allowed to deteriorate will give stability to the box and reduce the likelihood of damage and possible leakage.

Temperature

One of the most important things in a beer cellar is maintaining an even temperature. Temperatures should be between 13 and 15°C (55–58°F) to prevent spoilage. If temperature is not at the right level and constant, cask beers will go sour very quickly and taste of vinegar. If cask beers are too cold they can become cloudy – this is called 'chill haze'.

Factors that determine good beer cellar management

- Good ventilation to maintain the air quality, prevent dampness and the growth of mould.
- Effective lighting so stock and equipment can easily be located and maintained in a safe environment.
- Walls and ceiling must be kept clean and maintained.
- The floor should be kept clean, dry and free of rubbish.
- Even temperatures of 13–15°C (55–58°F) to prevent the spoilage of stock.
- Avoidance of strong draughts and wide ranges of temperature.
- Beer left in pipes after closing time should be drawn off.
- Care should be taken that the cellar is not overstocked as stock takes up space and costs money.
- All spiles removed during service should be replaced after closing time.
- Any ullage should be returned to the brewery as soon as possible.
- Reordering should be carried out on one set day every week after checking the stock of beers, wines, minerals, etc.
- Strict rotation of stock must be exercised, with new bottle crates or cases being placed at the rear and old stock pulled to the front for first issue.

3.2 POURING TECHNIQUES AND PRESENTATION METHODS

Each establishment will have its own range of glassware for the service of drinks. Examples of glasses for the service of drinks are shown in Figure 6.25. It is also common to use branded glassware for branded products as a company standard.

Cocktail glasses: for cocktails generally and smaller: for Pink Lady and White Lady

The saucer: for Champagne cocktails and Daisies. Not really used much now

The tulip: all Champagne and sparkling wines and also for Buck's Fizz and the Grasshopper

The flute: for sparkling wines generally and also for Brandy Alexander and Kir Royale

Paris goblet: in various sizes and used for wines, waters and beers. Also used for Cobblers, Pina Colada and Green Blazer

Worthington: for bottled beers, soft drinks and for Pimms, Coolers and long drinks such as Fruit Cups

Rocks/Old Fashioned glass: also known as whisky glass, often used for any spirits and mixers. Also used for drinks such as Old Fashioned and Negroni

Highball/Collins glass: used for spirits and mixers and for Highballs, John Collins, Tom Collins, Mint Julep, Tequila Sunrise and Spritzers

Brandy balloon: small for brandies and for B & B and brandy and liqueur-based cocktails, for frappés and for liqueurs. Larger for long drinks such as Pimms

Sour glass: for spirits and mixers and for sours and as an alternative to rocks glass

Martini Cocktail glass: for Dry, Medium and Sweet Martinis and Manhattans but also used for other cocktails

Slim Jim: for spirits and mixers and for sours and as an alternative to highball glass

Copita (sherry): mainly for sherry but also used for sweet wines

Elgin: traditional glass used for sherry in single and double measure (Schooner) sizes. Also in smaller version used for liqueurs

Port or sherry (dock) glass: used for both ports and sherries and also for sweet wines

Lager/pilsner: different sizes used for bottled and draught lager beers

Beer (straight): traditional beer glass in different sizes for half and full measures of any beers and also beer based mixed drinks

Beer (dimple): traditional beer glass in different sizes for half and full measures of any beers and also beer based mixed drinks, including Black Velvet and also Pimms

▲ **Figure 6.25** Examples of drinking glasses and their uses

Pouring beers and ciders

Draught or bottled beer and cider should be poured slowly down the inside of the glass, with the glass held at a slight angle (see Figure 6.26). This is especially important where a beer may produce a large head, for example Guinness or stouts.

▲ **Figure 6.26** Service of draught beer

Keg

Draught beers should have a small head on them. The bar person should ensure that he or she serves the correct quantity of beer with a small head and not a large head to make up the quantity required. A beer in good condition will have a head, or froth of the beer, clinging to the inside of the glass as the beer is drunk. This is sometimes called lace on the glass. Some establishments will also train staff to create a pattern in the froth to tie in the brand, such as a shamrock for Guinness.

Bottles – crown cap and corked

▲ **Figure 6.27** Service of bottled beers

- Remove the crown cap with a bottle opener, or if a cork has been used a corkscrew.
- Hold the bottle and the glass at an angle to each other. The neck of the bottle should not be placed in the beer when pouring.

- Pour the beer slowly so as not to form too much of a head.
- As the bottle is emptied the glass should be upright in the hand.

If a bottled beer has a sediment, a little beer must be left in the base of the bottle to ensure that the sediment does not go into the poured beer.

Cask beer

Cask beer is served straight from the cask. Care must be taken to draw off the beer slowly to avoid taking any sediment in the cask. Usually the cask will be sat on a sprung rack and this will tilt according to the amount of liquid still remaining in the cask. Less liquid in the cask will mean the cask has a steeper angle to its tilt to encourage the sediment to stay in the bottom of the barrel.

Cans

Inside some cans there is a widget that is designed to aerate the beer when the ring pull is pulled. The widget rises up through the liquid, and the gas, previously under pressure, forces the beer through slits. The beer then becomes aerated and therefore thicker, similar to hand-dispensed beer from a pump. Care needs to be taken not to shake the can before opening and all cans should be wiped over with a clean cloth to remove any dust or residue on the exterior of the can, especially by the opening, to reduce the risk of any external contaminants getting into contact with the beer.

Tilting the can and glass towards each other when pouring will reduce the amount of foam and standing time required for the beer to settle before consumption.

Wines including sparkling wines

By the glass

Wines are mostly offered in 125 ml or 175 ml measures. With the exception of sparkling wines, it is often better to serve the wine in a glass larger than the measure. This allows the aroma to develop in the glass and the wine to be better appreciated. Many establishments now also pour a measure of wine into a small carafe or pitcher for the service of wine by the glass. This then allows the customer to pour the wine into their glass as required.

Wines may be served in the types of glasses indicated in Table 6.19.

▼ **Table 6.19** Types of glasses used for serving wine

Type of wine	Type of glass for serving
Champagne and other sparkling wines	Flute or tulip-shaped glass
German and Alsace wines	Traditionally long-stemmed German wine glasses but nowadays a medium-size wine glass
White wines	Medium-size wine glass
Rosé wines	Flute or medium-size wine glass
Red wines	Large wine glass

▲ **Figure 6.28** Bottle types and glasses for wine

From the bottle

Service of white wine

Obtain the wine from the bar or storage area. Check that the order is correct and that the wine is clear and at the correct service temperature: 10–12.5°C (50–55°F). Take it to the table in an ice bucket/cooler and place the ice bucket in a stand.

Figure 6.29 shows service from a bottle with a cork. For bottles with screw caps, the opening procedure is to hold the whole length of the seal in the opening hand and to hold the base of the bottle in the other hand. The closure is held firmly in the opening hand with more pressure from the thumb and first finger around the cap itself. The bottle is then sharply twisted using the hand holding the base. There will be a click and then the upper part of the screw top can be removed.

If a fresh bottle is required, then fresh glasses should be placed upon the table, and the host asked to taste the new wine before it is served.

1   Present the bottle to the host with the label showing – this allows them to check that the correct wine is to be served. Ensure the correct glasses are placed on the table for the wine to be served. For white wines, make sure a clean napkin is tied to the handle of the ice bucket – this is used to wipe away condensation and water from the outside of the bottle before pouring the wine.

2   Using a wine knife, cut the foil all the way round, below or above the bottle rim, at the top of the bottle (some bottles have small caps rather than foils). The top of the foil only is then removed, and the top of the cork is wiped with the napkin.

3   Remove the cork using a wine knife. Smell the cork in case the wine is 'corked'. For white wines, place the cork in the ice bucket. If the wine is a high-quality vintage wine, then the cork would generally be placed on a side plate at the head of the host's cover. This cork should have the name and year of the wine printed on it. Wipe the inside of the neck of the bottle with the napkin. Wipe the bottle dry.

4   Hold the bottle for pouring so that the label may be seen. Use the waiter's cloth in the other hand, folded, to catch any drips from the neck of the bottle. Give a taste of the wine to the host, pouring from the right-hand side. He or she should acknowledge that the wine is suitable, i.e. that it has the correct taste, bouquet and temperature.

5   Serve ladies first, then gentlemen and the host last, always commencing from the host's right. However, nowadays service often follows from one customer to the next, anti-clockwise.

6   Fill each glass two-thirds full or to the widest part of the bowl – whichever is the lower. This leaves room for an appreciation of the bouquet.

7   Replace the remaining white wine in the wine bucket and refill the glasses when necessary.

8   On finishing pouring a glass of wine, twist the neck of the bottle and raise it at the same time to prevent drops from falling on the tablecloth.

▲ **Figure 6.29** Service of white wine

Service of champagne and sparkling wine

The same method is used for opening all sparkling wines. The wine should be served well chilled in order to obtain the full effect of the secondary fermentation in the bottle – effervescence and bouquet. Dessert wines, champagne and other sparkling white wines should be served at 4.5–10°C (40–50°F).

The pressure in a champagne bottle, due to its maturing and secondary fermentation, is about 5 kg per cm² (about 70 lb per sq in). Great care must therefore be taken not to shake the bottle otherwise the pressure will build up and could cause an accident.

Sparkling wine should be served in a flute or tulip-shaped glass, from the right-hand side of each customer. It is also worth considering lifting and holding the glass by the stem so as to pour the wine more easily and quickly, and to reduce the frothing of the wine.

1 After presenting the bottle to the host, the wine is ready for opening.

2 The neck of the bottle should be kept pointed towards a safe area in the restaurant during the opening process to avoid any accidents to customers should the cork be released suddenly.

3 The thumb should be held over the cork with the remainder of the hand holding the neck of the bottle.

4 The foil around the top of the cork is separated from the foil around the neck of the bottle by pulling on the tab on the foil, or by using a wine knife to cut it. The foil is not removed.

5 The wine cage is untwisted and is carefully loosened, but not removed.

6 Then, holding the cork and the cage in one hand, the bottom of the bottle should be twisted with the other hand to slowly release the cork.

7 The cork is removed.

▲ **Figure 6.30** Opening sparkling wine

Service of red wine

The basic procedure for the opening and serving of red wines is the same as for white wines described above. Red wines should be served at 15.5–18°C (60–65°F). Some young red wines may also be drunk cool at about 12.5–15.5°C (55–60°F).

If the red wine to be opened is young, the bottle may stand on an underplate or coaster on the table and be opened from this position. This adds to the overall presentation of the bottle and may prevent drips of red wine from staining the tablecloth. Although there is no technical reason why red wine should be served with the bottle in a wine basket or wine cradle, these are used in a number of establishments for display/presentation purposes. They also assist in retaining the sediment, found in some older red wines, in the base of the bottle.

The cork should be removed from the bottle of red wine as early as possible so that the wine may reach room temperature naturally. If the wine is of age and/or is likely to have heavy sediment, then the wine should be decanted. It should be placed in a wine basket when first presented to the customer. Placing the bottle in a wine basket helps to keep the bottle as horizontal as possible, comparable to its storage position in the cellar, in order to prevent the sediment being shaken up. The wine should then be opened and decanted. Alternatively, if the wine is ordered in advance, it can be left standing (unopened) for a few days before opening to allow any sediment to drop to the bottom of the bottle.

At the table – decanting by the bottle

Decanting is the movement of wine from its original container to a fresh glass receptacle, leaving the sediment behind.

There is a trend to decant younger red wines because exposure to air improves the bouquet and softens and mellows the wine. Decanting also enhances the appearance of the wine, especially when presented in a fine wine decanter. However, the permission of the host should always be sought before decanting a wine in the restaurant.

1   Extract the cork carefully. The cork may disintegrate because of long contact with alcohol, so be careful. Place a single point light behind the shoulder of the bottle, a candle if you are decanting in front of customers, but a torch, light bulb or any light source will do.

2   Carefully pour the wine into an absolutely clean decanter. The light will reveal the first sign of sediment entering the neck of the bottle.

4   The wine should always be checked to make sure that it is clear before being presented at the table for service.

3   As soon as sediment is seen, stop pouring into the decanter but continue pouring into a glass. The latter wine, when it settles, can be used as a taster or for sauces in the kitchen.

5   If the wine is not clear after decanting then it should be decanted again into a fresh decanter, but this time using a wine funnel that has a piece of fine muslin in the mouth of the funnel. If the wine is still not clear it should not be served, and a new bottle of the wine selected. It is also more common now for a wine funnel to be used as part of the decanting process generally.

▲ **Figure 6.31** Decanting wine

Very old red wine can break up with too much exposure to air. These wines can be left to stand for a few days to allow the sediment to settle in the bottom of the bottle. The bottle is then opened before the meal is served and the wine is poured very carefully straight into the glass, with the bottle held in the pouring position as each glass is approached. This prevents the wine slopping back to disturb the sediment. Sufficient glasses should be available to finish the bottle, thereby ensuring that the wine does not re-mingle with its sediment during the pouring process.

Different settings

Venues may offer different bars for various purposes of service. See Table 6.20.

▼ **Table 6.20** Settings

Type of bar	Explanation
Dispense bar	This offers service to restaurant staff or to event wine waiters. It removes the need for a bar within the dining area and reduces queuing time. It may be situated at the end of an existing bar or even dispense directly from the cellar
Customer bar	This is the traditional style bar where the customer approaches the bar, orders their drink and it is served and paid for
Function and event bar	These can be either fixed, in-situ bars or movable temporary bars. They can be cash only, account only, or part-cash and part-account bars. Often at large events the host will offer a free bar, on account for the pre-dinner drinks, and revert to a cash bar after dinner. The bar staff must be mindful of any limit set on the 'free bar' and later of anyone who is not authorised trying to gain additional drinks on a private tab that has not been authorised Event bars do not hold the full range of products as held in the main bars due to their size and this also assists in stock control and profitability

Service of spirits, liqueurs and fortified wines

Spirits

Spirits can be served either as a long or a short drink. As a long drink the spirit is measured and poured over ice into a 'Slim Jim' or other tall glass. A mixer will then be partly added or topped up to the customer's preference, and garnished as appropriate. A neat spirit (straight up) or on the rocks (over ice) would be served in a tumbler.

▼ **Table 6.21** Classic spirit mixers and garnish

Spirit	Glass	Mixer	Garnish
Gin	Slim Jim	Tonic water	Slice of lemon
Whisky	Tumbler or Slim Jim	Water, ginger ale, soda water	
Rum	Tumbler or Slim Jim	Cola, fruit juice	Slice of orange
Vodka	Slim Jim	Tonic water, lemonade, fruit juice	Slice of lemon or fruit to match juice

Liqueurs

These sweetened and flavoured spirits may be served by the glass or, in a restaurant, they may also be served from a liqueur trolley at the table.

If a customer asks for a liqueur to be served frappé, for example crème de menthe frappé, it is served on crushed ice and a larger glass will be needed. The glass should be two-thirds filled with crushed ice and then the measure of liqueur poured over the ice. Two short drinking straws should be placed into the glass before the liqueur is served.

If a liqueur is requested with cream, for example Tia Maria with cream, then the cream is slowly poured over the back of a teaspoon to settle on the top of the selected liqueur.

Basic equipment required on a liqueur trolley:

- assorted liqueurs
- assorted glasses – liqueur/brandy/ port
- draining stand
- 25 and 50 ml measures
- service salver
- drinking straws (short-stemmed)
- jug of double cream (for topping drinks such as Tia Maria)
- teaspoons
- ice
- wine list and check pad.

Other beverages served from the liqueur trolley include brandies and fortified (liqueur) wines such as port or madeira.

▲ **Figure 6.32** Bar trolley for the service of liqueurs

Fortified wine

Fortified wines are best served slightly cool in copitas (the small glasses used in Spain for pouring sherry – or, as the Spanish call it, jerez) or any small wine glass.

Port is served at room temperature or cool if it is white port.

Accompaniments

Coasters, cocktail napkins, cocktail sticks, straws, umbrellas, cocktail gherkins, maraschino cherries, fruit slices, wedges, peanuts, crisps and savoury snacks should all be ready to offer with a drink at the point of service. This will add value to the customer experience, increase reputation and repeat business.

Mixers

The choice of mixers to go with spirits often comes down to a customer's preference. Stocking mixers that complement your spirit offer will require some knowledge of the botanicals and ingredients used to produce the spirits. Select mixers that bring out the flavours of the spirits and balance the drink flavours, e.g. tonic water, soda water, ginger ale, cola, fruit juice, lemonade, bitter lemon. The garnishes should be fresh and seasonal.

Styles – on the rocks, straight up

A neat spirit (straight up) or on the rocks (over ice) would be served in a tumbler.

Cocktails

Glassware

Cocktails should always be served well chilled in an appropriately sized glass with the correct garnish, straw and umbrella, according to the policy of the establishment. Many cocktails are served in a traditional V-shaped cocktail glass (often called a Martini glass) but, if the cocktail is a long drink, then a larger glass such as a Slim Jim or Highball will be better suited. The key consideration here should be the presentation of the cocktail as seen by the customer.

Methods of cocktail-making

There are four main methods for making cocktails and mixed drinks: shaken, stirred, built and layered. See Table 6.8 on page 236 for a description of each method.

Garnishes and accompaniments

Adding visual interest and even a touch of style, cocktail garnishes are a standard component to most mixed drinks. A cocktail garnish is an ornamental item used to add character and a bit of flavour to a mixed drink.

Cocktail garnishes can vary widely but are most easily classified into two types: edible and inedible. Commonly comprised of citrus fruits, vegetables and savoury items, edible garnishes receive most of the attention, while inedible garnishes like umbrellas, straws and even sparklers have become more popular.

▼ **Table 6.22** Basic cocktail garnishes

Garnish	Description
Individual fruits and vegetables	Maraschino cherry is popular for the Manhattan and Old Fashioned. Martini and Gibson are traditionally served with an olive or onion
Herbs	Using herbs as a cocktail garnish adds an attractive element and unique flavour to many different drinks. Clean and select herbs carefully, to extract the best aroma and flavour. Place them in your hand and slap your hands together before placing them in drink
Citrus twist	The basic citrus twist is commonly used to impart light flavour to a cocktail and can be created using several different methods. Cutting a piece of zest from a fresh lemon is by far the easiest approach. It's important to minimise the amount of the bitter white pith taken when you cut the twist. Once cut, the zest is twisted above the cocktail to express the oils on to the cocktail and the remaining fruit rind can be rubbed around the rim of the rim of the glass and either inserted into the drink or discarded
Wedge	A wedge is a section of cut fruit that can be either placed on the rim of the glass or squeezed and placed into the cocktail. A simple complement to many drinks, the wedge is often cut as an eighth of an entire fruit with an additional incision made in the middle of the wedge to make placement on the rim easier
Fruit wheel	Primarily used for ornamentation, the wheel is a sliced fruit or vegetable that's placed on the rim of the glass. Occasionally combined with other items, the fruit wheel is often removed before consuming the drink
Flag	Flag garnishes are somewhat loosely defined, and include vertical items like celery, scallions and pieces of fruit combined on a skewer with items like skewered berries that are placed at the top of the glass. Great for creating a dramatic visual impact, flags can also be used to indicate what's contained within the drink
Rimmed glass	There are two methods to rim the edge of the glass: • moisten the rim of the glass with liquid (e.g. water, fruit juice or egg white) and place the overturned glass on a small plate containing the desired material (e.g. salt, sugar or spice). This will adhere the material to the rim, but it will also be inside the glass and will affect the flavour of the drink. • prepare the glasses in advance by moistening the outer rim of the glass and then gently rolling it through the material at an angle to prevent anything from getting into the glass

Accompaniments

Cocktails are often accompanied by small cornichon gherkins which are very salty. Also, olives and peanuts. The saltiness offsets the sweetness of the cocktail but also makes the customer thirsty and therefore desire more drinks.

Other non-alcoholic cold beverages

Glassware

Staff need to ensure all glassware is clean and polished before service of cold beverages. Due to this style of drink being refreshing and hydrating, depending on the style of glassware used by the establishment, it would be normal practice to serve water and juices in a long glass over ice.

Aerated waters

Aerated waters may be served on their own, chilled, in either Slim Jim tumblers, wine goblets, Highball glasses or 34.08 cl (12 fl oz) short-stemmed beer glasses, depending on the requirements of the customer and the policy of the establishment. They may also accompany other drinks as mixers, for example:

- Whisky and dry ginger
- Gin and tonic
- Vodka and bitter lemon
- Rum and cola.

Natural spring waters/mineral waters

Natural spring or mineral waters are normally drunk on their own. Some mineral waters may be mixed with alcoholic beverages to form an appetising drink. In all cases, they should be drunk well chilled, at approximately 7–10°C (42–48°F). If drunk on their own, they should be served in an 18.93 cl (6 $\frac{2}{3}$ fl oz) Paris goblet or a Slim Jim tumbler. Examples include Apollinaris, Buxton, Perrier and Badoit.

Squashes

A squash may be served on its own diluted by water or lemonade. Squashes are also used as mixers for spirits and in cocktails or used as the base for drinks such as fruit cups. A measure of squash should be poured into a tumbler or 34.08 cl (12 fl oz) short-stemmed beer glass containing ice. This is topped up with iced water or the soda siphon. The edge of the glass should be decorated with a slice of fruit where applicable and drinking straws added.

For service from the lounge or restaurant, the wine butler or lounge waiter must take all the items required to give efficient service on a service salver to the customer. These items will include:

- straws
- jug of iced water (on an underplate to prevent the condensation running on to the table)
- small ice bucket and tongs (on an underplate because of condensation)
- soda siphon
- a coaster on which to place the glass in the lounge.

The coaster should be placed on the side table in the lounge and the glass containing the measure of squash placed on the coaster. The waiter should then add the ice and ask whether the customer would like iced water or soda to be added. Drinking straws should be placed in the glass at the last moment if required. It may be necessary to leave the iced water and ice bucket on the side table for the customer. If this is the case they should be left on underplates.

Juices

Juices are held in stock in the bar as either bottled/canned/carton or freshly squeezed.

All juices should be served chilled in a 14.20 cl (5 fl oz) goblet or alternative glass.

Tomato juice should be served chilled on an underplate with a teaspoon. The Worcestershire sauce should be shaken, the top removed, placed on an underplate and offered as an accompaniment. The goblet may have a slice of lemon placed over the edge as additional presentation.

If fresh fruit juice is to be served then the service should be similar to the service of squash described above, except that a small bowl of caster sugar on an underplate with a teaspoon should be taken to the table.

Syrups

Syrups are never served as drinks in their own right. They are concentrated, sweet, fruit flavourings used as a base for cocktails, fruit cups and milkshakes or mixed with soda water as a long drink.

Garnishes and accompaniments

Garnishes for non-alcoholic drinks are commonly fruit- or vegetable-based, such as a slice of orange in orange juice, a stick of celery in tomato juice.

Customers should be offered the choice of ice and lemon/lime/orange or other appropriate fruit to garnish their drinks, as well as ice, as some customers prefer not to have either in their drinks.

A straw and swizzle stick are traditionally provided but to reduce the use of unnecessary plastic an environmentally friendly alternative should be sought.

Nuts, olives and other salted snacks may be offered to customers as standard or be available to order. These should be served in small dishes and if appropriate cocktail sticks and a small cocktail napkin should also be offered.

Hot beverages

Crockery and glassware

The service of hot beverages requires the appropriate crockery and glassware to be used. Staff need to ensure sufficient stock are clean, polished and placed where they will be readily available during service. If chips or cracks are found then the items should be put aside, the damage recorded and then disposed of.

▼ **Table 6.23** Glassware and crockery for hot beverages

Beverage	Glassware and crockery
Coffee	Coffee may be served in cups, demi-tasse (half cups) usually for espresso, mugs, tall glass latte/hot chocolate glasses with a handle The use of small coffee cups (demi-tasse) has declined for conventional coffee service although they are still sometimes used in event catering. These cups are also used for espresso Mocha is served in the same way as hot chocolate All crockery should be made of strong and durable materials to withstand the heat of the liquid as well as withstand cleaning in a dishwasher
Tea	Tea is usually served in a teacup with a saucer or in a mug, depending on the style of the establishment If the company has a brand logo on its crockery/glassware, then this should be facing the customer when the beverage is served Teapots can be either metal or ceramic porcelain. These should be in good condition and if chipped or cracked must be discarded. Teapot sizes range from individual one-cup pots up to industrial 20-cup pots
Hot chocolate	Hot chocolate is most often served individually in special heat-resistant glasses that fit into a special holder with a handle. It can also be served in a mug Hot chocolate may also be presented in a pot or jug for the customer to pour into a teacup Usually white sugar and sweeteners are offered for the customer to add, so the glasses or mugs are usually presented on side plates or saucers together with a teaspoon. Teacups are presented on saucers together with a teaspoon
Malted drinks	Other hot drinks, including malted drinks such as Horlicks and Ovaltine, are served in the same way as hot chocolate but without any additional cream or toppings
Tisanes (fruit or herbal teas)	These are becoming popular; they contain no caffeine or tannin and are consumed either hot or cold, without the addition of milk. Service is the same as for normal tea as above or in a tea glass
Alcoholic hot drinks	Drinks such as mulled wine, glühwein, wassail (mulled cider) and hot buttered rum are usually served during the winter and regional recipes are often favoured. They can be served in mugs or latte glasses

▲ **Figure 6.33** Service of hot chocolate in a glass with additional toppings

Equipment for tray service

See Table 6.18 on page 253 for the equipment required for the tray service of coffee or tea. Variations of this basic equipment will depend on the type of coffee or tea that is being served.

See Unit 207, page 309 for information on serving tea and coffee for table and assisted service.

Accompaniments

▼ **Table 6.24** Accompaniments for hot beverages

Accompaniment	Method
Sugar	Sugar comes in a variety of styles and service styles: white, brown, cubed, loose, crystals, on sticks, in sachets. Every establishment will have its own service standard and choice of the style of sugar offered to accompany the hot beverage provision
Cream/milk	Whipped cream to go on top of hot chocolate and coffee can either be whipped by the establishment or for convenience and waste reduction aerosol cans of cream can be purchased. Creams can be flavoured with vanilla, caramel, toffee, etc., similar to syrups to put into coffee for flavour
Milk	This can be offered fresh in small jugs, either hot or cold, to be added by the customer or in sealed cartons of fresh or UHT
Lemon	Usually sliced and de-pipped and offered with light teas such as English Breakfast, for a refreshing drink

3.3 COMMON FAULTS AND INCIDENTS ASSOCIATED WITH BEVERAGE SERVICE

Beer faults

Although thunder has been known to cause a secondary fermentation in beer (affecting its clarity), faults are usually a result of poor cellar management. The common faults in beer are described below.

▼ **Table 6.25** Common faults with beer

Fault	Description
Flat beer	Flat beer may result when a wrong spile has been used – a hard spile builds up pressure, a soft spile releases pressure. When the cellar temperature is too low, beer often becomes dull and lifeless. Dirty glasses, and those that have been refilled for a customer who has been eating food, will also cause beer to go flat
Cloudy beer	This may be due to too low a temperature in the cellar or, more often, may result from the beer pipes not having been cleaned properly
Fobbing	This generally refers to excess foaming while pouring draught beer. This results in product loss. This can be due to incorrect line sizing, incorrect line pressure, uptake of carbon dioxide at the point of origin (i.e. the keg or serving vessel) during or prior to dispense, unclean beer lines, improperly cleaned and rinsed glassware, incorrect beer temperature at the point of dispense (i.e. warm beer), or defects in the beer line

Wine faults

Faults occasionally develop in wine as it matures in bottles. Nowadays, because of improved techniques and attention to detail regarding bottling and storage, faulty wine is a rarity. Some of the more common causes of faulty wine are shown in Table 6.26.

▼ **Table 6.26** Common faults with wine

Fault	Description
Oxidation	This is caused by bad storage leading to too much exposure to air, often because the cork has dried out. The colour of the wine browns or darkens and the taste slightly resembles that of Madeira. The wine tastes 'spoilt'
Corked wines	These are wines affected by a diseased cork caused through bacterial action or excessive bottle age. TCA (*trichloro anisole*) causes the wine to taste and smell foul. This is not to be confused with cork residue in wine, which is harmless
Sediment	This is organic matter discarded by the wine as it matures in the cask or bottle. It can be removed by racking, fining or, in the case of bottled wine, decanting

Hot beverage faults

▼ **Table 6.27** Common faults with coffee, tea and hot chocolate

Fault	Description
Temperatures	Water has not reached boiling point
	Infusion time too short or too long
	Coffee kept at wrong temperature
	Brewed tea being kept too long before use or kept at wrong temperature
	Coffee sediment remaining in storage or serving compartment
	Temperature of the liquid used being insufficient to dissolve the hot chocolate powder or granules
	Poor storage has affected the commodity being used
	Dirty equipment: no regular cleaning or maintenance; limescale build-up
Strength and quality	Water not fresh
	Insufficient or too much coffee used
	Stale or old coffee/tea used
	Incorrect grind of coffee used for equipment in operation
	Coffee not roasted correctly
	Tea reheated
	Incorrect amount of drinking chocolate (powder or granules) to liquid (water or milk)
Milk	Milk is not fresh

Types of incidents

▼ **Table 6.28** Common types of incidents

Incident	How to avoid incident
Incorrect orders and complaints	Check the order with the customer
	Ensure this is recorded at the point of order, either electronically or in writing
	Check the beverage against the order before serving to the customer
Order of service	Cold items should be assembled on the tray or service point before the hot items are prepared. This will ensure all are served at the correct temperature to the customer
Spillages and breakages	Ensure cups and glassware have a heavy base which increases their stability and do not over-fill
	When carrying items on a tray place heavy and hot items nearest to the side carried against the body and ensure an even weight distribution over the tray. This makes the try easier to hold on one arm when offloading the items
	Never over-fill the tray as this increases the likelihood of items falling over or off the tray
Faulty equipment	If equipment becomes defective it should be removed immediately, and sent for repair if possible
	When the above is not practical, equipment should be disconnected from any power supply and a notice displayed to show it is out of order awaiting repair or replacement
	Using faulty equipment increases the risk of injury to customers and staff as well as damaging reputation and lowering standards

4 LEGISLATION FOR THE RESPONSIBLE SERVICE OF ALCOHOL

4.1 ALCOHOL CONTENT AND EFFECTS OF ALCOHOL

Alcoholic content

There are two main scales of measurement of alcoholic strength. These are:

1 Organisation Internationale Métrologie Légale (OIML) Scale (European) – this ranges from 0% to 100% alcohol by volume (ABV).
2 American Scale (USA) – this ranges from 0° to 200°.

The OIML Scale gives the ABV in the drink at 20°C. ABV indicates the amount of pure alcohol in a liquid. For example, a liquid measured as 40 per cent alcohol by volume will have 40 per cent of the contents as pure alcohol. Under the American Scale, alcoholic strength of 80° equals 40 per cent by volume.

The alcohol by volume (ABV) is usually listed on the label of the drink. The strength of different percentages by ABV are listed in Table 6.30.

▼ **Table 6.29** Approximate alcoholic strength of drinks (OIML scale)

0% alcohol	Non-alcoholic
not more than 0.05%	alcohol free
0.05–0.5%	de-alcoholised
0.5–1.2%	low alcohol
1.2–5.5%	reduced alcohol
3–6%	beer, cider, FABs* and 'alcopops'**, with any of these being up to 10%
8–16%	wines, usually around 10–13%
14–22%	fortified wines (liqueur wines) such as sherry and port, aromatised wines such as vermouth, vins doux naturels (such as Muscat de Beaumes de Venise) and sake***
20–70%	Spirits usually at 40%; liqueurs very wide range

* 'FABs' is a term used to describe flavoured alcoholic beverages, for example Bacardi Breezer (5.4%)

** 'Alcopops' is a term used to describe manufactured flavoured drinks (generally sweet and fruity) which have had alcohol, such as gin, added to them. They are also known as alcoholic soft drinks or alcoholic lemonade. Usually 3.5 to 5% but can be up to 10%

*** Sake is a strong (18%), slightly sweet, form of beer made from rice

Effects of drinking too much alcohol

Drunkenness

While alcohol can initially make someone happy and sociable, as a person becomes more drunk they may become disorientated and have difficulty walking and speaking coherently. The effects of drunkenness include blurred vision, slurred speech and being unsteady. Alcohol also depresses the brain and nerve function, affecting a person's judgement, self-control and motor skills.

Most of the alcohol consumed passes into the bloodstream, from where it is rapidly absorbed. This absorption may be slowed down if the drink is accompanied by food, but the amount of alcohol consumed will be the same. The liver must then burn up almost all the alcohol consumed, with the remainder being disposed of in urine or perspiration (sweat).

It takes approximately one hour for the liver to burn up one unit of alcohol; if it has to deal with too much alcohol over a number of years, it will inevitably suffer damage.

Social implications

Even moderate consumption of alcohol can affect work performance in several ways:

- **Anti-social behaviour**: violence related to alcohol usually happens because of a lowering of inhibitions and normal attitudes and actions when sober. In addition, vomiting, urinating and causing disturbance contributes to anti-social behaviour while under the influence of alcohol.

- **Nuisance**: alcohol can reduce a person's ability to be competent in their role, causing nuisance in the workplace by others having to either check or redo work. In addition, a person under the influence of alcohol has a reduced ability to gauge when their behaviour is no longer acceptable or appropriate.
- **Absence from work**: there is ample evidence that people with alcohol dependence and drinking problems are on sick leave more frequently than other employees, with a significant cost to employees, employers, and social security systems.
- **Work accidents**: in Great Britain, up to 25 per cent of workplace accidents and around 60 per cent of fatal accidents at work may be linked to alcohol.
- **Productivity**: heavy drinking at work may reduce productivity. Performance at work may be affected by both the volume and pattern of drinking. Co-workers perceive that heavy drinkers have lower performance, problems in personal relationships and lack of self-direction, though drinkers themselves do not necessarily perceive effects on their work performance.
- **Unemployment**: heavy drinking or alcohol abuse may lead to unemployment, and unemployment may lead to increased drinking.
- **Social issues**: drunkenness accounted for 339,000 estimated admissions related to alcohol consumption in 2015–16 according to the NHS statistics report on alcohol in May 2017. The ratio of admissions was 61% male to 39% female.
- **Family issues**: Table 6.30 identifies a range of issues affecting families.

▼ **Table 6.30** The impacts of alcohol on families

Family issues	Explanation
Parental responsibility	Drinking can impair how a person performs as a parent and a partner, as well as how she or he contributes to the functioning of the household. It can have lasting effects on their partner and children, for instance through home accidents and violence
Birth defects	Children can suffer Foetal Alcohol Syndrome (FASD) when mothers drink during pregnancy or the father has a history of alcohol abuse
Home social environment	After the birth, parental drinking can lead to child abuse and have numerous other impacts on the child's social, psychological and economic environment
Impact of drinking on family life	This can include substantial mental health problems for other family members, such as anxiety, fear and depression
Drinking outside the home	This can mean less time spent at home. The financial costs of alcohol purchase and medical treatment, as well as lost wages, can leave other family members destitute
Financial burden and safety	When people drink it often affects their family or partners, who may need to contribute more to the income of the household. There is also the potential for an increased risk of violence towards family members, partners or friends

Health issues

Short-term effects

When alcohol is consumed, it is carried around the body in the bloodstream and affects every organ in the body. On average, it takes about one hour for your body to break down one unit of alcohol.

However, this can vary, depending on:

- your weight
- your gender
- your age
- how quickly or slowly your body turns food into energy (your metabolism)
- how much food you have eaten
- the type and strength of the alcohol
- whether you are taking medication and, if so, what type.

It can also take longer if your liver is not working normally.

One unit of alcohol is equal to 10 ml (liquid) or 8 g (weight) of alcohol. This is roughly equivalent to:

- ½ pint of ordinary beer or lager
- one glass of wine (125 ml)
- one glass of sherry (50 ml)
- one measure of vermouth or other apéritif (50 ml)
- one measure of spirits (25 ml).

If you:

- drink a large (250 ml) glass of wine, your body takes about three hours to break down the alcohol
- drink one pint of beer, your body takes about two hours to break it down. One pint of strong lager is equivalent to three units, so this will take longer. However, this time can vary, depending on the factors mentioned above
- have a few drinks during a night out, it can take many hours for the alcohol to leave your body. The alcohol could still be in your blood the next day. This means that if you drive the day after an evening of drinking, you could still be over the legal alcohol limit.

Long-term effects

Heavy drinking can increase the risks of:

- anaemia
- cancer
- cardiovascular disease
- cirrhosis of the liver
- dementia
- depression
- seizures
- gout
- high blood pressure
- infectious diseases
- nerve damage
- pancreatitis.

For further information on alcohol consumption and on the short- and long-term effects of drinking alcohol, please see the Drink Aware website at:

www.drinkaware.co.uk/alcohol-facts/health-effects-of-alcohol

Changes in behaviour

Moderate alcohol consumption can have a relaxing effect and help people to integrate more easily with others. Conversely, high levels of alcohol consumption can lead to mood swings, paranoia, violent behaviour, and loss of inhibitions and rational decisions.

4.2 LEGISLATION RELATING TO THE SALE OF ALCOHOLIC BEVERAGES

Weights and Measures Act

All sales of goods by weight or measure should be in accordance with the legislative requirements of the Weights and Measures Act (1985) and the Weights and Measures (Packaged Goods) Regulations 1986. These usually require:

- a display of the prices and the measures used for all spirits, wines, beers, ciders and any other alcohol served
- the food and beverage items for sale to be of the quantity and quality demanded by the customer
- the use of officially stamped measures.

To comply with the law, whisky, gin, rum and vodka are sold in measures of 25 ml or 35 ml or multiples thereof. All other spirits do not require measuring under law but, in order to calculate sales and profits, it is usual practice to measure all spirits unless making a cocktail that is a mixture of three or more liquids, in which case the liquids used do not require measuring.

- Beer, wine and cider are sold in measures of ⅓ and ½ pints and multiples thereof.
- Wine by the glass is sold in measures of 125 ml or 175 ml and multiples thereof.
- Wine in a carafe or jug is sold in measures of 25 cl, 50 cl, 75 cl and 1 litre.

In England and Wales the Weights and Measures Act states that premises must display the notice shown in Figure 6.34.

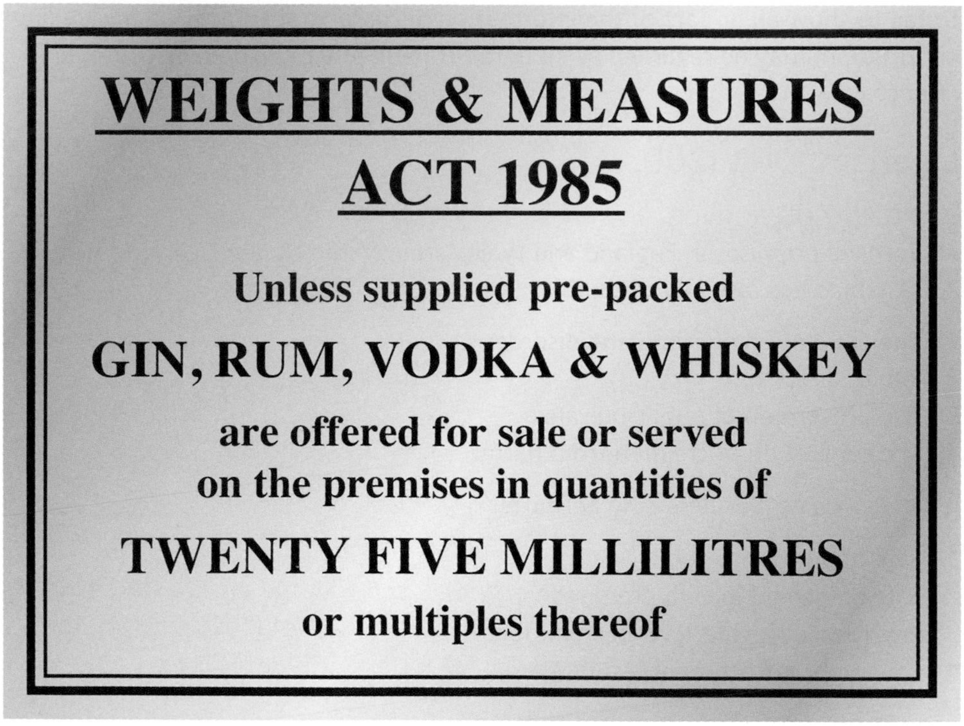

WEIGHTS & MEASURES ACT 1985

Unless supplied pre-packed

GIN, RUM, VODKA & WHISKEY

are offered for sale or served
on the premises in quantities of

TWENTY FIVE MILLILITRES

or multiples thereof

▲ **Figure 6.34** Weights and measures notice

A sign declaring this must be clearly displayed for any customer to read. Prices must also be clearly displayed for all alcoholic drinks sold on the premises.

Under the **Consumer Protection from Unfair Trading Regulations 2008**, menus and price lists must include all material information required by an average consumer to make an informed choice, which may include the following:

- accurate description of the name and brand of the drink, including alcoholic strengths (ABVs) where appropriate
- prices, inclusive of VAT. It must also be made clear if you have a compulsory service charge, a cover charge or a minimum charge per customer.

Where you have beer pumps and 'optic' stands you should ensure the advertising signs attached to these accurately indicate the brand of drink being dispensed.

How or where you display the information required above is not prescribed but it should be clear and easily readable by the average consumer. The best way to ensure that customers are given the required information is by using detailed menus or a clearly displayed price list, so there is sufficient information to enable a consumer to make an informed decision before they are committed to a purchase.

Bars should show the price list at the bar where orders are taken. In cafés and restaurants, the prices can be marked in menus or price lists. So that customers are informed from the outset, prices could be displayed in your window or the entrance to your premises.

To fail to show all or part of the information necessary, or to provide misleading information, may be regarded as an unfair trading practice and constitute an offence.

Licensing Act (2003)

Licensing objectives

All licensed premises in England and Wales are covered by the Licensing Act 2003, which has four **key objectives**:

1 The prevention of crime and disorder
2 Public safety
3 The prevention of public nuisance
4 The protection of children from harm.

It also contains four **licensing activities**:

1 Sale of alcohol by retail
2 Sale of alcohol in club premises
3 Provision of regulated entertainment
4 Late night refreshment.

The act requires a food service operation to:

- display a summary of the premises' licence, including the days and times of opening, the name of the registered licence holder, the licence number and a valid date
- display a price list of drinks
- adhere to restrictions on under-aged persons being served alcohol and employed to serve alcohol
- ensure an authorised person (or the Personal Licence Holder) is on site at all times.

Other types of licences include licences for music, both live and pre-recorded (these are issued by Phonographic Performance Limited (PPL) and Performing Right Society (PRS)), dancing, gambling, theatrical performance and television display. If you are showing broadcast or recorded films in a public space, you will also need to consider whether a licence for the copyrighted material is required – several companies such as Film Bank Media and the Motion Picture Licensing Corporation can provide appropriate licences. If you wish to show a film, you must enforce age restrictions in line with ratings from the British Board of Film Classification (BBFC). Breaching these guidelines is a criminal offence.

Regulated entertainment

This is broadly defined as any entertainment that takes place in the presence of an audience (whether members of the public or a club), or otherwise for profit, and where the premises has the purpose of providing the entertaining concerned. It may include:

- a performance of a play
- an exhibition of a film
- an indoor sporting event
- a boxing or wrestling entertainment
- a performance of live music
- the playing of recorded music
- a performance of dance.

In all cases, the supervisor and staff should be aware of the provisions and limitations of the licences held by the premises to ensure compliance.

Personal Licence

This is only required where alcohol is sold and allows someone who holds an accredited licensing qualification, and has applied for and been granted from their Licensing Authority a licence, to sell or authorise the sale of alcohol from a licensed premises in England and Wales. They must abide by the terms of a Premises Licence.

There are specific guidelines relating to the presence of the Personal Licence Holder on site. The Secretary of State makes the following recommendations in the National Guidance:

- The person(s) authorised to sell alcohol should be clearly identified.
- The authorisation should have specified the acts which may be carried out by the person being authorised.
- There should be an overt act of authorisation, for example a specific oral or written statement given to the individual(s) being authorised.
- There should be in place sensible arrangements for monitoring by the Personal Licence Holder of the activity authorised by him or her on a reasonably regular basis.

The guidance recommends that Personal Licence Holders give written authorisations to individuals that they are authorised to retail alcohol. This is known as 'delegated authority'

While this is not guaranteed to satisfy an enforcing authority, it does encompass the points in the guidance mentioned above.

Premises Licence

In order to retail alcohol, the business must have a Premises Licence. This is a licence granted to a building or area that carries out one or more of the four licensable activities as required under the Licensing Act (2003). It is granted by the Licensing Authority for premises in its area and continues to operate unless and until it is suspended or revoked. It may be issued for a specific time period.

These licences are applied for through the Local Licensing Authority and can take several weeks to obtain.

Designated premises supervisor

Every shift should ideally be supervised by at least one Personal Licence Holder. Without these licence holders the business is in contravention of licensing law and will not be able to retail alcohol until the correct licences are in place.

Opening hours

These will be shown on the operating schedule, a summary of which must be displayed on the premises where it can be easily seen by the public. This shows when the premises will be open and closed for one or more of the licensable activities. The schedule includes:

- Type of premises – for example a restaurant or supermarket.
- Facilities provided – such as bars, a beer garden, a supermarket with a café, night club with dance area.
- Activities – such as live music, cabaret, karaoke, dancing.
- Licensable activities – for example the sale of alcohol.
- Operating times for different days or weeks.
- Name and address of the Designated Premises Supervisor (DPS).
- Details of how you plan to meet the licensing objectives.

The opening hours granted to a premises allow opening during these times. It does not mean a premises has to be open, but that if it wishes to be open to trade it can do so during these hours unless a Temporary Event Notice (TEN) has been granted to extend the hours of trading.

These conditions apply to the whole of England and Wales.

The Prevention of Crime under the Licensing Act includes the prevention of immigration crime including the prevention of illegal working in licensed premises.

Consumption of alcohol by young people

Under the Licensing Act (2003) it is an offence to sell alcohol to anyone under the age of 18 years. However, a 16- or 17-year-old may consume beer, wine or cider if this is ordered and paid for by a responsible adult and is part of a sit- down, knife-and-fork style meal, and where the adult sits dining with the 16- or 17-year-old. A snack, such as a bowl of chips or a sandwich, would not be considered substantial enough.

Additionally, the 16- or 17-year-old should not be seated at the bar but in an area set aside for consumption of food as the main activity.

A Fixed Penalty Notice (£90) could be served if anyone should:

- obtain alcohol for a person under 18
- sell alcohol to a person under 18
- consume alcohol under 18
- allow consumption of alcohol under 18
- deliver alcohol to a person under 18
- allow delivery of alcohol to a person under 18.

30 What is the classic mixer for gin?

31 Cocktail garnishes can vary widely but are most easily classified into two types. What are they?

32 When serving beverages, name **two** precautions that should be taken to reduce spillages and breakages.

33 What does ABV mean?

34 What are the approximate alcoholic strengths of beer, fortified wines and spirits?

35 How long does it take on average for the liver to burn up one unit of alcohol?

36 List **two** health risks heavy drinking can lead to.

37 Give one example of what one unit of alcohol is equal to.

38 A premises that retails alcohol is required to have two specific licences. Name **one** of them.

39 Give one of the reasons why alcohol may be refused to be sold to someone on a licensed premises.

40 Name **one** serious consequence of not following legislation in a licensed premises.

BEVERAGE SERVICE

INTRODUCTION

The purpose of this chapter is to help you to develop and implement interpersonal and practical skills for a range of beverage service styles found within the hospitality industry.

This chapter will help you to:

- ensure you are displaying a professional attitude at all times
- respond to different customer situations
- know the equipment you will need to prepare different drinks
- know what skills you need when serving beverages.

1 INTERACTION WITH CUSTOMERS

1.1 PERSONAL PRESENTATION

Hygiene

It is important for all food handlers to take care with personal hygiene and to adopt good practices when working with food and beverages.

For further information see:

- Unit 205, page 158 for guidelines on creating and maintaining a professional and hygienic appearance.
- Unit 203, page 91 for guidelines on hand-washing.
- Unit 205, page 158 for advice on dressing as per establishment requirements and for advice on grooming.

Body language and posture

When dealing with customers staff should stand up straight and lean slightly forward to listen to what is being said. Standing with your feet slightly apart will aid in your balance, make you more relaxed and protect your back from straining. If you have to wait for any time while in view of customers do not stand with your arms folded or your back to the customers – think 'on-stage'.

For further information on body language, see Unit 201, page 23 and Unit 205, page 158.

When dealing with complaints stand calmly with your hands either clasped loosely or by your sides to show you are being passive, create a space between you and the customer, and if necessary step back to widen the gap.

If you feel nervous, try not to fiddle with your hair or clothing; take several deep breaths to calm yourself and smile, this will give the appearance that you are in control and give the customer confidence in your abilities, which in turn will give you more confidence.

Attitude

The correct approach to the customer is of the utmost importance. Staff should be able to anticipate the customer's needs and wishes without being servile. During service, a careful watch must be kept on customers to check the progress of the meal – this allows service staff to anticipate customer needs with minimal intrusion on their meal.

Remember, the customer contributes to the staff wages through payment of their bill and therefore deserves to be treated with respect and given the best service possible.

See Unit 205, page 159 for more advice on developing a positive attitude.

1.2 TRANSFER OF INFORMATION

The importance of transferring accurate information to customers, team members and other departments

Staff need to know the importance of clear communication between customers, team members and other departments. Ensuring all parties understand what is required, where and when, and any special requests or needs will contribute to the customer's experience and enhance the working atmosphere for staff.

Accurate communication will reduce the risk of customer dissatisfaction, reduce errors, reduce the risk of possibly serving something a customer may be allergic or intolerant to and reduce wastage, and therefore save money and increase profit.

See Unit 205, page 181, for information on the main methods of taking food and beverage orders.

Taking orders and special requests

Taking an order may be done verbally at the bar or may be written down in a check pad if the customer is in the lounge or restaurant. All checks should be written in neat handwriting and clearly set out. Abbreviations may be used when taking the order, as long as everyone understands them.

Special requests to accommodate the needs or individual tastes of the customer may include omitting or adding items to their food or drink order. For example, still or sparkling water, with or without ice, how a cocktail might be made and using specific brands of drinks.

For beverage orders, an efficient system must operate to ensure that:

- the correct wine and other drinks are served at the right table
- the service provided is charged to the correct bill
- a record is kept of all wine and other drinks issued from the bar
- management can assess sales over a financial period and make comparisons.

The usual system of control is a duplicate check pad. The colour of the check pad may be pink or white, but it is generally pink or some other colour to distinguish it from a food check. This acts as an aid to the cashier and the accounts department in differentiating quickly between food (white) and drink (pink) checks (see Figure 7.3 on page 303).

See Unit 202, page 43 for guidelines on supporting customers with additional needs relating to mobility, sight and communication difficulties.

Wine check

When the beverage order is taken, staff must remember to fill in the four items of information required, one in each corner of the wine check (see Figure 7.3 on page 303). These are as follows:

1 Table number or room number
2 Number of covers
3 Date
4 Signature.

Abbreviations are allowed when writing the order if they are understood by the bar staff and the cashier. When wines are ordered only the 'bin number', together with the number of bottles required, should be written down. The bin number is an aid to the bar staff and cellar staff in finding the wine quickly. Each wine in the wine list will have a bin number printed against it.

On taking the order, the staff should hand both copies to the bar staff, who retain the top copy. After preparing the drinks order, leave the duplicate copy of the order on the tray to enable the server to identify which drinks they need to collect and serve to the customer.

Briefings

Briefings are critical to ensuring the smooth running of service. Staff need to be briefed *twice* every shift, once when they come on to their shift – to allocate duties and to receive information of customers with special requirements, expected events or special groups and stock information. The second briefing will be just prior to service to advise staff of their workstations, any special requirements will be repeated, and additional service points will be raised. Uniforms and grooming should be checked to make sure that they meet the establishment's standards. The drinks list and bar menu (if applicable) will be discussed, highlighting allergens, substitutions and any special promotions. Any drinks that are not available will be confirmed to the staff.

A debrief at the end of service should happen to discuss any issues that arose during service. If necessary, notes of the issues will be written up and investigated further before the next shift. Staff who have performed well should be praised and any customer feedback, including compliments, should also be communicated to the team at this point. This will help all team members to improve and encourage them to give excellent customer service.

Product knowledge – opening times, services, facilities, menu, prices

Staff need to know not only the food and beverage on offer but also additional information regarding the premises – such as opening times, types of service on offer, other facilities and prices. Staff will be able to do their tasks more efficiently if they understand how the other departments in their organisation operate. In addition, a complete understanding of the products on offer will communicate to the customer that the establishment is organised and well run.

▼ **Table 7.1** Additional information regarding the premises

Product knowledge	Explanation
Opening times	The venue may have different opening times on different days of the week, it may have different rules for residents and non-residents and may offer different services within its premises. Hotel residents are by law allowed to consume alcohol 24 hours a day. Their guests may also consume alcohol if they are being entertained by the resident for the entire time of the non-resident's visit. Non-residents who are not guests of a resident may not consume alcohol past the hotel's permitted hours and should be informed in sufficient time that their alcoholic beverages need to be consumed by the end of permitted hours
Types of service	The establishment may have several restaurants offering different styles of food and beverage, ranging from a café, brasserie or snack bar to a full silver service restaurant. Breakfast may be served in a different area to dinner and the lounge may offer light snacks and drinks only. Therefore, it is vital that staff are aware of this information and the times when customers may use these facilities
Facilities	If the venue also offers other facilities, such as leisure, a casino, business services, conferencing, accommodation, etc., then staff should have knowledge of this and be able to either direct the customer or ask someone to further explain what is available to the customer
Menu and prices	A good understanding of the beverages menu and the prices will enable staff to assist customers with their queries and shows a professional attitude

Billing

Beverages ordered at the bar are often paid for there, but can be added to a bill if a large number of drinks are ordered and consumed, or if a meal is to be ordered and consumed later during the service period. This is often referred to as a 'tab'. This bill should be settled in the same way as a table bill before departure.

Stock levels

Stock is a valuable commodity and may have a limited shelf life. Use-by dates must be carefully managed to avoid unnecessary waste and therefore cost to the business.

A regular stocktake will ensure the correct level of stock for the business is maintained and will provide a check against inaccuracies and theft. Businesses will stocktake on a weekly or monthly basis depending on their policy. Spot checks can also take place at other times. If you are responsible for completing a stocktake, any discrepancies must be reported to your manager. For further information on stock, see Unit 208, page 315.

Waste and breakages

Wastage in food service comes from several areas:

- energy
- water
- food
- packaging.

To reduce the amount of waste at a premises the following should be considered:

- **Energy** – use low-energy equipment, such as chillers and fridges, to reduce the use of electricity. Ensure that there is sufficient air flow around appliances such as fridges and ice machines (lack of air circulation will result in machines working harder to remain cool and will waste electricity). Purchase energy-efficient equipment when you replace existing machines; most cost-effective modern models have low energy consumption.
- **Water** – sensor taps, flow-limiting taps and water meters remind users to reduce the amount of water they use in carrying out their duties.
- **Food** – waste fruits and vegetables (used to make drinks and garnishes) should be recycled for composting wherever possible.
- **Packaging** – recycle and reuse where possible. Purchase fruit and vegetables loose rather than prepacked or in recyclable packaging such as cardboard or hessian sacking.
- **Breakages** – these are costly to a business; all breakages should be recorded to assist in reordering of stock and to establish any trends of where and when breakages occur.

Types of communication used to transfer information

Body language and listening

See Unit 201, pages 22 and 23 for information on body language and listening.

Written, verbal and electronic communication

See Unit 205, pages 161 and 162 for information on written, verbal and electronic communication methods.

1.3 CUSTOMER INTERACTION

Communicate with customers, team members and other departments

Staff will need to communicate with many people throughout their working day, both internally and externally. To ensure a smooth service and maintain customer satisfaction, it is vital that communication is clear, and that information can be passed on or acted upon easily once communicated.

In person – meet and greet and through briefings

See Unit 205, page 163 for information and guidance on communicating with customers, team members and other departments in person.

Via the telephone – enquiries and orders

See Unit 205, page 163 for information and guidance on dealing with enquiries and orders via the telephone.

Writing – recording orders and bookings

See Unit 205, page 164 for information and guidance on recording orders and bookings.

How to respond to customers during service

See Unit 205, page 164 for information on responding to customers during service.

Dealing with incidents during service

- For information on dealing with customer illness and dress code, see Unit 205, pages 166 and 167.
- For guidelines on supporting customers with additional needs relating to mobility, sight and communication difficulties, see Unit 202, page 43.
- For guidelines on how to deal with customers who are suspected of having had too much to drink, see Unit 202, page 70.
- For guidelines on recording incidents, see Unit 202, page 71.

Under-age customers

Staff need to be aware that young people under the age of 18 may not purchase intoxicating drinks. However, if they are seated having a substantial meal and have a responsible adult accompanying them, also consuming a substantial meal, who orders them either beer, wine or cider and pays for the drinks, then this would be legal. Service staff should still ask for identification to confirm that the young person is 16 or 17 and if in doubt service should be politely refused.

2 BEVERAGE SERVICE SKILLS

2.1 PREPARE AND SET UP FOR SERVICE

Maintain cellar/storeroom

Cellars and storerooms can be dangerous places to work in because of the many hazards present. Correct working practice should be respected and followed at all times to ensure the safety of the employees and customers.

- Appropriate, protective clothing must be worn when working in cellars and storerooms. Safety goggles, steel toe-capped shoes, aprons and heavy-duty gloves should be available for employees to use.
- Gas cylinders should be secured to the cellar wall with a chain, safety strap or clamp when in use. Empty or unused cylinders should be laid down on the cellar floor to prevent them falling over.
- Carbon dioxide and nitrogen gases can leak from damaged casks or cylinders, joints and connections. Both these gases are odourless and, if inhaled, can cause a person to become unconscious. If a leak is suspected, the gas supply must be turned off immediately.
- Cylinders are high-pressure containers that are charged to 660 psi (pounds per square inch) and can be lethal if damaged. If a cylinder is damaged do not use it and inform your manager or supplier.
- Always use correct manual handling of casks, kegs and gas bottles, crates, boxes and heavy sacks. To prevent back injury kegs and barrels should be moved around the cellar by rolling them across the floor. Crates, boxes and sacks should be moved using an appropriate trolley or sack barrow. Heavy items may require two people to lift them safely.
- Casks remaining on the floor should be bung uppermost to better withstand the pressure.
- Boxes and crates should be stored off the floor on heavy-duty metal racking to allow for air to circulate and the floor to be easily cleaned.
- The cellar and storeroom floors should be washed down as required, but weekly with a dilute solution of chloride and lime (mild bleach) as a minimum.
- All cellar and storeroom equipment should be kept scrupulously clean. This includes measures, scales, scoops, funnels and tubing used for moving liquids from containers.
- Drink crates and boxes should be stored correctly so they do not topple over. Full crates or boxes should not be stacked on empty crates, as they will be top heavy and become unstable.
- Do not tamper with a cask or barrel. These are pressurised containers – whether they are empty or full. If a cask or barrel is damaged, do not use it and inform your manager or supplier.

▲ **Figure 7.1** Cellar equipment

A cellar should only be used for the storage of cellar equipment and drinks. Equipment that you would expect to find in a cellar is listed in Table 7.2.

▼ **Table 7.2** Cellar equipment

Recommended equipment	Use
Thermometers	Used to check cellar and beer temperatures
Humidity gauges	Used to check the humidity of the cellar
Stainless steel buckets	Used to collect **ullage** and to clean equipment
Brushes	Different sizes to clean beer lines and equipment
Mallet	Used to punch the **shive** on cask ales so a **spile** can be fitted to let the beer vent
Dipstick	Used to check the levels of beer
Mop and bucket	Used to clean the cellar floor
Cask taps, spiles, corks, bungs	Used to maintain the dispensing of beer

KEY TERMS

Ullage – missing liquid unable to be sold. Collected from drip trays or left in the bottom of kegs or casks.

Shive – a wooden disc placed within the opening of a beer cask.

Spile – a peg that fits the air hole of the shive.

Security procedures

A cellar should always be locked when unattended. Access may be restricted to key personnel to make the control of stock easier to enforce. Remember that the contents of a cellar are valuable and are susceptible to pilfering.

Cellar storage of beer

See Unit 206, page 254 for information and guidelines on cellar storage of beer.

Cellar storage of wine

Wines should ideally be stored in an underground cellar with a northerly aspect and free from vibrations, excessive dampness, draughts and odours. The cellar should be absolutely clean and well ventilated, with only subdued lighting and a constant cool temperature of 12.5°C (55°F) to help the wine develop gradually. Humidity should be kept between 45 per cent and 65 per cent to prevent dampness and the wine corks from drying out.

Wines should be stored on their sides in bins (this refers to a slot or shelf on a rack) so that the wine remains in contact with the cork. This keeps the cork expanded and prevents air from entering the wine – a process that quickly turns wine to vinegar. Wines should also be stored with labels uppermost. This ensures that the wines can be easily identified, and it protects the label by keeping it away from the base surface of the bin. It also ensures that any sediment is always located on the side of the bottle away from the label. This approach is also used for wines with alternative stoppers, such as screw tops.

White, sparkling and rosé wines are kept in the coolest part of the cellar and in bins nearest the ground (because warm air rises). Red wines are best stored in the upper bins. Commercial establishments usually have special refrigerators or cooling cabinets to keep sparkling, white and rosé wines at serving temperature.

Storage of other drinks

Spirits, liqueurs, squashes, juices and mineral waters are stored upright in their containers, as are fortified wines. The exceptions are port-style wines, which are destined for lying down, and these are treated the same as wines (see above).

Clean drink dispense lines

Keg beer lines should be cleaned once a week on average. This will prevent the build-up of yeast deposits that will eventually restrict the flow of the beer. Clean beer lines will keep the beer clear and bright. All cleaning chemicals should be kept in a separate, locked cupboard. Always check the manufacturer's instructions before using a cleaning agent. Before handling cleaning fluid, you should wear the appropriate protective clothing (PVC gloves, goggles and an apron).

How to clean drink dispense lines:

- Turn off the gas supply to the keg.
- Remove the keg couplers and clean them in a bucket of warm water with a cleaning fluid solution mix and rinse with clean water.
- Clean the cleaning socket that the keg coupler connects with, with a cleaning fluid solution mix and rinse with clean water.
- Connect each keg coupler to its correct cleaning socket and turn on the gas supply.
- Turn off the beer coolers to prevent the cleaning solution freezing in the beer lines.
- Fill the cleaning container with clean, cold water.
- Place buckets under the beer taps, remove the diffusers and draw the water through the beer lines until all traces of beer have been removed.
- Carefully follow the manufacturer's instructions, mixing the right amount of cleaning fluid for the size of your cleaning container.
- Draw the cleaning solution through the beer line.
- After about 15 minutes, draw fresh cleaning solution through the beer line.

- If the system is heavily soiled you may want to repeat this process a couple more times, but do not leave in longer than recommended by the manufacturer's instructions – refer to the cleaning fluid container.
- Thoroughly rinse the cleaning container and refill with clean, cold water.
- Draw the water through the beer lines until all traces of the cleaning solution have been flushed out.
- Reconnect the beer couplers, switch the gas back on, replace the diffusers and draw the beer through the beer line.

Cask-conditioned beer lines need to be cleaned more frequently than keg beer lines because live yeasts exist in the beer, so the beer lines will become contaminated.

- Turn off the flow of beer at the cask tap.
- Unscrew the line fitting from the cask tap and allow any beer in the line to flow into a clean stainless-steel bucket. This can be returned to the cask once cleaning has been completed.
- Place the end of the beer line in the cleaning solution.
- Draw the cleaning solution through the beer line using the hand pump on the bar.
- Leave for the recommended time.
- Place the end of the beer line in a container of fresh water and pull the water through the line until all the cleaning fluid has been removed from the beer line.
- Remove the beer line from the container of fresh water and draw through the water in the line.
- Reconnect the beer line to the cask and draw the beer through the line until it appears at the beer pump.
- Before dispensing beer from a recently cleaned beer line check that there is no trace of the cleaning agent. This can be achieved by sight, smell and taste. Serving beer with a cleaning agent present can cause sickness, diarrhoea and allergic reactions.

Temperature

Ideally, the bar fridges should be between 1 and 4°C to be able to serve well chilled drinks. For white wines, temperatures can be 8 to 12°C and for sparkling wines this can be 4 to 10°C.

Red wines, sprits and fortified wines are mostly kept at an 'ambient' temperature (not refrigerated).

Check cleanliness

The bar area should be checked for cleanliness; all surfaces should be wiped down with sanitiser, including shelves, racks and fridges, as required. All equipment should be clean from the previous service and uncovered when put into its correct position ready for service.

Rubbish bins should have been emptied and cleaned at the end of the last service; check this has been done – and that they have been lined with a clean bin liner. Empty bottle skips should be placed under the bar and the floor should be swept and mopped before service recommences.

All glassware and crockery if tea/coffee is made in the bar should be checked for cleanliness and polished as required. Cutlery as appropriate to the service style should be polished and stored near to the service point.

Replenish stock

Determining stock levels

For the establishment, the central stock levels needed to meet expected sales demand may be determined by using past sales data. As well as ensuring stock levels meet expected demand, using this historic data can also minimise the amount of money tied up in the stock being held. Good stock control can be supported by the application of a 'just in time' (JIT) approach to purchasing. JIT involves only ordering stock as required in order to meet the forecasted demand, rather than holding unnecessarily high stock levels, just in case.

All the individual outlets within an establishment – such as the lounge, lounge bar, cocktail bar, saloon bar, brasserie, dispense bars and floor service – should draw their stock on a daily or weekly basis from the cellar. Each outlet will hold a set level of stock or liquor called '**par stock**' that is sufficient for a service period – this can be a session or a day, or up to a week.

The level of the par stock will be determined by:

- the amount of storage space available in the service areas
- expected sales demand
- the time it takes for deliveries.

At the end of each service period, each individual outlet will **requisition** for the amount of drink consumed in that one service period to ensure that the stock level is brought back up to par.

Receiving stock

When receiving stock, it is important that the quantity, quality and use-by dates are checked. Use the delivery note to check against the order form because, once the delivered stock is signed for, it then becomes the responsibility of the establishment. Items that are damaged during transportation and delivery must be identified and the supplier will issue a credit note so the establishment does not get charged for these products. Prior to the delivery it is advisable to get the empty kegs, casks, crates and gas cylinders ready for collection. These are chargeable containers and should be returned to the supplier once they are empty for a refund. This also prevents a build-up of empty containers in your cellar.

Beverage control procedures

In any food service establishment where income is received from the sale of wine and drink, a system of control and costing must be put into operation. The system used will depend entirely on the policy of the establishment. Some or all of the record books listed in Table 7.3 may be necessary, depending on the requirements of the food service operation.

KEY TERMS

Par stock – set level of stock.

Requisition – complete an order for stock from the stores.

▼ **Table 7.3** Record books used in beverage control

Book	Used to record
Order book	Orders made to suppliers
Goods inwards/goods received book	Goods received from suppliers
Goods returned book	Goods that are sent back to suppliers
Returnable containers book	Returnable containers sent back to suppliers
Cellar ledger	Stock movement in and out of the cellar
Bin cards	Stock of individual lines in the cellar
Requisition book	Restocking orders for individual service areas
Daily consumption sheets	Usage of stock in individual service areas
Ullage book	Breakage, spillage and wastage
Off-sales book	Items sold at off-sale prices
Transfers book	Movement of stock between different service areas

Although referred to as books here, most modern systems are computer-based. However, the basic processes are the same whatever method is used to record the data. A summary of the basic steps in bar and cellar control is given in Figure 7.2.

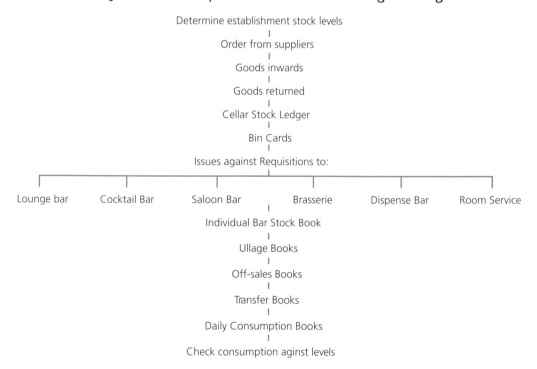

▲ **Figure 7.2** Basic steps in bar and cellar control

Stocktaking

All drinks are valuable commodities and have a limited shelf life. Use-by dates must be carefully observed and managed to avoid unnecessary waste that is costly to the business. Regular stocktakes will ensure the correct level of stock for the business is maintained and will provide a check against inaccuracies and theft. Businesses will conduct stocktakes on a weekly or monthly basis depending on their policy. Spot checks can also take place at other times. If you are responsible for completing a stocktake, any discrepancies must be reported to your manager.

Service equipment and accompaniments

Prepare the bar service top according to the standards of the establishment. This may include some or all of the following items:

- cutting board
- fruit knife
- Angostura bitters
- peach bitters
- fruit, such as lemons, oranges, apple
- Worcestershire sauce
- cucumber
- cocktail sticks
- fresh eggs (for cocktails)
- Maraschino cherries
- mixing glass and bar mixing spoon
- straws
- Hawthorne strainer
- tea strainer
- wine funnel
- wine coasters
- olives
- spirit measures
- cocktail shaker/strainer
- soda siphon
- nuts and crisps
- ice bucket and tongs
- coloured sugar.

2.2 TAKE AND PROCESS ORDERS

Prepare the room for service

Customer areas

Prior to service, the customer area should be checked to ensure the following has been done:

- Carpets should be vacuumed.
- Hard floors should be mopped clean.
- Furniture should be checked for cleanliness and vacuumed/polished as appropriate.
- Table surfaces should be cleaned/clothed.
- Menus/drinks lists should be placed on to tables.
- If flowers are placed on tables, these should be fresh, and water topped up as needed.
- Table numbers if used should be placed where they can be seen from the service point.
- Windows/glass/sills/mirrors should be polished and free of any marks.

Service area points

▼ **Table 7.4** Service area checklist

Service area	Checklist
Payment points	These will need to be checked that there are sufficient stocks of the following: • a copy of the booking sheet • details of any special requests • check/order pads • till rolls • fully charged credit/debit card machines • check the float in the till and the drawer is properly organised • pens • bill wallets/folders/plates

Service area	Checklist
Reception areas	These are the first areas a customer will see when entering the premises and need to be checked to ensure the right impression is given: ● clean and well-maintained floors, surfaces and walls ● coat hangers and tickets for safe storage of customers' coats and belongings ● clear signage for the toilets, exits and any other customer areas
Still room	This needs to be stocked with all items required for service, including: ● tea ● fruit teas ● tea strainers if loose leaf tea is used ● coffee ● decaffeinated coffee ● hot chocolate ● filter papers if used ● white and brown sugar ● artificial sweetener ● fresh milk ● fresh cream ● cups and saucers ● tea/coffee/latte spoons ● latte glasses ● sweet meats/petit fours ● biscuits ● service trays ● small napkins

Tables

When setting up the bar area check the tables to be used are clean, check for stability and report any maintenance issues. If they are to be covered check that the cloth is the appropriate size and does not trail on the floor.

Check the booking information to see if any tables have been reserved and place a reserved sign on the table(s) if necessary.

Ambience

Ambience in a food service area is created by ensuring that:

● the room is correctly set with everything the establishment has decided should be in the room
● the heating and lighting are appropriate for the time of day and season
● the music is suitable for the venue and at a suitable volume
● the decor reflects the style of the venue.

Promotional materials

▼ **Table 7.5** Promotional materials

Material	Description
Menus	Menus must be clear in detail and show the price of items, ingredients, the amount of alcohol by volume and a statement of the size of measures used in the establishment. There should also be a statement of how much VAT is and that it is included in the price stated. If there is a service charge, this must also be clearly stated on the menu
Table talkers	These are promotional offers and must contain the same information as a menu but will be for the promotional offers only. These are a good way to increase sales during quiet periods. They may be for food as well as drink offers to encourage cross-selling

Communicate product knowledge to customers when taking orders

Product range

The range of products on offer will vary according to the size and style of the venue. Chain or group bars will offer the same drinks across all their bars while individual operators may specialise in certain styles of drinks – for example, cocktails, real ale, whiskies, gins or wines.

The purpose of a wine and drinks list is similar to that of the food menu – it is a selling aid that provides information to the customer. It should be designed in such a way as to encourage the customer to want to open it and explore its contents. Careful thought is also needed in its planning, design, layout, colour and overall appearance to ensure it complements the style of the establishment. The design considerations are similar to those given to food menus (see Unit 204, page 125). Adequate information that is easy to find and follow will make the customer feel more at home and will assist in selling the wines and drinks on offer.

Bar and cocktail lists

These lists may range from a basic standard list offering the common everyday aperitifs – such as sherries, vermouths, bitters, a selection of spirits with mixers, beers and soft drinks, together with a limited range of cocktails – through to a very comprehensive list offering a good choice in all areas. The format and content of the list will be determined by the style of operation and the type of customer that the establishment wishes to attract. Depending on this, the emphasis may be on:

- cocktails: traditional or fashionable
- malt whiskies
- beers
- wines
- non-alcoholic drinks.

Bar and cocktail lists can be printed, written on a chalk board, on an overhead sign, or on a tablet such as an iPad. The customer may wish to enquire as to the ingredients and making methods to assist them in making an informed choice. Staff must know what ingredients are used by the bar person to assist customers in making their choices.

It may be possible to vary the chosen item available – letting customers know that the bar can be flexible will enhance their experience.

Staff should be able to explain not only ingredients but also preparation methods, size of the prepared drinks and recommend what food would complement the drinks to enhance the customer experience as well as upsell for the venue.

Alcohol/unit content

All menus should display the alcohol by volume (ABV) (that is, the alcoholic content) of the drinks. This is not, however, required for a cocktail; because it contains three or more liquids, they may not all be alcoholic and the spirits used do not need to be measured, the calculation of the ABV in a cocktail would be difficult.

All bottled drinks have their ABV printed on the label, and hand-drawn or pumped beer should have the ABV displayed on the pump.

The amount of alcohol being consumed is a measure of both the strength of the alcoholic drink and the amount or volume of the drink being consumed. To calculate the alcohol unit intake for wines:

$$\text{The number of units of alcohol} = \frac{\text{the specific percentage of alcohol (by volume)} \times \text{amount of wine in millilitres (ml)}}{1000 \text{ ml}}$$

For example, for a 75cl bottle of wine at 12% alcohol by volume, the calculation will be:

$$\text{The number of units of alcohol} = \frac{12\% \text{ ABV} \times 750\text{ml}}{1000} = 9 \text{ units}$$

Therefore, this 75 cl bottle of wine will give 6 × 125 ml individual glasses of wine and each glass will contain 1.5 units of alcohol (9 units in the whole bottle divided by the 6 glasses).

Further examples for calculating the alcohol unit intake for other drinks are:

- Lager at 5% alcohol by volume × 50 cl measure = 5 × 500 ml ÷ 1000 = 2.5 units per half-litre measure
- Spirit at 40% alcohol by volume × 25 ml measure = 40 × 25 ml ÷ 1000 = 1 unit per 25 ml measure
- Sherry at 18% alcohol by volume × 50 ml measure = 18 × 50 ml ÷ 1000 = 0.9 unit per 50 ml measure

For information on liquor licensing and law relating to underage drinkers, times that alcohol can be served, reasons for use of legal measures, and when to refuse service of alcohol, see Unit 206, pages 276 to 282.

Service measures

Characteristics

Within the beverage service industry, staff need to be aware that products and services have variables, and these are characteristic to the product or service being offered at the time.

For example, making beverages to different tastes such as strong or weak, with milk or cream. Some items such as tea and coffee can be served either hot or cold; cold drinks can be served with or without ice.

In addition to the variables of service there could also be the time it takes to prepare and serve a beverage – for example, five minutes for a cocktail or other beverages that are freshly prepared to order such as iced tea, jugs of Pimm's or Sangria.

It is important that service staff are trained to be able to inform customers as to these characteristics to offer a high level of service and satisfy demand.

- **Allergen information**. See Unit 203, page 99 for information and guidelines on the requirements for food and beverage services to provide allergen information.
- **Special diets**. Customers may have food intolerances – for example lactose, coeliac, sulphites. Staff need to be aware and flexible in meeting customers' needs; effective communication with customers and the bar should aid in helping customers make informed decisions. If allergies and intolerances are communicated in advance to the establishment this needs to be passed on to the relevant departments and usually customers can then be accommodated with their special diet.

The bar or other beverage service areas will still contain the same potential food allergen hazards as in the kitchen. Cocktails and mixed drinks often contain multiple ingredients using many of the 14 allergens – such as egg, cream, nuts, fruit and garnishes. Clear identification and information needs to be easily available and being able to advise customers is very important. See Unit 203, List of allergens on page 99.

Provenance – origin, ethically sourced

Many customers are interested to know where a product has come from, if it is local to the venue, if it has been organically produced, ethically sourced and environmentally packaged. This information should be easily available to staff to inform the customer and often is printed on the menu to give further details to customers. Also see Unit 201, page 34 for more information on ethical sourcing.

Price

Under UK licensing law, prices for alcoholic drinks must be clearly displayed, where the customer can easily see them at the point of placing the order. In practice, bars tend to display the prices of all their food and drink on a board behind or near the bar to assist the customers in making their choices. See Unit 202, page 58 on the Consumer Protection from Unfair Trading Regulations 2008.

Types of information required for orders

▼ **Table 7.6** Types of information required for orders

Information	Explanation
Size of measure	When service staff take the customer's order, they should check the size of beverage the customer wants ● A glass or a bottle of water or wine ● Service of tea may be by the cup, mug or pot of tea for one or more persons ● For coffee, staff should check if the coffee measure is a single (standard strength) or a double (strong); this applies especially if the customer is ordering an espresso

Information	Explanation
Accompaniments	When the order has been placed a check should be made if the customer would like any accompaniments – such as toppings to hot chocolate, hot water to water down tea, hot milk for coffee, syrups to flavour coffee, and if sugar is required
Dietary	Dietary requirements should be double checked in addition to allergies and intolerances. There could also be religious or disability requirements that may need to be accommodated, and this should be recorded on the order to assist in preparation and service of the items ordered
Brand	Brand names are often used as generic names for products on offer. If an establishment offers a certain brand and the customer requests another brand, service staff must make the customer aware of the brand available. Failure to do so would be mis-selling a product and could also be a potential risk to the customer
Table number/name	These should be added to the order to ensure service staff can correctly deliver and bill the customer for their order. Failure to do so can often lead to confusion and customer dissatisfaction
Timing of service	Service staff should endeavour to be efficient in their service but not to the extent that the customer feels rushed or, conversely, ignored. Gauging the service time may be left to the service staff or may be set within a venue's SOP manual
Consider legislation	Checking customers' ages when ordering alcoholic beverages is a mandatory requirement if staff suspect them to be under 18 years of age • Many venues operate 'Challenge 21' or 'Challenge 25' proof of age schemes and if in doubt staff should refuse service. Remember the law does not allow you to sell intoxicating drinks to ANYONE under the age of 18 years of age under the Licensing Act 2003 • Equally, if staff feel a person is drunk or that someone may be purchasing an intoxicating drink for another person whom they suspect is drunk, then the service of that alcoholic drink must be refused • For further information on the legal requirement see Unit 206, page 280

Take and process orders using different types of equipment

Staff may take customer orders using different types of equipment – for example, written checks (either in duplicate or triplicate) or on hand-held electronic devices (EPOS). See page 181 for more information on different types of equipment for taking and processing orders.

For beverage orders, an efficient system must operate to ensure that:

- the correct wine and other drinks are served at the right table
- the service provided is charged to the correct bill
- a record is kept of all wine and other drinks issued from the bar
- management can assess sales over a financial period and make comparisons.

For more information on taking orders, see page 179.

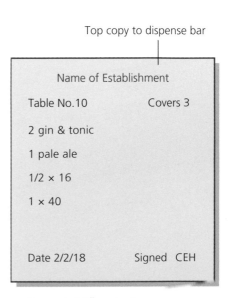

Top copy to dispense bar

Name of Establishment

Table No. 10   Covers 3

2 gin & tonic

1 pale ale

1/2 × 16

1 × 40

Date 2/2/18   Signed CEH

▲ Figure 7.3 Wine check

2.3 SERVE BEVERAGES AND ACCOMPANIMENTS

You will need to be able to present and serve a range of beverages using the appropriate service equipment.

Beers and ciders

Beers and ciders should be served at a temperature of 12.5 to 15.5°C (55 to 60°F), with lagers generally cooler than other beers at 8.0 to 10.5°C (48 to 51°F). Many different varieties of bottled beers are also served chilled. Draught beer and cider, on its route from the keg/cask to the pump, often passes through a chilling unit.

All glasses used should be spotlessly clean with no finger marks, grease or lipstick on them. Pouring beer into a dirty glass will cause it to go flat very quickly. See Unit 206, page 246 for information on different types of beer and cider glasses.

See Unit 206, pages 257 and 258 for guidelines on presenting and serving beers and ciders from a keg, bottle, cask and can.

Wines

The sommelier, wine waiter or bar staff must be able to advise and suggest wines to the customer as required. This means that the wine waiter must have a good knowledge of the wines on the wine list and be able to identify examples of wines that will match well with the menu dishes. Immediately after the food order has been taken the wine list should again be presented to the host so that he or she may order wine to accompany the meals that the customers have ordered.

There are seven key aspects of serving wines:

1. The wine waiter must be able to describe the wines and their characteristics honestly (bluffing should be avoided).
2. Always serve the wine before the food. Avoid any delay in serving the food once the wine has been served.
3. Serve wine at the correct temperature – it is better to tell the customer that the wine is not at the right temperature for service rather than resorting to quick heating or cooling methods, as these can damage the wine.
4. Treat wines with respect and demonstrate a high level of technical skill, supported by the use of high-quality service equipment. As the customer is paying for the wine and the service, they have the right to expect their chosen wine to be treated with care.
5. When pouring wine, the neck of the bottle should be over the glass but not resting on the rim in case of an accident. Care should be taken to avoid splashing the wine and, when pouring is complete, the bottle should be twisted and raised as it is taken away. This prevents drops of wine falling on the tablecloth or on the customer's clothes. Any drops on the rim of the bottle should be wiped away with a clean service cloth or napkin.

6 Do not overfill glasses. Fill glasses to the right level, usually to the widest part of the bowl or two-thirds full, whichever is the lesser. Sparkling wine served in a flute is usually filled to about two-thirds to three-quarters of the glass. Doing so helps the wine to be better appreciated and looks better too.

7 Avoid unnecessary topping up – it does not sell more wine and it often irritates customers. Another reason for being cautious about topping up wine glasses is that the customer may be driving. If wine is topped up constantly, the customer may not notice how much they are consuming. In general, it is preferable to ask the customer about topping up their wine.

See Unit 206, pages 258 to 263 for general information and guidelines on serving wines, champagne and sparkling wines by the glass, from the bottle and at the table, and on decanting wine by the bottle.

Different settings

See Unit 206, page 264 for information on bars in different settings, for example, dispense bar, customer bar, functions and events.

Functions and events

At large events where the customer has had the wine chosen for them to complement the set menu, the waiter will offer wines with each course and will carry both red and white as per the organiser's choice, which are then offered to customers to top up glasses as the meal progresses. The white wine is placed on the table in an ice bucket and the red wine is placed on the table. Alternatively, the wines can be stored on the sideboard and taken to the customers as required by the wine waiters. Care must be taken to not overfill glasses but equally to not let glasses become empty unless the customers decline more to be poured.

Spirits, liqueurs and fortified wines

See Unit 206, pages 264 and 265 for information and guidelines on preparing and serving spirits, liqueurs and fortified wines.

Cocktails/mocktails

Methods of cocktail making

See Table 6.8 on page 236 for information on the different methods of making **cocktails**, and examples of cocktails for each method.

Points to note when making cocktails:

- Ice should always be clear and clean.
- Do not overfill the cocktail shaker.
- Effervescent drinks should never be shaken.
- To avoid spillage, do not fill glasses to the brim.
- When egg white or yolk is an ingredient, first break the egg into separate containers before use.
- Serve cocktails in chilled glasses.
- To shake, use short and snappy actions.

KEY TERM

Cocktail – a short drink up to 10 cl. Often used to describe all types of mixed or long drinks.

- Always place ice in the shaker or mixing glass first, followed by non-alcoholic and then alcoholic beverages.
- To stir, stir briskly until the blend is cold.
- As a general rule, a mixing glass is used for those cocktails based on liqueurs or wines (clear liquids).
- Shakers are used for cocktails that might include fruit juices, cream, sugar and similar ingredients.
- When egg white or yolk is an ingredient, a Boston shaker should normally be used.
- Always add the garnish after the cocktail has been made and to the glass in which the cocktail is to be served.
- Always measure out ingredients; inaccurate amounts spoil the balance of the blend and taste.
- Never use the same ice twice.

Garnishes

See Unit 206, page 266 for a full list of cocktail garnishes and advice on serving.

Accompaniments

Staff should offer various accompaniments to enhance drinks and these should be appropriate to the chosen beverage. For information on accompaniments please refer to Unit 206, page 266.

Non-alcoholic cold beverages including juices and waters

Garnishes and accompaniments

See Unit 206, page 268 for information on preparing and serving garnishes and accompaniments to non-alcoholic cold beverages.

Hot beverages

Preparing and serving coffee

Methods of brewing can vary, ranging from instant coffee brewed by the cup, through to 1½ to 3 litre (3 to 6 pint) units and more, to machines that may produce large quantities for functions. Coffee beans may be purchased, and then ground according to requirements. The beans should not be ground until immediately before they are required as this will ensure maximum flavour and strength from the oils within the coffee bean. Pre-ground coffee normally comes in vacuum-sealed packets in order to maintain its qualities until use. These packets contain set quantities to make 4.5 litres (1 gallon) of coffee or 9 litres (2 gallons) of coffee, and so on.

When making coffee in bulk, 283 to 340 g (10 to 12 oz) of ground coffee is sufficient to make 4.5 litres (1 gallon) of black coffee.

- Assuming that cups with a capacity of 20 cl (⅓ pint) will be used, 283 to 340 g (10 to 12 oz) of ground coffee is sufficient to provide 24 cups of black coffee or 48 cups if serving half-coffee and half-milk.
- When breakfast cups, capacity 28 cl (½ pint), are used then 16 cups of black coffee or 32 cups of half-coffee and half-milk will be available.
- Capacity where demi-tasse (half cups) 10 cl (⅙ pint) cups are used is 48 cups of black coffee or 96 cups half-coffee and half-milk.

The rules to be observed when making coffee in bulk are as follows:

- Use freshly roasted and ground coffee.
- Buy the correct grind for the type of machine in use.
- Ensure all equipment is clean before use.
- Use a set measure of coffee to water: 283 to 340 g per 4.5 litres (10 to 12 oz per gallon).
- Add boiling water to the coffee and allow to infuse.
- The infusion time must be controlled according to the type of coffee being used and the method of making.
- Control the temperature since to boil coffee is to spoil coffee (it will develop a bitter taste).
- Strain and serve.
- Offer milk (hot or cold) or cream separately, and sugar and alternatives.

The best serving temperatures are 82°C (180°F) for coffee and 68°C (155°F) for milk.

Modern coffee service styles

- Espresso would be served in a demi-tasse, with a small teaspoon resting on the saucer.
- Cappuccino requires an oversized cup to accommodate the foamed milk and dusting of cocoa powder.
- Latte should be served in a tall latte glass with a handle and a long spoon, placed on a saucer for service.
- Americano should be served in a regular coffee cup with a separate serving of hot milk.
- Liqueur coffee is traditionally served in a glass goblet on a saucer.

See Unit 206, pages 250 to 252 for information on making coffee and Table 6.10 on page 239 for modern espresso-based coffee styles.

Preparing and serving tea

The type of tea used will of course depend on the customer's choice, but most establishments carry a varied stock of Indian, Ceylon, China and speciality teas, together with a variety of tisanes (fruit-flavoured teas and herbal infusions) available upon request.

The quantity of dry tea used per pot or per gallon may vary slightly with the type of tea used, but the following may be used as an approximate guide:

- 42–56 g (1½ to 2 oz) dry tea per 4.5 litres (1 gallon) of water for 24 standard teacups
- ½ litre (1 pint) of milk will be sufficient for 20 to 24 cups
- ½ kilogram (1 lb) sugar for approximately 80 cups.

When brewing smaller amounts in the still room, such as a pot for one or two, it is often advisable to install a measure for the loose-leaf tea. This ensures standardisation of the brew and control on the amount of loose tea being used. Alternative methods of pre-portioning tea may also be used, such as tea bags.

Because tea is an infusion, the flavour is obtained by allowing the tea to brew. The following checklist will enable good results.

1 Heat the pot before putting in the dry tea so that the maximum heat can be obtained from the boiling water.
2 Measure the dry tea exactly.
3 Use freshly boiled water.
4 Make sure the water is boiling on entering the pot.
5 Allow the tea to brew for 3 to 6 minutes (depending on the type of tea) to obtain maximum strength from the brew.
6 Remove the tea leaves at the end of the brewing period if required, but especially if making the tea in multi-pot insulated urns.
7 Ensure all the equipment used is scrupulously clean. Remember hard water resulting in limescale may affect your equipment and, in turn, your 'brew'. To overcome this safe water softeners are available.
8 Herbal teas vary in strength. Follow the instructions on the packaging to get the optimum brew from the tea.

Tray service for tea and coffee

For information on the equipment required for tray service of coffee and tea, see Table 6.18, page 253.

General points to note in laying up a coffee or tea tray are given below.

- Position the items to ensure an evenly balanced tray for carrying.
- Position the items for the convenience of the customer:
  - beverage on the right with spout facing inwards
  - handles outwards and towards the customer for ease of access.
- Ensure the beverage is placed on the tray at the last moment so that it is served hot.

Placement of tea and coffee cups from a tray

Figure 7.4 (a) shows the beverage equipment required, positioned on the service salver, assuming a table of four customers is to be served. Using this method, the server only has to make one journey from the sideboard/workstation to the restaurant or lounge table.

- The beverage service for each customer is made up of a teacup on its saucer, with a teaspoon resting in the saucer and at right angles under the handle of the cup.
- The beverage service is placed on the table from the customer's right-hand side, as the beverage ordered will be served from the right.
- The beverage service is positioned on the right-hand side of the customer with the handle to the right and the teaspoon set at right angles under the handle of the cup.

- While moving to the right-hand side of the second customer, the server will place a teacup on a tea saucer and a teaspoon in the saucer and at right angles under the handle of the cup. This beverage service is then ready to place on the right-hand side of the second customer – see Figure 7.4 (b).
- This procedure is then repeated until all the beverage services have been placed on the table for those customers requiring tea or coffee.

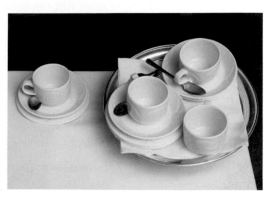

▲ **Figure 7.4 (a)** Service salver before the first cup and saucer are assembled

▲ **Figure 7.4 (b)** Service salver by the time the second customer is reached

When coffee is served after lunch or dinner, teacups are now more commonly used. The use of small coffee cups (demi-tasse) has declined for conventional coffee service although they are still sometimes used in event catering. These cups are also used for espresso.

Serving tea and coffee for table and assisted service

- Tea is not usually served but the teapot is placed on the table on a stand and to the right-hand side of the person who ordered. The customers will then help themselves. The cold milk and sugars (and alternatives) are also placed on to the table.
- Coffee may be silver served at the table from a service salver. However, this traditional method of serving coffee is not so common today. Generally other speedier methods are used, such as placing the cafètiere on the table together with milk and sugars (and alternatives) for customers to help themselves.
- Other methods of serving tea and coffee are:
  - Service from a pot of tea or a pot of hot black coffee held on the sideboard on a hotplate. Cold milk, hot milk or cream and sugars are placed on the table.
  - Service of both cold milk and hot milk or cream together with the tea and coffee from pots, one held in each of the waiter's hands. Sugars are placed on the table for customers to help themselves.
  - In event catering, where larger numbers often have to be served, the cold milk, hot milk or cream and sugars are often placed on the table for customers to help themselves. The tea and coffee are then served from a 1-litre-capacity vacuum flask, which may be kept on the waiters'

sideboard in readiness for replenishment should the customers require it. This method of holding and serving tea and coffee ensures that it remains hot at all times. (For examples of vacuum jugs for tea or coffee see Figure 6.20, page 250.)

When serving tea and coffee from multi-portion pots/urns it is usual to remove the tea leaves, coffee grounds or tea/coffee bags once the beverage has brewed, so that the tea and coffee does not become stewed.

Hot chocolate

Hot chocolate can be served with a topping of whipped cream, chocolate powder or shavings, marshmallows and a long spoon. See Unit 206, page 269 for more information on preparing and serving hot chocolate and other hot beverages.

Accompaniments

See Table 6.24 on page 270 for information on serving suitable accompaniments for hot beverages.

2.4 CUSTOMER BILLS AND PAYMENTS

Systems and equipment used for customer billing

See Unit 205, pages 206 and 207, for information on using a till, POS terminal, stationery and Chip and PIN machines for customer billing.

Methods of payment

See Unit 205, pages 207 to 208, for information on different methods of payment: cash, cards, cash equivalents.

Prepare customer bills for payment with relevant information

See Unit 205, page 209, for five types of information that should be contained on the customer's bill. Also, see Unit 205, page 209, for information on additional charges and prepayments.

Process customer payments in line with current legislation and procedures

Once the customer has received the bill and had time to check it, payment can then be taken in line with current legislation and procedures.

Offering a selection of payment methods – for example cash, credit card, debit card, contactless payment – will give customers more options for payment and make settling the bill a smooth and swift process.

All customers should be issued with a receipt. This will show what was consumed, the charges, a breakdown of VAT and service charges, as well as the date and time of payment. If there are any discrepancies, such as over-charges, then the refund should be shown on the receipt.

See Unit 205 for information on the following aspects of customer payments:

- Types of payment – page 207
- Documentation – page 212
- Cash equivalents – page 208
- Security checks – page 213.

2.5 CLEAR AREAS AT THE END OF SERVICE

At the end of service, the bar and seating areas will need to be cleared down, cleaned and restocked in readiness for the next service period. The following should be completed before anyone leaves the shift.

Bar

▼ **Table 7.7** Cleaning duties for the bar at the end of service

Item	Cleaning duty
Equipment	<ul><li>All used **glassware** needs to be put through the glass wash, polished and stored on plastic matting on the shelves</li><li>The **barista machine** should be switched off and stripped down. The group head and drip trays should be washed and left to dry in the air. The milk wand should be wiped clean and left in water (to soak off any milk residue inside the wand). Do not top up coffee beans until the next shift to preserve their freshness</li><li>Any blenders and cocktail-making equipment should be thoroughly washed and dried, and returned to their service point ready to use</li><li>Once the glasses have all been washed, the glasswasher should be emptied and rinsed, leaving the door ajar to allow any steam to escape. The drain plug should be removed, emptied and cleaned before leaving inside the washer</li><li>All crockery required for the next service should be replenished, with coffee cups being left on the top of the coffee machine ready to warm through when the machine is switched back on at the next shift</li><li>Any containers used for service of juices and syrups should be emptied, washed and left to air dry</li></ul>
Fridges	If necessary, these should be wiped clean and the stock replaced, all bottles should be front-facing if they are seen by the customer. Any food stuffs should be covered with cling wrap and date labelled
Ice machines	These should be checked to ensure the drain hole is clear and that the door is firmly closed; if this is not done then ice will not be made in time for the next service. Ensure the plastic or metal ice scoop is placed outside the ice machine or it will become buried under the newly produced ice
Consumables	Any dirty linen items should be placed in the dirty linen trolley for collection by housekeeping or the laundry. This includes tea towels, service cloths and aprons. Items such as straws, paper napkins, coasters, cocktail sticks should be tidied and spare stock placed nearby to be used to top up the stock at the beginning of the next shift
Accompaniments	Fruit, olives, gherkins, nuts and snacks should be put away in airtight containers, refrigerated as necessary. Sauces and condiments should be wiped clean and placed back in their service points
Restock/reorder	Any items that are running low should be brought from the storeroom and a requisition written up for items required to top up the stock levels for the bar. This requisition should be placed in the central stores or cellar before the end of shift. When the storeman/cellar man comes on duty they will compile the order ready for the next shift to collect and restock the bar in time for service

Item	Cleaning duty
Waste	Any rubbish should be removed from the bar at the end of the shift. Bin bags should be tied and lifted from bins, then taken to the appropriate area for disposal. If the venue is close to residential areas bottle skips should not be emptied outside after 11 p.m., this avoids upsetting neighbours and reduces complaints. Bins and skips should be cleaned and rinsed daily to keep them clean; this may be performed by porters during the day shift
Displays	Any display material should be checked for cleanliness, wiped down as required and stored away. If the display is not removable and has a high value, it should be in an area that can be secured while the bar is not in operation. If perishable items are used in the display, they should be removed and either refrigerated or disposed of as appropriate
Bar	At the very end of the closing down procedure the bar surfaces and floor should be wiped down or swept, then sanitised with the appropriate solutions for the surfaces being cleaned. Mops and buckets should be returned to the store or cellar to air dry
Secure	Finally all areas such as the cellar, storerooms and bar must be made secure ● The tills should be emptied of cash and left open ● The cash, sales readings and any other documents should be bagged and tagged and placed in the safe to be checked by a manager the next morning, if this has not been carried out by the supervisor at the end of the shift

Bar seating area

▼ **Table 7.8** Cleaning duties for the bar seating area

Area	Cleaning duty
Tables	Remove all glassware to the wash-up area, menus and drinks lists should be checked for wear and tear and wiped clean with anti-bacterial cleaning agent if necessary, placed in the bar ready for the next service. Strip any tablecloths or wipe down table tops with anti-bacterial cleaning agent
Seating	Wipe or dust hard chairs; upholstered chairs may need vacuuming and all chairs should be placed in their set positions as per the venue's layout
Floor	The floor should be checked for any forgotten customer items. If found, these should be recorded in the lost property book and safely stored away. The carpet should be vacuumed, and any hard floors should be swept and mopped using the appropriate cleaning solution
Consumables	Any foodstuffs left in the seating area should be either disposed of or stored away in their correct containers. Items such as napkins, sachets of sugar, sweeteners, salt and pepper or sauces should be replenished
Stationery	Menus and promotional materials should be checked to see if still current and either disposed of or restocked and made ready for the next service. If the venue uses a chalk or white board this should be checked to see if the items listed are still available or wiped clean ready for the next shift's menu

Consideration should be given to sustainability issues at all times, including the recycling of used items, the management of waste and the control of energy.

Test your learning

1 Identify **two** things that contribute to a person's presentation.

2 Give **two** examples of special requests that a customer might have when ordering beverages.

3 State the **four** things required when completing a check for a beverage order.

4 State **one** reason why briefings are important.

5 Give **three** examples of product knowledge that a service member should know.

6 State **three** things that can cause wastage.

7 Give **one** example of how a person under 18 might be served an alcoholic drink.

8 What is ullage?

9 What is the recommended temperature for a cellar?

10 Give **one** reason why beer lines are cleaned.

11 State **one** thing that regular stock checks can ensure for the business.

12 What is the ideal temperature of a bar fridge?

13 What does 'JIT' stand for?

14 State **four** examples of accompaniments used in bars.

15 Identify **two** things that contribute to the ambience of a food service area.

16 What is a 'table talker'?

17 What does 'ABV' stand for?

18 What is the definition of a cocktail?

19 List **two** tasks that should be carried out when clearing down at the end of service.

20 Give **one** reason why it is important to re-stock the bar and place a requisition for stock at the end of the shift.

FINANCE FOR FOOD AND BEVERAGE BUSINESSES

INTRODUCTION

The purpose of this chapter is to help you to carry out costing exercises, contribute to effective stock control and to maintaining the security of customer and business financial information.

The chapter will help you to:

- identify the costs that must be considered when running a business
- know the actions you can take to ensure the protection of the revenue of the business
- understand stock control and how to contribute to the requirements
- know how you can help to safeguard the financial information of your customers.

1 BUSINESS FINANCIAL CONTROLS

The main financial control methods covered in this chapter are:

- stock control
- costing and pricing
- revenue protection
- sales analysis
- securing financial information.

In addition, there are other control measures that apply to:

- order-taking methods (for food see Unit 205, page 180 and for beverages see Unit 207, page 302)
- billing methods (for food see Unit 205, page 206 and for beverages see Unit 207, page 310).

1.1 STOCK CONTROL

Importance of stock control for a business

Having effective **stock control** procedures is essential for any business.

KEY TERM

Stock control – maintain a level of stock in order to meet business demands.

▼ **Table 8.1** Successful stock management and the impact of poor stock management

Factors that contribute to successful stock management	Impacts of poor stock management
Designated suppliers with guaranteed quality specifications	Increased food costs due to poor supplier selection
Trained and designated staff allocated to the receipt and storing of supplies	Increase in waste due to overstocking and overordering of products
Standard operational procedures for handling stock and managing its storage	Loss of profits
Effective use of stock rotation techniques that ensure use-by and best-before dates are monitored and rotated accurately using 'First in, First Out' (FIFO) methodology	Theft and pilfering
Central ordering systems that can help monitor requisition requests and make efficient use of current stocks	Poor food safety and health and safety

Costs of sales

The costs of sales (also referred to as the food and beverage costs) are all the costs directly associated with selling a product, i.e. the purchase price of the ingredients required to make the dish or beverage. It is an essential factor when compiling menus, working out selling prices and achieving profitability. Effective stock control can help ensure that greater profit margins are achieved, that is the gross profit and net profits of a business:

- **Gross profit**: Total revenue less cost of sales.
- **Net profit**: Gross profit less labour costs and overheads costs.

When ordering and holding stocks of food and beverage it is important to factor your expected customer throughput and ensure you order stock to avoid wastage and/or overstocking as this will have a direct impact on the profitability of the business.

Stock rotation

Stock rotation can be described as the movement and replenishing of stock items with a focus on ensuring the older items are used before the newer. When rotating food and beverage products the following points should be considered:

- Use-by and best-before dates (see Unit 203, page 107).
- Availability of storage space and the ability to hold sufficient stock levels.
- Only stock that is required is held and stored.
- Minimise waste through effective stock management systems.
- Costs of holding stock (for example, cost of capital involved, storage space and cost of temperature control).
- Security of stock (reduce pilfering and theft).
- Stocktake records are kept up to date.
- Timings and frequency of deliveries.

If stock rotation procedures and monitoring are poor then there is a risk of financial loss that will directly affect the business profits.

Availability of dishes/products

Good stock control and management will ensure the smooth running of the business and will help guarantee the sustained availability of products for each department. Poor stock management can affect production and services areas.

▼ **Table 8.2** Effect of poor stock management on kitchen and restaurant/bars

Kitchen	Restaurant/bars
Unable to perform 'mise en place' duties	Limited choice leading to disappointment of customers leading to complaints
Delays in service	
Additional waste of products due to lack of dish ingredients	Embarrassment for staff
	Reduced ability to upsell
Poor stock rotation due to holding items that cannot be used due missing products	Loss of customer trust
	Staff will need to make more alternative recommendations
Staff frustration	
Reduction in profitability	Poorer customer meal experience

Business profitability

Good stock control contributes to business profitability by ensuring:

- correct cooking of food to minimise portion loss
- efficient preparation of raw materials
- correct preparation of beverages
- correct portion control
- minimal wastage, sufficient use of raw materials, utilising leftover food and other items
- reduced potential for theft
- accurate ordering and reordering procedures
- adequate stock-checking procedures
- reference marks to standardised recipes and methods
- accurate forecasting
- sound planning of products to be sold.

Cash flow

Cash flow can be defined as the net movement of money into and out of a business. That is, the money available after the costs of business have been accounted for.

Key to the success of the cash flow process is a controlled and accurate stock control system. The purchasing of goods must be well planned and monitored, and the use of the bought resources must be maximised to ensure minimal waste and maximum yield. Failure to maintain a good cash flow will result in loss of profits, wastage of products, the unavailability of dishes on the menu and poor customer satisfaction.

Customer satisfaction

Good stock management means that customer satisfaction will be maintained and enhanced as the food and beverages on offer will be:

- at the specified quality
- available
- consistent in content, presentation and service for each visit.

Business reputation

Maintaining enhanced levels of customer satisfaction will also have a positive effect on the reputation of the business. Increased sales and profits will in turn provide more job security for staff.

Stock control procedures

An organised storeroom is essential in order to maintain the unified process of control throughout the establishment. A clean, orderly store, run efficiently, is essential in any food service business for the following reasons:

- Stocks of food and beverages can be maintained at the correct and safe level, so eliminating the risk of running out items.
- All food and beverages entering and leaving the stores can be properly monitored to help prevent wastage.
- The percentage profit made by each department can be calculated.
- Use of an electronic point of sale (EPOS) system can help with stocktaking and reordering. For more information see Unit 205.

Stock reordering

For the establishment as a whole, central stock levels are required in order to meet expected sales demand. Past sales data will also help to determine stock levels required.

To calculate the stock level required, a useful formula is:

$$M = W (T + L) + S$$

Where:

- M is the maximum stock level
- W is the average usage rate (over the review period)
- T is the review period (time interval between orders)
- L is the lead time (time it takes for the order to arrive)
- S is the safety stock (buffer or minimum stock level).

An example for bottles of wine is:
- W = 24 bottles per week
- T = 4 weeks
- L = 1 week
- S = 1 week's usage of 24 bottles

Therefore:

$$M = 24 \times (4 + 1) + 24 = 144 \text{ bottles}$$

Minimum stock (buffer or safety stock) is calculated as follows:

$$L \times W = 1 \times 24 = 24 \text{ bottles}$$

ROL (reorder level) is calculated as follows:

$$(W \times L) + S = (24 \times 1) + 24 = 48 \text{ bottles}$$

The same basic approaches can be applied for all food and beverage items whether based on purchasing units, such as bottles as above, or quantities (litres/gallons, kilograms/pounds) or items such as tins, jars and packets, all with specified sizes.

Using this approach can enable food service operations to determine the stock holding that will meet the needs of the expected demand, while at the same time minimising the amount of capital tied up in the stock held (in the stockroom). Good stock control can also be supported by the application of a 'just in time' (JIT) approach to purchasing. JIT involves only ordering stock as required in order to meet forecasted demand, rather than holding unnecessarily high stock levels, just in case.

First in, first out

First in, first out (FIFO) is a term used to describe stock rotation and is applied to all categories of food. It simply means that foods already in storage are used before new deliveries (providing stock is still within recommended dates and in saleable condition). Food deliveries should be labelled with the delivery date and preferably the date by which they should be used. This information is used along with food labelling codes, such as use-by and best-before dates, and written stock records to form part of a food safety management system.

Signs of food spoilage may include an appearance different from the food in its fresh form – such as a change in colour, a change in texture, an unpleasant odour or an undesirable taste. The item may become softer than normal. If mould occurs, it is often visible externally on the item.

Spoilt foods should be recorded in a waste control book. They must be disposed of carefully to avoid any cross-contamination. Excess wastage should be reported to management as this could be a result of poor stock control and is controlled as part of the Food Safety Management System.

Stocktake

The main objectives of taking stock are:

- to determine the value of goods held in stock
- to compare the value of goods actually in the stores at a particular time with what should be there
- to calculate the rate of stock turnover.

▼ **Table 8.3** Stocktaking

Different values	How to calculate
Book or cash value	Value of opening stock + purchases received during the period – stock used in the same period
Physical stock holding	Counting the physical opening stock (in terms of units, for example kilograms, packets, jars, tins or bottles), adding the purchases and deducting the closing stock will give the usage. Checking this against the recorded usage will highlight any differences and indicate the efficiency of the stock control system.
Rate of stock turnover	Cost of stock used during the period, divided by the average value of the stock for the period, gives the number of times the stock has been turned over during the period.

For example, in a 28-day trading period, the **cost of stock** used was £4000. The **opening stock** on day one was £1800 and the **closing stock** on day 28 was £1000.

Average stock holding is: opening stock plus closing stock divided by 2 =

$$£1800 + £1000 / 2 = £2800 / 2 = £1400$$

Stock turnover is: cost of stock used divided by average stock holding =

$$\frac{£4000}{£1400} = 2.86$$

This means that in the 28-day trading period the stock turnover was 2.86 times.

Higher stock turnover can indicate good purchase control and likelihood of more fresh ingredients being used efficiently. Lower stock turnover can indicate more convenience materials are being used or poor stock control.

The rate of stock turnover will vary depending on the frequency of delivery, the commodity, the size of storage space available and the amount of money the establishment is prepared to tie up in food stocks.

Typical stock turnover figures for a month are at least 20 for perishable items (that means deliveries most days) and 4 for non-perishable items with deliveries, for example, once per week.

The process of stocktaking also:

1 identifies slow moving items; those items that are in stock and for which there has been no demand since the last stocktaking
2 allows comparison of usage of food with food sales; to calculate the food and beverage cost percentage and gross profit
3 acts as a deterrent against loss and pilferage.

Stocktaking will typically be done every trading period (for example, each month, every four weeks), or more frequently if a problem has arisen. Ideally, the stocktaking should take place at the end of a trading period and before the operational start of the next trading period. This can mean that the stocktaking will take place late in the evening or early in the morning. Stocktaking can be done electronically either by typing in codes or via a barcode system. Electronic systems can simultaneously calculate the physical stock held as well as the value, both per stock item and total stock holding.

The end-of-year **stocktake** is usually done in greater detail and with more thoroughness than for a trading period. Professional external stocktakers can also be used, particularly for the end-of-year stocktake.

Delivery of goods

Orders are usually requested via a purchase order. This states the item or items required, amount, size, weight and other pertinent information.

KEY TERM

Stocktake – checking the levels of stock to determine the value, to check what has actually been used, and to calculate the rate of stock turnover.

The goods delivered must be checked against the delivery note to ensure that all the goods listed have been delivered. The stores person may carry out an extra check by checking the delivery note against the copy of the original order in the order book. This is to ensure that the items ordered have been sent, in the correct quantities, and that extra items have not been sent which were not requested on the order sheet, as these incur extra cost.

Receiving practices vary with different organisations. The general principles of control are:

1 Check delivery note to see if the products delivered agree with it.
2 Inspect products/raw materials to determine if they are in agreement with the purchase order and specification.
3 Tag all meats with date of receipt, weight and other information needed to identify the delivery properly.
4 List all items received on the daily receiving report.
5 Accept the products/raw materials by signing the delivery note and returning a copy to the driver/delivery person.
6 Store or deliver goods to the correct place.

Good principles of receiving are important for control. These are:

1 Being ready and prepared for the delivery.
2 Checking the incoming goods thoroughly against the purchase order and the purchase specification. Opening cases if they appear to be damaged or tampered with. Dating all canned goods before storing.
3 Weighing items separately. When receiving bulk items, remove excess paper, ice, etc., before weighing.
4 Weighing meats and tagging them. This practice prevents disputes with the supplier about over- and under-weights. Tagging also reduces the chance of spoilage or excess weight loss. It also simplifies calculation of food costs, since a good record of meat withdrawals can be obtained from the tags taken from meat as it comes from the inventory.

Recording incoming deliveries is as important as checking quality and quantity. The form or style of doing this may vary but the intended principles are the same.

Documentation

Delivery note / invoice

When the goods are delivered to an establishment they should be accompanied by either a delivery note or an invoice. Whichever document it may be, the information contained should be exactly the same, with one exception: invoices show the price of all goods delivered whereas delivery notes do not. All deliveries are recorded in the goods inwards book, although this process is now usually computer-based.

Statement

At the end of a trading period, which can be from one week to several weeks, suppliers will issue a statement of account. This will detail the cost of all purchases made, less the cost of any returns, less the payments made and then state what is to be paid to them. There is also likely to be considerations over issues such as not paying on time.

Requisition

Each food and beverage department should use a method of requisition to draw (receive) items – for example, from the cellar when the bar needs restocking with soft drinks. Requisition forms may be distinguished by colour or serial number and are normally supplied in triplicate. The copies are sent out as follows.

1 **Top copy**: to the stores
2 **Duplicate copy**: to the control department
3 **Triplicate copy**: used by each department to check its goods on receipt from the stores.

The following information is listed on the requisition form:

- Name of the department
- Date
- List of items required
- Quantity and unit of each item required
- Signature of the authorised person, who may both order and receive the goods.

The purpose of the requisition is to control the movement of items from the stores into the department and to avoid too much removal of stock at one time, thus overstocking the department.

The stores person will not dispatch any items unless he or she receives an official requisition form. The form must be correctly filled in, dated and signed by a person in authority (from the department concerned). The stores person will have a list of such signatures for comparison and should not issue any stock unless a person on the list signs the requisition sheet.

Credit notes

Records of any returns made to suppliers are written in the goods inwards book or in a separate goods returned book. When goods are returned, the supplier will issue a credit note. This is a statement of what money is owed to the operation. These credit notes are then used as payment against future purchases.

Security

Stockrooms and storage areas should be secure at all times. Stock is valuable, and access should be limited only to those with authority to enter them. A requisition for stock items should be countersigned by a senior member of the department and stock should only be issued to an authorised staff member on production of the official requisition. A copy of the requisition form should be retained by the stockroom and reconciled with stock movement when a stock count is made.

Technology

As with many functions, computerised systems are often used for purchasing, stock control including stocktaking, **stock reordering** and payment systems.

KEY TERM

Stock reordering – ensuring that new, replacement stock is ordered at the right time.

1.2 COSTING FACTORS

Costing factors that influence food and beverage pricing

There are various pricing methods available to food service operators, but whichever methods are used, there should always be a clear pricing policy or objective in mind. These pricing objectives might include the following:

- Sales volume maximisation, where the pricing objective is to achieve the highest sales possible.
- Market share gain, where the objective is to increase the number of customers relative to the total possible market and the competition.
- Profit maximisation, where the pricing objective is to achieve the highest profit possible.
- Market penetration, where the pricing objective is to move from a position of a zero or low market share to a significant market share.

Once a clear pricing policy has been established, the pricing methods most suitable can be drawn from the various methods available; this is often a combination of a range of pricing methods.

Cost plus

This is the most common pricing method. The ingredient cost is established, and the gross profit is added. This is also referred to simply as cost+. The result is a selling price that gives the operator the required profit for that dish or beverage (although this will only be a profit if the dish is actually sold).

The **cost plus** method is attractive because of its simplicity. However, there are problems with this method:

- It makes the assumption that the required profit can be achieved by making it a set percentage of the selling price on all items (often 65 to 75 per cent).
- It ignores price sensitivity (how much a customer will pay) and demand (how the price affects the demand), and that value for money must be factored into the pricing decision.
- It fails to account for different restaurant types and different menu categories, and does not take into account that each dish/beverage is only part of a collection of items purchased to produce the meal experience.

Applying a standard gross profit to all items will make the selling prices look strange. The prices of low cost items will appear to be far cheaper than the prices for higher cost items. Therefore, when this method is used, it is usual to apply different gross profit percentages to different food or beverage items. This approach then ensures that the prices appear more balanced throughout the menu or the wine list.

Often a combination of different pricing methods is used. In addition to cost plus, these can include:

- **Competitive pricing**: This method is based on looking carefully at what the competition are charging and aiming to price at the same level or a slightly lower price.

KEY TERM

Cost plus pricing – adding to the cost of an item a fixed percentage to achieve the selling price.

- **Backward pricing**: This method requires an accurate estimate of what people are likely to spend in the future. The product and services are then designed to match what the market will bear – in other words, what the customer is prepared to pay for the product or service within that particular market segment.

Gross operating profit and net profit

There is a relationship between the costs of running the operation, the revenue that is received and the profit that is made. In food service operations there are three elements of cost:

1 **Food or beverage costs**: often called cost of sales.
2 **Labour**: wages, salaries, staff feeding, uniforms.
3 **Overheads**: rent, rates, advertising, fuel.

There are also two types of profit:

1 **Gross profit**: total revenue less cost of sales.
2 **Net profit**: gross profit less both labour costs and overhead costs.

Revenue, or sales, in food service operations is always equal to 100 per cent. Thus, all elements of cost and profits in a food service operation are always calculated as a percentage of the total sales figures. This is different to many retail operations, where the cost of sales figure is taken as 100 per cent, so the gross profit percentage is then worked out as a percentage of the cost price. The relationship between the **element of costs** and profit in food service operations is illustrated in Figure 8.1.

Food and beverage costs	Cost of sales
Labour costs	Gross profit £
Overhead costs	
Net profit	
Total sales	Revenue 100%

▲ **Figure 8.1** Summary of the relationship between revenue, costs and profits in food service operations

Fixed, variable and stepped costs

Costs can also be classified:

- **Fixed costs**: These are costs that have to be paid even if there is no business. These include costs of direct labour, insurance, rent and rates.
- **Variable costs**: These are costs that will change according to the level of business. These costs include utilities (gas, electricity, water) and raw materials.
- **Stepped costs/semi variable**: There is not always a direct relationship between the level of business and the variable costs. Sometimes increases in costs are semi-variable and these are sometimes called stepped costs.

> **NOTE**
>
> In kitchen operations gross profit is sometimes called kitchen percentage or kitchen profit.

KEY TERMS

Gross profit – sales less cost of sales.

Net profit – sales less labour and overhead costs.

Revenue – total amount of money received – always equal to 100% – cost and profits are always calculated as a percentage of sales.

Element of cost – food and beverage costs, labour costs and overheads.

Fixed costs – do not vary with level of business.

Variable costs – vary directly with the level of business.

Stepped costs – costs that increase in jumps as the volume of business increases.

This is where the costs are increased, e.g. employing another member of staff, but the profit to meet that extra cost will not be achieved until the sales have increased. This type of cost can also be when, for example, providing for events and banqueting.

Other factors that affect pricing

In addition to costs of ingredients and beverages there are other factors that affect pricing. These are summarised in Table 8.4.

▼ **Table 8.4** Other factors affecting pricing

Factors	Explanation
External influences	Changes in the rate of Value Added Tax (VAT), increasing costs of materials and changes in the charges for fuel and waste disposal. For further explanation of how VAT is applied, see Unit 201, page 13
Market conditions	Changes in the local competition, customer spend, trends, fads and fashions, changes in potential customers, customer mix, customer feedback and level of customer loyalty are all market conditions which can affect pricing
Dynamic pricing	This is where prices are changed according to the level of demand. If the demand increases, then it is possible to consider increasing prices. During slack periods, special offers can be considered, which in effect lower prices
Loss leaders	These are items that are sold at a loss but are offered in order to encourage other business, for example including a bottle of wine with a meal package when the customer spends a specified minimum amount. These can also be used as sale promotion activities, such as specially priced seasonal menus, menus with wine flights, and time-based offers to encourage trade during slow periods, for example including additional elements at specific times or pre- and post-theatre deals

KEY TERMS

Market conditions – level of industry competition and level and nature of customer demand.

Dynamic pricing – changing prices according to the level of demand.

Loss leaders – items sold at lower price to attract business and encourage other sales.

Calculate selling prices of food and beverage items

One of the pricing methods shown on page 322 is cost plus. This is the most common method of pricing. When the cost of producing a dish or a beverage is calculated it must include all the ingredients, including any garnishes. The percentage of gross profit required is then applied.

For example, a main course meal that has an overall food cost of £9.50 and a gross profit margin requirement of 70%:

- First calculate the food cost percentage. This is 100% revenue less 70% gross profit = 30%.
- To calculate the selling price: Selling price = £9.50 divided by 30% multiplied by 100% = £31.66.
- In addition, VAT needs to be added. The current rate of VAT is 20%.
- So, the selling price will be £31.66 plus 20% of £31.66. This is £31.66 divided by 100% and then multiplied by 120% = £37.99.

1.3 REVENUE PROTECTION

Causes of revenue loss

The causes of **revenue loss** are summarised in Table 8.5.

▼ **Table 8.5** Causes of revenue loss

Cause	Description
Theft	Theft, either by staff or by customers, can result in loss of food and beverages, stock, equipment or cash
Cover for staff illness	Additional labour costs are incurred when members of staff are off sick. This means that either additional staff have to be employed or existing staff have to be paid to work additional hours
Customer complaints	These could result in refunds to customers and potential future loss of business if negative reviews are posted on social media or on review sites such as TripAdvisor or OpenTable
Unbilled items	These are items which have not been included on customer bills
Food/beverage wastage	This can be caused by overproduction of food or beverages, or spoilage through poor stock control
Deposits	These are advance payments, for example for functions and parties, which have not been charged. These are essential to cover possible losses in case of cancellation or customers not turning up
Price reductions	These are used for promotional purposes such as early bird deals, or because an item is overstocked, or because of product perishability: inability to sell tomorrow the rooms or restaurant seats which were not occupied today

Recording revenue loss

In order to calculate the true revenue and profits, records need to be kept of all losses.

▼ **Table 8.6** Recording revenue loss

Type of record	Description
Wastage book	Food service areas should always record food and other wasted materials so that the cost can be calculated and action can be taken to reduce waste Each beverage sales point should also have a suitable book for recording the ullage. This is the amount of beer wasted in cleaning pipes, measures spilt, perishables, or anything that needs a credit
Stock control records	Accurate stock control records should include: • discrepancies in the amount of physical stocks • its selling price cash value
Cash reconciliation	At the end of each service period, the amount of payments received must be checked against the till records to ensure the two figures balance. Any discrepancies must be recorded
Breakages	There can be breakages in a number of places, including the stores, in food and beverage production areas and in the service areas. In all these areas it is necessary to have a breakages book to record all instances and what was broken as well as its selling price cash value

KEY TERMS

Revenue loss – caused by either increases in costs or lower than expected revenue

Recording revenue loss – process to ensure all waste is noted, costed and action able to be taken to reduce it

KEY TERMS

Sales analysis – process of calculating and evaluating a range of sales performance information.

Audits – checking if targets are being met.

Break-even analysis – finding the point at which the sales revenue exactly equals the total costs.

Till readings – summary of trading for a specific service period recorded on the till.

1.4 PRINCIPLES OF SALES ANALYSIS

Sales analysis techniques

Audits

It is common for **audits** to take place on a regular basis, usually by people not directly involved in the day-to-day running of the operation. Audits can also be carried out by external agencies and are usually very thorough. Reports from the audit go to senior management and will be used identify where performance lies – and where the business is not meeting its targets (and showing possible reasons for both of these things). For more information on the different types of audit, see Unit 202, page 73.

Break-even analysis

Break-even analysis is one of the most common tools used in estimating potential profitability. This is valuable to the business in general and also when calculating for special events and banqueting. This analysis is used to identify at what point all costs are covered and what actual cash profit is being made. It is also used to indicate what the profitability levels (or losses) might be for various levels of sales. The analysis can also be based on the number of customers, if an average sale per head figure has been estimated. The break-even point is where the sales revenue exactly equals the total costs: below that point the sales are not covering the costs and the business is making a net loss; above that point the business is making a profit.

Till readings

At the end of a specified service period summaries can be produced from **till readings**. These are also known as restaurant analysis sheets, bill summaries or records of restaurant sales.

The purpose of the sales summary sheet is:

- to check and ensure the revenue matches the items sold
- for the reconciliation of items with different gross profits
- to provide sales mix information
- to provide records of popular/unpopular items
- to provide records for stock control.

It may also include breakdowns of individual staff sales or specific till sales.

There are many different formats for sales summaries which are often electronically produced. Depending on the needs of the establishment, the information may include:

- date
- address of food and beverage outlet (if more than one exists)
- period of service
- bill numbers
- table numbers
- number of covers per table
- bill totals
- analysis of sales – for example food, beverages, or more detailed, such as menu and wine and drinks list items
- various performance measures (such as the cashier's name).

Year-on-year forecasts

It is common for operations to have forecasts (or budgets) for revenue, cost and profits. Actual performance is then checked back against the budget. Action is then taken to find out why there are differences and work to correct them. Comparison also take place against the performance at the same time last year, for example January this year with January last year. Although this approach is common it can have problems. The number of Sundays, for instance, can have an effect if the operation is closed on a Sunday. Bank holidays can also be at different times of the year, as can various festivals. For this reason, rolling totals of 12 months are often used. Thus, the total revenue and other measures at the end of January are the totals for the 12 months to date. These are then compared to the total revenue and other measures for the 12 months up to the end of December. This type of 'year-on-year' comparison gives a far better indication of actual trends than a comparison of month to month.

Average spend per customer (or per head, ASPH)

This is a calculation of the average amount spent per person during a service period. It is calculated by dividing the total sales by the number of people or covers served. If an operation knows its total revenue and the number of customers or number of checks over a specific period, then it is possible to calculate the **ASPH** and the average check figures. For example:

If:

Total revenue (£) =	1000
Total number of customers =	500
Total number of transactions =	100

Then:

ASPH = £2.00 (total revenue divided by the number of customers)

Average check = £10.00 (total revenue divided by the number of transactions)

Average group size = 5 (total number of customers served divided by the number of transactions)

This example also shows the calculation used to determine the average size of a group of customers. This can be useful information. Knowing that larger or smaller groups of customers make up a significant part of the market can help in the planning of the restaurant and kitchen layout, for example, or focus the advertising and promotion.

The importance of carrying out sales analysis to a business

Sales analysis is essential as it helps to identify how the business is doing and the trends in what customers are buying.

Monitoring sales analysis allows for demand forecasting, budgeting and **setting targets**.

KEY TERMS

Year-on-year forecasts – setting business performance targets and comparing the outcomes year on year with the forecasts.

Average spend – total revenue divided by number of customers for a given service period. The term 'average spend per head (ASPH)' is also widely used.

KEY TERM

Setting targets – identifying measurable things to be achieved by the business.

Demand forecasting

Sales analysis is essential as it helps to identify trends in what customers are buying. **Demand forecasting** helps to identify:

- popular/unpopular items on the menu/drinks lists
- records for stock control – for example, to help predict future demand
- changes in customers' interests
- where profits/losses are being made.

Having this information allows future forecasting of the nature of the business and the potential revenue. This can then help with forecasting, volume of customers, number of covers for different service periods, purchasing and storing ingredients and other commodities, also with ensuring that there are adequate stocks of linen and paper and other consumables, and adjusting selling prices as required.

Budgeting

When demand forecasting, **budgeting** has to take place. This is to ensure the operation will have the right number of staff in place and also the right levels of stock to meet the expected demand.

Setting targets

Having a detailed knowledge of past performance can assist in creating measurable objectives of a food and beverage operation. These are commonly expressed in the form of targets. Examples of measurable targets are revenue, costs, profits, average spend per head, number of customers. Other targets include those for social responsibility. Operators use targets to assist in making reasoned and objective evaluation of the performance of the operation, so that informed decisions can be made regarding the future of the business.

2 SAFEGUARDING FINANCIAL INFORMATION

2.1 SECURING FINANCIAL INFORMATION

Security of customer and business financial information

Under the General Data Protection Regulation (GDPR), customers have a right to expect that data about them is secure and is only used for the published business purposes (see GDPR, Unit 202, page 58). There is a general requirement to ensure that:

- **business information** on customers is kept up to date, fairly, lawfully and securely
- **customer information** is not passed on to third parties without prior consent from the customer
- staff are aware of the importance of the protection of customer information and the procedures to follow to ensure it is held securely.

Ensuring the security of financial information includes:

- **Use of passwords/pass codes** for specific people and ensuring these are kept private and changed regularly.

- **Limiting access/levels of authority** for dealing with incidents such as refunds, taking till readings and agreeing discounts.
- **Secure reservation and payment information** through limiting access, ensuring protection of internet and network connections and maintenance of equipment.
- **Management procedures or standard operation procedures (SOPs)** that cover all aspects of financial security, ensuring staff are trained to meet the standards required and that regular audits of compliance with procedures are carried out.

Payment point security

Ensuring the security of your **payment point** includes:

- **Secure** mobile payment terminals, known as Process Data Quickly (PDQ), and other payment machines through limiting access, ensure protection of internet and network connections and the maintenance of equipment.
- **Uplifts** of cash and other payment materials (such as vouchers) payment records are collected under secure conditions and through having designated people responsible and having requirements for checking and countersigning.
- **Limiting access** to payment point areas and equipment to specified people.
- **Staff training on security procedures** including action to be taken over unauthorised staff gaining access to secure areas, suspicious persons and incidents of theft.
- **Checking floats** and having designated people responsible for checking and countersigning.

KEY TERM

Payment point – place in the establishment where billing is created and payments are made.

2.2 CONSEQUENCES OF UNSECURED FINANCIAL INFORMATION

If financial information is not kept secure, this can lead to serious consequences for both the business and for the individual. These include:

- **Loss of reputation** can come through customers finding out that the secure access to their financial data has been potentially, or actually, compromised. A loss of reputation is difficult to recover from as customer trust in the business can be severely damaged.
- **Loss of revenue** can come from not ensuring the information is available when required, and not controlling access to information.
- **Fraud** can be caused either by customers using, for example, stolen or cloned credit cards or by staff using the financial information for illegal activities such as transferring money to other accounts or purchasing items outside the business.
- **Legal intervention** by enforcement authorities, such as police, environmental health and trading standards, which can then lead to prosecution. Legal intervention can also come from failure to comply with the General Data Protection Regulation (GDPR), which can lead to large fines and imprisonment (see also GDPR in Unit 202, page 58).
- **Unwanted reviews** in the press, on social media and on review sites.
- **Loss of employment** will result from the loss of business and damage to the reputation of the business. The operation will have to address the issues to improve and regain the business and/or customers' loyalty or make job cuts to save the business.

Test your learning

1 State **three** reasons why stock control is important to a business.

2 What does FIFO stand for?

3 What is a credit note?

4 If for one month the opening stock was £15,000, the purchases during the month were £2500 and the closing stock was £13,000, what is the cost of stock used for that month?

5 Identify **three** factors that influence the pricing of food and beverage items.

6 Briefly explain the cost plus pricing method.

7 What are the **three** elements of cost?

8 What are the **two** types of profit?

9 Identify **two** factors that can affect pricing.

10 If the cost price of an item is £5 and the gross profit is set at 70%, what will the selling price be?

11 Identify **three** causes of loss of revenue.

12 State **one** method for recording revenue loss.

13 Give **one** reason why sales analysis is important to a business.

14 What does ASPH stand for?

15 Give **two** reasons why it is important to ensure the security of financial information.

Glossary

À la carte menu items individually priced, and a type of service in which the cutlery for each course is laid just before each course is served

Aboyeur or barker the person who is in charge of and controls the hotplate during the service period

Active listening head nodding, gestures and repeating back phrases that are heard to ensure confirmation or understanding

Aerated water a beverage that contains carbonic gas. Examples are tonic water, soda water, dry ginger, bitter lemon, cola and lemonade

Allergen something that causes an allergic reaction such as swelling, itching or rash

Anaphylactic shock a very serious allergic reaction for which medical treatment is required

Appetiser starter courses

Apprenticeship gaining a qualification while in employment

Arabica a mild coffee blend

Aromatised wine wine that has been flavoured and fortified

Assisted service the customer is served part of the meal at a table and obtains the other part through self-service from some form of display or buffet

Audits checking if targets are being met

Average spend total revenue divided by number of customers for a given service period. The term 'average spend per head (ASPH)' is also widely used

Bacteria organisms harmful to humans

Balanced diet a diet which contains the correct amounts of all of the food groups

Barista a bartender who makes hot and cold drinks and alcoholic beverages

Bartender/bar person staff working in bar areas serving wine, drinks and cocktails

Beer line plastic hose connecting the keg or cask (barrel) to the beer engine or dispensing unit

Blend a tea composed of a variety of different types of tea

Bouquet aroma/smell

Break-even analysis finding the point at which the sales revenue exactly equals the total costs

Broaching head fitting that connects the beer gas lines on the keg

Budgeting setting amounts for costs against revenue targets

Buffet customers select food and drink from displays or passed trays; consumption is either at tables, standing or in lounge area

Built ingredients and ice are put into the glass one after the other

Business information includes information about staff, revenue and costs

Captive market the customer does not have a choice of operation

Carvery some parts of the meal are served to seated customers; other parts are collected by the customers

Cashier responsible for billing and taking payments

Casual work not employed on a regular basis

Catering offering facilities to people, especially the provision of food and beverages

Chemicals include cleaning fluids, disinfectants, machine oil, insecticides and pesticides

Cider alcoholic beverage obtained through the fermentation of apple juice, or a mixture of apple juice and up to 25 per cent pear juice

Cocktail a short drink up to 10 cl. Often used to describe all types of mixed or long drinks

Commercial sector includes hotels, restaurants, bars and clubs. These businesses need to make a profit so that the business can survive and grow

Consortium a group of independent hotels that make an agreement to buy products and services together

Contracting/outsourcing obtaining services from an outside supplier

Control measures ways of minimising risks and hazards

Corporate social responsibility (CSR) business objectives which aim to make an organisation work in more ethical ways

Corporation tax a tax on business profits

Cost plus pricing adding to the cost of an item, a fixed percentage to achieve the selling price

Cost provision a budget that an organisation must work within

Cost-provision sector businesses in the public sector that do not need to make a profit. Includes hospitals, schools, colleges and prisons

Costs of materials and providing the service

Counter service self-service by customers from a buffet or counter

Cover place setting

Covering letter accompanies a CV and explains why you are suitable for the job on offer

Covers number of people to be served

Cross-contamination when bacteria are transferred from contaminated food (usually raw food), equipment or surfaces to ready-to-eat food

Crumbing down removing bread crumbs and other debris from the customer's table

Curriculum vitae (CV) lists your contact details, educational qualifications and work history, your interests and any other activities in which you participate. It is used when applying for a job to demonstrate your skills to potential employers

Customer information includes personal details, as well as records of financial dealings, such as bill and payments

Customer process the experience the customer undertakes

Customer relations the relationship between customers and the food and beverage service staff

Customer service specification written statements of both technical and service standards, sometimes referred to as 'service offer' or 'customer contract'

Customer-to-staff ratio the number of staff required to serve a specific number of customers

Cutlery refers to all items used as eating implements – spoons, forks and knives

Danger Zone temperatures between 5°C and 63°C. It is possible for bacteria to multiply between these temperatures

Decanting the movement of wine from its original container to a fresh glass receptacle, leaving the sediment behind

Demand forecasting making an estimate of the expected level of business

Demographic changes differing patterns of population statistics

Dietary requirements customers may have a range of dietary choices based on vegetarianism, medical requirements (including food intolerance and the prevention of allergic reactions), ethical considerations or lifestyle choices

Distillation process used to increase the alcoholic strength of a liquid

Due diligence ensuring that a business has taken reasonable care and done everything it can to prevent food safety problems

Duty rota allocation of days and hours on duty for members of staff

Dynamic pricing changing prices according to the level of demand

Electronic point of sale (EPOS) system that allows orders to be sent to departments for preparation, for billing and for re-ordering of stock

Element of cost food and beverage costs, labour costs and overheads

Employee a person who works for the organisation

En place the traditional term used when all the preparatory duties have been completed

Environmental health officer (EHO)/ environmental health practitioner (EHP) responsible for food safety standards and enforcement

Ethical issues purchasing products from sustainable, local and reputable suppliers

External customers customers from outside the organisation

Fanning a lower grade of tea, mostly used in tea bags

Farinaceous dishes pasta and rice dishes

Feathered game birds such as partridge, grouse, woodcock, quail or pheasant

Fermentation the conversion of sugar into alcohol and carbon dioxide

First in, first out (FIFO) using the stock to ensure that the stock first received is the stock that is first used

Fixed costs do not vary with level of business

Flatware spoons and forks

Flush a picking of tea

Fobbing excess foaming of beer

Food intolerance when a person reacts to eating certain foods, causing difficulty with digestion and having an unpleasant physical reaction to them

Food poisoning an illness of the digestive system that is the result of eating foods contaminated with pathogenic bacteria and/or their toxins

Food safety putting in place all of the measures needed to make sure that food and drinks are suitable, safe and wholesome through all of the processes of food provision

Foodservice means the same as catering. This word is becoming used more often

Fortified wine wines such as sherry and port, which have been strengthened by adding alcohol

Franchise an agreement where a person or group of people pays a fee and some set-up costs to use an established name or well-known brand

Franchisee the franchise user

Franchisor the branded company franchise provider

Frappé served on crushed ice

Full-time employee employment of usually 35 or more hours per week

Furred game includes venison and hare

Grade particle size of a tea leaf, used to describe the quality of tea

Gross Domestic Product (GDP) a measure of the value of goods and services in a country during a period of time

Gross profit sales less cost of sales

Guéridon service a movable service table or trolley from which food may be served

Gyle cap dated label or plastic cap that shows the date when beer was brewed and tagged or casked

Hazard anything that can cause harm

Head waiter has overall responsibility of the staff team in the restaurant

Hollow-ware items other than cutlery, for example teapots, milk jugs, sugar basins and serving dishes

Hors d'oeuvres traditionally a selection of salads, fish and meats

Hospitality the friendly and generous treatment of guests and strangers

Hospitality industry any business that provides for its customers any combination of drink, food and accommodation

Host/greeter receptionist who is responsible for greeting customers when they arrive

Hotplate or pass the meeting point between the service staff and the food preparation staff

Indirect employment employment in support services

Infusion hot liquid production method using herbs, peels and roots to extract flavour

Internal customers staff in other service areas, such as kitchen staff, bill office staff, dispense bar staff and still room staff

Just in time (JIT) only ordering stock when it is needed

Keystone disc in the base of a beer cask in which the beer tap is installed

Layered or poured when liquids with different densities are floated one on top of the other

Level of service can be between limited and high level of personal attention

Lifestyle preferences food and beverage consumption based on ethical sourcing

Limited liability company the amount that the owners of the business will have to pay to cover the business's debts if it fails or is sued is limited to the value of the shares each shareholder (owner) owns. Company documents are available to the public

Liqueur sweetened and flavoured spirit

Loss leaders items sold at lower price to attract business and encourage other sales

Low alcoholic beverage containing between 0.5 and 1.2 per cent alcohol

Maceration cold liqueur production method using soft fruits to provide flavour and aroma

Managers staff responsible for making sure the operation runs smoothly and within budget and may be responsible for future planning. Examples are head chef, restaurant manager and reception manager

Market conditions level of industry competition and level and nature of customer demand

Maturation period of time to allow cheese to develop and ripen

Meze a type of à la carte menu, Turkish, Greek and Middle Eastern in origin and with small dishes that are ordered together

Mise en place preparation for service

Mixologist bar person who specialises in mixing and serving drinks, especially cocktails

Mixology cocktail making

Muddled some ingredients (for example fruit, leaves and sugar) are crushed at the bottom of the glass before other ingredients are added

Mutuality of obligation employer and employee have specific rights and responsibilities

Net profit sales less labour and overhead costs

New World wines wines produced outside of Europe, in countries such as the USA, Australia, Argentina, Chile and South Africa

Non-alcoholic beverage or soft drink not containing any alcohol

Non-captive market the customer has an open choice of opportunities

Old World wines wines produced in Europe

Operational staff practical, hands-on staff, including chefs de partie, section chefs, commis chefs, waiters, apprentices, reception staff and accommodation staff

Outside catering off-premises catering

Par stock set level of stock

Partnership two or more people working together as the proprietors of a business

Part-time employee regular employment of usually less than 35 hours per week

Patent still (continuous, column or Coffey still) method used to produce light spirits

Pathogen harmful bacteria

Pay As You Earn (PAYE) the scheme operated by HMRC to take tax from employees as they earn

Payment point place in the establishment where billing is created and payments are made

Perry obtained from pear juice and up to 25 per cent apple juice

Personal development plan a plan designed to monitor and measure an employee's performance

Personal presentation includes all aspects of how an employee appears to the customer, including hygiene, grooming, dress, body language, posture and attitude

Personal protective equipment (PPE) protective clothing and equipment used for tasks that may pose a risk or hazard

Personal selling when food and beverage service staff contribute to the promotion of sales

PESTLE stands for Political, Economic, Sociological, Technological, Legal, Ecological. A model used to classify influences on a business

Physical contamination when something gets into food that should not be there

Porter helps with cleaning duties and moving equipment and stock

Post mix aerated water served from a dispensing gun; the carbonated water is added to the syrup after the syrup leaves the container

Pot still method used to produce heavy flavoured spirits, for example, brandy

Poultry includes chicken, duck, goose and turkey

Poured another name for layered cocktails

Private companies companies that cannot sell shares

Private sector organisations that aim to make a profit

Prix fixe menu with one dish on offer for a set price

Professional bodies draw membership from various professions at various levels and provide a range of support for both their members and the industry

Profit the difference between revenue and cost

Public limited companies (PLCs) companies that can sell their shares to the public

Public or secondary service sector industries where the provision of accommodation, food and beverages is not the principal business; provision by the state or local authority

Recording revenue loss process to ensure all waste is noted, costed and action able to be taken to reduce it

Recycling reprocessing materials so that they can be reused

Requisition complete an order for stock from the stores

Revenue total amount of money received

Revenue loss caused by either increases in costs or lower than expected revenue

Risk the chance of somebody being harmed by a hazard

Risk assessment identifying hazards and actions required

Robusta a harsher, bitter coffee blend that contains more caffeine

Runner does some of the service, clears tables and does much of the cleaning and preparatory work

Sales analysis process of calculating and evaluating a range of sales performance information

Seasonal work fixed-term contract for employment during business periods such as summer months or the Christmas period

Seasonally sourced fresh food products purchased during the season when they are naturally ready to be used

Semi-captive market customers may choose, but once the choice has been made then the food and beverage available becomes limited to that provided by the location

Service enhancements when food and beverages are served from trolleys such as cheese, sweet, carving or drinks trolleys

Service plate used by the server during service

Service salver a round, silver or stainless steel tray used to carry glasses and cutlery

Service sector food and beverage operations that provide a service to other businesses where hospitality is not the primary business

Service sequence stages in the service of a meal

Setting targets identifying measurable things to be achieved by the business

Shaken the ingredients are placed in a cocktail shaker with ice and shaken

Shive a wooden disc placed within the opening of a beer cask

Silver service presentation of food by waiting staff, using a spoon and fork, on to a customer's plate, from food flats or dishes

Single point service the customer orders, pays and receives the food and beverages at one point

Small- to medium-sized business enterprises (SMEs) companies with fewer than 250 employees

Smoothies drinks made using a blender

Social media internet-based platforms for communication, such as Facebook, Twitter and YouTube

Social responsibility concerns about sustainability and the environment

Sole trader an individual who owns a business, takes all the risks, is liable for any losses and keeps any profits

Sommelier/wine waiter serves alcoholic and non-alcoholic drinks during the service of meals

Spear head external fitting on a keg in which the broaching head is attached

Spile a peg that fits the air hole of the shive

Spore protective shell which allows cells to protect themselves from heat or freezing

Standards of service how well the level of service is achieved

Station waiter provides a service to a group of tables called a station

Stepped costs costs that increase in jumps as the volume of business increases

Still room provides items of food and beverages needed for the service of a meal not found in other major departments such as the kitchen, larder and pantry

Stillage wood or metal rack, on which a barrel is stored so that sediment settles to the bottom

Stirred the ice and ingredients are placed into a mixing glass and stirred

Stock control maintain a level of stock in order to meet business demands

Stock reordering ensuring that new, replacement stock is ordered at the right time

Stocktake checking the levels of stock to determine the value; checking what has actually been used, and calculating the rate of stock turnover

Straight-line counter all foods are displayed on one long counter and customers move along the counter in order

Sub-contractor a company or person who carries out work on behalf of the company

Supervisory staff oversee the work of the operational staff

Table d'hôte a type of cover in which the cutlery for the whole meal is laid before the first course is served

Table d'hôte or menu du jour menu with a specific set price and number of food courses

Table service the customer is served at a laid table. This type of service, which includes plated service or silver service, is found in many types of restaurant, in cafés and in banqueting

Table theatre a service enhancement in which food and beverages are served from trolleys. These can include cheese, sweet, carving or drinks trolleys and also guéridon service

Tapas a type of à la carte menu traditionally eaten in Spain, with snack-size dishes that are ordered together to make a meal

Target an outcome for an employee to work towards as part of their development

Taxation compulsory payments collected by central, devolved and local government which contribute to the state's revenue

Tender when companies compete to win a contract

Till readings summary of trading for a specific service period recorded on the till

Tisane a flavoured tea or herbal infusion

Toxin poison

Trade bodies associations of employers or specific types of suppliers

Trancheur a specialist carver

Tuber vegetable grown beneath the soil

Turnover the amount of money a company makes

Ullage unable to be sold. Collected from drip trays or left in the bottom of kegs or casks

Underflat also called an underliner

Upselling another name for personal selling

Value Added Tax (VAT) a tax on the final consumption of goods and services

Variable costs vary directly with the level of business

Varietal the grape used to make a specific wine

Vegetarianism not eating meat or meat-derived products

Vinification wine making

Vintage wines grown and made in a particular year

Viticulture the cultivation of grape vines

Vitis vinifera main vine species for grapes used for wine making

Wave service service of whole tables, one at a time and proceeding across the room

Work ethic a positive attitude and competence in contributing to the success of the business

Work experience being in a workplace for a set period to see how you get on

Worker someone who works within the organisation, but is employed by another company

Year-on-year forecasts setting business performance targets and comparing the outcomes year on year with the forecasts

Index